POLITICAL JUDGMENTS

POLITICAL JUDGMENTS

Dick Howard

ROWMAN & LITTLEFIELD PUBLISHERS, INC.

ROWMAN & LITTLEFIELD PUBLISHERS, INC.

Published in the United States of America
by Rowman & Littlefield Publishers, Inc.
4720 Boston Way, Lanham, Maryland 20706

3 Henrietta Street
London WC2E 8LU, England

British Cataloging in Publication Information Available

Library of Congress Cataloging-in-Publication Data
Howard, Dick, 1943–
Political judgments / Dick Howard.
p. cm.
Includes bibliographical references.
1. Political science—History. 2. Political science—Philosophy.
I. Title.
JA83.H697 1996 320'.01'1—dc20 95-26274 CIP

ISBN 0-8476-8162-9 (cloth : alk. paper)
ISBN 0-8476-8163-7 (pbk. : alk. paper)

Printed in the United States of America

∞ ™ The paper used in this publication meets the minimum requirements of
American National Standard for Information Sciences—Permanence of Paper
for Printed Library Materials, ANSI Z39.48–1984.

Contents

Part III. Political Theory or Theory of the Political?

Acknowledgments

Many discussions, arguments, disagreements, and agreements went into the chapters that compose this volume. Some of the chapters appeared individually over the years, in contexts that I explain in the introduction. In addition to the editors and collaborators of those journals, and those working with the journals where translations (or original versions) of these essays appeared, I should thank particularly Renzo Llorente who, while working on his own intriguing project on the division of labor, was able to take time to help (critically) rework these chapters and to prepare them for publication. The index, which should help make serviceable this sometimes diverse collection, is due to his creative, critical, and research-oriented mind.

The separate chapters of this volume, which have been revised (and in some cases translated by the author), appeared in the following publications, to whom grateful thanks are owed for permission to reprint.

Chapter 1. Written for the German publication of these essays, published under the title *Die Politisierung der Politik* (Frankfurt am Main: Suhrkamp Verlag, 1996).

Chapter 2. Originally published as "Rediscovering the Left," *Praxis International* 10, no. 3/4 (1991); reprinted in *Russia and America in the 21st Century: Perspectives of Russian and American Philosophers*, edited by William Gay and Tatjana Alekseeva (Lanham, Md.: Rowman & Littlefield, 1994).

Chapter 3. Originally appeared in the *Journal of the British Society for Phenomenology* 14 (January 1983); reprinted in *The Politics of Critique* (Minneapolis: University of Minnesota Press, 1988).

Chapter 4. Originally published as "Pourquoi revenir à la Révolution américaine," *Intervention*, No. 15, January-March 1986; translated by James Clarke and republished in *The Politics of Critique*.

Chapter 5. Originally published in *Thesis Eleven*, No. 36 (1993).

Chapter 6. Originally published in *Thesis Eleven*, No. 33 (1992).

Chapter 7. Originally published in *Philosophy and Social Criticism* 8, no. 4 (1981); reprinted in *The Politics of Critique*.

Chapter 8. Originally published in German in *Die Frankfurter Schule und die Folgen*; English translation by author published in *Critical and Dialectical Phenomenology*, edited by D. Welton and J. Silverman (Albany: SUNY Press, 1987).

Chapter 9. To appear in special issue of the *Cordozo Law Review* on Habermas's *Facticity and Validity*, promised publication 1996.

Chapter 10. Originally published in French in *Les Temps modernes*, November 1983; English version in *The Politics of Critique*.

Chapter 11. Originally in *Autres Temps*, June 1992; translation for this volume (modified) by author.

Chapter 12. Unpublished in English; German translation in *Aesthetik und Kommunikation*, Heft 84, Jahrgang 23 (February 1994).

Chapter 13. Originally in *Autres Temps*, French reprinted in *M*; revised translation by author in *German Politics and Society* No. 28 (Spring 1993). German variant in *Berliner Debatte. Initial*, April 1993.

Chapter 14. English version in *Constellations* 1, no. 2 (October 1994); originally in French at Colloquium of Collège International de Philosophie; German version in *Berliner Debatte. Initial*.

Introduction

Political Judgments

This book was first published in German as *The Politicization of Politics*. The first chapter explains the internal coherence and the external context that unite these apparently diverse essays into a coherent whole; it also explains my claim that politics today needs to be "politicized." In preparing this new English-language edition, a different title captured more closely the intent of both the book and each of the chapters that compose it. By changing the title of this edition (while preserving the discussion of politicization), I hope to make clearer the kind of theory proposed here. This is not a book of philosophy, although it discusses philosophers and their work; it is not a book of history, although it analyzes historical experiences and their results; and it is not a book of politics, although it engages contemporary political problems and proposals. It is a book of political judgments, which are specific types of claims whose rather idiosyncratic mode I will clarify in these introductory remarks. In the process, I will suggest also why the rediscovery of political philosophy in the recent past needs to be supplemented by another kind of political reflection if it is to continue to bear fruit (rather than remain the private property of academic institutions).

This volume is conceived as a whole whose once-independent parts are enriched by their placement within the broader context. Some chapters are rather scholarly: the nonphilosopher may find the Hegelian antecedents and the democratic premises of Jürgen Habermas's recent legal theory tough going; the nonhistorian may not immediately see the need to spend so much time with the institutional structures of the ancien régime; and despite my double return to Kant, some readers may argue that I presuppose too much background knowledge. Other chapters are more attuned to recent public debates; they discuss contemporary implications of problems that need to be probed also for their own sake. The reader may find that I cover too much ground too quickly, for example in my attempt to right what I call "two hundred years of error," or that I belabor the obvious. Other chapters may give rise to other complaints. Of course, were I to start from scratch, I would have written a different book. However, I did not write the other book; and if I had, it would not be this book, and it would not express these political judgments. It would be a unified statement, inviting the reader to read differently.[1] This self-evident remark has implications that are not trivial.

There is a reason to publish collections of political judgments rather than waiting for their crystallization in a single, and unique, political statement. I return to this reason repeatedly under the heading of *democracy*. Political judgments are the language of democracy; they are what makes it different from previous political regimes. In a democracy, there is no privileged standpoint from which an ultimate and definitive judgment could be attained. There is no point in time, no place in space, no a priori validity that can be maintained within the constant flux of democratic opinion. At the same time, and for the same reason, there is a constant quest to find just such a definitive standpoint, to unify partial visions in a perspective on their totality, and to adjust reality and its representations to one another. Democracy preserves its form and its substance as long as that quest is seen for what it is—not wrong but never realizable; a necessary search for a sense that must remain always open to criticism; and the search for a unity that does not abolish the difference from which it emerges. If uncertainty weighs too heavily, the quest becomes an obsession, unity excludes diversity, and criticism appears to play into the hands of an undefined enemy, then democracy turns toward what I call an *antipolitics*, the culmination of which is the totalitarian illusion that society has been able finally to coincide with its political representation. This is the modern form of the Platonic illusion that knowledge has come to power and rules with the force of law in a society that is transparent to itself.

If democracy depends on political judgments, what gives an author the right to judge? What do I presume of myself, and of my readers, when I write? Why should others be interested in my particular problems or solutions? For that matter, why should I care that others share my judgments? Why should I take seriously the judgments of others? The questions are not new; Plato's *Republic* was only the first polemic in a long tradition for which democracy is the reign of opinion:

inconstant, disorderly, and above all confused. In that tradition, what counts is truth, which is universal and is unchanged by the fact of being known by one, many, or none. Politics becomes the province of "selfless servants" of truth. As a result, the domain of the political is accorded no autonomous standing—save in the scandalous exceptions grouped under the rubric "Machiavellianism."[2] And judgment either is reduced to the ability to subsume particular evidence under already known and universal rules, or is disdained for its abstract and formal character and replaced by a search for immediate and concrete intuitions. At best, judgment is associated with the Aristotelian concept of *phronesis* but is still assimilated to an ability to find one's way in the shadowy world of opinion and moral casuistry. At worst, at the threshold of the modern democratic era, Kant's *Critique of Judgement* had to face up to the dictum *de gustibus non disputandum*, there is no disputing about taste, and to refute its implication that judgment was not even a proper matter for philosophical reflection.

Political judgments assume a basic democratic right that is often forgotten: *the right to error*. This right is based on a double presupposition. First, at the level of philosophy, judgment becomes possible only when one has abandoned what phenomenologists call the "natural attitude"; it assumes that there is a difference between the way things appear and the way they truly are (or can become). If the way things truly are is not the way they appear, then the claim to know them as they truly are also assumes the risk of error, of misjudgment, or of mistaking what we want for what really is. Without this right to error, philosophy is impossible; we remain among the shadows of Plato's Cave, where disagreement is possible but truth is not. Second, at the level of politics, the consequences of this right to error are the inverse of its philosophical premise. In a democracy, those with whom we disagree politically are not *guilty* of error; our task is not to condemn them but to convince them. We know that we can convince them because democratic citizens who claim the right of error assume at the same time responsibility for their judgments as judgments—that is, as philosophically fallible. This explains the uniqueness of political debate within a democracy, and points to the reason why the quest for a philosopher-king is condemned from the outset.[3]

The political apprenticeship in the right to error is the subject matter of my historical analyses of the American and French Revolutionary experiences in part 2; the philosophical methods that permit the responsible debate that tries to avoid or to correct error is the subject matter of the philosophical passage "from Marx to Kant" in part 3.

Experience on the one side, philosophical procedure on the other: their synthesis is suggested by the contemporary political judgments grouped in part 4, whose discussion concretizes such themes as guilt, responsibility, sacrifice, and judgment itself. Such a synthesis is not a final resting place; it does not put an end to the need to make and to assume political judgments. That is why, in the preparation of this English edition, I resisted the temptation to replace some of its political judgments by more recent ones.[4] The reason that I did not make these changes even though they might have made me look wiser or more politically perceptive explains two further aspects of political judgments.

The right to error means that political judgments are partial in both senses of the term: they are not neutral but must take a stance; and they can concern only a part, never the totality, of experience. That is why a book composed of political judgments can treat such diverse themes, and why it must do so in a language and with a rigor that is adequate to the object being treated—whether it be the philosophy of Kant or the institutions of the ancien régime. Political judgments are not all contemporary to one another; they are not all made in a single instant. They are partial in the further sense that they have a past, which they cannot deny and for which they are responsible. However, they are not condemned simply to repeat that past, as if it were an eternal verity (or damnation). That means that a book of political judgments is not a single unitary statement (which is the reason that this book could not have been rewritten as a single judgment, as I mentioned a moment ago). That is why it brings together judgments concerning not only a wide range of issues but also those that were made from different temporal perspectives, and others not originally intended for an American public and written in a different idiom.

Turning to the contents of these political judgments, the experience that unites them is the claim that the revolutions of 1989 in Eastern Europe have returned the question of the political nature of democracy to the head of the contemporary political agenda. Yet, five of these fourteen chapters were written before 1989. While I cannot claim prescience—that would not be a judgment, after all—my concern with the phenomenon of totalitarianism, the metaphorics of the French Revolution, and the originality of the American Revolution point out another aspect of political judgments: their existential foundation.[5] In my case, it was the good fortune of having certain kinds of experience, combined with persistence in trying to form my own judgments about it, and the readiness of friends to respect independent judgment (and to practice it themselves) that were crucial. I try to describe this experience in the comparison between the European and American Lefts (in chapter 11) and to reflect on it in relation to the Marxian legacy (in chapter 2). The existential claim that the unity of these political judgments lies in a life-experience does not imply that I am the only one who could (or should) publish a book of political judgments—on the contrary. Political judgments bring together diverse aspects of a life's experience in a way that casts new light on the apparently separate parts that are now seen to form a whole. They permit an author to find new sense in his or her work. This introduction is thus not just a self-presentation but also an invitation to others.

There is one final aspect of *my* volume of political judgments that needs to be explained. If 1989 put the final nail in the coffin of Karl Marx, on which I had been hammering since my 1973 critique of Rosa Luxemburg, why do I claim that now more than ever one has to take Marx seriously? Not as political guide nor as a scientist, Marx the philosopher of modernity remains relevant because he shows the necessity of seeking the synthesis that democracy makes impossible. It is not important that Marx erred in thinking that he had found that synthesis. The right to error remains in force for Marx as well. It is only when one has sought, as he did, to realize the seamless synthesis that will put an end to difference that one can come to recognize why that final unification is impossible (as he did not). Acceptance of the demand to go beyond the world as given, and recognition that such transcendence can never be fully realized, is the precondition for recognizing why politics must be politicized, why political judgments are always necessary and yet never definitive, and why responsibility is the premise of solidarity among individuals insistent on asserting their rights to their own individuality.

*   *   *

I should note that I have modified these chapters where it seemed necessary in order to facilitate comprehension, to make the prose more readable, or to add information that had been lacking. I did not rewrite substantively, nor did I try to make 100 percent certain—as one would do in a single judgment—that I had used concepts in a wholly consistent manner over the period of years during which these materials were written.

Others will have learned the art of political judgment in other schools, with other teachers and texts. I hope that they will think seriously about the invitation to see what would happen to their own political judgments if they were to find their way between two covers.

Introduction

I suspect that the results would be of interest, to them and to the rest of us.

Notes

1. The reader will find that when I speak of judgments in this volume, I am referring in fact to a specific kind of judgment whose nature and legitimacy were first made clear by Kant's distinction between subsumptive judgments (which begin from a universal rule and place particular facts underneath it, thus determining that this winged creature is a bird) and what are called reflective judgments (which begin from a particular and seek to find a universal adequate to it, as in the claim that a painting is beautiful, even though we know of no universal rule that defines the beauty of an artwork). Political judgments are reflective judgments, as will be seen. Such reflective judgments are both possible and necessary in a democratic society, as I will show in a moment.

2. Claude Lefort points to the historical function of this category. Insofar as politics, and particularly democratic politics, is based on the kind of knowledge that characterizes the world of opinion, it is an uncomfortable domain in which indeterminacy rules. The idea of a "Machiavellian" politics implies that it is indeed possible to acquire a mastery over ends, over the choice of the means to achieve those ends, and even a mastery of one's own self. Yet, as Lefort shows, it is just the impossibility of such a mastery that is the principle of Machiavelli's political thought (Claude Lefort, *Machiavel. Le travail de l'oeuvre* [Paris: Gallimard, 1972], e.g., 73–92).

3. I should insist that there is a difference between political judgments, as I am presenting the concept here, and political opinions. In assembling this volume, I asked myself whether I should reprint some of the shorter, more popular (op-ed) work that I have published during this period. However, such opinion pieces are based on a different kind of appeal: they seek to convey a single emotion or intuition, they have the structure of an essay that embroiders around a unitary theme, and they aim at communicating to the reader an insight that stands out sharply before fading away in the face of the next opinions that succeed in penetrating the readers' certainties.

4. Thus, although I tried to apply some of the ideas in this volume to the victory of the Republican Party in the 1994 elections, I kept the discussion of the challenges facing Bill Clinton after his election in 1992; and in the same chapter, I also retained the analysis of the Europe of Maastricht even though I had just finished an analysis of the challenges facing Europe in the fall of 1995. The former article has been published as "Clinton à mi-parcours," *Esprit*, March 1995, 144–59, and in German translation as "Die Politisierung der Politik und die Halbzeitwahlen 1994," in *Aesthetik und Kommunikation*, Heft 89, Jahrgang 24 (May 1995): 45–55.

5. To avoid any misunderstanding, I do not claim that political judgment is the province of what some have called the "public intellectual," and still less what an earlier tradition called the "organic intellectual" or the "ideologue." Political judgments are not a form of praxis, as conceived for example in the Hegelian-Marxist tradition; their function is not to make conscious those potentialities that were unconscious, to strip the blinders of opinion from naive eyes so that they can see a truth that the author of the political judgment knows already.

Part I

What Is the Political?

1

Politicization of Politics

What were the revolutions of 1989? What is the democracy whose worldwide triumph they announced? The second question is only a different formulation of the first, as I will try to show. The answer to both questions helps to explain why the triumphant democracy of 1989 is in disarray today—and not only in the former Soviet empire. European unification, which seemed poised to move to a new level after the signing of the Maastricht treaty, has stalled; and the election of Bill Clinton in 1992, which seemed to indicate a renewal of the belief that government can do good, did not produce a "Kennedy-effect" that would renew American political life. The 1994 midterm congressional elections renewed a rather different type of politics. The problem is not only conjunctural or pragmatic; it is structural and it is philosophical. Precisely for this reason, I will argue that the 1989 overthrow of an ancien régime and the emergence of democracy as a problem has the potential to put an end to what I call "two hundred years of error." Philosophical reflection on the revolutions of 1989 can elucidate the conditions of possibility for a rediscovery of the political, and with it the structure of democratic politics. To understand the challenges of the present, a reconsideration of past possibilities and failed choices is necessary.

Marxists are not the only ones who think of modern political history in terms of metaphors taken from the French Revolution. The father of the post-1989 economic "shock therapy," Jeffrey Sachs, uses the same imagery to denounce the defeat of his allies in Russia, comparing Yeltsin to the Girondins, and recalling that the Gironde was replaced by Napoleon.[1] However approximate his history, Sachs's metaphors are interesting. But to understand the paradigmatic role of the French Revolution, and of its American predecessor, one needs to undertake

3

a philosophical analysis of *the political* as it has emerged with our modernity and has determined our understanding of democracy. The democratic politics whose conditions of possibility were created by the two great eighteenth-century revolutions has too often been deformed by what I call an *antipolitics*. This antipolitical orientation will be seen to be shared by the Marxists, who seek to "realize" what was begun in 1789 but left unfinished or aborted in 1793, and by those who appeal to the market as a neutral institution regulating the relations of individuals whose freedom it leaves untouched. None of the diverse forms of antipolitics can be assigned exclusively to the Left or the Right. Rather, as chapter 2, "The Marxian Legacy and the Problem of Democracy," suggests, the Left can be better understood as the partisan of the political, the Right as supporter of antipolitics.

Neither revolution nor democracy is defined by some material structure or set of institutions, actions, or events that could be described by an outside observer. That does not mean that these conditions can be ignored; the revolutions of 1989 did depend on concrete changes in both the personnel who held power and on the institutional structures through which power was exercised. Similarly, specific constitutional frameworks and juridical protections are necessary for democratic politics to function. But can one say that the American Revolution was not democratic—or not a revolution—because it did not establish immediately full citizen participation in politics, let alone abolish slavery? Would one say that the French Revolution was neither revolutionary nor democratic because it culminated in the Reign of Terror or in the Napoleonic empire? The same indeterminacy holds when the historian tries to specify the temporal moment in which the revolution occurs. Is the American Revolution defined by the Declaration of Independence? the victory over Great Britain that realized independence? the Constitution? the Civil War, which finally liberated the slaves? As "Origins of Revolution" (chapter 3) indicates, the same problem is posed by the French Revolution. Revolution is not a thing or an event; it is an origin—the origin of the political.

What is the political?[2] If a simple definition must be given at the outset, it could be said that the political is the way in which a society and its members come to understand themselves as *this* society rather than an accidental coexistence of random particular movements that have temporarily congealed under the pressure of outside and accidental forces. The political is then the process by which a society expresses its autonomy—*auto-nomos*—giving itself its own laws. This structure can be formulated by the philosopher in Kantian terminology: the political is the condition of the possibility of politics. After the historical facts are established, patterns brought to light, and choices defined and described, the philosopher asks how these facts, patterns, and choices became possible. The philosopher insists on the difference between the condition and that which it conditions—on the difference between the political and politics. This is not to deny that politics is about "who does what to whom," as Lenin famously put it. It implies that the dimension of meaning must be introduced in order to explain the dynamism that makes the "facts" appear to call for action—for politics. Without that dimension of meaning, how can the suddenness with which the totalitarian systems collapsed be understood? What else could explain the political effects of the "antipolitics" by which civil society sought to free itself from totalitarian rule?[3] Similar questions have to be asked of the French and American experiences two centuries ago: neither revolution was preordained— nor was either a simple accident. That is why the philosopher insists on the radical possibilities inherent in the project of defining the political.[4]

It is not the philosopher who defines the political, nor can its definition be established once and for all. The philosopher can only analyze the structure by which, in specific conditions, the political is defined. The distinction between the political and politics creates the space in which democracy becomes possible. To preserve that space, something like what Habermas calls a liberal or democratic culture is necessary.[5] The creation and preservation of a democratic culture is itself a daunting political task. It is necessary to avoid the always-present temptation either to reduce the political to politics (and then to reduce politics even further, to the social, or the economic) or to overcome their distinction in a higher unity that eliminates divisions within the healthy body politic. That reduction and this overcoming illustrate antipolitics. The revolutions of 1989 have not been immune to the temptation of antipolitics, any more than were the revolutions that inaugurated the era of modern politics two hundred years ago, or than is contemporary Western democracy. The fact that the revolutions of 1989 were *antitotalitarian* gives them at least the possibility of avoiding (and helping the West learn to avoid) the antipolitical denial of the distinction between politics and the political. Because totalitarianism represents the most radical form of antipolitics, understanding its inner logic has implications for nontotalitarian societies as well.

The five chapters of this book that were written before 1989 were attempts to understand the implications of the critique of totalitarianism for the development of democratic politics.[6] Two of them are attempts to rethink the concept of revolution, as illustrated by the French and the American Revolutions. Another addresses the political claims of the Frankfurt School's critical theory and of Gadamer's hermeneutical attempt to analyze meaning in order to understand the limits of philosophical reconstruction and its difference from politics. These limits and this difference suggested the need for a reconstruction of Marx's philosophical premises, and of political attempts to inherit what I have called the Marxian legacy. They form the basis of my claim that the relation of the political to both politics and to philosophy is antinomical and can be clarified only by the movement from Marx to Kant. That philosophical argument was presented systematically in *From Marx to Kant* (1985), whose revised second edition was published in 1993. The present volume does not, however, simply repeat or apply old conclusions to new problems; in indicating to the reader what to expect in the following pages, I will try to explain as well why I have presented these chapters under the title "the politicization of politics."[7]

Making a Virtue out of Necessity

The title of this chapter is deliberately ambiguous. "The politicization of politics" could be taken as a declarative or descriptive statement, asserting that in modern conditions politics becomes autonomous and is freed (or forced) to follow its own immanent logic. In that case, the arguments presented here would be a reconstruction of the process of modernization along the lines of Max Weber or Niklas Luhmann. But the title also could be read as the imperative that politics must reflect on its own conditions of possibility if it is to fulfill truly and justly its function. In this latter case, the argument would be a critique of an incomplete modernization that remains to be realized, calling for something like another revolution. As in Kant's *Critiques*, the ambiguity lies in the genitive "of": is it modern politics that demands to be—or that has been—politicized? Or is it the political that needs to find—or has found—an institutional form adequate to modern conditions? In the former case, politics would be freed from its social—and especially from its economic—determination in order to realize its systemic function in modern societies. In the latter case, the sense of the whole, the meaning of the Good Life in the City, would need to find a new institutional embodiment. In either case, the theory that results would be critical. The object, structure, and grounds of legitimacy of that critical theory remain to be defined.

The conceptual framework developed here makes a virtue out of this ambiguity. The reader will encounter a succession of dualisms, whose ineluctable necessity gives them the systematic status of what Kant called an *antinomy*. Both poles can be shown to be necessary; yet they apparently cannot be realized simultaneously in some sort of higher synthesis. The most general expression of this antinomy is the opposition, and yet the mutual implication, of politics and the political. Thus, empirical political choices are caused by empirical considerations; but this simple causality neglects the normative sense by which the political binds rights-bearing individuals into an autonomous community that endures, evolves over time, and generates responses to new challenges. This normative aspect of the political calls for philosophical analysis. But the philosophical cannot be immediately identified with the political. These two poles will form instead another mutually reciprocal opposition, another antinomy (to which I return in a moment in the case of Marx). These abstract and general antinomies acquire particular forms in the chapters that follow. For example, I analyze the opposition and yet mutual implication of individual rights and communal solidarity, of democracy and the republic (or democracy and its totalitarian "realization"), of the social and the political; similarly, I present as antinomic the relation between the American and the French Revolutions, a "bourgeois" "first" revolution and its "double" or realized form, and the political theories of Marx and Kant; at another level, I study the relations of genesis and normativity, particularity and receptivity, judgment and will. This extension of the concept of an antinomy needs explanation.[8]

What makes these polarities, which are encountered first in empirical analysis, into antinomies? In each case, one pole, which is apparently complete and necessary, cannot be understood without reference to its equiprimordial other; the two cannot coexist peacefully, yet neither can be abandoned. Their opposition and their mutual implication are due to a systematic imperative. The most famous illustration is Kant's Third Antinomy in the *Critique of Pure Reason*. A world that the understanding has shown to be governed by causality would leave no place for morality, whose foundation is the freedom of the will. The systematic imperative demands that both causality and freedom be preserved. Kant's resolution of the antinomical conflict made a virtue out of necessity; as he put it in the preface, he sought "to destroy [metaphysical] knowledge in order to preserve [moral] faith." This solution could be read as establishing a peaceful coexistence, or even an indifference of the two poles to each other. Kant's successors, however, tried to make necessity into a virtue by claiming that the opposition was only apparent, and that a higher stage of Reason or History would overcome it. In so doing, they developed the implicit systematic presupposition of Kant's critical philosophy. The result was an idealism whose systematic unity destroyed the antinomic structure that was their premise. This attempt to overcome the antinomies was not wrong; indeed, it showed that only through the attempt to overcome them do these polarities become antinomic. This is why I claim that only when one has shown the *philosophical* strength of Marx can one return to Kant; only then can one see that, and how, Kant provides the philosophical method for achieving the *political* goals of Marx.

The most successful attempt to go beyond the Kantian dualism prior to Marx belongs to Hegel. For the problems that concern us, his *Philosophy of Right* is paradigmatic. Hegel's premise is expressed in the famous assertion (in his preface) that "the actual is the rational and the rational is the actual." Beginning from the free will, Hegel develops a systematic theory of the increasingly rational and self-reflective stages through which the will actualizes its freedom in the world. In the legal sphere of abstract right and in the domain of morality, the individual develops, enriches, and preserves his or her individuality. However, this individuality can exist only within the framework of a presupposed society and culture, which Hegel calls *Sittlichkeit*, and whose rationality is developed, enriched, and preserved in the domain of the family, in the relations of civil society, and finally in the state. What is the relation between the legal and moral spheres in which individuality finds its rational content and the spheres in which the *sittliche* community achieves its rational form? Does the one presuppose the other? Do they both presuppose that world-historical development into which Hegel's description of the rational state culminates? If "world history is the court of the last judgment," as the *Philosophy of Right* concludes, what becomes of the claim to universal validity of the philosophical system?

The interpretation of Hegel's solution to the Kantian antinomies need not concern us here.[9] His turn toward history points to the place of Marx in any systematic attempt to understand the relation of philosophy and the political. The rigor of Marx's attempt to overcome the antinomic structures is impressive. Because I return to it at several points in the following chapters, I will be brief here. The logic of

Marx's passage from philosophy to political economy, and to his theory of proletarian revolution, is suggested by a Note to his Doctoral Dissertation in which he stressed the need "for philosophy to become worldly and for the world to become philosophical." Both sides of the demonstration were necessary; philosophy could only be truly philosophical insofar as it added "the critique of the weapons" to the "weapon of critique." At the same time, the world had to be shown to need philosophy in order to become truly (*für sich*) that which it is only in principle (*an sich*). This quest for systematic completeness and necessity is the premise that transforms the polarities from which we began into antinomies. But Marxism can become another idealism if it denies the autonomy of its own antinomical presuppositions in the quest for a dialectical totalization that becomes, ultimately, the totalitarian form of antipolitics.

Why, then, do I take Marx so seriously? Why do I make these philosophical claims whose formulation in Lukács's *Geschichte und Klassenbewußtsein* (1923)[10] has been refuted, surpassed, or simply forgotten? The answer is suggested in chapter 10, "From Marx to Kant: The Return of the Political," when I present a Marxist interpretation of Kant and then suggest in successive subsections that "if Kant were a Marxist . . . he would not have written the *Critique of Judgement.*" Only when the systematic demands of philosophy (and the logical structure of the political) are developed to their necessary and complete consequences can the temptation either to unify difference in a higher synthesis or to withdraw into a contemplative relativism be avoided. That is, the Marx whom I introduce represents the imperative of post-Kantian philosophy to seek systematic completeness. This Marx incarnates what I call *the philosophical*. This Marx succumbed to the temptation to reduce the political to politics (and, in the last—"philosophical"—instance, politics to economics) because he did not see that the philosophical and the political relate to one another antinomically. When the philosophical is taken alone as the standard by which politics is to be judged, the result denies the autonomy of the political and, as a result, imposes a totalizing reason on the interests and autonomy of that which stands outside of its framework.

But the question remains: why introduce Marx in a book that tries to draw some of the consequences of the revolutions of 1989? The answer explains my stress on the logic of totalitarianism. I do not only criticize totalitarianism for its violations of human rights, human dignity, or communal autonomy. I do not simply oppose to it a self-evident liberal or democratic politics, as if totalitarianism had been imposed from outside by the bayonets of the Red Army. Totalitarianism is the extreme form of antipolitics, which is a temptation that is present in democratic political systems as well. At the most general level, antipolitics is constituted by the attempt to overcome the antinomies between the philosophical and the political, and between the political and politics. The development from Kant to Marx illustrates the way that such an attempt is built into the antinomic relations. More generally, a polar relation or opposition becomes an antinomy only within the framework of the systematic attempt to overcome it, because only then does each pole have to reflect on its own autonomy, becoming for-itself or explicitly what it was only in-itself. That is why the completeness and rigor of Marx's system stands as the best (but not the only) illustration of the philosophical roots of the antipolitical temptation. But antipolitics is not simply a theoretical error that can be overcome by enlightenment; to avoid it, one must make a virtue out of the necessary antinomical structures of modern political life. The critique of totalitarianism that is made possible by taking seriously the *philosophical* program of Marx points to the need to look differently at the nature of the political and its relation to the origin of modern politics.[11]

Origins of the Political

The revolutions of 1989 have put an end to what I have called two hundred years of error. Totalitarianism attempted to realize democracy by uniting politics and the political, overcoming the opposition between the democratic individual and the community of which he or she is a member. In this case, the political is defined as the way in which a society and its members come to understand themselves and their relation to one another as the result of their own choice, of their autonomy. When this symbolic or normative dimension that gives meaning to the community is identified with a concrete set of political structures or procedures, there is no longer any place or space for the individual to engage in autonomous self-interpretation or critical reflection. The choice of totalitarian antipolitics arises when the tension between the free individual and the autonomous community is felt to be unbearable; as a result, a synthesis is sought, but its cost is, finally, the loss of both freedom and communal autonomy, and with this comes the eradication of the culture of democracy. The point to be underlined here is that this totalitarian adventure was not an accident, an historical aberration, an irrational folly or childhood illness against which humanity has now been safely vaccinated. This is why the revolutions of 1989 have to be seen in a larger perspective.

The critique of totalitarianism as antipolitical has implications not only for the self-understanding of the societies that were liberated by its fall. The tension between politics and the political is present in Western democracies as well. Liberal political truisms, like faith in the neutrality of the market, the separation of the social and the political or the private and the public express antipolitical tendencies. Modern political techniques, such as the increasing usage of juridification and bureaucratic or technocratic solutions, perform a similar function. The same refusal of tension underlies appeals to values, to tradition or to ethnic or religious bonds. The appearance of these forms of antipolitics is no more surprising or illegitimate than is the attempt by various interests to make their weight felt on the political scene. The danger is their one-sided affirmation, their denial of the need to preserve the place of the political that makes society's self-interrogation and self-critique possible. The fate of the revolutions of 1989 will depend on their ability to maintain the autonomy of the political, as will the future of the Western democracies. They must learn this lesson from the revolutions of 1989 if they are to avoid the forms of antipolitics that have come to dominate that which passes for politics among them. This is what is meant by the need for the politicization of politics.

The challenges facing the post-1989 world can be put into perspective by returning to the era opened by the American and the French Revolutions. These ruptures created a new political *Gestalt* that is characterized by the presence of the antinomies to which I have just referred.[12] The modern individual was liberated from the traditional bonds of community and from the representation of the world as an organic and hierarchical totality. How could that individual find his (and eventually her) place among other individuals who were equally free to search for their own self-realization? How could the pursuit of individual interest, particularly if it affected other individuals and their rights, be justified? What is the responsibility of the individual to other individuals? Could a framework be found, a new kind of solidarity, within which individuality could find a place without losing its individuality? How can a communal solidarity generate normative validity without endangering the rights of the individual whose free will must be realized in a social unity that is not simply accidental? Such questions are familiar to the philosopher; they date back to the origins of the *Polis*. Their modern formulation oscillates between the search for a republican polity and the affirmation of a democratic society.

These questions, and their derivatives, confront not only the philosopher; the historian also encounters them, as does the practical politician. Whereas totalitarianism sought to overcome the antinomies, antipolitics tries to avoid them. The earliest figure of antipolitics is furnished by the two forms of nineteenth-century liberalism—the Anglo-American and the Continental. The former appeals to the neutrality of the market, assuming that the freedom of the individual will be justly realized by its abstract, neutral, and objective logic. The latter develops Benjamin Constant's distinction between the freedom of the Ancients and that of the Moderns by separating the conditions of political life in common from that of private individual rights. In both cases, the antinomic tension is replaced by an appeal to the pole of private rights and the individual quest for happiness. On the other side stand the various forms of socialism, which, beginning with Babeuf, sought to go beyond merely formal individualism to actualize material social justice. Similarly, the conservative reaction to the egoistic individualism unleashed and legitimated by the revolutions attempted to avoid the antinomies of modern democratic politics by recovering traditional communal hierarchies of value.

The political (as distinct from the philosophical) logic of antipolitics is usually illustrated by the course of the French Revolution. But "Origins of Revolution" (chapter 3) shows that a closer look at that history poses more questions than it answers. What was the French Revolution? Was it the emergence of the masses, with the storming of the Bastille, the Great Fear, the *journées*? Was it the Declaration of the Rights of Man and the attempt to work out the institutional forms in which these rights could coexist with the rights of others? Or was the French Revolution an aborted attempt to realize the revolutionary triad of liberty-equality-fraternity? On that more-radical reading, the French Revolution was only a first step, the posing of a task for those who (after the claim that the Russian Revolution of 1917 was its realization has been finally refuted by 1989) have today inherited its legacy. That would imply that the French Revolution was incarnated in its most resolute actors, the Jacobins; and that Lenin's definition, in "One Step Forward, Two Steps Backward," is historically correct: the Bolshevik is a Jacobin irremediably attached to the working class. But this interpretation leaves us again face to face with the inheritance of totalitarianism and—working as historians for the moment—we cannot appeal to philosophy for a critique of the logical foundation of that extreme form of antipolitics.

The misleading metaphorics of the French Revolution can be avoided by taking seriously the American Revolution. That means, first of all, asking (as we do in chapter 4) in what sense was the American Revolution revolutionary? The path that led the colonists from the assertion of the Rights of an Englishman to their Declaration of Independence poses the question of why they were driven to radicalize their demands to the point of rupture. They did not start from a teleological theory of history or from a utopian projection of what should be. This is what makes their politics political; in pursuing concrete aims, and in defending their interests, they discovered the political as the horizon that gave sense to their claims. They had to invent a theory that permitted them to understand, and also to convince their fellow colonists, of the validity of their judgment of events. On this basis, a common citizenship could emerge; a shared experience that could claim universal validity among them was reflected in the creation of a democratic political culture. There was no reason to think, in 1761, when the Seven Years' War ended in North America, that the colonists would demand independence. Fifteen years later, through successive radicalizations of their reflection on who they were and what kind of society they wanted, Tom Paine's *Common Sense* spoke for, and to, all of them: they had generated a common sense of themselves in the course of a series of particular resistances that were transformed from a stubborn negation of British arbitrariness into a normative political affirmation of a solidarity for which no sacrifice was too great. They would hang together rather than live apart.

The political theory by which the Americans justified their demand for independence was based on the idea of an essential opposition between power, which seeks to expand, and liberty, which must constantly defend itself. The Americans knew also that individuals are vain, self-seeking, and easily corruptible. They can fall victim to the lures of power, the allures of honors, or the material benefits bestowed on them by those in power. That is why their Declaration of Independence insisted on the need for a separation from a corrupting court and king. Once free, however, and in the economic and political turmoil created by the War of Independence, they found that their own self-chosen authorities could be equally dangerous. During the crisis years they came to realize that their image of an essentially good people, united in the defense of liberty, was not a theory but an ideology: it was another form of antipolitics. How could they understand the instability, inequity, and interest-domination of their new political world? In their search for self-understanding, they sought to apply their own theory to their new situation, this time as a critique of its ideological presuppositions: how could the people, who now were in power, not realize the common good? Their answer is articulated by the Constitution of 1787, whose premise is radically new: "the people" is not—and should not be—a single collective and unified subject oriented wholly to the general good. That would be a form of antipolitics, in this case, one that points toward the totalitarian form. Instead, their new republic had to be founded on a democracy, a plural society whose inherent divisions and tensions meant also that it remained open constantly to the new.[13]

The American result is conceptualized (in chapter 5) as a "double revolution" whose structure differs from the French model in which a bourgeois or formal revolution of liberty is followed by a social revolution that brings equality as the premise for the realization of true fraternity in which difference is abolished in a shared synthesis that eliminates conflict. In the American case, the presupposition of the unity of the people was put into question by the reality of the politics exercised by the empirically existing plural people during the crisis period. This second revolution illustrates the way in which the political is the presupposition of actual politics. It is a self-reflection, an immanent self-critique. Its institutionalization by the Constitution of 1787 maintains the plurality of the people, and ensures that no group, no institution, and no branch of government can claim to act in the name of "the" people.[14] On this basis, the Americans were able to develop the first system of political parties, to effectuate the first peaceful transfer of power from one political party to another, and to find unity in their own division. The unity that held them together was their modern self-understanding as reflected in a *republican* Constitution, whose application by the Supreme Court could oppose the will of the majority in order to protect the rights of the minority or the single critical individual—and thereby to preserve the plurality of the *democratic* society.

The chapters in which this American political history are presented here illustrate the successive radicalizations by which politics is reflected upon at the level of the political.[15] The events and institutional crystallizations that took place between 1761 and 1800 illustrate the positive interaction and continued tension between a democratic society and a republican polity. The process is traced immanently; the goal is to show the political logic of this revolutionary radicalization. The first chapter, "Why Return to the American Revolution?" (chapter 4), begins from the question of whether the American Revolution was indeed a revolution. Written before 1989, it tries to show how the preservation—rather than the overcoming—of the antinomic relation between republican and democratic institutions could lead to a radical politics that could have an application in the contemporary West. The second chapter, "Liberalism, Democracy, and the Theory of the Double Revolution" (chapter 5), was written after 1989. It was intended as a reflection on the difficulties facing the societies that had liberated themselves from totalitarianism. Its "American" formulation of the concept of the double revolution—and on the temptation faced by even American historians to revert to the French model in which 1793 (or 1917) would follow 1789—was intended to suggest that this same self-reflection was necessary in the East.[16]

However, the American Revolution cannot stand alone as the origin of the political; nor can the solutions it invented—which were unable to confront the moral challenge of slavery and the economic challenge of industrialization—be thought of as the ultimate resolution of the antinomy of politics and the political. That is why I return to the French Revolution in "Constitution, Representation, and Rights" (chapter 6), again reading immanently the historical record. The difference between politics and the political reappears, and the representation of the political affects political events and choices. The analysis of the political structure of the ancien régime from which the modern individual liberates himself poses the question of why the French Revolution could not invent institutions adequate to the new political world to which it gave birth, how it had to radicalize itself continuously, and why it has nonetheless remained the model of modern revolutions. In addressing these questions, the political historian encounters repeatedly the philosophical structure of the political. The conflict of the two wills liberated by the revolution—the will of the individual, consecrated in the Declaration of the Rights of Man, and the unitary will of the sovereign nation, affirmed against the representative claims of the monarchy—reappears in "Toward a Politics of Judgment" (chapter 14), as the basis from which a politics of judgment, which thematizes the common sense of the American Revolution, can emerge.

Political Theory or Theory of the Political?

Political theory presupposes what it needs to prove: the nature of the political. The problem is not that political theory is ahistorical (although it often is). Even when the dynamics of history are taken into account, for example by Marx, political theory is antipolitical. Although the Kantian question of the "conditions of the possibility" of politics points to the need to distinguish politics from the political, it presupposes that the empirically given form of politics, whose conditions of possibility it seeks to understand, defines the political. However, we have seen that revolutions are only the extreme case of the constant challenge to redefine the political, and thus politics. In what sense was the attempt to create an autonomous civil society in Eastern Europe political? In what sense are the new social movements of recent years political? Similar questions can be asked of the role of economic interests, moral concerns, cultural autonomy, or the individual right to private liberty. History shows that any of these domains of life can become political even though it was not originally taken as part of politics. This occurs when the conditions of the possibility of their self-affirmation challenge the previously assumed definition of politics and put into question the nature of the political, which was the foundation of that form of politics. The resulting tension between politics and the political opens up a public space in which society (and its members) can reflect on what it is and on what it wants to be.

The explicit difference between politics and the political that emerges from the new attempts to define the political becomes antinomical when the attempt is made to overcome this difference. We have seen that Kant's successors were driven by the quest for systematic completeness to try to find a unity in which all particulars would have their rational place. They assumed, as the philosophical Marx put it, that "reason has always existed but not always in a rational form."[17] In this case, however, political theory is identified with philosophy; it is taken to be the expression of a latent reason whose actualization is the task of the praxis of political vanguards who claim to know the path that necessity must follow. As such, political theory becomes an ideology. Those who act in its name become its servants—the same "selfless servants" of whom Plato's *Republic* spoke at the beginnings of political theory, and who reappear as faithful members of the totalitarian party at its end.[18] Because they assume that they know already the nature of the political, the theory-praxis problem appears to them as a problem demanding simply a mechanical adaptation of the world to their theory rather than posing the challenge of how to judge the particular situation with which they are confronted. The result is that political theory separates itself from the political world of which, or for which, it claims to be the representative.

The practical expression (or the politics) of this kind of political theory takes the form of enlightenment. In its premodern form, it is based on the assumption that "to know the good is to do the good." With the birth of modernity, the external guarantee that the now autonomous and free individual subject will be receptive to the enlightened politics of political theory could no longer be taken for granted. Chapter 7, "Politics of Modernism: From Marx to Kant," shows that the rationalism of the *Lumières* cannot be maintained after revolution has dissolved social unity into a plurality of rights-bearing individuals whose relation to one another poses the question of the political. The enlightenment's version of the critique of ideology, which separated the theorist from a world in which he (or his theory) was not a participant, had to be reformulated as a permanent and immanent self-critique. This was the great advance of Marx's concept of ideology, which presents capitalism's self-reproduction as just such a self-critique. However, as we have seen, the systematic imperative led the philosophical Marx to postulate the proletariat as the *real* subject-object of history whose unity would overcome all contradictions. My claim is that the resulting antipolitics can be avoided, and Marx's insight into the nature of ideology can be salvaged, by a return to the antinomical Kant.

The critique of ideology that replaces the rationalist philosophical politics of enlightenment draws on the analysis of antipolitics. Ideology is defined as the attempt to overcome the antinomical tensions that we have seen to constitute the immanent structure of modernity. Capitalism's attempt to define the social world in economic terms, to reduce all values to exchange-value, to eliminate the novelty that it constantly produces is only one illustration of a structure that penetrates all of the domains of modern life. The lawyer defines the world through the lens of the law, the scientist thinks it through her concepts, the consumer through his. This reification that reduces difference to unity was defined by Herbert Marcuse as "one-dimensionality," and it had been the object of the Frankfurt School's critical theory. The Frankfurters' attempt to salvage difference and to preserve the autonomy of critique culminated in Adorno and Horkheimer's *Dialektik der Aufklärung* whose pessimism suggested that escape from ideology and the preservation of autonomy was possible only for a theory that, in Adorno's later phrase, preserved its radicality because the moment for its realization had been missed. Although Adorno's "negative dialectics" sought to avoid the idealism of Hegelian-Marxism and to remain true to the paradoxical structure, in the last resort, of modernity, for it the critique of ideology became itself a politics. The grounds of this inversion of the place of politics and philosophy are suggested by Gadamer's hermeneutical attempt to reclaim tradition for modernity. Usually written off as a conservative, Gadamer confronted the Frankfurt thinkers, reaffirming a lesson learned by the young Marx in his critique of his Left-Hegelian friends who also confused philosophy and politics. Just as with those whom Marx called the "theoretical" and the "practical" parties, so here neither philosophical form of enlightenment as politics (see chapter 8) can stand on its own; each sunders the antinomic totality and finds itself doing the opposite of what it intended.[19]

The philosophical critique of ideology does not see that capitalism does not have or apply an ideology in order to veil its reality; capitalism is ideology. It is the attempt to define all meaning—including that of the political—in terms of economic production and reproduction. In this way, capitalism denies the self-critical nature of modernity just as does the antipolitical totalitarian attempt to overcome its contradictions. Neither ideology recognizes that the immanently self-critical structure of modernity is simply the expression of its democratic nature. It is this insight that permits Jürgen Habermas's *Faktizität und Geltung* (see chapter 9) to move beyond both the first generation of critical theory as well as his own earlier attempts to formulate a theory of the political.[20] Rather than analyze modernization as a socioeconomic process in the course of which the political is differentiated from society in order to become an autonomous steering mechanism, Habermas insists on the need to combine "a discourse theory of right" with a "communication theory of society" in order to articulate a critical theory of democracy. His theory remains in the Frankfurt tradition insofar as it builds from an immanent critique; but it goes beyond it by joining together the processes of modernization with those of democratization. The pessimism that Frankfurt critical theory inherited from Weber can then be replaced by a positive account of the rationalization of the life-world.

Despite his recognition of the primacy of democracy, Habermas remains a political theorist whose politics is defined by the task of enlightenment. He admits that democracy cannot live without democrats; yet his political theory of "liberal culture" presupposes what it needs to prove. Habermas stresses the role of the "new social movements" in defining the political; and he articulates and maintains the tension between the imperatives of the system and the reproduction of the life-world. His democratic theory of law is presented as playing a "hinge" function, mediating between these two spheres without conflating them; the political result is presented in the image of a life-world that imposes what he calls a siege on the system. In this sense, he preserves the antinomical structure of the political, which he defines as occupying the dimension of "verticality" as opposed to the "horizontal" relations within society. He sees how the need to articulate demands in the language of the law in order for them to be "heard" at the level of the system, which is the place where change can actually occur, makes possible also a rationalization of the life-world through the systemic process that he calls "counter-steering." At the same time, his philosophical interweaving of a legal theory, a social analysis, and a political project recalls Hegel's *Philosophy of Right*. But just this similarity puts into question Habermas's presupposition of a liberal culture, which, as we saw with Hegel's *Sittlichkeit*, is articulated by the same systematic account that it makes possible. What is this liberal culture? How does democratic society reproduce itself? How can it avoid the snares of antipolitics? The familiar problems return once again.

Habermas's commentaries on the revolutions of 1989, and his reflections on the anniversary of 1789, make clear that for him the realization of the Enlightenment defines both democracy and modern liberal culture. His analysis of the revolutions of 1989 as a kind of "revolutionary catching-up" (*nachholende Revolution*) is based on the idea that Soviet-bloc societies had never been touched by the possibility of democratic politics. That the revolutions of 1848, for example, did not succeed in opening these parts of the world to stable democratic institutions is an empirical fact of politics. The philosophical issue is different, as was suggested by the claim that the American and French Revolutions presented the origins of democratic politics even though the Americans did not abolish slavery, or give women (or eighteen-year-olds) the vote, and even though the French Revolution gave way to the Terror, the Empire, and the Restoration. Russia was not a complete democracy, but serfdom was abolished in 1863, liberal Westernizing individualism did compete increasingly with appeals to the Slavic soul, and a revolution did break out in 1905. Similar tendencies, often more pronounced, could be found in east-central Europe before communism came to power in 1948. The point is, once again, that the totalitarian temptation is immanent to the self-critical, antinomic structure that emerges with the end of a hierarchical and organic representation of the world, and that makes possible both the politics of democracy and the tension that can lead to antipolitics. It is not enough to say, with Habermas, that Enlightenment defines the political; and that politics are then to be judged by the degree of their adequacy to this presupposed goal. Such a definition of the political leaves unclear the relation between the life-world and the liberal culture, which is both the presupposition and definition of the nature of the politics implied by Habermas's political theory. There is no reason why an Eastern European politics of the life-world could not take an (atavistic or populist) antipolitical form as a reaction to the abstract imperatives of the logic of the market. That is why I return to Kant at the end of this section (chapter 14) to stress the *republican* moment of democratic politics. This is the legacy that 1789 offers to the heirs of 1989.[21]

Unlike Habermas, Kant could not presuppose the existence of a liberal or democratic culture in his pursuit of a politics of enlightenment. A Kantian account of how such a culture might be created suggests another reason for the move from Marx to Kant (see chapter 10). Kant's 1784 essay, "The Idea of History from a Cosmopolitan Point of View," invoked international relations in order to suggest how a republican politics might be produced. His argument, however, was formulated before he had developed his concept of reflective (as opposed to subsumptive) judgment in the *Critique of Judgement*. That is why a Marxist like Lukács could argue that Kant's philosophical revolution had to be completed by Marx; it is also why I insist, in chapter 10, that if Kant were a Marxist, he would not have written the *Critique of Judgement*. The theory of reflective judgment permits a different reading of Kant's political proposals, for example, as he reformulated them in "Perpetual Peace" (1795). The question now is, how do those kinds of particulars that cannot be subsumed under pregiven laws emerge? What kind of particulars call for the experience of reflective judgment? Consideration of international relations provides one element of an answer insofar as change at this level can affect the way in which domestic relations are perceived.[22] What is illustrated in this process is the means by which *defining the political* presents the matter for politics. Political judgment as reflective creates the public space (and republican framework) in which the individual can validate his or her rights within the framework of a community that is constituted in that very same exercise. In this way, the vicious circle in which political theory presupposes what it wants to prove can be replaced by a theory of the political; reflective judgment suggests the method by which, in modern conditions, the political is defined.

Political Judgment

The political theorist who was criticized a moment ago because he applies ideology-critique to a world external to his theory avoids the need to judge particular events and to interpret their singularity for and with a community that must confront them. In so doing, the political theorist is subsuming particulars under pregiven laws. However, as opposed to the premises of natural science or of traditional society, there is no guarantee in the world of modernity that others will accept the validity of these particular judgments. As the American Revolution illustrated, political judgments are accepted only by a common sense that is produced through self-critical public judgments of events and conditions. In this way, a receptivity is produced, a shared sense whose function was seen in the reception of Tom Paine's *plaidoyer* for an independent republic in 1776. This moment of receptivity must supplement the moment of particularity that poses the question of the political. The two moments are interdependent; they present another variant of the antinomic structure that founds modern politics. Particular interests, grievances, or causes do not, on their own, give rise to political actions; there must be present also a public that is receptive to the particular claims if their realization is to be legitimate rather than the result of external manipulation. However, receptivity alone does not suffice; a receptive public confronted with issues that are of a type that does not demand reflective judgment can fall victim to populist demagogy that seizes on systemic issues that belong to the technical domain of political steering (e.g., budget deficits) or to concerns of the life-world (e.g., values) to pursue its own agenda.[23]

The antinomic moments of particularity and receptivity that constitute the reflective judgment present an interpretive framework for contemporary political choices. I began with my own experiences, which led me to ask in chapter 11 if the American and European Left are involved in the same struggle. The American New Left took form in the Civil Rights movement, which exemplified the interplay between particularity and receptivity. In what sense were sit-ins political? How did these particular demands for rights awaken a sense of injustice and a receptivity to change on the part of the public? In Europe, meanwhile, another kind of New Left was emerging. Emblematically, while both the American and German Lefts were organized under the label SDS, the Americans were Students for a Democratic Society and the Germans were the Sozialistischer Deutscher Studentenbund. Yet in that heady year 1968, their actions transformed the political culture of both nations. In the years that followed, both lost their creative force because, instead of continuing to define the political, they adopted a pregiven "revolutionary" definition of politics. A third Left also began to emerge in 1968: not the Euro-communism crushed by its so-called fraternal allies in Prague, but an antitotalitarian Left that looked to a democratic politics to insure individual rights and leave society free to give itself the forms that it wished. That third Left was not understood by the Western Lefts—indeed, many have still not understood it.[24]

It is tempting to interpret the revolutions of 1989 in terms of the model of reflective judgment, with its moments of particularity and receptivity crystallizing in a common sense whose self-evidence explains the rapidity with which the seemingly omnipotent totalitarian party was swept away without violence. The dissidents of the previous years had stood up to oppression, had sought to "live in truth" (V. Havel) and to assert their rights as individuals. But could these particular actions, this attempt to define the political, engender the necessary moment of receptivity? There was apparently no public space, no liberal culture that could hear their voices, see their actions, and share their experience. Yet the attempt to create a civil society independent from the state did proceed, differently in different political cultures, for example in Poland, Czechoslovakia, or Hungary. It is quite tempting to interpret this process in terms of a politics of judgment, and to see analogies to the end of the Old Order in 1776 or 1789. Yet this is only one side of the story. The opposition to totalitarianism was often more of an ethical assertion of the individual will than it was a political formation of public judgment.[25] The rapidity with which many leaders of the opposition disappeared from the political life of their nations in the years following 1989, and their inability to adapt to the conditions of a democratic politics, recalls the problems encountered by the politics of will that emerged in the French Revolution. How can the individual will coexist with the will of the nation? The answer depends on the politicization of politics.

The proposed move from Habermas to Kant suggests a different formulation of the challenges facing the revolutions of 1989. How can a political culture be created after forty years during which the only option for the individual was the ethical politics of will? The problem becomes more difficult when it is admitted that totalitarianism was not imposed from the outside on a unanimously resistant people; it was supported from within, enthusiastically by some, passively by others, and even with a certain civic courage by those who tried to make the best of the cards history had dealt them.[26] This sometimes active, sometimes passive support for the Old Order explains why I pose the question of guilt in "Guilt and the Birth of Democracy" (chapter 13). Although I treat it in the specific context of the former East Germany, and by comparison with Karl Jaspers's reflections on the problem in the wake of Nazism, the dilemma is more general. As the conflict of the two politics of will in the French Revolution showed, a revolutionary rupture with the past makes all traces of that past appear guilty; and once the legitimacy of the revolutionary present is defined by its negation of the past, any critical opinion can be denounced as supporting the guilty past: as treason. To avoid the kind of spiral experienced by the French Revolution that culminated in a law of suspects that decreed that those who are not fully with us are secretly our enemies, it is necessary to move toward what chapter 14 calls a politics of judgment.

The critique of totalitarianism as well as the experience of the American Revolution suggest a way to transform the guilty past into an element of the democratic present. The question of guilt can be reformulated as the problem of corruption by applying the theory of the American colonists who recognized that power is expanded not by force but by corrupting a self-interested, easily beguiled, and irresponsible citizenry who will do its bidding in exchange for material reward or social honors. The critique of totalitarianism adds to that account of the American experience the idea that guilt as corruption is also a corruption of the political, a destruction of the antinomic structure within which democracy can function, the option for security rather than the uncertainty and risks of life in a democratic society. On this basis, the actions and omissions of those who lived under the old regime can be judged publicly—not in a court of law (although actual crimes must be punished) but in the court of public opinion. This kind of judgment is at the same time constitutive of a democratic public that comes to know what it means to take responsibility for one's particular actions. The different modes of behavior under the Old Regime can become the subject of political judgment insofar as that regime is now distinct from the present; at the same time, the present can never simply overcome, forget, or master once and for all its past. Solidarity can exist only with those who are different from the individual and who nonetheless recognize a responsibility for common belonging.

The judgment of the corruption of the political adds to the politics of judgment the notion of responsibility. What is judged is not the will of an individual, nor the results of the action of an individual will. The question is neither ethical, existential, or legal, as if one could be found guilty for not "living in truth." The political culture that is needed to maintain a vital democracy must be based on a kind of receptivity that cannot be led astray by the kind of populist demagogy that replaces reflective public judgment by the subsumption of political choice under technical imperatives (e.g., reduce the budget deficit) or absolute moral values (e.g., abortion is always killing). By contrast, a democratic form of receptivity depends on the existence of a sense of responsibility whose foundations can be seen in the *act* of reflective judgment. It claims not only to be true; it appeals also to an other whom it wants to convince of the rightness of its assertion. To appeal to an other is to recognize his or her autonomy; but it is also to express a sense of responsibility toward another individual. Whereas the politics of enlightenment does not need to engage the otherness of the other, who—in Habermas's phrase—has only to "catch up," the politics of judgment occurs only when I assume a responsibility toward that other in a nonpaternalistic manner radically different from that of the Enlightened Despots whom Kant already had so bitterly opposed.[27] The acceptance of my judgment by another individual does not mean that she becomes like me; that would deny her autonomy, which was what made necessary the reflective form of the judgment in the first place. The existence of a shared or common sense does not exclude the autonomy of the individual, which is, in fact, its premise. Responsibility is not obedience to a pregiven and universal ethical imperative but the creation of a political bond based on mutual recognition by autonomous individuals.

In this way, the contemporary politics of judgment returns to the structure of the political as it emerged in the wake of the American and French Revolutions. Judgment does not replace the (individual or collective) will; it is its precondition. The formulation of a politics of judgment avoids the antipolitics that was born at the same time. It gives particular interest its legitimate place in the political process without permitting that interest to deny its role as political; and it leaves space for the quest for a common identity without opening the possibility of an atavistic ideology. The solidarity based on responsibility toward other autonomous individuals with whom one shares a common public space is the precondition for confronting the fundamental political question facing not only the revolutions of 1989 but also the contemporary West: the issue becomes the choice between a politics of sacrifice or the sacrifice of politics (chapter 12). The old welfare state and the safety net that it provided cannot be re-created or reinvigorated; it is overburdened, indebted, and inefficient, and its political foundation has been put into question by the realities of an interdependent world order.[28] The invocation of an imperious external necessity in order to impose sacrifice on the citizenry is an antipolitics that can give way to demagogy; it is based on the subsumption of the given conditions under pregiven lawfulness (called necessity). While it may succeed for a time, it cannot produce the normative legitimacy that makes sacrifice into an act of solidarity that revivifies the political and makes it possible for society to confront the new challenges that will confront it without giving up its democratic foundation.

The lessons and logic that emerge from reflection on the revolutions of 1989 help to clarify the nature of the disarray in which democracy finds itself today. Democracy is a fragile creation, constantly self-critical, subject to the ideological temptations of antipolitics; democracy is never achieved fully or finally. The need that I called making a virtue out of necessity in order to sustain its antinomical tensions does not legitimate the politicians' appeal to external necessities to justify their actions and omissions. If they try to do so, the politicians act like the political theorists of enlightenment who presuppose what they want to prove. In this context, the Maastricht Treaty on European Union and the election of Bill Clinton, which apparently signified a rebirth of the political, are seen to be less hopeful signs than one might have thought at first glance. They express an antipolitical appeal to external necessity rather than the judgment of how particular conditions demand public reflection and particular sacrifice. If this imposition of shared sacrifice is to be supplemented by a solidarity based on responsibility, a new or renewed democratic political culture must be created. Whether this will occur remains an open question. It is, in effect, the question of the politicization of the political—the recognition of, and refusal to submit to, the antipolitical temptation, which is the lesson to be learned from the critique of totalitarianism.[29]

Notes

1. The first citation is found in the *New Republic*, 31 January 1994; the second is from the *New York Times*, 21 January 1994, A 10. Sachs's own proposals for the former empire are explicitly antipolitical in the sense that I will be using the term here.
2. No single definition of the political can be offered, as if one were dealing

with an intemporal essence; indeed, as will be seen, I talk frequently about *defining the political*. My use of the term is not indebted to Carl Schmitt but to its French usage in the critique of totalitarianism, particularly in the writing of Claude Lefort, Cornelius Castoriadis, and Paul Thibaud.

3. I am using the notion of antipolitics in this sentence in the sense of György Konrad and *not* in the specific meaning that I am giving to it in this volume. Konrad's notion, and that of the antitotalitarian movements in Eastern Europe before 1989, has been thematized and theorized in Jean Cohen and Andrew Arato, *Civil Society and Political Theory* (Cambridge: MIT Press, 1992). As I suggest below, and in chapters 13 and 14, the difficulties facing attempts to translate this antipolitics after 1989 pose important political and philosophical problems.

4. It should be stressed that defining the political is not the task only of revolutionary politics. Indeed, in an essay reprinted in *Defining the Political* (Minneapolis: University of Minnesota Press, 1989), which examines the political origins of democracy, I begin from the question of how radical politics is possible when one no longer believes in "the" revolution.

5. On this notion, see chapter 9 as well as the arguments in part 3 of this introduction.

6. This point is stressed particularly in chapter 14, where Ulrich Beck's point that the German Left never took seriously the logic of totalitarianism is cited. Similarly, in chapter 11, when I try to explain why the promising beginnings of the American New Left were deformed, the failure to understand the challenge of totalitarianism is seen to be a crucial element. By contrast, the "second Left" in France developed precisely on the basis of such a critique, and it correctly criticized the pacifism of the German Left in the 1980s debate over the installation of the Cruise and Pershing missiles which, arguably, was one of the external influences on the fall of totalitarianism. The French influence on my own work, and my experience in Eastern Europe, explains why I can republish these pre-1989 essays in a volume that seeks to understand the implications of the revolutions of 1989.

7. This title was suggested to me by Raimund Fellinger of Suhrkamp Verlag; it served as the title of the German edition of this book. For the systematic philosophical argument to which I allude in the text, see my *From Marx to Kant*, second ed. (London: Macmillan, and New York: St. Martin's Press, 1993).

8. It could be said that Kant's antinomies, as presented in the *Critique of Pure Reason,* are not in fact antinomical since his solution to them shows that they result from a confusion of the claims of understanding with those of reason. The same might be said of the examples I have just given: why should they not simply coexist peacefully, side by side? The point, as I will show in a moment, is that dichotomies or dualisms can *become* antinomic in specific conditions.

9. As will be seen below, and in chapter 9, Habermas's *Faktizität und Geltung* poses the problem anew.

10. Reprinted in Georg Lukács, *Werke*, vol. 2 (Neuwied: Luchterhand Verlag, 1968). English translation by Rodney Livingstone (Cambridge: MIT Press, 1971).

11. By underlining "philosophical" here, I am accepting the distinction proposed by Miguel Abensour's "Réflexions sur les deux interprétations du totalitarisme chez Claude Lefort" in *La démocratie à l'oeuvre. Autour de Claude Lefort* (Paris: Editions Esprit, 1993), 79–136, which differentiates a political critique of totalitarianism as a new historical form of political domination and a philosophical critique, which is not circumscribed by the empirical form of any given totalitarian system but puts into question the very nature of the political.

12. What of the English revolution of 1640, if not that of 1688? Michael Walzer has argued in *The Revolution of the Saints* (Cambridge, Mass.: Harvard University Press, 1965) that it is around the former revolution that one can trace what his subtitle calls the "origins of radical politics." The problem, however, is suggested in an earlier article that develops his thesis, "Puritanism as a Revolutionary Ideology" (in *History and Theory* 3, no. 1 [1963]). As a form of religious belief, Puritanism cannot be said to be modern or furnish a model for modern politics. Walzer's interpretation is quite possibly based on an interpretation of totalitarianism that is indebted to J. L. Talmon's the *Origins of Totalitarian Democracy* (New York: Praeger, 1960), which I find oversimplified.

13. In part 3 of this introduction, I argue that political theory is inadequate insofar as it presupposes what it needs to prove: the nature of the political. But I assert as well that the American experience of a "double revolution" in which a critical self-reflexion on the premises of the revolution takes place is necessary if the revolutions of 1989 are to succeed in instituting a new democratic political order. See also on this concept, chapter 5.

14. This claim is developed in my study *La naissance de la pensée politique américaine* (Paris: Ramsay, 1987), and elaborated in the afterword to its English translation, *The Birth of American Political Thought* (Minneapolis: University of Minnesota Press, and London: Macmillan, 1990). At one level, American political history can be read as a competition among the branches of government (including the federal states), which claim to be the true representation of the will of the American people as a whole. A recent illustration of this thesis is provided by a former member of the cabinets of Lyndon Johnson and Jimmy Carter, Joseph Califano, who sees the present ills of American politics as due to the fact that an "imperial Congress" has come to replace what was called in the 1970s an "imperial presidency." Califano's "Imperial Congress" was published in the *New York Times Magazine*, 23 January 1994. For a different argument, see Michael Lind, "The Out-of-Control Presidency," *New Republic*, 14 August 1995, 18–23. Lind's argument makes use of arguments similar to the ones that I develop here, citing, for example, *Federalist 63*. His article is worth reading for its analysis of the conjunctural roots of the present political stalemate in the United States.

15. In *The Birth of American Political Thought*, I make this process explicit by dividing each historical period into its "lived experience," its "reflection," and its "conception," which, in turn, becomes the first stage of the next period. To each of these moments I add, under the title "History Rethought," a discussion of the political presuppositions of the historiographers who have interpreted these developments.

16. I should underline that this idea of a second revolution is based on the American experience. Andrew Arato has pointed out that in post-1989 Hungary, elements of the nationalist right wing have suggested the applicability of the French model: for them, 1989 was "only" a bourgeois or formal revolution, which needs to be "realized" by a truly national revolution (Andrew Arato, "Revolution, Restoration and Legitimation: Ideological Problems of the Transition from State Socialism," Working Paper No. 156 [New York: Center for Studies of Social Change, New School for Social Research]).

17. Marx to Arnold Ruge, September 1843, published as part of "Ein Briefwechsel von 1843" in the *Deutsch-Französözischen Jahrbüchern*, and reprinted in Karl Marx, *Frühe Schriften* (Stuttgart: Cotta-Verlag, 1962), 448.

18. The argument that political theory destroys its own presuppositions from Plato onward is developed in Sheldon Wolin's *Politics and Vision* (Boston: Little, Brown, 1960). The critique of the party militant that I suggest here is presented by Claude Lefort; I develop its outlines in chapter 14. As already suggested, this temptation is present also in the French and American Revolutions; but the Americans avoided it through their "double revolution."

19. For Marx's explanation, see the Note to his dissertation, which the editors call "Das Philosophisch-Werden der Welt als Weltlich-Werden der Philosophie" (*Frühe Schriften*, 71–73), where the two parties are called "liberal" and "theoretical," and "Zur Kritik der Hegelschen Rechtsphilosophie" (*Frühe Schriften*, 495-96). At the end of this latter text, Marx introduces his theory of the proletariat as overcoming the antinomy. A similar inversion is present in Marcuse's attempts to understand the nature and place of a radical art, as illustrated in chapter 7, below.

20. I would claim that this attempt to define the political has been at the foundation of Habermas's work since *Legitimationsprobleme im Spätkapitalismus* (Frankfurt am Main: Suhrkamp Verlag, 1973), which I discussed in *The Marxian Legacy* under the title "A Politics in Search of the Political." Similarly, in his *Theorie des kommunikativen Handelns* (Frankfurt am Main: Suhrkamp, 1981), as I argue in the afterword to the second edition of *The Marxian Legacy*, the same problem reemerges when Habermas can only define the need for political action as the reaction to a "challenge" (*Herausforderung*) to the life-world. As I argue in chapter 9 below, *Faktizität und Geltung* comes closer to an adequate formulation.

21. This republican structure should not be equated with contemporary "communitarian" critiques of liberalism that Habermas rightly criticizes nor is it simply the ancestor of Rawls's deontological theory of justice. The relation

of a republican politics to a democratic society (or culture) proves to be antinomical; neither can stand alone but they cannot be conflated. That is why the claims to realize a People's Republic or even a Democratic Republic are simply disguises for totalitarian antipolitics. With this danger in mind, one can interpret positively Habermas's insistence that he is presenting two distinct theories: that of a democratic (or discourse) theory of law (or right), and that of a communication theory of society. The "hinge" function of the law serves to maintain the distinctness of the two projects.

22. One reason for my stressing the role of international relations is that I wrote that essay at the time when the struggle over the Euro-missiles was taking place. As I have already suggested, that challenge to totalitarianism was one ground for the domestic and foreign policies of Mikhail Gorbachev, whose ultimate result was the revolutions of 1989. Despite my criticisms of the political logic by which the Maastricht Treaty proposed to advance European unification (chapter 12), it is possible that Maastricht could have positive implications along the lines suggested here. At least that was the argument that I suggested in "France, Germany and the Concept of Europe" (1985), reprinted in *Defining the Political*.

23. Habermas's *Faktizität und Geltung* provides the analytic tools to avoid this danger. In addition to the distinctions already mentioned, Habermas's democratic theory insists that "all of those potentially concerned" must take part in defining the political. Receptivity cannot be simply presupposed; the life-world is not the same as the "liberal political culture" that is crucial for Habermas.

24. This is the case particularly in Germany, where the critique of totalitarianism had not taken root, and where the post-1989 liberation of the former German Democratic Republic has at times been interpreted as the expression of material greed symbolized by the desire for the imported bananas of which the West Germans are the world's great consumers. The same critique applies to much of the American Left. Left politics does not entail a denial of the place of interest; it is not a new form of moral asceticism.

25. This assertion would be difficult to justify (or falsify) empirically, but the conceptual distinction needs to be made in order to see how the ethical affirmation of the will can define the political under certain conditions, but how its separation from the political, its absolutization, makes it incapable of participation in democratic politics. A similar argument is suggested by my critique of the interpretation of the French student revolt of 1968 as "political" and that of 1986 as "ethical." That essay, which was not titled "Ethics *or* Politics" but "Ethics *and* Politics," is reprinted in *Defining the Political*.

26. The problem can also be presented as that of the emergence of new elites and the nature of their legitimacy. Posed in this manner, it reflects back on the Western democracies as well, as Tocqueville had seen in *Democracy in America*. Is the notion of a "democratic elite" a contradiction in terms? The addition of the concept of responsibility to the notion of reflective judgment in this discussion of guilt is a first step toward replying to this question.

27. On this latter point, see my essay on the work of Ingeborg Maus, "Just Democracy," in *Constellations* 2, no. 3 (1996). Ingeborg Maus's reinterpretation of Kant's political theory in *Zur Aufklärung der Demokratietheorie* stresses the antipaternalism of Kant's position and its relation to a modern theory of democracy. I might mention in this context that the first essay in which I develop some of the ideas behind this volume is "Enlightened Despotism and Democracy," originally published in 1977 and now reprinted in *Defining the Political*.

28. Pierre Rosanvallon argues in *La troisième crise de l'Etat Providence* (Paris: Fondation Saint-Simon, 1993) that the contemporary welfare state is based on a concept of solidarity derived from the notion of a collective insurance policy in which individuals who are abstractly identical are faced with a threat that could hit any one of them at any time. This kind of welfare state, whose emergence in France is traced by Francois Ewald's *L'Etat providence* (Paris: Grasset, 1986) to the need to develop insurance against accidents at work, can no longer justify its appeal for sacrifice in a society where some have jobs and educational qualifications that make them immune to the danger of falling through the social safety net. Rosanvallon does not explain what kind of "new solidarity" could emerge, and how it could emerge, but his analysis of the "crisis" is telling.

29. In the case of Clinton, I propose some directions in which this process might be developed in terms of what I call a "middle-class politics." I need not emphasize that this is a judgment, as are other political assertions in this volume; they are offered as arguments about the political, not as sociological observations to which it could be replied, for example, that "of course all practical political battles are won at the middle." It might be objected that my emphasis elsewhere in this volume on the role of new social movements and "the party of disorder" imply that the political can be defined anew only from outside of the established political order. By including this discussion of Clinton and Maastricht, I have tried to underline the fact that politics cannot be redefined simply by an act of will that anyone can undertake at any time. Conditions of receptivity are necessary. On the other hand, necessity does exist: the task of political judgment is to redefine the political implications of that necessity. Politics is not continual invention; autonomy is not solipsism. Radical politics is not radical because it avoids or ignores the political system; it is radical because it insists on the democratic politics that modernity makes possible.

2

The Marxian Legacy and the
Problem of Democracy

After 1989, there is no reason to adhere to old conceptual frameworks; the time is ripe for iconoclasm. Let me propose, therefore, that Marxism and the free-market faith share something in common. Despite the difference in the content of their goals, they share a common perspective that I designate here as that of "the party of order," and that I analyze more generally as antipolitics. Because neither can understand the phenomenon of democracy, their quarrel over content disguises a secret connivance. The result has been two hundred years of error, a series of errors that stem from the inability to recognize, and to live within, the tensions and paradoxes of a modern democracy. The problems that emerged with the birth of modernity, at the time of the American and the French Revolutions, have not been so much addressed as avoided by the proponents of socialism as well as those of free-market capitalism. The revolutions of 1989 permit us to begin anew, if we can understand the nature of the problems that we have to confront.

The challenge that we are facing is not just conjunctural; it is the structure of modernity that is called into question by the very gains that made it possible. The modern individual is a being who has "a right to have rights" (Arendt), but whose really existing rights are guaranteed nowhere, by no external force, be it God, nature, material necessity, or rational choice. It is the emergence of this individual, and the problematic of rights, that justifies calling the events of 1989 by the name "revolution." If the new situation is revolutionary, then we have to rethink the nature of that concept as it has come down to us from the nineteenth century. If we do, then the dilemma of the former

31

opposition in the lands where "really existing socialism" (Bahro) has been shown to have been naked can be rethought: what it took to oppose totalitarianism is not necessarily the basis for the creation of modern democracy. It will appear that the old leftist dream of a "Third Way" has no future because it had no really possible past.

However, neither Marxism nor the free market can be thrown out, as if they were somehow proven false by reality. The challenge is to understand how the (erroneous) question to which they provide the (correct) reply could have emerged. This is where the phenomenon of "cognitive dissonance" emerges. What kind of theory cannot be challenged by reality? What kind of practice makes theory necessary at the same time that, as practice, it can never be reduced to, or completely absorbed by, its own necessary theory? These questions are not abstract. Their paradoxical formulation here needs to be explored against the background of the old certainties and the new doubts and challenges.

Cognitive Dissonances after 1989

Should the "events" of 1989 surprise a serious leftist? I call these massive changes "events," in scare-quotes, to play on the way the French avoided coming to grips with their own, apparently inexplicable, experience in May 1968 when a student protest was transformed into a paralyzing general strike only to be followed by elections that brought a massive victory to the party of order. Further, using the term "party of order" rather than "Right" or "conservative"—let alone "capitalist"—recalls that in the same year of 1968, the ruling Communists brought what they called order back to Prague on the heavy treads of Warsaw Pact tanks. The hydra-headed, polymorphous enemy that haunts the nights of the party of order is not the Left or socialism—or communism—but *democracy*. This assertion may appear self-evident; who, after all, ever came out against democracy? Well, to be honest about it, many of us in the West did—hedging our criticism by saying that we opposed only the formal democracy that we denounced as ideological. But the fate of "really existing socialism" forces us to think again. We do not undertake this rethinking as political virgins. We have a past and we live in a present; we have to proceed from the cognitive dissonances that they induce.

The serious leftist who is also a philosopher must confront Marx and his legacy by rethinking Marx's place in the history of philosophy. It quickly becomes clear that Marx's understanding of the history of philosophy presupposes and depends on a philosophy of history. Marx's attempt to stand Hegelian idealism on its head, to give the dialectic a third turn that would really make "the actual the rational and the rational the actual," was the theoretical foundation of his self-conception as philosopher of revolution.[1] He was not wrong to make this claim; leftists who are philosophers continue to seek that reconciliation or unification of the real and the ideal, the individual and the community, freedom and necessity. When they come to power—before they get cynical and their philosophy becomes a simple rhetorical exercise—their theoretical claim to be the bearers of this revolutionary reconciliation makes them into a party of order. Even before they come to power, however, this theoretical heritage produces cognitive dissonances. Revolution and democracy become mutually exclusive political concepts.

The model of Rosa Luxemburg can serve as a key to understanding the ambivalent and ambiguous place of democratic politics within a leftist movement. Luxemburg was a radical critic of the antidemocratic aspects of the Bolshevik seizure of power in 1917, as she had been the critic of Lenin's reshaping of the party nearly fifteen years earlier. At the same time, her status as a democrat who was also an emphatic revolutionary was confirmed in her last article, written from the ruins of the Spartakus uprising in January 1919. Her title "Order Reigns in Berlin" was not merely rhetorical; after this allusion to the proclamation that followed the defeat of the Polish revolt in 1831, she wrote, "And so run the reports of the guardians of 'order' every half-century. . . . And the rejoicing 'victors' do not notice that an 'order' which must be periodically maintained by bloody butchery is steadily approaching its historical destiny, its doom." Rosa Luxemburg expected the revolution to carry out history's sentence. Assassinated the next day, she became the first icon for those who refused to identify Leninism with the Marxian legacy.[2] The relation between her revolution and a radical but still democratic politics remained to be explored by her heirs.

Seeking to inherit the Marxian legacy, many Western leftists experienced cognitive dissonance in their first debates with their socially critical peers from the East. What we thought was "Left" was for them support of the established order; what they took as "radical" was for us support of the principles of our own order. A classical illustration of this involved Rudi Dutschke, who led a delegation from the Berlin SDS to meet with student rebels in Prague in early 1968.

The Western Left was busy discovering Marxism; the Czechs were concerned with such supposedly formal freedoms as the right to demonstrate publicly or to form associations free from the tutelage of the authorities. Despite the obvious basis for misunderstanding, dialogue took place: enemies of an order that decried them as "anarchists," both sides were seeking to give new life to democracy. As their situations differed, so did their remedies. That was to be expected: democracy is not a universal form, self-identical and unalloyed. While this shared democratic *ethos* showed itself on the streets during that heady year of 1968, it was not formulated theoretically—at least in the West, where the glorious notion of revolution overshadowed the democratic demands.

Both sides might have turned to Rosa Luxemburg, another so-called anarchist. In "Order Reigns in Berlin," she had described revolution as "the only form of 'war' . . . in which the final victory can be prepared only by a series of 'defeats.' " Despite this suggestive image, which points to a normative learning process that is necessary for the creation of a democratic political culture, Luxemburg did not identify revolution with the democracy that haunts the party of order. She was still a Marxist for whom the "haunting" specter was Marx's; his theory was her revolutionary guarantee. She appeals constantly to text and verse, for example in her critique of Eduard Bernstein's revisionism, where she is content to have shown that "in its essence, in its bases, opportunist practice is irreconcilable with Marxism." Similarly, in the depths of a world war, her *Junius Pamphlet* insisted that "Marxist theory gave to the working class of the whole world a compass by which to fix its tactics from hour to hour in its journey toward the one unchanging goal."[3] There are, of course, counterexamples in her theory as in her practice. For now, the point is that one cannot resolve cognitive dissonance by invoking democracy as a *passepartout* that trumps all other positions or a synthesis that magically unites politics, society, and economy.

Democracy does not eliminate real difference, even among its own supporters. Another example of cognitive dissonance, from another part of the world, testifies to the need to *learn* democratic politics. A liberal reader of the *New York Times* might not have been surprised by the following passage in an article about El Salvador: "We used to march chanting, 'Socialism, Socialism,' " said Rev. Rogelio Ponceele, a Roman Catholic priest who has lived and worked with the largest guerrilla faction for almost a decade. "Now we march chanting, 'Democracy, Democracy!' " But what if the reader read on, to discover that the thrust of the article was that, after a decade of struggle, the guerrilla troops are not ready to follow their newly converted leaders? The *Times*'s explanation is that there is a gap between the educated leaders and the "poorly educated peasants who joined after suffering from rightist repression."[4] Rosa Luxemburg would suggest a different reading. "Democracy" is more than a slogan uniting the excluded against the party of order. In her polemic against the Leninist party, she added to the genetic argument that "the proletarian army is first recruited in the struggle itself," the normative qualification that "only in the struggle does it become aware of the objectives of the struggle." This insistence on democratic learning processes reappeared in her defense of the program of the Spartakus League in 1919, when she insisted that "the masses must learn to use power by using power."[5] Such sentiments lead to the accusation of "spontaneism." What must one learn to be a democrat who is heir to the Marxian legacy?

The party of order accused the New Lefts of the 1960s of being "anti-intellectual." In my own attempts to reply to this criticism, I encountered another case of cognitive dissonance. As I read Richard Hofstadter's *Anti-Intellectualism in American Life*, I was surprised to find myself, again and again, siding emotionally with the anti-intellectuals' rejection of the desiccated, formal, and increasingly atomized society that relentlessly conquered all aspects of life. This instinctive populist response was buttressed by an encounter with E. P. Thompson's *The Making of the English Working Class*; and it found a more theoretical justification in Polanyi's *The Great Transformation*. The premodern idea of a "moral economy" protected from the invading efficiency of the modernizing state was appealing because it pointed to the source of a native radicalism promoting collective values in the face of the egoistic individualism of a market society. It seemed to offer support to Rosa Luxemburg's "spontaneist" politics in her pamphlet *Mass Strike*, whose foundation was that "the masses will be the active chorus, and the leaders only the speaking parts, the interpreters of the will of the masses."[6] Luxemburg had also insisted that I read my Marx. I had found in *The Communist Manifesto* a hymn of praise to what Schumpeter called the "creative destruction" of capitalist modernization and a critique of that "moral economy" denounced now as "the idiocy of rural life." Marx had no hesitation in praising the achievements of the "revolutionary bourgeoisie"; but he wanted to go beyond them. He could have recourse to that magical Hegelian notion of an *Aufhebung*—preserving while raising to a higher level—of these achievements. This was no more convincing than playing the "trump card" democracy. It furthered cognitive dissonance.

Beyond Democracy: Totalitarianism?

At first glance, Rosa Luxemburg can continue to illustrate the cognitive dissonances encountered by post-totalitarian leftist politics. The challenge is not to formulate a democratic constitution or to articulate social rights whose unerring enforcement would serve to guarantee a democracy. The countries we call democratic have different constitutional frameworks, and they guarantee more or less consistently the political rights of their citizens. This political liberalism cannot be identified with democracy.[7] The rights that appear today as essential to liberal societies are often of recent vintage—for example, the right of women or eighteen-year-olds to vote—and the same rights are not present in all the liberal societies—for example, privacy protection or abortion rights. The rights that we do have in these societies are sometimes violated; the political system does not always function as the constitution promises. Rosa Luxemburg knew this; when she presented the program of the Spartakus League, she insisted that "far more important, however, than what is written in a program is the way in which it is interpreted in action."[8] This does not mean that rights and their guarantee are merely formal or that they can be written off as "bourgeois." The variety that characterizes the liberal rights suggests that while these rights have a material foundation, their guarantee lies in the openness of these societies to an historical struggle whose central variable is rights. It is this openness that justifies calling these societies democratic. Democracies are inherently historical societies whose future remains open, founded, as Luxemburg said, only on how rights are "interpreted in action."

The fact that formal liberal rights are insufficient on their own seems to imply the need to ensure their material foundation. But this separation of a material foundation from the rights it is assumed to guarantee often has had unfortunate political consequences. It seems to imply that rights can be temporarily suspended in order to build the foundation that will make it possible for all citizens to enjoy them. Two alternatives seem possible: "democratic socialism," the famous Third Way so long sought by so many on the Left; or the attempt to return to the pretotalitarian autochthonous developmental process that wants to continue the peculiar history of each nation as if there had been no interruption. These options both assume that totalitarianism was imposed on society from without, by external political fiat and without the at least tacit complicity of the population. In the first case, this political imposition is said to have been made necessary by the inability of the indigenous bourgeoisie to assume its historical role; in the second case, totalitarian politics appears to have broken into a (relatively) harmonious endogenous development. Both positions would do well to recall Rosa Luxemburg's warning to the Spartakus League not to imitate "the bourgeois revolutions in which it sufficed to overthrow that official power at the center and to replace a dozen or so persons in authority."[9] The quest for a Third Way assumes that politics can do everything; the return to historical continuity treats politics as epiphenomenal. A new politics has to unite the two levels, but not by simple addition. This is where we must leave Rosa Luxemburg.

I have overschematized the positions of those seeking a Third Way; and my characterization of the attempt to erase the totalitarian interlude from national history neglects the very different political options that have emerged in Eastern European contexts. My excuse is my "Luxemburgism." Rosa Luxemburg pointed repeatedly to the need to navigate between "two reefs": "abandonment of the mass character or abandonment of the final goal; the fall back into sectarianism or the fall into bourgeois reformism; anarchism or opportunism."[10] She thought she could synthesize them in the "mass strike" where "the economic struggle is that which leads the political struggle from one nodal point to another; the political struggle is that which periodically fertilizes the soil for the economic struggle. Cause and effect here constantly change places."[11] But this appealing synthesis is still produced by *addition*. Its political result appears in Luxemburg's alternative to Lenin's Bolshevik party. She insists that her party "gradually becomes the haven of the different dissatisfied elements of society, becoming a party of the people opposed to a tiny minority of capitalist rulers."[12] This is not a new politics. The politics that I called "Luxemburgism" is based on the existence of a democratic society; but here she is appealing to the motor of an autonomous capitalist economy.

The challenge is to conceptualize the politics, or the political culture, of a democratic society. Marx is more helpful than his political heirs. Hegel had taught him that the birth of a civil society, which is neither reducible to the private sphere nor capable of being absorbed by the political state, is the mark of modernity. Although Marx's later work reduced its anatomy to mere economic relations, he often showed an awareness of the complexity of civil society. The two tendencies can be seen in *The Communist Manifesto*. Marx's description of what he calls the "revolutionary" achievement of the bourgeoisie can be reduced neither to economic relations (as the material foundation of rights) nor to political imperatives (rights themselves). "All fixed, fast-frozen relations, with their train of ancient and venerable prejudices and opinions, are swept away," writes Marx. "All new-formed ones become antiquated before they can ossify. All that is solid melts into air, all that is holy is profaned, and man is at last compelled to face with sober senses, his real conditions of life, and his relations with his kind." New needs can now arise; new forms of communication produce a new civilization; cities "rescue" the peasantry from "the idiocy of rural life." Aside from the familiar rhetoric, this analysis could well have been written by Tocqueville.[13] But Marx then explains away this social revolution as the result of the contradiction between feudal property relations and productive forces that must "burst them asunder." He rapidly generalizes his economistic model to portray the coming of the proletarian revolution, along the lines suggested by Luxemburg's "party of the people." This permits him apparently to achieve two goals, both of which remain to haunt us: it provides a material foundation for the normative freedoms Marx wants to see realized; and its appeal to a philosophy of history based on the genetic progress of a class struggle that will ultimately reconcile and unify them all avoids the threat that historical change could threaten those freedoms. The former founds what appeared in Luxemburg as an additive politics, while the latter closes off that open future necessary for the politics of democratic rights.

If Marx is read through the eyes of Tocqueville, the action of what Marx called the "revolutionary" bourgeoisie can be seen as producing a democratic society. The elimination of "solid" certainties and the profanation of the "holy" signify the end of a society in which each knows his place and calling; the modern individual is born, and must face, with "sober senses," the problem of who he is, and with whom he will relate. Marx does not talk about rights here; his earlier work had led him to believe that they were only formal. But his own contrast of bourgeois and feudal society could have led to a different conclusion. Feudal rights were ascriptive; they were imposed by God and by the "solid" nature of things. The modern individual confronts a world without foundation; if that individual has rights, their foundation can only be political; they are won through struggle. This suggests that capitalism's constant revolutionizing of social relations poses a challenge, constantly renewed, to newly won rights of the individual. Capitalism is not simply a mode of production; the history of class struggle must be reinterpreted as a history of the politics of rights; and, unlike the economistic history to which Marx appealed, this history can never end in a grand synthetic unification. In a democratic society whose foundation is the modern individual who can appeal to no fixed material or transcendent, genetic or normative, final ground of rights, history remains open and politics remains necessary. Democracy is not formal but the lived experience of a struggle for right that can never end.

This reading suggests a different framework for understanding the emergence of totalitarianism, which is not simply imposed from without on an unwitting citizenry. The social democracy whose foundation is the radically free individual is uncomfortable; men and women are free atoms, alone together in that infinite space so feared by Pascal. They know that the rights they may have, like the place they may occupy, may be "swept away" or "become antiquated before they can ossify." It is this lived experience that makes rights appear to be merely formal and democracy a luxury. The demand arises for "real" democracy and/or true community; division is intolerable, a threat to one's very being. This picture can be overgeneralized; its details need to be analyzed for each concrete situation. The quest for roots, something "solid" and even "holy," arises; a movement emerges, be it fascist or communist.[14] But this does not imply a leap to a qualitatively new moment in history. Totalitarianism is not beyond democracy; it is immanent within the logic of democracy—as was the "mass strike" that sails magically between Rosa Luxemburg's two reefs. Both democracy and totalitarianism are founded on the experience of social division in a society of individuals; democracy seeks to preserve that division, while totalitarianism wants to overcome it in a new unity. Totalitarianism appears to be the logical solution to the tensions of democratic society. In this sense, totalitarianism is an antipolitics.

The claim that totalitarianism is immanent to democracy is not simply the inversion of the common thesis, spoken today with triumphalist accents, which sees the two as polar opposites. Democracy is not a state of affairs; it is not simply the static liberal ideal of the constitutional protection of basic rights. The picture painted by Marx, seen through Tocquevillean eyes, is not that of a stable society. It would be better to describe a dynamic of democratization, referring to a process whose origins lie in the modernization that eliminates the certitudes of the Old Order.[15] Totalitarianism is not the kind of antipolitics that east European oppositionists such as G. Konrad sought to theorize as a new political stance within and against totalitarianism. *That* antipolitics is an instance of what I refer to here as a democratic politics of rights. Totalitarianism only pretends to achieve the unity of society; its politics imposes unity vertically with the result that it atomizes constantly any attempts by groups within civil society to constitute themselves horizontally. This explains the fact that the Czech radicals, in their encounter with the German SDS in 1968, insisted on the importance of the right to free assembly. The apparently paradoxical insistence on the immanence of totalitarianism to democracy forces us to make clear not only the distinction of liberalism and democracy; its implications make clear also the error of what I called Rosa Luxemburg's "additive" politics, which separates political form from social content.

The implication of this argument is that totalitarianism can never be fully realized, even though it remains a constant temptation because of the inherent instability of democratic society. Its own logic turns against it. If it were indeed achieved, its very foundation—the society of individuals who seek constantly their own roots and their own rights—would be obliterated. The project is self-contradictory. It would result in just the kind of sullen withdrawal—or oppositional antipolitics—that has been seen in Eastern Europe. James Madison confronted a similar problem in his famous tenth *Federalist Paper*. To cure the ill of "faction," he wrote, one could destroy "the liberty which is essential to its existence," or one could give "to every citizen the same opinions, the same passions and the same interests." The first would be "worse than the disease," the second is not only "impracticable" but a denial of the "first object of Government."[16] Madison's solution was to multiply the number of factions, so that each checks the threat from the other, preserving a democratic society within the framework of a representative republic. Once again, we have to pay attention to the words. Madison's democracy was not based on popular sovereignty; his insight was that a representative republican state is necessary in order to preserve a democratic society. In order to clarify this notion, we need to see why the radical and rapid collapse of the totalitarian states would certainly not have surprised Madison. This will make possible at the same time the development of the other side of the claim advanced here: that capitalism, too, represents the party of order whose true enemy is democracy.

The Modern(izing) State

Madison's rejection of the image of a united democratic sovereignty has a further implication. If the new democratic society was the result of the action of the revolutionary bourgeoisie, Marxist economism makes sense. But the same emerging democratic society was also analyzed by Tocqueville as the product of the modernizing state seeking to assert its absolute sovereignty. Claude Lefort argues that the distinction between the two approaches explains why Marx did not take seriously the autonomy of democratic society.[17] The theory of history sketched in *The Communist Manifesto* passes from feudalism to capitalism without stopping to consider as a distinct moment the absolutist state, whose notion of sovereignty remains dominant in modern times.[18] As a result, when Marx analyzes the French Revolution and the Declaration of the Rights of Man, he cannot take seriously the conquest of these rights, which appear to him to be only formal. The freedom to do whatever does not harm others appears to him only to protect the egoistic monad, rather than to liberate the individual from hierarchical society and to open up the possibility of forming new social bonds. The same holds for the distinction between the public and private spheres, which is not the formality mocked by Marx but rather the guarantee of a right that makes the individual free. Freedom of opinion and of its communication are again not simply formal; they imply that knowledge will not remain the monopoly of those in power. The right to security is not only Marx's protection of capitalist property; it is a right that protects the citizen from arbitrary action by the government and thereby affirms the autonomy of the individual. Marx's one-sidedness even leads him to ignore the historical implication of the presumption of innocence, which for Claude Lefort is "an irreversible acquisition of political thought."[19] One did not need to stress the import of these rights to the Czech radicals of 1968 or to their heirs.

However one analyzes the relation of the absolutist state and the "revolutionary" bourgeoisie in the various national histories, one point remains common to all. Centralization and the new concept of sovereignty destroyed the hierarchical and ordered cosmos inherited from traditional society. A new matrix emerged; the individual and a politics of rights became possible. The emerging individualist society may ally with the monarch against the aristocracy; or it may join the aristocracy in attacking the monarchy. More important than the economic forces here is the new configuration that opposes the society to the state. But this polarity should not be identified with a Marxist history of class struggle whose goal is to achieve an eventual synthesis—let alone the elimination of one of the poles to the benefit of the other. The figure is more complicated because the society that is being considered here is a democratic diversity of individuals whose unity and division are structured by the system of rights guaranteed by the state. Because these rights serve to preserve diversity as well as unity, they are the object of a struggle that can never end. The sovereignty of the state is affirmed in the protection of these rights and the guarantee of a space in which society can seek to affirm new rights. This was Madison's definition of "the first object of Government"; but it has a European ancestry in the absolute state, whose first great theorist, Jean Bodin, titled his treatise *The Six Books of the Republic*.

This framework permits a reinterpretation of the history that has produced both capitalism and totalitarianism. The modernizing state—not Marx's economistic revolutionary bourgeoisie—applying its new conception of sovereignty, creates the conditions for social democratization. It produces a society marked by individualism, difference, and division; it is, also, a society in quest of community, identity, and unity. The nation-state can only apparently, and briefly, provide that link; its normative position as guarantor of rights demands that the state stand outside of society; if it claimed to be identical with society, it would inevitably appear, sooner or later, to have taken sides in the struggle inherent within democratic society and would pay the price in the coin of lost legitimacy. It can avoid that accusation only if it claims to incarnate some necessity or value immanent to society. With this step, it is on the road to totalitarianism; its claim to be identical with society is not based on democratic diversity but rather appeals to a putative unity, furnished by a mystical *Volk* or by a logic of history's necessary path, which only the Marxist communist or the fascist *Führer* can know.

The same dilemma that can lead to the pretended totalitarian solution to the tensions of modern democratic culture faces capitalism as well. What is surprising is that capitalism makes the same claim to social immanence. The neutral market replaces the neutral state; economic interests are substituted for political rights. Like totalitarianism, capitalism is an antipolitics; it denies its own nature as political. The enemy of capitalism is not the proletariat but that democracy whose politics is founded on the Rights of Man. Capitalism, like totalitarianism, seeks the elimination of social division; it can only control the effects of its constant revolutionizing of social relations by reducing them all, ultimately, to identical quantitative form.

The struggles that Rosa Luxemburg called "anti-capitalist" can be reinterpreted within the framework of democracy and antipolitics. Of course, these contests concern interests; Madison's analysis of factions recognized that "from the protection of different and unequal faculties of acquiring property, the possession of different degrees and kinds of property immediately results," and that "the most common and durable source of factions has been the various and unequal distribution of property." Indeed, the development of interests seemed to him the mark of "civilized nations."[20] But interest and even unequal possession of property are not identical to capitalism. Rather, the challenge posed by popular struggles is anticapitalist in the specific sense suggested here: they put into question the claim that the capitalist economy provides that immanent unity that the birth of modern, individualist, and democratic society had destroyed. These movements are affirming the historically open and democratic character of a society in which political struggle is legitimate. They are affirmations of rights or, as Lefort and Hannah Arendt put it, of "the right to have rights." It does not follow that all popular movements should be supported; that decision must be the object of democratic politics. It does follow, however, that any such movement that refuses to take part in that democratic process on the grounds that its values or goals represent the immanent truth or unity of society are to be rejected.[21]

Party of Disorder

This discussion took its starting point from the conflict between the party of order and those New Leftists whom I called democrats. I used Rosa Luxemburg, that most rigorous—and therefore most contradictory—of the heirs to the Marxian legacy as a backdrop for an attempt to provide a wider framework in which the Marxian legacy—and the problem of post-totalitarian societies—could be interpreted. The hypothesis suggested by Claude Lefort, that both capitalism and totalitarianism are attempts to provide an immanent closure that unites the moments of genesis and normativity in a divided society that cannot justify its unity by an appeal to transcendent norms, permits a reinterpretation of the history of popular struggles over the past two centuries—the two hundred years of error to which I referred at the outset. It suggests, on the one hand, that these movements can—but need not—move in a direction that lends support to the totalitarian solution. That would explain why so many—including the peasant Salvadorians to whom I alluded, along with the sophisticated German SDS visiting Prague—can find themselves allied with political choices whose ultimate results they would come to deplore. The history of fellow traveling, which Lefort describes as the party of the *bien-pensants*, can be understood from this perspective.[22] There remains that anti-intellectual temptation of a moral economy, whose persistent appeal points to a final cognitive dissonance to which I did not allude at the outset: the East German experience.

Why were those oppositional groups whose courageous stance showed the nakedness of the totalitarian claims unable to play a political role once the regime collapsed? It appears that, given the totalitarian claim to immanent necessity, only a moral stance could challenge its legitimacy, just as it took a moral certitude to support the individual refusal to accept the total regime. To be more than an individual refusal, the opposition had to assume that it spoke for a collectivity that had been suppressed and that would emerge full-blown once the oppression was lifted.[23] But this opposed one absolute to another, one totality to another. When the regime fell and society found itself on its own, the opposition could not accept the legitimacy of a politics whose foundation is the plurality of factional interest. The greatest strength of the opposition became the source of its weakness. It could not understand the materialism that was unleashed in the wake of the fall of the Old Order; and it could not accept the calculating politics of the Western Social Democrats whose wager that the economic costs of reunification would drive the voters to its side. But on what basis could the opposition criticize such self-interested behavior? Did it not have to appeal, implicitly or explicitly, to a concept of unity, to the idea of a society that would be at last, by means of the proper knowledge and behavior, reconciled with itself beyond its divisions? Did it become, in spite of itself, a part of the party of order?

Although the opposition in the East was called democratic, its basic tendency was moral. In its experience, politics and parties were simply the first step on the path to corruption. The democratic label could be affixed to it insofar as the form of its challenge—in the wake of the Helsinki Accords—was the demand for rights. The Western signatories at Helsinki conceived these rights within the frame of liberalism. The identification of liberalism with democratic society has led to much confusion. Rights must be won, and be defended, politically. What is the source of such a politics? Reread through the eyes of Tocqueville, Marx provides part of the answer. His revolutionary bourgeoisie was acting from the clearest of material interests; and yet its action opened the space in which the modern individual could come to exist within a democratic society. Of course, that society was not as democratic as one would like—although it was too democratic for many of its unwilling creators, such as those denounced by Marx in *The Eighteenth Brumaire*. It was a society that could become more democratic, despite the best efforts of the party of order. But there is no revolutionary bourgeoisie in Eastern Europe. Can one assert that the transformation of absolute sovereignty into popular sovereignty, which inaugurated what Robert R. Palmer called "the Age of the Democratic Revolution," is being repeated in post-totalitarian societies? If so, what form will its new politics assume?

The renewed dialogue between East and West permits both sides to rediscover what it is that made their politics "Left." As in 1968, the radicals East and West can find common ground only around the challenge to realize democracy. As in 1968, they are the party of disorder. This time, however, the Eastern critique of totalitarianism and the Western critique of capitalism have to work in tandem: the West can learn from the East that its own democracy is not simply the formal system of liberal rights, while the East can learn from the West that capitalism is simply another way of dissolving the qualitative differences that must emerge in democratic societies into the quantitative neutrality of the market.[24] Both systems are the enemy of democracy; and democracy, in turn, has now an historical and theoretical foundation that avoids the reproach of formalism and abstractness that made for the appeal of Marxism. The moralist temptation must be seen to be only another way to take the side of the party of order. Now that history no longer provides us with a vector of truth, and now that rights are constantly up for challenge, there is no single politically correct position; there is only politics. Paradoxically, in the West, this has led to a hardening of positions; ideology seems to count for more than critique; one needs to assert one's identity and to validate it by being on the right side. However, politics are only defensible by argument, program, and practice. The party of disorder has its programs; it takes to the streets, the platform, the public space because it has concrete goals, and arguments to defend them. It knows that society must be governed, decisions made, resources allocated; but it knows too that these are *political* choices, not answers to Marx's "riddle of history." The party of disorder does not reject but thrives on cognitive dissonances. Perhaps that is why, in the end, it remains, although critically, within the Marxian legacy.

Notes

1. This was Lukács's claim in his 1923 classic *History and Class Consciousness*, trans. Rodney Livingstone (Cambridge: MIT Press, 1971). I traced Marx's consistent progress from philosophy to political economy in *The Development of the Marxian Dialectic* (Carbondale: Southern Illinois University Press, 1971). At the same time, I was preparing an edition of the political writing of Rosa Luxemburg, whose philosophical importance had also been stressed by Lukács's book. Rethinking this philosophical and political constellation led me to the concept and problem of the Marxian *legacy*.

2. Luxemburg's article is translated in *Selected Political Writings of Rosa Luxemburg*, ed. Dick Howard (New York: Monthly Review Press, 1971). My understanding of the notion of a Marxian legacy, which I prefer to the usual concept of Western Marxism, is sketched in my own book of that title, whose first chapter presents the contradictory character of that legacy by reexamining Luxemburg's life and thought more critically than I did in the introduction to her *Writings*. (See *The Marxian Legacy*, 2d ed. [Minneapolis: University of Minnesota Press, and London: Macmillan, 1987].) I will use Luxemburg as a kind of pole for reflection in the first parts of this essay because—as opposed to Marx, for whom an autonomous political theory is impossible in capitalism and not necessary in socialism—she stands for that aspect of the Marxian tradition that at least sensed the need for a properly political theory.

3. Citations from Luxemburg, *Selected Political Writings*, 130, 325.

4. Lindsey Gruson, "Among Salvadoran Rebels, A Split Over Rights Accord," *New York Times*, 11 August 1990, 2.

5. The first citation is from "Mass Strike, Party, and Trade Unions," in *Selected Political Writings*, 270; the second citation is from "Our Program and the Political Situation," in *Selected Political Writings*, 406. The citations could be multiplied and counterexamples given, as I do in *The Marxian Legacy*.

6. "Mass Strike, Party, and Trade Unions," 270.

7. This distinction is stressed in Jean Cohen's "Discourse Ethics and Civil Society," *Philosophy and Social Criticism* 14, no. 3-4 (1988): 315–37.

8. "Our Program and the Political Situation," 380.

9. Ibid.

10. "Militia and Militarism," in *Selected Political Writings*, 142; and again in "Organizational Questions of Russian Social Democracy," 304.

11. "Mass Strike, Party, and Trade Unions," 241. It would be more accurate to use the concepts of genesis and normativity here, but Rosa Luxemburg

was not concerned with such nuances. That is why her alternative to Lenin's theory of the political party is weak.

12. "Organizational Questions of Russian Social Democracy," in *Selected Political Writings*, 303.

13. Tocqueville's analysis of democracy as a social structure, and his attempt to formulate a properly political theory that could permit its fruitful unfolding while avoiding its negative potentials bears rereading today—as French thinkers such as Claude Lefort, François Furet, and Marcel Gauchet have shown. In the present context, it should be recalled that Tocqueville's task, in the wake of the French Revolution of 1830 in *Democracy in America*, and then in the wake of both the revolutions of 1848 and Bonaparte's coup of 1851 in *The Old Regime and the Revolution*, was to understand how the social victories inaugurated by 1789 could be preserved by political means. Those who are faced with the results of the democratic revolutions of 1989 might read him with profit.

14. The issue of nationalism could be posed within this general framework as well. However, one would have to distinguish the form of nationalism that emerged in the nineteenth century, as an answer to the social challenge posed by the revolutionary bourgeoisie, and twentieth-century nationalisms that emerge to face the erosion wreaked by the economic processes of capitalism. The reemergence of nationalism in post-totalitarian societies would represent a third variant within this framework, as will be suggested below.

15. To avoid any historical misunderstanding, I should emphasize that totalitarianism becomes a possibility in situations where the democratic process is beginning to take hold. One would cite examples like Russia, Weimar Germany, Republican Spain, perhaps even Sun Yat Sen's China. On the other hand, even within societies where democracy has become a learned mode of political culture, radical movements calling themselves "Left" have constantly to face the fact that they find themselves denouncing formal freedoms, ideological manipulations, and the quotidian quest of electoral politics for a mythical center. Established democracies, like France and Italy, or even the United States during the Great Depression, can give birth to movements whose tendency is totalitarian. One will try to distinguish, for example, between "social rights" and "political citizenship," and suggest that the latter is not enough. The slope is slippery because democratic society is not a state of affairs but a constantly repeated challenge that can never be put to rest by the discovery or production of the ultimate foundation.

16. Alexander Hamilton, James Madison, and John Jay, *The Federalist*, ed. Jacob E. Cooke (Middletown, Conn.: Wesleyan University Press, 1961), 61. On the uniqueness of the American experience, and its relevance to today's debates, see Dick Howard, *The Birth of American Political Thought*, trans. David Curtis (London: Macmillan, and Minnneapolis: University of Minnesota Press, 1990).

17. My debt to Lefort for the previous sketch of the relation of democratic

48   *Chapter 2*

society and totalitarianism should also be acknowledged. For details and references, see *The Marxian Legacy*, chapter 7, and the afterword to the second edition.

18. Michelet was the first of a long line of nineteenth-century historians, which included the radical republican Quinet and the socialist Jaurès, to recognize that the notion of popular sovereignty that founded the French Revolution was rooted in the logic of the ancien régime. Absolute sovereignty, one and indivisible, is claimed also by revolutionary democracy—and by the antidemocratic theory of Carl Schmitt.

19. Claude Lefort, *L'invention démocratique. Les Limites de la domination totalitaire* (Paris: Fayard, 1981), 61.

20. Hamilton, Madison, and Jay, *The Federalist*, 58, 59.

21. This is why *The Federalist* insists on the republican form and argues constantly against the excesses of democracy. When he analyzed the danger of "faction," Madison defined it as "a majority or a minority," and it is clear that he worried more about the former than the latter. For a further argument, see my essay "The Political Origins of Democracy," whose first section is titled "Politics after 'the' Revolution," and whose concern is to articulate a "post-revolutionary politics" by developing the relation between republican politics and democratic society. The essay is found in *Defining the Political* (London: Macmillan, and Minneapolis: University of Minnesota Press, 1989), chapter 15.

22. Lefort takes the term from Solzhenitsyn's *Gulag Archipelago*, where it is applied to the still-orthodox denizens of the camps, and extends it also to those Western intellectuals whose mania for orderly systems to avoid grey zones fits well with a moral desire to think well of themselves (see *Un homme en trop* [Paris: Editions du Seuil, 1976] and *The Marxian Legacy*). I return to this point in chapter 14, "Toward a Politics of Judgment."

23. This assertion, based on the East German experience, cannot be generalized to all east European oppositionists. Konrad's "anti-politics" thought of itself as a morality of participation; the very name of the Polish opposition, "Solidarity," points in the same direction. The goal in both cases was the creation of an autonomous civil society. The difficulty, however, is that both strategies were conceived *within* the framework of the (weakened or "Helsinkized") totalitarian state. It is not clear how they can develop in the new, post-totalitarian context.

24. This is an idealization, as if my attempt to present a normative framework were also an empirical description. Nonetheless, even the radical free-marketeers in the East remain part of the party of disorder, as do those in the West who are not ready to join in the quest for a mediocre *république du centre*.

Part II

The Birth of the Political

3

Origins of Revolution

The Place of Philosophy

Marx saw himself as the first modern revolutionary. His contempt for utopians and humanitarians of varying stripes and dreams was matched only by his disdain for those whose arguments lacked the rigor of science. His preface to *Towards a Critique of Political Economy* (1859) provides an autobiographical description of how Marx came to his revolutionary stance. Marx mentions a manuscript that he and Engels composed in 1845 that was "left to the gnawing criticism of the mice." This manuscript was posthumously published as *The German Ideology*. Marx says that it was not published at the time because its authors had achieved their goal—self-understanding. The implication appears to be that the ideology against which Marx and Engels defined their own position was the philosophical tradition culminating in Hegel and his followers. The further implication—over which much polemical and political ink has been spilled—was that the work preceding, or perhaps also including, *The German Ideology* is somehow non-Marxist because it is too philosophical. One then opposes a humanist youth throwing about concepts like "alienation" or "radical needs" to a "scientific" grey-bearded revolutionary. Depending on one's temperament, one can use the humanist-philosopher to criticize the results of so-called socialism, or the results to criticize the philosopher's inaction or inadequacy.[1]

As revolutionary, the scientific and the humanist Marx in fact face a common problem. Revolution is distinguished from revolt; it is not an accident, an irrational product, or a mysterious treasure. Modern revolution claims to be necessary—either rationally (logically) necessary or materially necessary. Thus, in Marx's case, there is first a kind

51

of logical (or ontological) argument involving the structures of alienated labor that works by means of negation and the negation-of-the-negation; and there is then a kind of materialist demonstration offered in the theory of necessary capitalist economic crisis. Between these two extremes, one finds, for example, in the first part of *The German Ideology*, a kind of world-historical panorama portraying the necessary progress of humanity as it continually creates and satisfies new needs. Each of these arguments for the necessity of revolution is a theory. Each leaves open the question of the relation of theory to the actual practice of the revolutionary.

The theory/practice problem is specific to modern revolution. When Kant wrote "The Old Saying: It May Be True in Theory But It Doesn't Work in Practice" in 1793, he broke new ground. Marx later confronted the problem in its classical form in his doctoral dissertation on Greek philosophy. In one of the Notes appended to his doctoral dissertation, Marx speaks of the task of "making the world philosophical and making philosophy worldly." The quest expressed here is not new with the modern revolutionary; the dualism of Is and Ought, Real and Ideal, Genesis and Validity has stood at the origin of Western philosophy. What is new, however, is the solution that Marx offered only a few years later in 1843. What Marx called the "riddle of history" is to be solved by the really existent proletariat, which is produced "artificially," notes Marx, by a specific social formation whose negation it incarnates. The proletariat is an object that can become a subject, a product that is its own producer, a reality whose demands are for the ideal. It expresses the riddle *and* the solution. If philosophy is understood as the grappling with the classical dualisms, then the proletariat is the elimination of philosophy, its overcoming, and the destruction of all metaphysical speculation.

Even when he first proposed this proletarian politics, Marx knew that it contained an ambiguity. He knew that the proletariat was not the same as those poor who, the Bible tells us, will always be with us. Their poverty is natural and transhistorical. The proletariat was produced by a specifically modern capitalism, which, in the Germany of the 1840s, had only begun to gain a foothold. Hence, Marx refers to the "formation" of this proletariat and stresses that it is produced "artificially." One can understand Marx's subsequent turn to the study of political economy as a way of demonstrating the material or economic logic by which such a proletariat—which will solve the problems of philosophy and the riddle of history—will be formed. But there is a further aspect to Marx's argument. The proletariat that will be formed by the capitalist economic development is only an object, a product; it must be brought to consciousness, to subjectivity. In 1843, the only image Marx could find for this process was that of the "lightning of thought," which would have to strike this "naive soil of the people" and make it conscious of its revolutionary potential for true self-realization of all humanity. From this point of view, the analyses of alienation, the formation of radical new needs, or even the specificity of Marx's critique-theory are the elaboration of his first insight. In a word, the proletariat contains within its own definition the dualism that it seeks to eliminate; but just this dualism would plague it and its theories.

The "specter haunting Europe" with which the *Communist Manifesto* (published in 1848) begins is a curiously chosen image that expresses the ambiguity of Marx's proletarian political solution. Obviously, the materialist who felt that he had overcome philosophy-as-ideology considered this specter to be something quite real. But what? The proletariat, one would think; or at least the proletariat-as-in-formation. Yet the next phrases of the *Manifesto* explain that every opposition party in Europe finds itself labeled and branded as "communistic," and that this means first that the ruling class acknowledges communism as "a Power," so that, second, the present *Manifesto* should be published in order to demystify this specter by explaining or describing what communism really is. These two aspects of the specter are then discussed theoretically in the first two sections of the *Manifesto*. What emerges there is simply an elaboration of the ambiguous dualism that constitutes the proletariat: the first section shows how the bourgeoisie produces "its own grave-diggers" in the process of seeking to increase constantly its own profits, while the second section talks about the communists who know "the line of march, the conditions, and the ultimate general results" of the movement, and whose task is the "formation of the proletariat into a class." How do these two moments fit together?

Although he rejected philosophy and its dualisms, Marx nonetheless elaborated a specific style of theorizing. Nearly everything he wrote was titled or subtitled "a critique." The critique style of theory explains the surprising praise that Marx bestowed throughout his life on the "civilizing process" of capitalism. It also explains why his life's work was a book called *Capital*—subtitled "A Critique of Political Economy"—and not a volume called *Socialism*. Writing to Lassalle (22 February 1858), Marx explained that the goal of *Capital* was to be "a presentation, and through the presentation a critique of what is presented." Critique, in other words, is the *self*-critique of the object it describes. Theory is not applied from without; it is not an abstractly universal criterion applied to a particular social system. Critique is immanent; revolution is inexorable; the bourgeoisie produces "its own grave-diggers" in an economic system that carries the socialist future "in its womb." This style of theory fits perfectly the ambiguity of the proletariat. It presents spectrally, as in a revealing mirror, the true essence, the facts, of a social system that seeks to veil itself in ideology. The demystification of the critique will then correspond to the real experience of real proletarians; the "lightning of thought" will strike, the hour of revolution will have arrived when the object produced by capitalism becomes the subject of a new history.

This theory as immanent critique is the key to the optimism of the modern revolutionary. Possessing—or better, possessed by—this self-critique of capitalism, *he* becomes the real, incarnate bearer of the ideal, the unity of the traditional dualism. He does not have to argue, convince, or judge; all he does is speak the facts, the very capitalist facts by which capitalism condemns itself. The revolutionary can thus be apparently quite modest, even democratic and tolerant. The *Manifesto* insists that the communists are not separate from or opposed to other working-class parties, nor are they the representatives of any interests but those of the proletariat as a whole. They can represent the whole, Marx thinks, because of their theory that gives "understanding [of] the line of march, the conditions and the ultimate general results of the proletarian movement." But this apparent modesty, this empirical, democratic tolerance is in fact their greatest *hubris*. No philosopher would make the claim to be the real expression or the voice of the social totality; that is usually reserved for the caricature of Hegel imagining himself as secretary of the World Spirit. The *Manifesto* transforms this Hegelian philosophical secretary into the secretary-general of the party.

My claim is not, or not simply, that a certain kind of immanent critique theory had to have certain political consequences; people are not consistent with theories when it comes to action. Further, the essential ambiguity of Marx's critique or proletarian theory meant that it was open to various interpretations, only one of which has been alluded to thus far. Because the proletariat was supposed to become the real unity of the philosophical dualisms it was only *potentially* the "solution to the riddle of history." Philosophical considerations thus remain relevant.

Philosophy and Historical Action

The ambiguity of the proletariat stems from the fact that it is on the one hand the product of capitalism and therefore an object, and on the other hand, at least potentially, it is a subject capable of understanding and transforming the alienated and/or exploited world whose reproduction depends on its alienated labor. Depending on which of these two aspects of proletarian politics is stressed, one can become either a "reformist" or a "revolutionary." If the necessary character of capitalism's self-critique is the center of one's preoccupations, then political action consists of working with the current of history without rocking the boat. One then attacks the voluntarism of those who want to go too far too fast—while risking the danger that one's own gradualism in fact works to temper the decline and to put off the final victory. The situation is the inverse if one tries to be a revolutionary. Here, too, the results of one's action may be the opposite of what one sought because one will have opted for the wrong priority in the dualist world of proletarian politics.

The history of the Second International, of its demise with the outbreak of world war, and of the creation of the Third International (and re-creation of the second) after 1917 could be retraced in terms of these two options. That, however, would not be of great interest here; and, moreover, it would lead to multiple scholastic nuances since each party was building from a common source: the ambiguity of Marx's own theory.

Lenin's theory of the revolutionary party in *What Is to Be Done?* (1902) is consistent with the interpretation I drew in the preceding discussions from the *Communist Manifesto*. Lenin suggests that although the proletariat is quite aware of its exploitation (but *not* of its alienation or new needs, as in the young Marx), its immediate reaction to this is only defensive. The everyday experience of capitalism leads only to "trade union consciousness," the attempt to make the best of a bad lot within the confines of established social relations. Therefore, the task of the revolutionary party is to intervene, politically, from outside, with the aid of its theory that permits it to teach—more precisely, to lead—the proletariat to transcend its immediate interests toward a "political class consciousness" that recognizes the necessity of total social transformation. One could say that is precisely what the Bolsheviks did in 1917. The agent of the Russian Revolution was not so much the proletariat as the Leninist party. (Whether this party in fact articulated the true aspirations of what proletariat there was in

Russia at the time is not important here, nor are the "circumstances" that are claimed to have prevented it from realizing those aspirations. Important is only Lenin's going beyond economic immediacy and its immanent logic to introduce what he called the political dimension of revolution.)

Although Lenin's theory of the party is prefigured in the *Manifesto*, another of his formulations is significantly pre-Marxist. His 1904 pamphlet, *One Step Forward, Two Steps Backward*, continued the Russian debate to which *What Is to Be Done?* was a contribution by adding the historical specification that the revolutionary is a "Jacobin indissolubly connected to the interests of the proletariat." The need to refer to history for justification is interesting. It implies a break with the immanent logic of the critique theory. It could be used naively (or meanly), as when one looks to history for edifying examples that explain present choices.[2] This is how Stalin used it, for example, to justify his alliance with Zinoviev and Kamenev against the leader of the Red Army, Trotsky, who was pictured as a new Bonaparte. This was how Trotsky in his turn used it from exile a few years later when he called the advent of Stalin a repetition of the overthrow of Robespierre and the Terror in the French Revolution during the month of Thermidor. But there is more to be said about historical action and about its interpretation.

Marx's own writing of history was (usually) less naive and edifying than his successors'. It was he who criticized the French revolutionaries for dressing up in the garments of the Roman past in order to hide from themselves the radical implications of their own actions. It was also Marx who denounced nineteenth-century revolutions for cloaking themselves in the garb of the French Revolution. And it is to Marx that we owe the recognition of the past as weighing "like a nightmare on the brain of the living." What Marx-the-historian saw was the essential ambiguity of action, its open-endedness and multiplicity of meaning. Historical actions in this sense do not have a cause; they have what I call an *origin*, which is structured by the tension seen of the dualisms that constituted classical philosophy and that the proletariat is supposed to overcome.

Action and Origins

What do the modern revolutionary whose justification is the self-critique of the facts themselves and the revolutionary who returns to an often mythologized but nonetheless real event share with each other? Why are these two attitudes often combined in one and the same person? From the standpoint of history as edification, the French Revolution is originary in that it proves that the historical continuum can in fact be broken, that new beginnings are possible. Before 1789 a theory of immanent self-critique could not have been revolutionary. Before 1789 the most audacious critic could not present an immanent critique.

On a theoretical plane, 1789 points to problems for the immanent critique theory. Can one use the transition from feudalism to capitalism as the model for a leap beyond capitalism? Was the French Revolution "bourgeois" because its principal actors and their goals were bourgeois; or was the (unintended?) consequence of the revolution the emergence of a bourgeois society? Further, what is one to make of the fact that bourgeois societies were born in other countries without the aid of a revolutionary midwife?

The problem for the immanent critique theory is that if the revolution is a leap then it cannot be caused by pregiven material fact or the immanent logic of social conditions. If it were explained by such a reduction to the facts, then it would not be a revolution and the origin of a new history. On the other hand, revolution cannot come from nowhere, from voluntarism and willpower. There must be some material basis for its advent. We are caught, once again, in the Marxian version of the philosophical dualism. One sees how the Marxist can take either side when he confronts the French events. The analysis may point to the way in which political transformations of the super-structures—the end of feudal privilege and development of contract law, for example—create conditions for the emergence of a capitalist economy. However, as one looks more closely, the other side of the coin quickly presents itself. The revolution is said to have been "merely political" because it does not destroy but only transforms the mode of exploitation of the population. The debate can continue, but its point is lost.

The modern revolutionary who looks to science and critique and the edifying revolutionary who turns to history for examples share the belief that actions have causes, or *real* origins. One finds vivid expressions of this in Marx, for example when he insists in *The German Ideology* that "it doesn't matter what this or that individual proletarian thinks or does but what the class is and *must* do." What is being stressed here is the idea of origin as generating action, as the genesis of practice. The other side of the coin stresses the normative model of origins, assuming human rationality and the need for legitimation of the actions to be taken. Normative legitimation is then provided by the representation of the historical event as real: the impact of David's painting, *Oath of the Horatii*, or the reception of classical republican history in general, on the French revolutionaries could serve as an illustration.

Both explanations are symmetrically incomplete because they make the same mistake: they take the origin as real. Before explaining the nature of this mistake, and why it is a mistake, we need to make an excursus into the historiography of the French Revolution. Lenin's invocation of those events in "One Step Forward . . ." is just one example of the manner in which the French Revolution—however one chooses to define its nature and scope—has colored the way in which we think about time and history. The French Revolution meant that the leap, the rupture, was possible; it meant that new problems, crises, and possibilities could be recognized for the first time. The revolution was thenceforth a constant presence, for the revolutionary or the conservative or the reactionary who conjured it up or away.

The French Revolution as Origin

The originary character of the French Revolution can be seen in the paradoxical fact that its promise has remained necessarily unfulfilled. The promise is not simply an object of contemplation or a mirror for one's self-legitimation; nor is it an external, utopian standard permitting condemnation of the present; nor is it the positive ideology of liberty-equality-fraternity as human values. All these were roles that the Greeks or Romans could and traditionally did play prior to 1789, since no one dreamed of an actual return to the Golden Age, however and wherever they pictured it. The French Revolution, on the other hand, has had a different kind of follower. It was present as an immanent threat or hope whose metaphorics and historiography were also a political statement. It was present, in a word, just like the specter invoked by the *Manifesto*.

The Revolution had no single concrete result that could have marked its success and thereby justified a halt in the process. Freeing people from the bonds of feudal and corporate traditionalism, the Revolution sought to create the world anew. It invented its own calendar, created a new system of weights and measures, initiated new feast days and holidays, sought to found a new religion. Real motives and interests existed, but they could only be expressed in the new revolutionary language, as can be seen in any of the great debates of the times. Only the cold shower of the Terror, and the appearance of Bonaparte with the promise of empire, could bring the festival of continual creation to a halt—and even then the debate about the phases, duration, and results of the Revolution continue among the historians and politicians. Thus, the most reflective of recent French historians, François Furet, asserts:

> The history of the French 19th century in its entirety can be considered as the history of a struggle between the Revolution and the Restoration across episodes dated 1815, 1830, 1848, 1851, 1870, the Commune, the 16th of May 1877. Only the victory of the republicans over the monarchists at the beginning of the Third Republic marks the definitive victory of the Revolution in the depths of the country: the lay teacher of Jules Ferry, that missionary of the values of 89, is the symbol more than the instrument of that long victorious battle. The integration of the villages and peasantry of France into the republican nation through the principles of 89 would thus have taken at least a century. . . . The victory of a republican Jacobinism which was so long tied to the dictatorship of Paris, is only gained when it is supported by the majority vote of rural France, at the end of the 19th century.[3]

But, Furet continues, even the victory of the republic has not exhausted the originary character of the revolution, which lives on in the twentieth century as the ideal of "the" revolution that is necessary because the realization of the nineteenth century's republic has not satisfied the undefined and undefinable expectations placed on it.

The manner in which the nineteenth century conceptualized the Revolution as the demand for the real instantiation of the republic suggests that one function of the originary event is to create a real rupture in the historical continuum of experience. The result of the rupture is not only chronological, it is also social. Nothing can be taken for granted in a society riven by the self-questioning that its broken historical self-image entails. Social hierarchy that had been accepted unquestioningly and envisaged as an integrated spatial order of groups coexisting next to one another is transformed into social division and competition for dominance. In this sense, the Revolution as a real event posits or creates a revolutionary temporality, setting forth the New not as an essence or structure already existing potentially and ready to be realized but as a problem or question. This is why, when the republican formulation of the origin is realized by the end of the nineteenth century, the question does not simply fade away; history does not end in normalcy; the origin remains as a problem, formulated now as the question of "the" revolution. The implication is that the treatment of the French Revolution as a *real* origin is deceptive insofar as its reality can never be pinned down anatomically to a fixed set of events or demands that could be realized in the way, for example, that the physical properties of a newly discovered entity can be exhaustively analyzed and its uses fully elaborated, or a building constructed from a blueprint. Thus, in the case of the French Revolution, Furet points to problems of chronology: did it begin, as Tocqueville suggests, as early as 1787, when the bankruptcy of monarchical politics was evident? Or was it the call for free election of the Estates General, or the transformation of the Estates General from a traditional tripartite body deliberating separately to a unitary body, or the storming of the Bastille that was crucial? When did it end? With Thermidor, the Consulate, the Empire, the Restoration? Was the end symbolized by the abandonment of the new revolutionary calendar? Or, could one read the entire nineteenth century as the prolongation of the Revolution (as the demand for the Republic)? Or, does it continue into the twentieth century (as the search for "the" revolution)? The historian's question poses the theoretical problem of origins.

When the French Revolution is taken as a real origin of the present and its problems and questions, the event serves as the basis of what Furet calls a "discourse of identity," or what I call an edifying view of history. Every historical period, and even the different social strata within a period, can be situated and its functions identified by relating it to the originary event. Ethnography, too, illustrates this edifying discourse of identity. The functioning of the originary myths of a society at once explain the genesis of its social order while giving normative justification to those social structures. Usually, the identification proceeds smoothly as a glorification of the continuity of past and present that orders the different social functions within the group according to a spatial coexistence. At other times, such as the Renaissance, the quest for identity entails a rupture that puts into question the adequacy of the present to the normative image of the past as superior to the present. In this case, the critical power of the fact cannot simply be integrated into the spatially ordered functional whole. The new fact introduces discontinuity between genesis and validity, and thereby poses the temporal question of the possibility of a new arrangement. In this sense, it poses the question of origins rather than claim knowledge of real origins or material causes.

The edifying discourse of identity that looks to the French Revolution as real origin is fundamentally different from the smooth integration offered by the myth *and* from the kind of discontinuity illustrated by the Renaissance image of the classical age. In both of those cases, the origin is fixed, identified, and static. The origin there is external, not immanent, as in the modern claim. The immanence of origins—from the city of God to the history of man—is the source of our modern notion of history as well. The French Revolution is an origin that self-consciously reflects on itself as origin, which questions itself continually, debates with itself as it progresses, takes each accomplishment as a temporary phase in a total rupture with all fixation on the past.[4] This mode of action as a continual process of creation (and destruction of the past) is isomorphic to the specific historicity of capitalism whose rapacious and iconoclastic character prevents the fixation of origin as unique and permanent. Capitalist society is the continual overcoming of the present in the form of expanded reproduction. This is why Marx praised it in the *Manifesto*, seeing it as immanently revolutionary as opposed to the structure of traditional societies. Thus, in reply to the above question of the way in which the revolution inaugurates, or consecrates, the capitalist mode of production, the answer must not be the reductive thesis of a materialism, as if the Revolution somehow permitted the breakthrough of material forces that had been lying dormant in the womb of an anachronistic superstructure, *nor* that the Revolution created superstructures that somehow permitted the growth of these material forces. The assertion must be that capitalism and the French Revolution have what Max Weber called an "elective affinity" because of their shared ideological form of temporality.

The edifying discourse of identity supposes a real origin that can be fixed and identified as either a genetic source of the present or a normative standard of judgment on the present. The ideological structure of capitalism that both denies and affirms the continual production of novelty accounts for the continual effectiveness of the revolutionary invocation of the French Revolution in the nineteenth and twentieth centuries. The failed revolutions try to relive the originary event as their real model, as Marx continually observes. Even the successful ones are only temporary halts whose institutionalization and fixation in terms of the balance of real social interests shows itself inadequate to the temporality of the originary thrust. No more than the capitalist can copy previously successful modes of production can the revolutionary copy previous revolutions. If the transition to socialism is the move to a new form of social relations, it cannot follow the model of the French Revolution as real origin. Revolution against capitalism entails a different temporality and a different relation to origins.

Philosophy and Revolutionary Origins

Contemporary philosophers, in the wake of Heidegger and Freud (as well as the modernist movements in the arts), have devoted much effort to exorcising the myth of real origin. Logically, an origin cannot be real or realized. If the origin is a real presence, generating a series of events as its result, then it is either itself caused by something, or if it is a "first cause," the events that follow it are merely Spinozistic accidents with no independence or reality of their own; they cannot be taken as the realization of the origin. No event or thing can exhaust or satisfy the origin; each measure is a partial realization and determination of it; but were it fulfilled, it would be a cause not an origin. The origin must be absent. However, one must be careful. If the origin is taken as a real absence, then it can never be realized because any satisfaction would be a delimitation of the radicality of the origin; its realization would be its destruction, and thus the elimination of its originary function. The situation is similar to the concept of essence of Hegel. Either the origin manifests and realizes itself, in which case it loses its power as originary; or it remains an originary but undefined source and goal, in which case there is nothing more that can be said of it. Yet, if not real, the origin still has its effect. What is its mode of existence?

Freud comes to the aid of the philosopher. Just as Furet showed the social function of the notion of origin in the "discourse of identity," so too can we see origin's function for the individual in the psychological phenomenon of identity. The progress of Freud's discoveries maintains the notion of origin while progressively questioning its reality. Early on, Freud believed the accounts of his hysterical patients who explained the source of their troubles in a real event, usually of a sexual nature (or in a real lack or need, again sexual). Gradually, he came to realize that this "event" was more often than not a fantasy, or a fantasmatic embroidering revealing *and* concealing something that gave the patient a fundamental set of meanings or an identity in terms of which life is lived and events interpreted. The identity of the individual, the origin of this particular individuality, is thus imaginary. This imaginary origin is, of course, very real in the life of the individual, generating a series of otherwise inexplicable actions and serving to give meaning or validity for the individual to congeries of events that, to the outside observer not privy to the imaginary identity, appear random. Thus, the paranoiac's self-identity generates modes of behavior that become self-validating and justifies these behaviors in a narration that, once the premise is shared, makes perfect sense. "Cure" for Freud, like philosophy for Heidegger, consists not of eliminating the problem of origins or identity but of destroying the illusion of their reality. It is not thought on the reductionist midwife model, nor that of causal science; a specific mode of judgment is involved, to which I can only point here.[5]

An origin is the dynamic interplay of presence-absence, a revealing that must also conceal. If the origin were fully present, there would be nothing for it to originate; there would be a plenitude that "was, is, and will be" (as Rosa Luxemburg spoke of the revolution in her last article, written in the ruins of the failed German rising of 1919). But in that case, the question of origins would never be posed. If the origin were fully absent, the situation would be structurally identical. If I were the individual who I was, am, and will be, then I would have no history, just as I have no history if I am no one, simply a product of my circumstances. The same holds true for the historical event: the French Revolution is neither wholly determined and complete nor simply the product of forces existent outside of it. The revealing-concealing nature of the origin has the same structure in both cases. I am, and the Revolution is, what is done in the material world; but consideration of these behavioral traits does not exhaust the significance of either me or it. For the psychoanalyst, what appears as the same action performed by several individuals can have a variety of different psychodynamic explanations; actions are overdetermined, not reducible to a linear model of cause and effect. The same overdetermination holds true for the historian's account of action. The presence-absence dualism to which the philosopher points is simply his version of the tension of genesis and normativity to which I have frequently called attention in the preceding pages. The conclusion is the same: neither side can be privileged, and the tension must be maintained.

The specificity of the French Revolution as origin, and the source of its elective affinity with capitalism, lies in its nature as an action that is its own origin. There is nothing outside the Revolution, nothing that does not get its meaning from this source. The Revolution generates actions from its own momentum; and these actions are in turn legitimized by their revolutionary origin. The part is infused with the sense of the whole, which can tolerate nothing outside itself. The Revolution must continually seek after closure and totalization in order to maintain its identity; anything outside of it threatens its very existence. Thus, with Furet, one might date the end of the Revolution at the moment when, after Thermidor, with the advent of the Directory, legitimacy was no longer earned by direct appeal to *le peuple* as immanent origin and norm but was referred to a constitutional legality, established by actions safely in the past and external to the present. With the appeal to constitutional legality the question of origins loses its radical, threatening character. The nineteenth-century attempt to realize the promise of the Republic, and the twentieth century's quest after "the" revolution are, from this point of view, simply the completion of the system, not its overthrow. The nineteenth-century demands took the Revolution as an origin in the genetic sense, whereas the twentieth century took it as an origin providing normative validity and, hence, different demands. In either case, however, what must be stressed is the elective affinity not only of capitalism and the French Revolution, but also of both of them with the revolutionary proletariat of Karl Marx when that proletariat is taken as a real origin in either the genetic or the normative sense.

The philosophical (and psychoanalytical) notion of origin both permits the identification of the error that takes the origin as real and, more important, suggests a rather different research agenda for those interested in political change. I say "research agenda" quite explicitly because the first and most important lesson from the foregoing analysis is the danger of taking one's theory as an Archimedean point from which to move the world. To say that there is no real origin is also to say that there is no revolutionary subject, no bearer of the future of humanity, no savior. Learning to act in the immanence of the present and learning to think within the paradoxical constraints of modernity's continual questioning of principles and its paradoxical because unrealizable quest for origins, are the first steps.

Origin of the Political

If the elective affinity or structural isomorphy among the French Revolution, the advent of capitalism, and the Marxian revolutionary proletariat is accepted, the first consequence is that each of them has to be reevaluated. More particularly, the usual picture of a capitalist economic system taking root and form in an archaic society that it then transforms and dominates is misleading on several accounts. I would claim, rather, that one can trace the emergence of a series of new political problems in the late eighteenth century as the different national variants of the modern state take form. These political problems can be conceptualized through the work of the philosophers in the tradition inaugurated by Kant (and closed by Hegel-Marx); they can be recognized in the legal and constitutional issues that were summarized at the time under the banner of republicanism; and they can be traced in the growing administrative centralization and complexification that passed under the banner of Enlightened Despotism. In each of these instances, the solution that vanquishes its opponents is the creation of an independent ("capitalist") economic sphere. Capitalism thus appears to be the solution (or pretended solution) to a series of political problems. These political problems lose their distinctiveness—their political nature—once capitalism becomes the reigning center of life, a kind of "real origin" that both generates actions and gives normative legitimacy or meaning to these same actions. The political does not, however, simply disappear.[6]

The political questions that the advent of capitalism (as well as, in their own ways, the French Revolution and the Marxian revolutionary project) covered over must be rediscovered and reactivated. The rediscovery passes along the path taken by Marx himself: the tradition from Kant to Hegel. However one may criticize Marx, his work encapsulates the wealth of the tradition of German Idealism; the contradictions and difficulties of Marx are not due to some subjective failing on his part that we latecomers could somehow correct with hindsight. Retracing the path of German Idealism should not be—as it usually is, especially since Lukács's masterful "reification essay" in *History and Class Consciousness*—the demonstration that the telos of that movement, its unity and totality, is summed up in Marx. On the contrary, the path of the movement must be from Marx to Kant if one is to rediscover those political questions that, in the work of Marx, are occluded by the dominance of the capitalist economy. By the same token, the reactivation of these rediscovered questions demands the same movement from Marx to Kant. The modern revolutionary, from whose claims these reflections began, cannot serve as role model. His assumptions are, in fact, part and parcel of the economic logic that destroys the independence of politics. Insofar as one assumes that

Lenin's Bolsheviks are true to that model, their apparent success at modernizing economically the backward Russian territory shows them to have been simply more efficient (or ruthless) than run-of-the-mill capitalists.

By using the category "modernity" to describe what is usually simply called capitalism, I want to suggest the need to analyze a broader field than the merely economic. Modernity is that form of social relations (and relations to nature) that emerges when all tradition and all external origins of legitimation are destroyed and when the genesis of events is no longer explicable by a causal logic. Modernity is defined by the immanence of origins; it is a sociocultural formation that continually questions itself and its identity. Social relations, defined by the immanence of the question of origins, are by their very nature political. Modern politics is the manner in which a society reflects—and acts—upon the immanence of its own origin, on the fact that the members of society must define continually, in word and deed, the kind of society they are and want to be. The old hierarchies and distinctions among individuals that were legitimized by gods or nature or reason—by an external origin—can no longer be accepted. Above all else, this means that modern politics must be democratic, deliberative, and public (or what the eighteenth century called "republican"). The principle of immanence means, furthermore, that modern politics can never come to some ultimate solution or arrangement where participation and debate are no longer necessary. That would mean fixing a point or principle as a *real* origin, a cause that nolens volens becomes external to the system over which it exerts its perhaps enlightened but surely despotic power. Decisions of social justice or questions of economic interest must therefore be formulated and resolved as political in this modern sense—and the inverse mode must be avoided, that is, the political must not be reduced simply to the economic.

The danger for modern politics is to act as if its origins were real; that is, to stress either the genetic or the normative at the expense of the other. A constitution, bill of rights, and other normative mechanisms cannot replace the genetic processes (including the economic ones) that constitute civil society, any more than the genetic procedures can determine the normative. Political liberalism and economic liberalism must not exclude each other. Put in a different manner, the danger is the dominance of the social reformers, but it is equally the victory of the animadversions of the neoconservatives. The usually proposed "Third Way" via bureaucracy or technocracy is equally to be excluded. The logic of origins shows the impossibility of the assumption that modern society can be dealt with quantitatively if only the proper common denominator can be found. Although it tends toward unification at one pole, modernity refuses a politics that, in the guise of science and technology, destroys its own preconditions.

Finally, there is a positive conclusion. If we can show that modernity is structured by the tension of genesis and normativity that poses the question of immanent origins, which in turn defines the parameters of democratic politics, it follows that the task of the revolutionary is to discover and to create ways to preserve this originary questioning. Not that we take the world in our hands; not that we form a new party; but rather, to paraphrase the young Marx of 1843, that we look at what people are already in fact doing, and show them through our critical questions and actions the originality of their own action.[7] The attempt to reduce social movements to the logic of cause and effect and the definition of social questions as concerned with either (economic) genesis or (political-legal) normativity are moves that the established powers encourage precisely because they reduce the radical question of democracy and origins to the solvable and familiar. In the context of modernity, revolutionary politics is revolutionary because it is political.

Notes

1. The *locus classicus* of this debate is the controversial work of Louis Althusser, especially the essays collected in *Pour Marx* (Paris: Maspero, 1965) and the collective project coordinated by Althusser, *Lire Le Capital* (Paris: Maspero, 1965). One should not forget, however, that Georg Lukács had been able to reconstruct the Hegelian-philosophical elements of Marx's theory already in his 1923 classic, *Geschichte und Klassenbewußtsein* (reprinted in Georg Lukács, *Werke*, vol. 2 [Neuwied: Luchterhand Verlag, 1968]) prior to the publication of Marx's early humanist manuscripts.

2. I will shortly be using François Furet's term "discourse of identity" to adumbrate or replace this term. However, "edifying" history is of course a well-known genre and the butt of many a critic, though it has not usually been, save perhaps by Hegel, dealt with as here.

3. François Furet, *Penser la revolution française* (Paris: Gallimard, 1978), 16–17. Furet has since elaborated this argument in *La Revolution, 1770–1880* (Paris: Hachette, 1989).

4. Compare the following passages from *The Eighteenth Brumaire* in which Marx describes the revolutionary proletariat. They provide material for conclusions to be drawn shortly.

Proletarian revolutions . . . criticize themselves constantly, interrupt
themselves continually; in their own course, come back to the apparently
accomplished in order to begin it afresh . . . recoil ever and anon from the
indefinite prodigiousness of their own aims.

"Until," Marx continues, "a situation has been created which makes all
turning back impossible, and the conditions themselves cry out: *Hic Rhodus,
hic salta!*"

I separated the final line from the rest of the passage because it seems to me
that the reference to "the conditions themselves" marks a dangerous shift in
the structure of the argument, as should be clear from my criticisms of the
notion of real origins in the text.

5. See chapters 7 and 10 (on Kant) as well as the final discussion of the
"politics of judgment" in chapter 14.

6. Capitalism is thus a form of antipolitics, a theme that is treated in more
detail elsewhere in this collection.

7. From this point of view, see the brief work by Cornelius Castoriadis,
"Ce qui est important," written in 1959 for a small ultra-Left journal and
reprinted in his *L'experience du mouvement ouvrier*, 2 (Paris: UGE, 1974).
This short piece sums up, in an important sense, an elaborate theoretical
edifice to which I owe a great deal, including much of the interpretation of
Freud proposed here.

4

Why Return to the American Revolution?

We are experiencing a crisis of the political imagination. Witness the rise in "neos"—neoliberalism, neoconservatism—and the exhaustion of political combinations such as "social democrat" or "welfare state." At the same time, the era of the "post" dominates in the cultural domain. What is happening today is at best social, at worst psychological; and both are distinct from the political in their affirmed individualism and their tolerance of a pluralism that quickly risks becoming relativism, even nihilism.[1] This distinction of the social from the political is not introduced in order to disqualify the social or to deny the potential implicit in what are commonly called "new social movements." Rather, this distinction helps to formulate a question that cannot be posed if one accepts a definition of the social that affirms individualism as its basis and its principle. Are we witnessing the end of the autonomy of the political? Perhaps the political never really was autonomous? At any rate, we can ask whether it should be and whether it should remain so.

Contemporary Apolitical Politics

Suppose for a moment that the prevalent cynical attitude that nearly instinctively reduces the political to its social basis only expresses a partial truth; suppose that the infamous "dialectic of enlightenment," proposed politically by Adorno and Horkheimer, but since adopted by many thinkers grouped under the somewhat misleading name of postmodernism, does not culminate in the abandonment of the search for a meaning that explains and justifies our social being-together, and that the quest for autonomy is not a mere pretension of modernity.[2]

One could then try to transform a fault into a virtue by affirming that the political success of our forebears left us the heritage of a successful republican government within which social differences can be reconciled. This was the common attitude in the United States in the 1950s, when sociologists were congratulating themselves about the "end of ideology" and when historians were explaining the "liberal consensus" and celebrating "American exceptionalism." The same attitude could be found today among those who believe that the principal merit of the successful power shift in France in May 1981 was the elimination of the major differences between parties that, despite their labels, have come to represent what in the United States are called liberals, some a bit more on the Right, others on the Left. According to this argument, those who speak of a "crisis" are troublemakers influenced by ideas and ideologies foreign to the liberal community. If the arguments of these critics make any sense, this is due to the fact that their models are applied to societies that have not yet experienced the realization of the liberal revolution. Once this revolution has been accomplished, it seems that the autonomy of the political no longer has any meaning; and those who speak of crisis should come finally to understand that their discourse has neither object nor coherence.

This implies that those who speak of the crisis of political thought are those who do not accept liberal society as the realization of the political. But this way of avoiding real problems, which was typical in the United States during the 1950s, does not succeed in masking the conflicts that quickly passed into the political arena. The civil rights movement is an example, as is the nearly simultaneous emergence of a counterculture that—though driven to excess in the anti-Vietnam War movement—cannot be reduced to that movement or, for that matter, be blamed for its failure. That new culture was and remains highly ambiguous. Without going into detail, one can assert that its evaluation depends in the last instance on the relation between its particular forms of action and the normative moment that is the political. It has to be seen that the new culture was not only a sociological fact; it was founded on a universalizing demand whose expression exceeded the particular interests it expressed in its demand for justice and right. The failure (perhaps provisional) of this new culture is explained by the fact that its purely social self-understanding prohibited the explicit passage to the articulation of the universal that was nevertheless the motor and the source of its expression.

Another way out of the crisis of political imagination that is manifested in the contemporary assertion of the priority of the social over the political without putting into question its foundational principle is proposed by those philosophers and literary theorists who call themselves "deconstructionists." Just as the forgetting of Being, according to Heidegger, is said to explain the planetary domination of technology and its artificial logic, the crisis originating from the domination of the political over the social seems to have become so habitual that we find ourselves without ideas to oppose its infernal machinery.[3] It follows logically that the crisis is only "ontic" (i.e., concerning only the empirical forms of politics) and that the weakening of our imaginations is rather a good sign; vice becomes virtue, political production is replaced by a sort of social *Gelassenheit* (or a liberal laissez-faire). The universalization of the social thus furnishes a measure by which to judge the relative value of different social movements: those that seek to go beyond their own individualism toward any sort of universal are condemned: egalitarian socialism is rejected as much as is the conservative return to bygone values: consummate individualist anarchy is of no more value than the return to classical natural law advocated by Leo Strauss. The irony is that this universalization of the social, which has the advantage of accepting the necessity of a foundation for our social being-together, falls immediately into its opposite; everything is particular, nothing has an independent value—we have come to the end of history and of knowledge.

As if it recognized the difficulty of giving positive form to its criticism, this latter attempt to escape the crisis sought to change itself into a historical and political reason by an alliance of its Heideggerian or Derridean foundation with a critique of totalitarianism. That critique became common currency in France toward the mid-1970s, when the so-called new philosophy came into fashion. Disregarding the vapid and rhetorical philosophic character of this journalistic mode, it is important to underline the fact that it was new only because of its lack of historical memory. The critique of totalitarianism led, however, to reposing the question of democracy. The most profound analysis of their relation can be found in the work of Claude Lefort, who has reflected on this question since his essay "La contradiction de Trotski" published in *Les Temps Modernes* in 1948. This is not the place to review the path pursued by Lefort; I should say, however, that I am greatly indebted to him.[4] Instead, I will start from another analysis, which is also inspired by the reflection on totalitarianism and which is preoccupied by the ambiguities of democratic thought— namely, Hannah Arendt's essay *On Revolution*.[5]

Two Revolutions and Two Traditions

Hannah Arendt's thesis is at first approach apparently unproblematic. The American Revolution was above all a political revolution, whereas the French Revolution quickly became a social revolution. Political revolution ignores and leaves aside private life; the *res publica,* the public thing, is its foundation, its justification, and its goal. This "public thing" is by definition universal, shared by all; since private interests exist and are sustained only through the maintenance of political bonds, this pursuit of the common good can be said not to harm those interests. It follows that the republican politics that emerged from the American Revolution was not caused by the relative material equality that characterized the thirteen rebellious colonies; their struggle was not the political reflection of a social infrastructure. Arendt insists that the American Revolution was a political creation; for her, revolution is nothing other than this institutional creation.

While the argument is impressive, an analysis of the French Revolution puts it in question. At an empirical level it is evident that the French had to take social inequalities more seriously than the Americans did. The revolutionaries of 1789 were looking to found a constitutional republic; their successors, the Girondins, were following the same course. As for the Jacobins, was it their fault that the political revolution was abandoned to social individualism? That would be to attribute to them retrospectively Lenin's famous definition according to which a Bolshevik is "a Jacobin indissolubly bound to the proletariat." Moreover, the recent French critique of totalitarianism has devoted itself largely to refuting the Jacobin pretension to speak in the name of a political universal that is to be imposed on an inert society. The difference between the two revolutions must be situated elsewhere.

Jürgen Habermas proposes a comparison of the two revolutions on the basis of a distinction between two schools of natural law.[6] The Anglo-Saxon school of natural law is optimistic: that which is natural is good. But that good, natural society can be deformed or corrupted by an external intervention; the task of the political is to restore society to its natural freedom—a freedom that society alone is capable of administering. Good government is small government; it is laissez-faire government. In a word, the political is negative; it teaches the legislator to abstain from external intervention. The American Revolution was thus justified as a reaction against the political meddling of the English in the internal affairs of the colonies. As for the republican government that the Revolution produced, Habermas treats it as secondary; one could imagine other superstructures that would permit the free unfolding of society according to its natural motion. In contrast, Habermas continues, Continental natural law begins from the premise of a corrupted society, which it criticizes in the name of a state to be created (or re-created). It recognizes the reality of power and its capacity to influence in a positive or corrective manner. When it takes power, Continental natural law applies itself to the positive transformation of society; it is ready, in the Rousseauvian phrase, to force men to be free. Before the French Revolution, this type of natural law was expressed by that oxymoronic form of government called Enlightened Despotism. Its logic is explained by the fact that Continental natural law is rationalist; its Reason does not hesitate to construct a state capable of imposing itself upon the disorganized movement of society. One sees here a Jacobin interpretation of Rousseau. Revolution is the rational transformation of society by the state. As for the form of this state, it calls itself republican because the state acts in the name of the *res publica*; however, the *raison d'être* of this republican government is not political but social. Thus, the failure of the French Revolution can be explained by the fact that, in making explicit the priority of the social without acknowledging its particularity, the political found itself caught in the pincers of contradictory social demands.

Neither Habermas nor Arendt thematize the relation between the Republic and democracy—perhaps because Habermas remains a tributary of Marx's denunciation of politics as illusory, while Arendt tends to exclude the social from her conception of democracy because of her classical vision of politics. As such, the free play and egalitarianism of society in republican politics appears to be only the ideological form that legitimates in fact the domination of private interests. In order that a society be democratized, its political structure must also be democratized. That, apparently, can happen only when society itself—incarnated, according to Marx, in the proletariat—takes political power. The paradox is that this taking of political power by society results in the disappearance of the distinction between the social and the political—either in the form of the total domination of the political (which calls itself "democratic," even if it takes the form of a Soviet-style "real democracy"), or in the form of the domination of the external constraints imposed by actual society on the freedom of the political. The demand for democracy is thus confused with a demand for transparency (from the social to the political, or from the political to the social), which results in the totalitarian fantasy of a complete and seamless identity of society with itself. This totalitarian tendency inherent in the logic of democracy brings us back to our point of departure—the crisis in political imagination. Paralysis not only comes from the manifest failures of the socialist state, as well as of the welfare state, but also is founded on a certain lucidity with regard to the political ambiguities of democracy. If democracy is defined as social activity and if a republic is understood as the political form that preserves the public space where this social activity is carried out, then the complete realization of social democracy would destroy the republican public space. The danger is that this recognition of the "dialectic of democracy" can be directed against democratic politics.[7] This is why it is useful to reexamine the American Revolution, which started from a conception of political freedom and produced a unique integration of the political with the social.

Two Republican Concepts of Freedom in America

When the Seven Years' War—which the colonists called the French and Indian War—ended in 1763, the thirteen English colonies of North America found themselves freed from external threats from the French, whereas the mother country found itself not only in debt but suddenly the master of a new empire. In order to deal with its debt, it had to reorganize its imperial relations. Economic exchanges between the colonies and England were structured in terms of a mercantilist politics. By definition, these relations had to work against the colonists' interest even before England found itself saddled with a new debt burden. But the colonists' reaction to this economic exploitation had to articulate and legitimate itself in political terms. Moreover, the colonists felt closer to the English than they felt to each other. This bond with England was maintained politically by the Whig ideology of freedom. Without the constraints that had been imposed by the presence of the French, the dialectic between material reality and its theoretical reflection was able to play freely—until it produced a double reversal.

Whig thought had been installed through a violent revolution that beheaded a king in 1649, and through a peaceful revolution in 1688 that called itself "glorious." In its most general form, Whig thought represents a world where power and freedom continually confront one another, the former seeking always to expand at the expense of the latter. Although it is power that plays the role of the aggressor, Whig ideology conceives of history as the long march toward freedom and its conquest of power. It draws sustenance from the constant increase of parliamentary power through successive confrontations with the monarchy that seem to supply the historical demonstration of the validity of its thesis. But, in retrospect, Whig ideology must be distinguished from Whig theory. The latter furnishes a hermeneutic permitting the actors to uncover the hidden ends of historical and contemporary actors, whereas the former justifies the hope that motivates these actors when they pass into action. Whig ideology can easily be combined with the classical idea of the republic. Republican government, in this case, would be the incarnation of triumphant freedom. It is here, with this postulated unity of the individual and the commonweal of the republic, that the ambiguity of Whig ideology is revealed. To conceive of England according to the republican model, it was necessary to indicate how each person's private activity converges in the common good. In order to do that, the classical concept of "mixed government" was applied. That political theory suggests that each social estate (i.e., monarchy, lords, and commons) is represented at the political level by an institution that incarnates its interests. Therefore, contemporaries said of England not only that it had a constitution, but also that it *was* a constitution. This image of a Whig social republic was able to serve as justification for the newly established order that took root in 1689 and that was consolidated by Walpole. Some critics nevertheless saw that its reality could only be fictitious, cloaking the true sources of power and the threats to freedom. A revival of Whig theory followed from this recognition; the new attitude took the name "Old Whig." The Old Whig critique reactivated the idea of a contrast and the competition between freedom and power; its denunciation of the abuses of power was often supplemented by an invocation of the idea of a republic carrying out the common good (a commonwealth)—whence the other designation of this school of thought, the "Commonwealthmen." The Old Whigs thus reactivated the political element that the merely social establishment of Walpole's Whigs tended to veil.

Given the geographical position and the economic structure of the colonies, Whig ideology in its formulation of the mixed social republic could not define the colonists' position within the new empire. On the other hand, the Old Whig critique served them well as an interpretive hermeneutic, given that the English were beginning to impose new constraints on their commerce and new taxes on their affairs. This is not the place to retrace once again the pamphlet-strewn road leading to the Declaration of Independence. It is important to stress that each step was the outcome of a reflection in the Old Whig style that sought to uncover and to denounce the appetite for power and the use of means that were a corruption of liberty by the British measures—even when those measures were anodyne and often justifiable from the point of view of the well-being of the empire to which the colonies did, after all, belong. As proof of the influence of Old Whig thought, one has only to reread the Declaration of Independence, in which the few general principles that preface the statement are followed by several detailed pages illustrating English misdeeds and demonstrating their intention of stifling colonial liberty. The debate over the Lockeian character of the doctrine of natural law invoked by the premises of the Declaration of Independence is less important than the recognition of the deep hold of this Old Whig hermeneutic on the political thought of the future revolutionaries.[8] If our contemporaries reduce the political to the economic, our ancestors were past masters of the inverse tactic. We should perhaps take them more seriously.

Another aspect of the application of Old Whig thought to the experience of the colonies explains the passage from revolt to revolution and also the republican hope of the new Americans. The colonies were very different from one another; animated by a jealous localism and often by an exclusionist religiosity, as well as by real differences of interest (for example, concerning the virgin land to the west), the creation of unity between 1763 and 1776 must be explained. The principal explanation is the experience of a common struggle; the colonists all shared an active concern for a freedom menaced by English power. This common struggle gave rise to what can be called a common sense, whose existence raises another important point. The first anti-English actions were led by the merchant elite, whose material interests were likely to suffer. This group was opposed to a local political elite whose power was consecrated by England and its king. The merchant elite mobilized the crowd—which was more than willing to comply. The experience of the two sides appeared promising to both. Members of the elite were learning not to fear popular participation, which showed itself to be controllable; the popular masses were learning about the pleasures of political action for the first time and about their own power. Across the thirteen colonies a common experience of critical demystification and of political action was leading toward the unity that was the revolution. The Declaration of

Independence was nearly anticlimactic from this point of view. It was the expression of what Tom Paine had come to call "common sense."

The conquest of independence did not consecrate the end of the political evolution of the new United States. Once declared, independence had to be given a political form. At first there were the thirteen state constitutions. Some were populist and participationalist (like Pennsylvania), whereas others preferred to copy the English model (like Maryland); the majority were unique creations (of which Massachusetts was typical). The government of this confederation of thirteen states, which in theory directed the war and was responsible for the repayment of foreign loans, had no constitutional existence at all. It was only after eighteen months of independence and war that a constitution was proposed to the states, and it was not until 1781 that it was legally implemented. That same year, the War of Independence came to an end; in 1783 the treaty of Paris, which ratified the victory, was signed. The economic inflation during the war was followed by a deflation; freed of the empire's mercantilist constraints, the economy was not able to find its own direction. Each state did what seemed best in its own eyes, but all experienced the same difficulty: the people, finally in power, were showing themselves to be fickle, the self-interested victims of their passions, an easy prey for demagogy. It was as if all the warnings of classical political thought that since antiquity had forecast the degeneration of democracy into anarchy, followed by the arrival of tyranny, were proving themselves to be true.

This image of a degenerating democracy was produced by a dominant class having much to lose if the situation did not improve. More important is the political theory on which such an image depends for its verisimilitude. If the people, at last in power, apply to themselves the principle of doubt at the base of the Old Whig hermeneutic, what will be its result? How could one understand the idea that freedom could oppress itself? The fault must be sought in the particular republican political form that American social democracy—or democratic society—gave to itself. It attempted to follow the English Whig model that balanced political institutions on the basis of a corporative relation of social estates in a socially mixed government. However, social estates no more existed in the now independent United States than did an external power against which freedom had to defend itself. Thus, the Old Whig hermeneutic maxim was no more adequate than was its Whig counterpart—and from its application came only the vision of a self-destructive democracy. In place of the Old Whig model that had dominated the prerevolutionary struggle, it is necessary now to imagine a positive principle in order to give an institutional form to the sovereign freedom that had conquered independence by 1783. The constitutions of the confederated states and that of the Confederation itself, were not sufficient for the realization of freedom because they were based upon an Old Whig principle and on a classical idea of the republic that the revolution had made useless and anachronistic. The revolution continued, even without its chiefs.

The new constitution produced at Philadelphia in 1787 was the result of a compromise between the material interests of individuals and of states. But it was founded also on the need to take into account a radical change of perspective. The mixed republican constitution was replaced by a system of checks and balances among the three branches of government. The governmental branches no longer were supposed to represent social interests; now they were to incarnate political functions; and each branch would represent, in this way, popular sovereignty in its entire freedom and autonomy. This representative political structure in which each branch totally represents popular will, while none exhausts its entirety, implies at the same time that no branch can claim to embody actually and fully the freedom that founds political action and makes it possible. This means that freedom is identical to the *res publica,* which implies in turn that no single group or branch of government can ever claim to possess the true nature of the sovereign people, any more than any political program can claim to be the full expression of a premodern social order that is passive and homogeneous.

This is not the place to analyze further the Constitution, still in force today; nor need one harp on the flaws that have appeared in the course of its implementation. Obviously, for example, the present bipartisan political system was not predicted by the Constitution; and the practice of judicial review by the Supreme Court is often criticized by one or the other of the political parties (depending upon whether the Court inclines toward a progressive or a conservative reading). More important is the result of the theoretical overthrow of the republican version of the Old Whig logic, which guaranteed that the place of power and freedom must remain empty. The Constitution as supreme law is itself subordinated to this sovereign but empty freedom. How does this freedom that, to use a significant phrase from Merleau-Ponty, is "everywhere and nowhere" express itself? Negatively, the function of this empty place is to articulate the moments of the political and to prevent the predominance of freedom over the state (i.e., anarchy) or of the state over freedom (i.e., despotism). Positively, the expression of freedom must permit the articulation of the relation of the political and of the social. This is where the history of the American Revolution meets our current crisis.

The American Revolution and the Current Crisis

The crisis of the contemporary political imagination is expressed in the fact that the political is either reduced to an expression or an appearance of the social or is replaced directly by the social. What is troubling in this structure is the absence of criteria for differentiating what is positive from what is ambiguous or simply negative in the plurality of the social. Everything that moves is not *ipso facto* to be applauded as a new social movement; every social movement that draws public attention is not *eo ipso* a political movement. The simplest solution would be to treat the republic as merely the political framework that permits and that legitimates the action of the social upon itself. The republican government of the United States differs from that which the French Revolution sought to bring about because the latter attempted to give real and immediate substance to the *res publica,* whereas the application of Old Whig thought to their political behavior during the Confederation period demonstrated to the Americans the impossibility of such a realization. Even so, this American republic tends to replace the practical concept of democracy—the regulated and legal action of society on itself—by the metaphor of a generalized "democratization" (extended today to family relations, school relations, etc.). In this context the rereading of the transformations of the American Revolution leads to a rethinking of the relation between social democracy and its political form.

The caricatural picture of the American Revolution depicts it according to Whig ideology. Since the advent of freedom is supposed to be necessary, that approach tends to ignore the conflicts, contradictions, and incoherence of the politics that accomplish it. Whig ideology also ignores the false consciousness of the actors who quite probably aim for ends other than those that they attain. The equation of freedom and democracy throughout the American Revolution was in no way necessary; it was neither sought by the majority of 1776 nor even by that of 1787. One is tempted, therefore, to explain the nature of democracy in America as Tocqueville suggested when analyzing its social foundation and establishment. Tocqueville's analysis appeals all the more to our contemporaries because he demonstrates the misdeeds of a social democracy that is willing to sacrifice liberty to the jealous quest for equality, to the point that there emerges a kind of dictatorship of opinion that takes the form of totalitarianism. But this totalitarianism is apolitical; it results from the absorption of the political in and by the social.[9] This raises the question: can one avoid the slide toward totalitarianism simply by the transformation or reorganization of the social? This difficulty, in turn, seems to bring us back to the model of the French Revolution that sought to impose reason on society from the outside. But are we condemned to this choice between two models, the one giving priority to society but incapable of explaining the motor of its change, the other insisting on the necessity of political intervention without being able to explain its social foundation?

Truly political change must be certain of the receptivity of the social to its decrees if it is not to become an enlightened despotism. On the other hand, change whose roots are purely social is not able to explain precisely what particulars are capable of bringing about this political transformation; it therefore risks supporting a social movement whose tendency is harmful to freedom.[10] These reciprocal limitations lead to a paradox: the action of society upon itself that we define as democracy poses a problem whose resolution can only be political, whereas the republican structure that the American revolutionaries identified classically as the political defines in fact the social form of a democratic society whose immediate reflections are political laws. This paradox returns us to our analysis of the American Revolution on the basis of two questions: that of the institutional articulation of freedom by a sovereign people, and that of the relation between the social and the political.

No one was seeking either independence or revolution in 1763; and those who were forced to declare themselves independent in 1776 resisted this step until the last minute. That resistance and those hesitations should be emphasized; they testify to the resistance of the social to political change. From the start, American society conceived of itself according to the English Whig-republican idea of a mixed constitution. The Declaration of Independence by that society involved putting into question its political self-conception. Once it was freed, society fell back on itself; the sovereign people in power provided it with laws that depended only upon its will. The resulting instability can be conceptualized in Old Whig terms; society understood itself on the basis of an analysis founded on the politicization of all social relations. Suspicion with regard to the aims of power, which fueled the anti-Federalist opposition to the 1787 constitution, shared also by the "nationalists" (who cleverly labeled their cause "Federalist"). They supported the new constitution because they were seeking to go beyond the anarchy that they claimed dominated the life of the Confederation. Thus, the centralization that the Constitution introduced was accepted only after bitter debate. It was only in the process of putting into practice the new institutions that it became clear that, as was seen above, the Constitution is articulated such that the place of power cannot be occupied. Such a constitution can function only within a society where private interests set the wheels in motion; there is no place for the kind of state-led initiatives that the rationalist-Jacobin French model seeks to realize.

The stages of the Revolution can be reconstructed as suggested above according to the logic of particularity and of receptivity that I have suggested. The Old Whig analysis is a political analysis that designates the social particulars that call for political action; the latter in turn prepares the social terrain to accept the measures that follow. Each reapplication or iteration of Old Whig political analysis revives the social, another of whose particular aspects will subsequently be put in question. From this point of view, it is the political that determines the action of the social. One can also invert the analysis. One could begin the analysis of colonial society by asking whether the English political measures could have succeeded; one would then study the political response that those measures roused, and their incapacity to express the social demand that is supposedly still only latent in the social. This type of study was briefly alluded to by the question of the political unification of the thirteen colonies and the republican form that their constitutions adopted.[11] After independence, one can study the manner in which the articulation of social interests prevents political reflection from procuring the requisite autonomy needed to preserve the freedom that guarantees the originary distinction of the social from the political. This obstruction, which lasted until there was a federal constitution, must be stressed; it shows the danger in not permitting the autonomous existence of a political moment. From this point of view, the creation of a strongly national federal government by the Constitution of 1787 should not be identified with a French-style Jacobin centralization. We saw that the structure of the federal government makes impossible such an aim, which looks, for example, at recent statistics for the justification of its own autonomy.

This reconstruction may sound abstract to the ears of those accustomed to hearing the synecdoche that attributes all evil and all good to "Washington." That objection brings us back to the crisis in contemporary political thought. What Washington manages to do in this or that situation can be understood to result above all from the separation between the social and the political that makes possible that autonomous action. It may be replied that the weight of society explains that in fact Washington is not always able to do what it wants. Perhaps it would be better to abandon the dichotomy altogether, even while insisting on the autonomy of the two domains that necessarily refer to each other. That would imply that freedom can be reduced neither to its social nor to its political form. Does the same hold true for the interests whose particularity suggests that they must be conceptualized as belonging to the social? Particularity, as we have seen, can only be determined from the standpoint of the political. This implies that the definition of democracy as society acting on itself does not suffice. Without the political reference, society, strictly speaking, does not exist as anything but an accidental accumulation of atomized individuals sharing neither a past nor a future—although the citizens may be quite unaware of this, save in specific instances of crisis that result in what can rightly be called a revolution.

Does this imply, then, that the solution to our crisis is found in a revolution? The comparison of the French and American Revolutions should caution us against the abuse of this concept. The essence of the American Revolution was not the seizure of political power with the aim of transforming society—and yet we still accord it the title of revolution. If our goal is not arbitrarily to remove this label from it, the concept of revolution must be redefined. It could be argued that a revolution occurs when the dimension of the political, or that of the social, that was kept hidden or repressed by the established order, regains its autonomy. Further, the success of this revolution depends on its capacity for preserving together both of these two elements. This suggests, finally, that the crisis we are currently experiencing is not to be overcome but rather to be thematized both with regard to its necessity and with regard to its specific logical structure. That, however, is a task of another kind. For the moment, the return to the American Revolution, like the theory of the Old Whigs, makes necessary a political analysis of the social relations of power that are occluded by the liberal-Whig or socialist-Marxist evasions of the implications of the autonomy of the political.

Notes

1. For example, a colleague who teaches sociology regularly asks his students at the beginning of the semester to describe themselves. Without fail,

he finds neither men nor women, rich nor poor, students nor workers, only psychological classifications. I'm generous, kind, critical, depressive—in short, the "social" is empty. It doesn't make sense anymore.

2. The logical consequences of this version of "dialectic of enlightenment" can be illustrated by Peter Sloterdijk's hugely successful popular essay *Kritik der zynischen Vernunft* (Frankfurt am Main: Suhrkamp Verlag, 1983), or better yet by certain "deconstructive" analyses inspired by philosophers such as Lyotard, Deleuze, Guattari, or Baudrillard.

3. This is the argument suggested in "L'Ouverture" by Jean-Luc Nancy and Philippe Lacoue-Labarthe in *Rejouer le politique* (Paris: Galillée, 1981). That talk marked the opening of a short-lived Center for the Philosophical Study of the Political in Paris. My analysis is in "The Origin and Limits of Philosophical Politics," in *The Politics of Critique* (Minneapolis: University of Minnesota Press, 1988). For a discussion of the more subtle application of deconstruction by Laclau and Mouffe, see "Another Resurrection of Marxism," in *Defining the Political* (London: Macmillan, and Minneapolis: University of Minnesota Press, 1989).

4. Lefort's evolution and his recent work are discussed in my *Marxian Legacy* (2d ed. [Minneapolis: University of Minnesota Press, and London: Macmillan, 1988]). See also "Liberalism, Democracy, and the Theory of the Double Revolution" below. For an overview of the journal *Les Temps Modernes*, and for Lefort's role in the split that led Merleau-Ponty to leave the editorial board, see Anne Boschetti, *Sartre et 'Les Temps Modernes'* (Paris: Editions de Minuit, 1985). Note, however, that the standpoint of Boschetti is that of the sociological theory of Pierre Bourdieu.

5. Hannah Arendt, *On Revolution* (New York: Viking Press, 1963).

6. In "Natural Law and Revolution," in Jürgen Habermas, *Theory and Practice*, trans. John Viertel (Boston: Beacon Press, 1973).

7. See the famous Trilateral Commission report on a "crisis of ungovernability" in democracies that would necessitate limiting democracy in order to preserve it. See M. J. Crozier, S. P. Huntington, and J. Watanuki, *The Crisis of Democracy: A Report on the Governability of Democracies to the Trilateral Commission* (New York: New York University Press, 1975).

8. See Dick Howard, "La Déclaration d'Independance," in *Dictionnaire des oeuvres politiques* (Paris: PUF, 1987). Hannah Arendt stresses the phrase "*we hold* these truths to be self-evident," and the insistence on offering to defend what "we hold" to be true before "a candid world."

9. Derridean-Heideggerian critics Nancy and Lacoue-Labarthe speak of this situation as a "soft totalitarianism." This designation adds nothing to the analysis. It would be better to speak of social or political forms of totalitarianism.

10. The Nazis, for example, insisted that they were a "social movement" and not an ordinary, self-interested, and divisive political party. This was one reason many of the older generation reacted negatively to the New Left of the 1960s, which insisted on its own "movement" character.

11. The best overall analysis of the social activity that leads to the political is found in Pauline Maier's *From Resistance to Revolution* (New York: Vintage Books, 1972). There are many specific studies of the social activity that became a political revolution; the first of these was written by Carl L. Becker, *The History of Political Parties in the Province of New York, 1760–1776* (Madison: University of Wisconsin Press, 1909), who posed the question of whether the Revolution concerned the question of "Home Rule" or "Who should rule at home?"

5

Liberalism, Democracy, and the Theory
of the Double Revolution

The idea of the "double revolution" was implicit in the successive stages through which the French Revolution was driven toward the Terror, whose legitimation was offered by Robespierre under the name of "revolutionary government."[1] After Thermidor had put an end to the rule of the radical Jacobins, the demand for another revolution that would complete the Revolution defined the identity of the true revolutionary. On the last of the revolutionary *journées*, 1 Prairial of the Year III, the masses who invaded the Convention demanded "Bread and the Constitution of 1793." Not long thereafter, Babeuf and the Conspiracy of Equals provided both the theory and the practice of the double revolution: the social and economic transformation that would follow on and complete the achievement of bourgeois liberties was to be lead by a dedicated, selfless conspiracy acting in the name of the people. Babeuf was to have numerous heirs in the nineteenth century. In the twentieth, the idea that something like 1793 had to follow and complete 1789 was made more palpable by the interpretation of the Russian Revolution of 1917 as the completion of what had been begun in eighteenth-century France. Caught up in the passions of the times, the great French historian Albert Mathiez could publish a pamphlet comparing Robespierre and Lenin—as if history had been waiting for its final consummation.

Two hundred years after the French Revolution began, the hope that another revolution would transcend its merely formal or bourgeois character by fusing liberty to social equality has apparently come to an end. The revolutions of 1989 can be understood as the condemnation of the second revolution in the name of those very bourgeois goals that animated the first. But if the liberty that has been won in Eastern Europe is defined and limited to only these older historical concepts, nothing prevents the reemergence of the quest for a "true second revolution"—but this time as one that argues that "really existing socialism" was not socialism at all, and that there is still hope for true social justice to be realized. (Or, alternatively, as in Hungary recently, a populist and nationalist right-wing movement could apply the schema of the double revolution to interpret 1989 as only a formal transformation led by an egoistic bourgeoisie that needs to be given "true" national content.[2]) That is why the Eastern European revolutions of 1989 cannot be understood simply as the triumph of (or return to) bourgeois or capitalist values; more than a victory of one side, these revolutions mark the defeat, from within, of the other side: of totalitarianism as a doomed political project whose logic must be understood if contemporary radical politics is to be rethought and the curse of historical repetition avoided.

The revolutions of 1989 have placed the concept of democracy in the center of political debate. While it is tempting to argue that the problem of instituting a modern democracy was already the crucial feature of the French Revolution, that claim cannot be defended here.[3] Rather, I want to propose a very different notion of the second revolution in order to provide a framework for understanding the radical implications of the democratic challenge. In this context, the work of Claude Lefort has been, and remains, pathbreaking.

The remarks that follow were presented originally at a three-day conference in his honor, held at the Beaubourg Museum in Paris in January 1992.[4] My assignment was to present the "American detour" in Lefort's work. It turned out that this was no detour at all; Lefort's analysis of totalitarianism, and his self-critical reflections on revolutionary practice—which had led to his original split with the *Socialisme ou Barbarie* group—had well prepared the terrain.[5] The double revolution is radical insofar as it is the self-critique of the revolution that made it possible.

The Critique of Totalitarianism

Reflecting in a 1975 interview on his political trajectory and his relation to and break with the group *Socialisme ou Barbarie*, Claude Lefort explained how and why his position had become more radical:

I wanted to question the fundamental principles of revolutionary action to which I had adhered for fifteen years. First and foremost, the very image of revolution. I discovered that the critique of bureaucracy that I had applied to the basic enterprise of *Socialisme ou Barbarie* had been left along the way. . . . I wanted to show that the concept of direction, or leadership, was linked to that of revolution. . . . The root of the illusion was the belief in a radical break between past and future, a break occurring in an absolute moment . . . in which the meaning of history is revealed.[6]

I will not trace here the critical persistence with which, as early as his essay "La contradiction de Trotsky" (1948), and through the polemic with Sartre and with those whom he then called the "progressive intellectuals" before discovering in Solzhenitsyn the more apt label of *bien-pensants*, Lefort obstinantly refused to pretend to be able to occupy the god's-eye view (*pensée de survol*) that Merleau-Ponty's phenomenology had already criticized and of whose political perniciousness he himself provides us with many examples.[7] My thesis will be that it is not possible to understand the theory of democracy without taking into consideration the evolution of revolutionary ideology—or of the ideology of "the" revolution.

Two more recent statements by Lefort will allow me to explain why this detour through America is useful for our purposes. The first comes from a self-interrogation on the meaning of his being a "philosopher." Lefort asks:

But how could I have attempted to assess . . . the meaning of the denial of social division by and in totalitarianism—the denial of the division between the State and civil society, of the division of classes, of the division between sectors of activity—but also the denial of the difference between the sphere of power, the sphere of the law, the sphere of knowledge (a difference which is constitutive of democracy)—without seeming to legitimate, or without myself worrying that this would legitimate, the existing divisions which characterize the established democratic regimes in which we live.[8]

Indeed, he goes on, how can one criticize totalitarianism and Marxism without thereby lending a helping hand to the oppressive regimes that appropriate for themselves the label of "democracy"? If the dream of the "good society" is abandoned, how can one do politics? Or even philosophy? Does knowing what one is opposed to, directly or through logical mediations, lead to a knowledge of what one wants or should want? This last question takes its full weight when Lefort observes, in "Reflection on the Present," that "it would be vain to look for [a reflection about the democratic regime against which totalitarianism arose] either in Souvarine, or in Simone Weil, for example, or in Adorno, Horkheimer, or Hannah Arendt.''[9] The criticism of totalitarianism remains valid for itself; but is criticism sufficient?

Liberalism and Democracy

Could one say that democracy did not become the object of a theoretical debate because it did not seem to be a political issue? That is what historiographical debates about the stakes of the American Revolution would lead one to believe. At the end of World War II, the thesis of American exceptionalism was unchallenged; it alleged that America was a fundamentally liberal society, and that no radical political idea—of either the Left or the Right—could find any durable support there. Accordingly, Louis Hartz or Richard Hofstadter reconstructed the country's political history around principles that they deemed Lockeian. Similar assumptions explain Daniel Bell's famous thesis about the end of the era of ideology. However, the idea that underlies all of these positions has been put into question by a remarkable historian, Gordon Wood, whose book, *The Creation of the American Republic* (1969), has been published in France in a collection directed by Claude Lefort, and to which Lefort has written an introduction. Lefort notes that even Wood expresses "reservations about the American political system." Indeed, he questions the "disconnection of the social and the political," whose result is an American "liberal tradition" that cannot "articulate a politics based on the opposition of interests.''[10] In other words, American liberal democracy is based on a rigorous separation between the political and the social, the public and the private, the person seeking the happiness hallowed by the Declaration of Independence and the citizen who has become passive. It is thus impossible to mobilize people to conduct a "great" political project—or even to awaken them to the call for a republican politics whose disappearance Gordon Wood seems to mourn. In other words, the dream of a second revolution remains present, if in an attenuated form, even in Gordon Wood's apparently antiliberal appeal to republicanism.

Claude Lefort only mentions these "reservations" in the last paragraph of his introduction to *The Creation of the American Republic*.

He admits that "the argument is powerful," but explains that he cannot discuss it in the framework of his introduction. He limits himself to a negative observation, which challenges the idea of what I just called a "great" political project. In its place, one should

> agree that, on the contrary, where there was a durable intertwining of political and social problems, in the wake of the French Revolution, the formation of ideology, by allowing a full-blown class antagonism and by creating a rift between bourgeois liberalism and proletarian socialism, was accompanied by a troubling uncertainty about the nature of democracy: its effect was to devalue rights and to produce an attraction to the idea of a power organically linked to society.[11]

The problem is the attempt to unify the social and the political; or, in other words, it is the classical ideal of a Great Legislator who would realize "organically" both society and power. But what Lefort's introduction seeks to demonstrate is that Wood presents American democracy as "a new form of society" that "has no paternity: it is not the work of a legislator"; as Wood's title indicates, it is a creation of and by the entire people. This was possible because the pretension of operating from a god's-eye view (*survol*)—which a "Direction" or leadership pretending to be revolutionary implicitly or explicitly claims for itself—was refused, and because "the image of the legislator disappears, and with it that of the best regime."[12] In this sense, Wood would appear to free us from the chains of revolutionary ideology, to liberate our imagination from the need to repeat and to complete the revolution.

American Revolution as Revolutionary

How can we respond to Gordon Wood's doubts? How can we avoid the snares of the liberal tradition? Lefort emphasizes that Wood uncovers two revolutions within the American Revolution. The first led to independence. It should be stressed that this revolution was not the result of a material necessity dictated by specific social conditions. Nor should one think that this revolutionary activity is explicable by Tocqueville's thesis about the influence of an originary equality that supposedly existed already in the colonies. Lefort points out that Tocqueville "tends to collapse the political and the social" when he implies that social conditions determine political forms.[13] What has to be explained in this first revolution, rather, is the practical and theoretical appearance of an ideology that "gives reasons for the onset of a revolution which the quarrels with the British Parliament alone are unable to provide."[14] From this emerges what Lefort calls a "will toward rupture and innovation," the quest for a new world with its "moral dimension and utopian depth."[15] How is it that the demand for the "rights of an Englishman" becomes the demand for rights per se? How can we explain the explosive effects of Tom Paine's *Common Sense*, which appeared from nowhere to fire the republican demand? Gordon Wood draws our attention to the Radical or Old Whigs, whose political self-understanding was based on a simple but profound understanding of the political: power and freedom are both necessary in any polity; yet they are fundamentally opposed to one another. Power tends, by its very nature, to expand; indeed, its very nature tends toward tyranny. But it can expand only at the expense, and with the complicity, of freedom, which must therefore always keep an eye open not only to the schemes of power, but also to its own sinful and corrupted nature. In this way, Radical or Old Whig thought is founded on a dynamic notion of politics that questions the intentions of the other but also remains always self-critical of itself. The result is an ideology that dominates the first period of the revolution, and that leads to independence.[16]

What happens to this ideology when the people—that is, freedom—have occupied the place of power? What can be the source of a conspiracy against freedom? Where does corruption lie? These questions lead to the second stage of the American Revolution, which is characterized by the application of the very ideology that made the revolution to the results of that revolution. What had happened was that the ideology of the first period—with its rejection of the schemes of the executive and court and its faith in the uncorrupted popular will—led to the creation of governments in which all power was given to a popular assembly. As Lefort points out, this structure was based implicitly on the image of a homogeneous people—the good people that had freed themselves from the yoke of the king. However, that image of a united society was quickly challenged in two ways by the ideology that had made the revolution. That ideology was essentially jealous of power; to protect itself even from its own assemblies, it insisted on frequent elections, which produced changing majorities and led to unstable and nitpicky legislation. In this way, the introduction of institutions designed to limit the political autonomy of the popular legislative assembly made obvious the division of society itself. The result, says Lefort, was that "at the same time as the institution of the republic calls forth an idealization of the assembly of the people, there arises a suspicion about the validity of representation. The result is the remarkable fact that the rise of democratic representation coincides with the very questioning of its rights and of the limits of its authority."[17] The assembly, which was supposed to incarnate popular aspirations, acted instead as a mirror that forced a self-critique. It was in fact "a denial, imposed by reality, of the theses of the first republicans" who still believed that their revolutionary society would return to its positive and unified nature.[18]

This reflection or doubling of the revolution gave rise to what American historians call the "critical period." Wood sees in it "the labor of society on itself" that will lead to the creation of a new science of the political. However, one must be careful here, for it is just this new science of the political about which Wood had also expressed his "reservations."[19] The creation of this new science borrows the dichotomy of power and liberty that grounded revolutionary ideology, but now it is the people as a majority, or more precisely democracy, which is denounced as the incarnation of a despotic power. The men who met in Philadelphia in 1787 to write a new constitution had to invent a new type of representation of the sovereign people. Lefort describes enthusiastically their theoretical premises: "Nothing could be more radical than this conception. Since the people can in no way alienate its own freedom, it can only delegate this or that part of its power, within determinant boundaries, and for determinant ends, to its representatives: the federal government and the state governments are similarly the elements of a vast system of representation."[20] Lefort admits, as does Wood, that there may be "an element of ruse in this reasoning." After all, at the same time that the people are granted their sovereignty, the concrete use of this sovereignty is prevented by the checks imposed by the new representative principle. Nevertheless, Lefort insists, this theory "is not any the less in keeping with the democratic spirit which had vainly sought to transform itself into practice."[21] With this, we are at the center of the debate concerning Wood's reservations about the American Revolution as well as the chances for meaningful social or political change within a contemporary American type of democratic republic.

It was necessary to invent a new idea about both the people and about power in order to go beyond the ideological representation of both of them in the first revolutionary period. If the people are now to be denied the exercise of power, this is not because they do not have the empirical competence to make use of it. Rather, it is because of the discovery that the people do not have the unity and homogeneity that revolutionary ideology attributed to them. The people come to recognize that they are divided, diverse, and condemned to remain so. Lefort emphasizes two results of this learning process. On the one hand, American identity "is detached from belonging to a localized territory, anticipating its further settlement on new territories"; on the other hand, the idea of "an ultimate authority, the Constitution, to which the governing and the governed are equally subjected" can appear in the place of the ideological representation of a united people for whom the common good is one and unique.[22] The disincarnation of power that is implied in the idea of a sovereign people that cannot be fully present in any institution and that can only delegate their power for specific ends is thus at the basis of both the expansive capacity of the newly freed thirteen colonies and of their translation of the theoretical idea of a "fundamental law" into a judicial practice that came to take the form of "judicial review." But how does this demonstration illustrate the democratic character of the double revolution? After all, it does not take much imagination to criticize expansion as "imperial" or to denounce judicial review as "nondemocratic."

American Revolution and the Origin of Democracy

As if he saw the problem without stating it explicitly, Lefort emphasized the fact that judicial review is based on a new vision of a social contract, one that is established among equals, rather than expressing the relation between a power and the people, as it was for the radical Whigs. This is why, he says, conventions and other popular manifestations such as illegal, often violent, and rebellious meetings come to acquire an institutional status during the debates over the ratification and the amendment of the Constitution (which led to the incorporation of the Bill of Rights, which the Framers had not felt to be necessary because their new institutions made the arbitrary exercise of power impossible[23]). Although Lefort does not refer here to Hannah Arendt, he describes the practical realization of an idea that was dear to her: conventions, in the plural, are a "way to institutionalize the Revolution . . . [which] bears in itself the virtuality of a *return to first principles*, as Machiavelli put it; these conventions protect the freedom to begin."[24] The implication is that the republican form is essential to the realization of American democracy to the extent that it makes explicit the political dimension of a society that now knows itself as divided and yet nonetheless unified. This republican form should not be identified with the classical republic, which, since Aristotle or Polybius, was founded on the organic image of a "mixed society" in which divergent social interests are linked in such a way as to form a whole that is in principle, or naturally, unified. Having been forced to get rid of this image of the naturally good and unified society, the Americans were no longer seeking to realize the "revolutionary" project of insuring the full presence of the people in the government by identifying the social and the political in one totality. Their democratic republic was representative in the "modern" sense of the term, as *The Federalist Papers* defense of the new constitution insisted forcefully.[25]

This is why it would be wrong to ask what is represented in this new democracy. Posed in that way, the question takes a god's-eye view (*pensée de survol*) and conceives of representation in terms of adequation between the representative and what is represented. Lefort, on the contrary, emphasizes the fact that "the conception of a generalized representation [by all of the institutions defined by the new constitution] was indicative of a mutation for which the simple concept of a republic does not fully account. It is this mutation that Gordon Wood . . . defines best by introducing the concept of the *disembodiment of government.*"[26] Furthermore, continues Lefort, "one should not conclude that power detaches itself from the people . . . since the people, even though they are excluded from political action, remain omnipresent. Everything takes place . . . as if the governed and the governors had traded roles."[27] Not only is power strictly delegated, its very expression in governmental institutions is fragmented in such a way that no instance can claim to be its complete incarnation. This disembodiment of power is at the basis of the checks and balances that form the basic structure of the constitution.[28] But, Lefort insists, this institutional structure is not simply a ruse to prevent the people from governing themselves; it also implies not only that social division is recognized and maintained but also that this division becomes the source of constant activity. That is why the American Revolution did not attempt to impose a conception of the public good on a recalcitrant people or try to "use force against human nature, as the republics of Antiquity [or the "revolutionary government" of the "second" French Revolution] did in violation of their own best interests." That is why Americans were able to recognize that "the existence of political parties is unavoidable and even necessary."[29]

But Gordon Wood's reservations are not yet fully answered. The birth of political parties representing private or economic interests cannot satisfy the American who mourns the disappearance of republican virtue or the revolutionary in search of great politics that is not limited to Lockeian liberalism. Lefort asserts that, beyond the transformation of revolutionary ideology, the passion for liberty has remained alive; but a critic may reply that this freedom is manifested only in the private life of the isolated individual. Lefort's answer is double. The constitution itself creates powers; it multiplies "the channels insuring the circulation of opinions, of beliefs and—no less important—also of societal interests . . . without ever permitting power to arise and to crystallize in one place."[30] To this invitation to social action that comes, as it were, from above, from the political, is added a second incitation that is rooted below, so to speak, in the philosophical or theoretical. The disembodiment of government—that "set of institutions governed by the principle that power must not actualize itself anywhere, that nobody, no group may pretend to occupy its place or appropriate its exercise"—as well as "the distinction and separation of power, law and knowledge of the ultimate goals of society," produce conditions in which the democratic debate can neither be avoided nor come to an even temporary end.[31] What we see here is the same critique that Lefort addressed earlier to the reading of Tocqueville that "tends to collapse the political and the social."[32] Whereas Lefort saw in Gordon Wood's work the antidote to such a reading, we can see today that the reservations expressed by Wood were based precisely on the fact that he, like our contemporaries, tended to forget that, as opposed to Lockeian liberalism, democratic society is only possible within a political framework that is open to challenges and change. It is as if, in spite of the implications of his own analyses, Gordon Wood shared the presuppositions of liberalism.

This is not the place to pursue further the distinction between liberalism and democracy, but reference has to be made to it insofar as Claude Lefort also makes use of Gordon Wood's analyses at the conclusion of a remarkable analysis of Guizot's "polemical liberalism" that seeks to draw the lessons from the failure of the French model of revolution.[33] The result of his analysis is that the idea of a liberalism that would exist only at the level of the political and of a democracy that expresses itself on the level of the social is only another hypostatization of the dichotomy expressed by the reservations of Gordon Wood and by the demands of the traditional proponents of the second revolution. It follows that what Wood should more properly have called the "democratic" creation of the American republic implies that democracy can only be conceived if it takes on, or learns the necessity of, the republican form—a form that, it should be stressed, is not eternal, as its comparison with the classical form of the republic proposed by *The Federalist Papers* indicates.[34] This is because the republican form makes explicit the permanent presence of the political. If it cannot prevent the positivistic tendency that separates the social from the political, at least it expresses a permanent warning against such a reductionist error. This is what seems to me to explain that, after the domination of liberalism in the period designated by Daniel Bell's notion of the "end of ideology," there arose the Civil Rights movement as well as a New Left whose principle actor had the name Students for a *Democratic* Society.

But the temptation presented by the political model of the French Revolution and the idea of an historical rupture cannot be discarded so easily. Lefort goes back to Tocqueville in "Réflexion sur le Présent" to defend him from having reduced democracy to the level of the equality of conditions.[35] On the contrary, the reason Tocqueville insists that democracy cannot "be maintained in the absence of civil and political liberties," while at the same time emphasizing that this democracy comes into being in an "irresistible" manner, is that he understood that politics is "a permanent invention, an 'art' " that belongs to "the essence of democracy."[36] Not only would it be an error to insist on the priority of the social, as if it were something wholly real; the social cannot be isolated artificially from the political, as is done by the hypostatized subject in the French model of revolution. A final contrast of the French to the American experience brings back the question of the relation of totalitarianism to democracy, from which we began: "France alone has seen its revolution separate itself from its actors; only in France was the revolution idealized, even personified; only in France was a mythology born and the type of the revolutionary hero created. . . . In short, the French Revolution gave rise to an imaginary stage on which, until recently, all the desires of those who, here and there, put their hopes in a radical change were projected."[37]

Such artificial dichotomies can be avoided if one imitates the American model of the double revolution that applies the revolutionary method to itself. This self-reflective and self-critical process, which underlies the whole of Gordon Wood's book and which deserves a detailed analysis on its own, is not without parallels to the philosophical attitude outlined by Lefort in the autobiographical passage about the nature of philosophy cited at the beginning of this essay. In a word, it consists of an apprenticeship to reality that can take place only through experience—an experience that is made possible by the rejection of revolutionary ideology, of the ideology of "the" revolution. Whether it is the American Revolution or the work of Claude Lefort, what is necessary is a "critique of the revolution," to borrow the title of Edgar Quinet's acute study of the French Revolution, which Lefort also republished in his collection.[38] This is the reason why, unlike the other critics of totalitarianism to whom Lefort referred, Lefort is led to put forward a theory of democracy as radical politics.

Notes

1. I will talk sometimes about a "double revolution," sometimes about a "second revolution." Generally speaking, the former refers to a self-reflection of the revolution on its own conditions and goals, while the latter suggests the self-realization of the revolution by radicalizing its initial aims.

Robespierre's words (25 December 1793) were as follows: "the goal of constitutional government is to preserve the republic; the goal of revolutionary government is to found it." Saint-Just had laid the practical basis for this theory in a speech of 10 October 1793 when he asserted that "[t]he laws are revolutionary but those executing them are not. . . . In the present conditions of the republic, the Constitution cannot be established. . . . It would become the guarantee of threats to liberty because it would lack the violence necessary to repress those threats. . . . It is impossible for revolutionary laws to be executed if the government itself is not constituted in a revolutionary manner." Revolution thus becomes regeneration; it knows no limits; as an end in itself it can be only total.

2. For the case of Hungary, see the critical analysis by Andrew Arato, "Revolution, Restoration and Legitimation: Ideological Problems of the Transition from State Socialism," Working Paper No. 156 (New York: Center for Studies of Social Change, New School for Social Research). Arato's presentation of the current debates in Hungary makes clear that the persistence of the schema 1789-1793 is not limited to leftists. However, the American variant of the second revolution will make apparent that the schema can be understood in a different context and as having different implications.

3. See "The Marxian Legacy and the Problem of Democracy," chapter 2 above.

4. The original French version is published in *La Démocratie a l'oeuvre. Autour de Claude Lefort*, edited by Claude Habib and Claude Mouchard (Paris: Editions Esprit, 1993).

5. On Lefort's development, see chapter 7 of *The Marxian Legacy* (London: Macmillan, and Minneapolis: University of Minnesota Press, 1988), as well as the afterword, which brings the discussion up to date. On the journal

and group *Socialisme ou Barbarie*, see in *Marxian Legacy*, chapter 8 on Cornelius Castoriadis, as well as the afterword.

6. *L'Anti-Mythes*, "Entretien avec C. Lefort," No. 14, November 1975, 10 (interview of 19 April 1975).

7. For example, his critique of Trotsky tries to "place Trotsky in his role as an actor in a situation which, when he wrote his book, he pretended too easily to be able to view as a whole" (in *Elements d'une critique de la bureaucratie* [Genève: Droz, 1971], 14). The critique of Sartre, significantly called "From the response to the question," ends with the reproach: "Did you not yourself thus seek to prove to yourself the validity of your choice? Did you even ask yourself the question that you had formerly posed so clearly: for whom does one write?" (*Elements*, 108). As for "The Method of the Progressive Intellectuals," it is denounced for its pretense of being "realistic" (in this case, for justifying the lesser evil of the Gomulka solution to the Polish crisis of 1956), and thus for speaking in the name of power, "an attitude," Lefort continues, "which would appear merely comical if it did not reveal a permanent attitude of the French left. That left, which has broken with the established bourgeois order, presents its communist opinions in order to tie itself to another order [i.e., the USSR] into which it reintroduces—but now as positive—all the characteristics that it denounced as negative in its own society" (*Elements*, 261). See also my comments on "the party of order" in chapter 2 above.

8. Claude Lefort, *Ecrire. A l'épreuve du politique* (Paris: Calmann-Lévy, 1992), 348–49.

9. Ibid., 371.

10. Claude Lefort, Introduction to *La Création de la République américaine* by Gordon Wood (Paris: Belin, 1991), 27–28.

11. Ibid., 28.

12. Ibid., 5, 6, 8, and 6.

13. Ibid., 7. The distinction between "the social" and "the political" would be possible only if one could assume a god's-eye view (*pensée de survol*) that was separate from both of them. The theme of "political society" is a constant debt to Merleau-Ponty's phenomenology. This theme is most clearly developed with regard to Tocqueville in the essays cited in note 32 below.

14. Lefort, Introduction, 13.

15. Ibid., 10, 11.

16. This is why the Declaration of Independence is largely devoted to cataloging a long list of grievances presented to "a candid world" in order to demonstrate a pattern of corruption from which it is imperative that the colonists separate themselves in order to insure their freedom. The "inalienable rights" to which the second paragraph of the declaration famously refers are prepolitical rights; the declaration and the revolution are political acts whose theoretical foundation is the Radical Whig conception of politics.

17. Lefort, Introduction, 15.

18. Ibid., 13, 16.
19. Ibid., 17.
20. Ibid., 19.
21. Both citations in Introduction, 19.
22. Ibid., 20.
23. There are in fact two points to be stressed here. If a list of rights were in fact to be incorporated in the Constitution, the Framers feared that the failure to consider some other rights would be used to prevent their later assertion, thereby blocking off the possibility of historical progress. Second, the new vision of the democratic social contract meant that rights were not something that was acquired by a sort of contract with an already existing power; rather, rights are that which permits free individuals to enter a social contract—and to acquire thereby new rights. This is what seems to be presupposed by Hannah Arendt's notion of a "right to have rights," which Lefort cites frequently.
24. The distinction between Arendt and Lefort would demand a study of its own. Ulrich Rödel notes (Ibid., 22) that Lefort does not seem to distinguish between the process of ratification by conventions and the role of the people in the process of amendment. Even though he insists on the republican form of American democracy, Lefort does not, for example, propose a theory of civil disobedience or emphasize the role of active minorities. Lefort does not speak (any more than does Wood) of the learning process that allowed for the birth of the American Bill of Rights, and that structured its specific form and content. On the other hand, what Arendt and Lefort share is the concern to institutionalize the revolution, and the interpretation of this institutionalization as "the freedom to begin." (I should express here my thanks to Ulrich Rödel for his critical comments on an earlier draft of this essay.)
25. The argument of *The Federalist Papers* on this point is most explicit in Number 63, where democracy in the ancient republics is said to be based on the full presence of all citizens in all actions of government whereas the modern republic being proposed for the United States is based on a representative democracy. For the details of the argument and its political implications, see *The Birth of American Political Thought* (London: Macmillan, and Minneapolis: University of Minnesota Press, 1989), especially 186–204 and 221–27.
26. Lefort, "Introduction," 24. (The phrase from Wood is found in the English original of *The Creation of the American Republic* at p. 608.) That Lefort emphasizes here a disembodiment of *government* may seem surprising; later he returns to his usual formulation, referring to "power" in this context. The reason is that, in the American structure, power lies with the sovereign people whereas government is divided, as we will see in a moment.
27. Ibid.
28. It should be stressed that it is these checks and balances rather than the traditional separation of powers that are crucial to the structure of American politics. The separation of powers presupposes an organic image of society whose static nature clashes with the dynamics of modern political society.

29. Ibid., 26. Concerning the birth of political parties, see *The Birth of American Political Thought*, cited above, especially 223–27.

30. Introduction, 26ff.

31. Ibid., 27.

32. Ibid., 7, cited above at note 7. For Lefort's reading of Tocqueville, which restores the complexity of his political thought, see "Réversibilité: liberté politique et liberté de l'individu," and "De l'égalité à la liberté," both in *Essais sur le politique. XIXe-XXe siècles* (Paris: Editions du Seuil, 1986).

33. See "Guizot: le libéralisme polémique," in *Ecrire*, 113–39. Several points from Lefort's essay should be mentioned, at least in passing. Lefort shows how Guizot proposes "the critique of a power which thinks of itself as separate from society and which claims to rule it from outside" (123). This self-image is shown to be that of the politician who is seeking to gain power, and who criticizes other "liberals," such as Benjamin Constant, who "mostly think in terms of defending liberties and who are taken aback at the idea of actually exercising power . . . because they reduce that exercise to the function of command and of coercion" (122). Guizot understands that this self-image of the liberal is illusory because it does not see that "power is produced from within society and that society can only discover the form toward which it tends, and thus stabilize itself, by means of its own action" ("Guizot," 122). It follows that "power can only be active as long as it draws the resources for its activity from the movement of society. . . . Its activity is proportional to its *receptivity*" (124, italics added). A government has authority over society only insofar as it is part of society and that it knows itself as part of society. "Thus," concludes Lefort, "we cannot limit ourselves to the idea of an autonomy of the political. Guizot suggests the image of a single space doubled over in such a way that, in one sense, politics implants itself in the social, and in another sense, the social implants itself in the political" (125).

34. I am not certain that Lefort would agree with this claim that, however, seems at least implicit in his reading of Gordon Wood. In other places, and more often, he tends to speak of democracy's representative character—which is also one of the central themes of Wood's study. (See, for example, in *Ecrire*, "Foyers du Républicanisme," 208, and "Trois notes sur Léo Strauss," 281.) In this context the following argument from *Ecrire* should also be considered.

Is it so difficult to hold onto two ideas at the same time? To recognize that the history of democracy cannot be separated from that of the state, of capitalism, of technology, and that it is ruled by principles which are specific to it. When we say that democracy is a form of society, this does not mean that it contains the signification of everything that happens in that society, or that shapes the life of a people. If we were to examine, for example, the phenomenon of the nation, we would have to agree that it is irreducible and yet intertwined with the development of democracy, that there exists a tension between identifying with the nation and a democratic ethics—a tension that is all the greater insofar as the nation finds itself ever less capable of closing in upon itself. (381)

This passage is found at the end of "Réflexion sur le présent," which I cited earlier in reference to the fact that criticisms of totalitarianism do not necessarily contain the guidelines for constructing a theory of democracy. The question raised there, it seems to me, is the one Weber called that of "elective affinities," or more generally the question of democracy's capacity to appropriate and to subordinate to itself other institutions and other logics.

35. *Ecrire*, 382.
36. Ibid., 382.
37. Lefort, Introduction, 8.
38. See Edgar Quinet, *La Révolution* (Paris: Belin, 1987). The original edition was published in 1865; the "critique of the revolution" was Quinet's reply to his critics on the Left, and was published as the preface to the fifth edition of the work in 1867. For an evaluation of the debate, and the splits in the French Left of the time, see François Furet, *La gauche et la révolution au XIXe siècle* (Paris: Hachette, 1986), which reprints the attacks on Quinet.

6

Constitution, Representation, and Rights

The quest for legitimate political representation was central to the French Revolution from its origin throughout its development. The gesture of 17 June 1789, by which the Estates General proclaimed itself the National Assembly, was followed on 20 June by the Tennis Court Oath, by which the deputies now claiming to represent the Nation promised not to separate until they had given France a constitution. Three days later, by the voice of Mirabeau, they affirmed their political legitimacy: "Go tell your master [the king] that we are here by the force of the people and that we will leave only by the force of bayonets."[1] But even before the street brought new actors to the stage, fissures could be seen in the Assembly's unity. Mirabeau's combative self-assertion was seconded by Sieyès: "Messieurs, we are today what we were yesterday. Let us deliberate." By what authority, on what issues? On 9 July, the representatives took the name Constituent National Assembly. What were they constituting and how? Was their constitution to represent the Nation; or was it to insure the legitimate rights of the people? If it was to do both, what was the relation between the ideal Nation and the real, empirical nation? And what was the relation between the rights of the people and those of the individuals who are the reality of that people? The concept of representation articulates the problems faced by the Revolution; it defines the space in which a new politics could take shape.

Modern politics lives still with the legacy of the French Revolution. Recent historians have attempted to inherit that legacy by returning to their nineteenth-century predecessors.[2] They take seriously the inaugural rupture with the past that defines the Revolution; but they do not assume that this implies that the Revolution is a unitary whole that could be studied for itself. On the one hand, they reject the

101

materialist interpretation that seeks a bridge between the old and the new because such an explanation would annihilate the phenomenon it seeks to understand by inscribing it in a continuous history whose sense cannot be questioned because we remain within its purview. A materialist theory leaves no legacy; its "revolution" was necessary, had to occur, and will succeed: it is not our legacy, we are its heirs. It defines our politics. On the other hand, the return to the nineteenth-century historians has political as well as theoretical grounds. These authors were politicians who turned to history to understand the meaning of the Revolution, which was their legacy. Like the actors they studied, they faced the Revolution as a rupture that was the origin of a new history. The Revolution for them was incomplete, contradictory, in quest of its own ends. Our late twentieth-century situation differs from theirs in one crucial sense: we have to inherit another legacy: 1917, which was not the realization of 1793, let alone of 1789.[3] We cannot conceive politics as constitutive of rights (of individuals, the people, or the nation); nor can we reduce politics to the defense of supposedly pregiven rights. We must rethink the concept of legitimate political representation.

The Old Regime was based on representative legitimacy; its political space was defined by what was called a constitution. The Revolution inverted the order of the Old Regime; its first task was to give itself a constitution to legitimate its politics. This entailed a paradox; the Constituent Assembly was both the subject and the object of its political initiative. This theoretical structure had practical consequences. The Revolution was an unmasterable interval between the Old Regime and the New Order that it promised to constitute or sought to represent. A threat for some, an opportunity for others, all admitted the need for its end in a legitimate political order.[4] With its work finally completed, and the assent of the king acquired, the Constituent Assembly took leave from the stage with the announcement, on 30 September 1791, that "the end of the revolution has come." The Legislative Assembly that was to be elected had thus been constituted as the legitimate representative of the new Nation. Yet, on the last day of its brief and unhappy life, before the new Convention would convene to write a new constitution for a now republican nation, that Legislative Assembly took a radical step: it secularized civil society, defining marriage as a civil contract and permitting divorce. This revolution would outlive all the political institutions invented between 1789 and 1815: it produced the *Code Civil* to regulate an individualist, egalitarian society. How was that society, which remains our own, to be represented as legitimate?[5] If the *Code Civil* is the result of the Revolution, what is its relation to that other lasting consequence of 1789: the Declaration of the Rights of Man?

Representing the Old Order

The self-understanding of the absolutist French state was articulated by two conceptual frameworks: Bodin's *Six livres de la République* (1576) and Loyseau's *Traité des seigneuries* (1611). On the one hand, the state was a thing, the *res publica*; on the other, it was a sovereign person possessed of a will and seeking to attain a goal.[6] The resulting structure is characterized by four features: spontaneity, unity, continuity, and power. Spontaneity implies that the state emerges from natural laws governing social development independent of human will. This state is the unity of a plurality of individuals; it is thus a legal subject different from and superior to the individual members. This implies that it is a corporation with its own will; and that will is expressed by a specific organ. Its corporate character implies that the state has continuity over time, regardless of the passing of its members. Further, past decisions are binding on the present because the state remains even if the form of government changes. Finally, this state must command absolutely within its boundaries. Although its power is exercised in three distinct functions—justice, legislation, and administration—it is by its nature indivisible. The Old Order was thus the unity of material and spiritual properties; it was a "regime" in the sense of a total way of life. Crucial to this structure is that the source of the legitimation of politics is transcendent to its agent.[7]

This definition of the state as a juridical person implies the need for a constitution whose function is to designate the real persons in whom the state is presently incarnate. This legitimate authority can be vested in a single person, or the rights of corporations can be recognized by the fundamental law. The customary French constitution defined procedures for government, the first of which was the Salic law. This insured the continuity of the state whatever the fate of its government; it meant that public order was maintained in an interregnum; and it avoided arbitrary attempts like that of Louis XIV to make his bastards legitimate heirs to the throne.[8] Most important, the Salic law meant that the state is superior to the king, and that there is a law higher than ordinary laws that royal politics cannot modify. This implied, further, that the king is not a private person but a public functionary, the "first servant of the state."[9] One should not interpret this as a modern notion; the French king remained the "mystical body of the monarchy"; his relation to the kingdom was viewed as parallel to that of Christ to the world[10]; in classical terms, he was the head, which knows and interprets the needs of the body even when these are unconscious.[11] As sovereign, the king is absolute and yet bound by the fundamental law of the state.

In practice, the concepts of the state and the sovereign (or monarch) interpenetrate such that each strengthens the other. The state is responsible to the individuals who are its body; it must maintain peace, union, and the justice that consists in free disposition of property. Although the sovereign is not subject to the commands of others, and can break the law by simply asserting "For such is our pleasure," he is nonetheless bound by the laws of God and nature (and by the fundamental law). Further, the sovereign as the incarnation of the state is a public person whose power does not reach into the private sphere.[12] This distinguishes absolute rule from the tyranny that arises when the monarch's actions make the people no longer subjects but slaves without personal freedom or control over their own properties. Such tyranny violates the natural law that made us all free; it is the result of force and arbitrariness. This distinction became important when the king saw the need to concentrate power in order to meet challenges confronting the state. He could expand his power by means of "commissaries" who administer in his name. Such agents of the sovereign, for whom the constitution has no explicit place, are in a peculiar situation: as agents, they could always be overruled (as could their opponents, the parlements); but also as agents, they were mere instruments for the execution of the decisions of another: they were not responsible. The state was thus strengthened by the agents of the sovereign at the same time that royal power could grow by appeal to necessities of state.

The relation between the French state and its sovereign was not so harmonious as constitutional theory pretended. Henri IV acknowledged the fundamental law by accepting Catholicism; but he set about quickly to reinforce his own sovereignty. To finance that adventure, the "Paulette" was invented in 1604, guaranteeing the integrity of the "offices" that the king sold to the ambitious, who then owned them as private property protected by fundamental law. But the king could, in turn, try to limit this autonomy by using the revenues collected from the sale of offices to pay the nonresponsible royal commissaries to work for the centralization of the state around his own sovereign person. But Henri's assassination put an end to his ambitious program; under his successors, the officers of the parlements got the upper hand, and appealed to the fundamental law to justify blocking the royal will. "The Parlement declared that since Philippe le Bel and Louis le Hutin had declared it to be established in Paris its duty was to preserve the Constitution of the State, to verify the laws, ordonnances and edicts . . . and other important affairs of the kingdom.''[13] The royal reply appealed to its own version of the historical constitution: the monarchy deals with affairs of state, while the parlements are limited to matters of individual justice. The quarrel continued as the state grew. The centralizing commissaries could be accused of arbitrary intervention in offices whose autonomy was the guarantee of justice; or they could be justified as an antiaristocratic critique of and intervention against privilege on the part of selfless rational agents of the state. Ultimately, force would decide the better argument.

The first battle was the Fronde. The parlements joined with the nobility against the centralizing sovereign. The parlements inverted the traditional doctrine according to which the king alone could will for the state. They argued that the king as a finite human could err whereas the parlements, as a corporation, carried the continuity of the state. Their political position was strengthened by the fact that Mazarin was both a foreigner and a cardinal; their theoretical claim was that they represented France in a genealogical line dating to the annual assemblies under the Franks that had become impossible once Charlemagne increased the size of the kingdom. This theoretical equation of the parlements with the people implied further that the king was merely the physical body of the state whose soul is justice, public order, and customary law. This implied that the king is sovereign only with the agreement of the parlements; and further, that if he is assassinated or a minor, sovereignty remains with the parlements.[14] But this bold theoretical move went too far; the parlements could now be divided from their noble and popular allies to whom the promise of an Estates General able to override laws and ordinances would appeal.[15] The parlements' claim to represent the fundamental law destroyed the unity of the Fronde. With Mazarin's death, Louis XIV took up the reins of power and ruled absolutely, with appeal neither to the Estates General nor to the parlements.[16]

Louis XIV's attempt to rule absolutely even after his death showed that the contradictory legitimation of power-centers had not been overcome by his long rule. His attempt to legitimate his bastards was overruled by appeal to the fundamental law of the kingdom; the regent allied with the parlements to increase his own authority. Although Louis XV resumed the absolutist pattern, the parlements were not silenced. The need to increase revenue for the centralizing state was met by their opposition. The king claimed that public order and justice emanated entirely from him and his commissaries; he insisted that the parlements' role was not to formulate law but only to offer advice before registering royal decisions. Although the intendants worked to rationalize administration, their actions were challenged by the parlements' repeated appeal to customary justice.[17] In this context, the Maupeou reforms were correctly perceived as a royal revolution. Their pretext was a parliamentary attempt to censor the king's agent in Brittany, the duc d'Aiguillon. The king insisted that he alone was responsible for administration. The parlements persisted, attempting to re-create the alliance that had produced the Fronde. Maupeou exiled them and created reformed institutions of justice that depended directly on the crown. Despite protests and theoretical arguments that justice can be preserved only by officers independent of the monarch, the battle was nearly won when, suddenly, Louis XV fell ill and died at age sixty-four. His twenty-year-old grandson won popular support with his decision to restore the parlements.[18]

While the material constraints on the parlements and the new king remained constant, the theoretical principles to which each appealed had lost their hold on reality. Parlement's popularity was not based on the customary constitution whose principles it claimed to represent but on opposition to the rationalizing central government.[19] The crown, on the other hand, could not simply impose its will, nor could it call for an Estates General to grant it the needed powers, since that would deny rights that it claimed as inherent in the very nature of sovereignty. The expedient proposed by Calonne in 1787 was the Assembly of Notables, which would function as a sort of crown council. This group proved less pliant than expected; Calonne was replaced by Loménie de Brienne who functioned as the agent of the Notables against the monarch. "Sovereignty had passed to the Notables," writes Mousnier, "the Revolution was made . . . an aristocratic revolution instead of the royal revolution of Maupeou."[20] Reforms were introduced: the penal code was revised, non-Catholics were granted civil rights, and administration was made more efficient; but the need for new revenues remained. The parlements again failed to understand the situation. They rejected a proposed stamp tax as a "perpetual" imposition to which popular, not simply parliamentary consent was necessary, and demanded the calling of an Estates General. Equally blind to the new reality, the king and the notables did not see that this meant that parlement had abandoned its fundamental claim to legitimacy. Instead, parlement was exiled, and a play of force similar to the Maupeou reforms resumed. Parlement was accused of seeking to add legislative power to its judicial role. It replied that the nation must agree to new taxes, for the king is only the administrator, not the owner of the public fortune.

The Old Regime did not have long to live; its demise came amidst a crisis of its own self-representation. Financial difficulties, new social forces, even bad weather were involved; so was misjudgment, by the king and by his ministers. The Estates General was to have been a delaying tactic; each side wanted to use it for its own ends. As Tocqueville notes, parlement and monarch had taken turns instructing the people, the one teaching the vices of royalty, the other the crimes of aristocracy. Opinion gained new legitimacy. [21] With it, the idea that the nation should participate in its own affairs came to be heard. But what was the "nation"? In the Fronde, the parlements had claimed to represent the historic entity "France." Now the thirteen parlements of the kingdom claimed to stand as one; in exile, their popularity was based on their role as legitimate political actors. Yet within a year the parlements were as dead as the regime they thought they were combating. The relation of the parlements and the sovereign had been defined by reciprocal dependence; the former were necessary to prevent abuse by the latter. Although claiming to represent the fundamental law and private property, the parlements were in fact an aristocracy whose privilege depended ultimately on the king. In rebellion against the monarch, they were rejecting their own legitimacy as well as that of the monarch. Both revealed themselves as particular institutions claiming to represent a universal. After the fall of the Old Regime, the Revolution would seek to constitute that legitimate universal by defining the Nation that opinion had put in the place of the state of the Old Regime and its royal representative.

Constitution of the New

The interdependence of the state and the sovereign, which characterized the Old Order, was based on a specific notion of representation.[22] The monarch was the representative of the state, the particular incarnation of its universality. He could reign absolutely without becoming tyrannical so long as he did not violate the fundamental laws. These laws, also called the constitution, constituted him as king. The parlements could appeal to this same constitution to claim that interference in their autonomy was just such a violation, since they owned their office as a legitimate property. This led to an irresolvable clash when, at the time of the Fronde and then in the years leading to 1789, the parlements went one step further to insist that they represented the fundamental law as such. The result was a competition for legitimacy between two forms of representation. To whom and to what could each appeal? Appeal to the state by the monarch, or appeal to the fundamental law by the parlements became abstract once the Estates General was called. The unity of the political head and the incorporated body on which the Old Order was founded had no room for this new actor.[23] The Estates General could be seen as the representative of an undefined Nation over against a weakened monarch and a parlement that had made itself irrelevant. But one should not give in to the temptation to read history retrospectively.

Who or what was the Estates General? If it was representative of an ordered corporative state unified by its constitution, it was a rival to the monarch, capable of stepping into his place. To do so, however, it would need to produce a new constitution to replace the customary fundamental law. How could such a constitution become legitimate? The representative relation had to be conceived in new terms. In the Old Regime, the representative and that which he represented were external to one another; the king represented a state that would continue to exist after his demise, and the orders represented a corporate society whose existence was independent of its transitory members. In practice, however, the competition between the centralizing monarchy and its nonresponsible commissaries had weakened the autonomy of the corporate order; and the new force of public opinion turned increasingly against so-called aristocratic privileges that had lost their function. If this meant that the Estates General represented the claims of a society that was tending toward egalitarian relations, its political implication was that the externality of the representative structure of the Old Regime could not be maintained.[24] There was no need for an external power to constitute the social hierarchy and to grant to society its political legitimacy. Representative and represented had now to be conceived as immanent to one another. This implied that the constitution and the action of government existed on a common level. In this horizontal space, a modern concept of politics could emerge. Before it could appear, however, the adaptive potential of the old concept of vertical representation had to be exhausted.

The formal call for the meetings of the Estates General made these abstract questions concrete. The king let the initiative slip away; Brienne convinced him to pose the question of the form of the Estates General to the country as a whole. In a country where concrete political experience was limited, public opinion was easily dominated by general, speculative ideas. Concrete or pragmatic arguments were replaced by abstract reflections on the nature of legislative power in general, then on the nature of government as a whole, and finally on the foundations of society itself. The debate began with citations of Montesquieu; by its end Rousseau dominated.[25] At the same time, the form of representative government became a problem of arithmetic: would the representatives of the Third Estate be doubled? If doubled, would the Estates meet jointly or in separate chambers? Did the Third Estate represent the weight of number, while the others represented the corporate institutions of the Old Regime? Was the Third to share in government—to be "something" in the terms of Sieyès's influential pamphlet that sought to define it, or was it to be "all," excluding privilege altogether, as Sieyès had argued in 1788?[26] The king compromised again, doubling the representatives of the Third Estate but leaving open the question of the vote. Tocqueville describes the inevitable result: victory was placed before the eyes of the Third Estate, which had been given time to discipline itself, to test its unity, and to heat its desires to the point of action. Political representation in a society founded on equality would be based on number. But how could number become the new Nation?

The logic of the Old Order still dominated the thinking of the political actors. The Third Estate had to legitimate itself as representative without accepting the old corporate society. The Nation had to be given substance. The architecture of the meeting rooms suggested a tactic. After meeting jointly with the king, the three orders—aristocracy, clergy, and the Third Estate—were to deliberate separately. Space had been constructed for the clergy and the nobility; but the size of the Third Estate forced it to remain in the common meeting hall. At its first meeting, on 6 May, the Third Estate took the name "Assemblée des communes." However, it did not begin formally to deliberate because that would imply that it was a separate order, only a part of the Nation. For the next month, it attempted to convince the others to unite with it. Finally, on 11 June, the self-designated Commons (as the Third Estate now called itself) voted to request formally its reunion with the other estates. Significantly, this motion was made in the name of "the representatives of the nation." On 15 June, Sieyès argued that it would be unjust for the representatives of 96 percent of the people to be inactive because of the resistance of the rest.[27] After two days of debate, Sieyès's proposed title, "Assembly of the known and verified representatives of the French Nation," was rejected in favor of the straightforward label "National Assembly." The new Assembly then voted that it alone could raise taxes, and that it, not the king, was responsible for the national debt. This implied the logical identity of the new Nation and the state of the Old Order. In so doing, the National Assembly, in effect, put itself in the place of the king.

The monarch had to react to this challenge. He promised to come to the Estates General on 23 June. Architecture again intervened. To prepare the royal session, workers had to close the common room, leaving the Third Estate no place to meet. This led to the Tennis Court Oath. When the king appeared on the twenty-third, he made concessions on taxes, decentralization, and the press, but refused to permit the orders to meet together. His presentation was a classical Old Regime *lit de justice*; the king concluded that he alone knew the wishes of the people and would do them. Mirabeau's response to the agent who sought to impose the royal decision referred to the king as "your master," implying that he was not master of the National Assembly, whose president, Bailly, added, "I think that the assembled Nation cannot receive orders." Sieyès's proposal to "deliberate" followed. The king capitulated on the twenty-seventh; the orders would meet in common. But the Tennis Court Oath had changed the object of deliberation. The representatives had not only sworn to remain together and affirmed that the National Assembly existed wherever they were, but also swore not to separate until a constitution was established. The politics of the National Assembly was thus not to be limited to the kind of reforms proposed by the king on the twenty-third; it would give the Nation a new constitution, inaugurating a new form of political representation.

The National Assembly and the king were not alone on stage. As during the Fronde, the princes sought to take advantage of a weakened monarch, and looked for popular support. The Palais Royal became a center of agitation. Newspapers were founded, beginning with Mirabeau's *Lettres à ses commettants* and followed in September by Marat's *L'Ami du peuple*; the public was to be more than a passive spectator.[28] On 9 July, the National Assembly made its goal explicit; it took the name of the Constituant National Assembly or simply Assemblée constituante. The Bastille, the Great Fear, and the creation of autonomous municipal governments gave new significance to this title.

Whom did the members of the Assembly represent? They had been elected under the Old Regime, in their regions and by their orders, often on the basis of an imperative mandate whose terms were consigned in the *Cahiers de doléances*. How could they claim to represent a Nation? With conditions outside raising fears of anarchy or civil war, was their task actually to constitute the nation?[29] In that case, their constitution would not be a framework within which politics becomes legitimate, as in the vertical structure of the ancien régime; it would be itself a politics, but one that needed to ground the legitimacy of its active intervention that sought social transformation. That would conserve the structural logic that had characterized the French state since Bodin and Loyseau. The relation of the National Assembly to the Nation would invert that of the king to the state; customary law would be replaced by a rational constitution. This logic gave political force to the concept of natural law and furthered the attack on privilege in the name of equality. But it entailed an ambiguity in the relation of the Declaration of the Rights of Man—and of those rights themselves—to a political legitimacy still conceived as representative.

The structural constraint imposed by the tradition of the French state produced a contradiction in the politics of the Revolution. The relation between the state and the government—Rousseau's universality of the General Will and particularity of the executive—had to be regulated by a fundamental law that defines the space within which politics is legitimate. When the Nation is substituted for the state, and the National Assembly for the executive, the relation of representation is no longer unilineal or vertical. The National Assembly plays a dual role: it must constitute the Nation and it must will for the new nation; it must be at once universal and particular. If the basis of its universality is its claim to represent the Nation, how could it make room for the particular decisions necessary to a politics that will constitute the new nation? The Old Regime had avoided this dilemma by appeal to customary law as a transcendent foundation legitimating royal decisions. The Revolution could appeal only to natural law, which was immanent to its politics. If tyranny consisted of the king's assumption of rights belonging to the state in defiance of fundamental law, how could the new National Assembly avoid the reproach of tyranny when it attempted to concretize natural law in particular instances? The confusion between politics as constituting the Nation and politics as expressing particular needs within a legitimate order is the result of this conceptual dilemma.[30]

The constitutional draft submitted by Mounier in the name of the first committee on 9 July began with an implicit admission of the difficulty. It insisted on the need for "a precise idea of the sense of the word *constitution*," but quickly added that such a constitution had to be adaptable to "a kingdom inhabited by twenty-four million men." The moderate Mounier stressed that the French "are not a new people recently emerged from the depths of the forests to form an association." But events had outpaced moderation; after the Bastille and the Great Fear came the night of 4 August. As a "national" assembly, the deputies could not appeal to the king against the threat posed by anarchy that was felt to be the inevitable consequence of an unconstituted people; they had to act on their own. They interrupted their debate on the specifics of a constitution to decree the "destruction of the feudal order." More than just the end of privilege, the night of 4 August consecrated the advent of that society of numerical equality toward which the centralizing monarchy had tended.[31] By eliminating the old corporate structures, the National Assembly recognized at the same time the natural rights of the individual. In the "kingdom inhabited by twenty-four million men," all were equal insofar as all were individuals. The logic of the night of 4 August made the National Assembly literally constitutive; seeking to associate the monarch in its action, this Constituent Assembly proclaimed Louis XVI the "Restorer of French freedom." But besides the logic of natural law, the other constitutional logic was also present; the nation needed a constitution to make legitimate its politics. Two months later, after the Paris women had forced him to abandon Versailles, Louis became merely the "king of the French." But what made these twenty-four million individuals a unitary Nation, a collective individual? And were their rights founded by that Nation, or were they rights given by nature? In the latter case, how do such natural rights acquire a political form?

Although the now Constituent Assembly did not speak for all of the French, or speak with one voice, it was carried forward by the political logic of its new order. A first large emigration followed the fall of the Bastille; moderates like Mounier departed after the Paris women had forced the return of the king; and the same popular pressure was said to have transformed Mirabeau into a partisan of a monarchical democracy.[32] The now Constituent Assembly continued its efforts to constitute the reality of the new order. Provincial assemblies were eliminated, church properties were placed "at the disposition of the nation," the traditional parlements were abolished, and geographical and administrative divisions were constructed on an abstractly rational basis. The nation would be constituted by equal individuals whose formal and juridical identity insured its unity and, thereby, its own individuality. The Constituent Assembly made explicit the logic of its politics at its penultimate session on 29 September 1791; Le Chapelier proposed to forbid popular societies like the Jacobins as particularist infringements on the universality of the Nation. The inability to slow the rush of constitutional labor and to close the Revolution was implicit in this refusal of the right of existence of parties.[33] The quest for unanimity and the need for unity made particular interests illegitimate. Yet some provision for dealing with particular rights in a nation of individuals was necessary. The interplay of monarch and parlements within the constitution of the Old Regime had served this function; the New Order would have to find an equivalent. Could the imperatives of the Nation, whose opposition to the particularism and privilege of the Old Order made possible the modern individual, clash with the rights of the individuals who constituted the actual nation?

The Right of the New

The awkwardness of the institutional solution at which the Constituent Assembly finally arrived is evident in the Constitution of 1791. Article 3 of chapter 2 declares, "There is in France no authority superior to that of the law. The king reigns only by it, and he can demand obedience only in the name of the law." As if it feared that this limitation would be violated, the assembly followed this provision with two articles concerning the oath to be taken by the monarch; article 6 then declared, "If the king puts himself at the head of an army and uses its force against the Nation, or if he does not formally oppose such an enterprise undertaken in his name, he will be considered to have abdicated the throne."[34] The suspicions of the assembly were well-founded. Indeed, the Constitution was accepted by the king only after the failure of his flight at Varennes, and on the basis of the fiction that he had been kidnapped. In the meanwhile, the Constituent Assembly had continued to legislate the nation into existence. At each step, opposition had emerged; the assembly itself was divided, participation decreased within and pressure increased from without. The Constitution alone could not provide the needed political legitimacy; the nation demanded that its particular needs be represented. What made these demands legitimate? What was the political status of the famous activist *journées* when the nation directly imposed its will on its representatives? The dilemma of the Constituent Assembly is apparent in its greatest and most lasting achievement, the Declaration of the Rights of Man and of the Citizen.[35] Its premise is that "the ignorance, forgetting or disdain for the rights of man are the only causes of public unhappiness and the corruption of governments." It proposes to present these rights solemnly so that "the acts of the legislative authority and those of the executive can be compared at every moment with the goal of all political institutions." In this way, "the demands of the citizens will henceforth be founded on simple and incontestable principles." This implies that the individual is a legitimate political actor; and it seems to make a place for the revolutionary *journées* when it adds that this citizen action will result in "the maintenance of the Constitution and the happiness of all." But this supposes a harmony between individual rights and the unity of the Nation that is not made explicit. Instead, the Declaration makes provision for the legitimate role of government. Article 12 explains the need for a "public force" which serves to guarantee rights; and Article 13 adds that its cost is to be born equally by all "according to their means." But Article 14 seems to put the supposed harmony into question: "The citizens have the right to determine by themselves or by their representatives the necessity of the public contribution, to freely consent to it." Article 15 is more explicit still: "Society has the right to control the administration of all public agents." This implies that although government is instituted to protect the rights of the individual, it does so only insofar as that individual insures that his representative represents truly. As with the relation of the Nation to the real nation, there is a conceptual slippage. The individual protected by government is the abstract "man" whose rights the Declaration defines; the individual who protects himself is the "citizen" or the "society" that surge forth in the *journées*. The logic of the Old Order reappears: the rights of "man" have the transcendent status of the state, while the role of the citizen or society is analogous to the monarch. Just as the king found it convenient to appeal to necessities of state to increase his power, so the Revolution will appeal to extralegal necessity. But while the Old Order could defend itself by appeal to the parlements and fundamental law, the egalitarian society of the Revolution had no such possibility since "man" was both immanent to it and yet its transcendent justification.[36]

The need for revolutionary legitimacy was made more acute by the logic that permitted the Constituent Assembly to substitute the Nation for the state of the Old Regime. The Declaration proclaimed both the rights of "man" and those of the "citizen." The distinction is not drawn explicitly, but the necessity of inverting the constraints of the structural logic of the Old Regime suggests an interpretation of its implications. The Nation obeys the same contradictory, immanent, and transcendent logic as "man." Article 3 of the Declaration makes this explicit: "the principle of all sovereignty resides essentially in the Nation." Its next sentence defines legitimate government: "No body, no individual can exercise an authority which does not emanate explicitly from [the Nation]." The Old Regime state had recourse to its constitution to define representative legitimacy. The Declaration proposes a different principle. Article 2 insists, "The goal of all political associations is the conservation of the natural and imprescriptible rights of man." Since article 1 had declared that "men are born and remain free" and article 2 made freedom one of the four natural rights, article 4 had then to define positively this freedom that article 3 had specified only negatively. It is the right "to do anything which does not harm the other." This right "to do anything" was a rejection of the corporative society of the Old Order[37]; the new political question was how to define "harm" to the other. Article 4 explains that a limit on freedom can be decided only by the law; and article 5 specifies that "the law has the right to forbid only actions harmful to society." But "society" is not defined here, any more than it was in the previously cited article 15. Article 1's admission that "social distinctions can be founded only on common usefulness" might be introduced here in order to clarify the issue. Authority can be delegated legitimately only in the form of law, and only when it works for the common good. But if this supposition that there exists a common good (a *res publica*) is not a recourse to the constitutional premises of the Old Order, then it can only be the premise of a republic, which none of the members of the Constituant Assembly was seeking.[38]

The difficulty arises from the fact that the Declaration was trying to do two things at once: it had to found the sovereignty of the Nation in order to make good its rupture with the Old Order; and it had to establish the relation of the individual to the actual nation that legitimately exercises this delegated sovereignty. Article 6 poses this dual task: "The law is the expression of the general will. All citizens have the right to participate personally or by their representatives in its formation." The general will expresses the sovereignty of the Nation; the citizens' participation in it puts them (rather than the government) in the place of the Old Regime monarch. That was why article 3 stressed the need for explicit delegation, which is reaffirmed by the concern in articles 13–15 that government must be responsible to the citizens (or society). Article 16 confirms this interpretation when it insists, "A society in which the guarantee of rights is not assured or the separation of powers determined does not have a constitution." Both sides are thus present. The guarantee of rights—including the presumption of innocence (article 9), freedom of opinion (article 10), and freedom of communication (article 11)[39]—insures the participation of the citizen that makes delegation legitimate; the separation of powers insures against the usurpation of arbitrary power in the name of the Nation. But this protection of individual rights is achieved at the cost of denying the unity of the Nation (whose unique sovereignty article 3 proclaimed); not only is its power separated, but participation by real individuals threatens its universality.

The well-known "slippages" of the Revolution, as one interest or faction after another laid claim to the title of representative of the Nation, can be interpreted as the result of the ambiguous political role of the Constituant Assembly, which had at once to constitute a Nation and at the same time to provide it with a Constitution making legitimate ordinary politics.[40] Two crucial early debates illustrate the contradictory logic of the Constituant Assembly. The first concerned the imperative mandate. Lally-Tollendal spoke for many when, on 26 June, he requested permission to return to his constituency to ask permission to participate in the new assembly. In the ensuing debate, Sieyès won massive support for his argument that there was no reason even to debate the issue; the action of 17 June, which declared the National Assembly, implied that its work was founded on a new principle of representation. In becoming a National Assembly, they had agreed that the Nation was the abstract unity that had replaced the state of the Old Order; there was thus no reason to consult one's actual constituents. Two months later, after it had decreed the death of the feudal order, the Constituant Assembly had to decide the constitutional place of the king. The logic of the Nation that had been applied to the question of the imperative mandate implied that the relation of the king to the representative assembly would be like that of the parlements to the king; and on this basis the moderate monarchist Malouet argued in favor of a suspensive veto for the king. But the real debate was between the partisans and opponents of an absolute veto; they applied a different logic, appealing to the real nation rather than to the fictive Nation. Barnave asked how the people could, "the day after its victory, share the exercise of sovereignty." Sieyès rejected the idea that the executive could override the will of the people or appeal to the people against the will of their representatives. On the other hand, Mounier still defended the absolute veto on the grounds that without it "the government would no longer be monarchical but republican." This threat came too soon to be heard, as did its counterpart from the other side, when Pétion argued that the sovereignty of the real nation over itself demanded a direct democracy.[41] But one should not conclude hastily that Pétion pointed to the future trajectory of the Revolution; the logic of the Old Regime, and of the Nation, remained to put into question the new direct democratic logic of the nation and the politics of the *journées*.

The contradictory role of the nation was inscribed in the Constitution of 1791, and in the future of the Revolution. Its final section addresses the problem of constitutional revision. Its first article reveals the embarrassment of its authors: "The Constituent National Assembly declares that the Nation has the imprescriptible right to change its Constitution" to which is added the qualification that "nonetheless, considering that it is more in conformity with the national interest only to use the right to reform for those articles which experience will have made evident the disadvantages by the means given in the Constitution itself, decrees that it will be preceded by an Assembly for Revision which will have the following form." The awkward grammar, and the eight articles that follow—which make revision nearly impossible— express a recognition that there is a difference between the real nation whose right to change its constitution is granted, and the abstract universal Nation referred to as the "national interest." When the events of 1792–93 made revision imperative, the Legislative Assembly that was elected once the Constituent Assembly had completed its labors had no choice but to call a new Constitutional Convention. The Revolution began anew, but the conceptual problems it faced in attempting to create a space for legitimate politics remained the same. The Nation triumphed over the nation, and the rights of "man" over those of the individual. The Directory was incapable of inverting the path; in the end there were only the *Code Civil* and our political legacy: the Rights of Man.

Representation and Modern Politics

The Revolution constituted the modern French Nation and the Rights of Man, but it was driven to treat that nation and those rights as real (or as ideals to be realized). The zigzag course between abstract universal and concrete particular is explained by the need to overcome the Old Regime whose vertical articulation of the logic of representation defined the space of legitimate politics. The self-affirmation of the National Assembly accomplished *de facto* that task; when it sought *de jure* legitimation as a Constituent National Assembly, contradictions emerged. The representational logic of the Old Regime still governed the attempt to formulate a constitution that would make possible political legitimacy. As a result, the Declaration of the Rights of Man appears as the attempt to provide the political equivalent of the Old Regime's fundamental law. The problem was that the externality of the representative to the represented could no longer be assumed. The contradictory logic that appeared in the analysis of the Nation and of Rights reappeared in the constitutional process because of the immanence of representation and the represented. The constitution had to be at once normative and genetic, universal and particular. What was at one moment normative—the Nation, the rights of "man"—could at another moment become genetic—the nation and individual or social rights. The Revolution became a politics legitimated only by itself—the immediate spontaneity of the *journées*; only the positive classifications of the *Code Civil* could survive it.

The politics of the Revolution was originary.[42] It could not come to an end until the novelty of its structure was recognized. The attempt to realize the political Revolution by overcoming the divisions of society condemned it to discover constantly new demands, to criticize its partial successes, to become that revolutionary government that the radical Jacobins had opposed to mere constitutional government. This was in part the revenge of the representational logic of the Old Regime; in part it was due to an inability to understand the new political history of which the Revolution was the origin. But how can that history be represented? The proposal that emerges from this philosophical reinterpretation is that the duality encountered in the fundamental concepts by which the Revolution sought to understand itself need not be overcome. That duality is a contradiction only insofar as it is assumed that politics seeks to restore a unity in which the representative relation realizes the unilinear and vertical correspondence claimed by the Old Regime. Within the immanence of the modern history originated by the French Revolution, representative and represented are constantly changing places; sometimes the accent is on the process by which norms are generated; other times it is the norms that demand realization. Complete identification of the particular and the universal is impossible and even pernicious. The challenge is different; the reversibility of the normative and the genetic is no vice.[43] The question is rather: What are the particulars for which normative legitimation is and must be sought? How can norms become the particular occasion generating public action? The *Code Civil* gives no answer; the Rights of Man pose and repose the question anew. The concept that "man" as a simple human being has rights—and not the specific content that one or another period gives to those rights—is what remains revolutionary, down to our own day.

The French Revolution was unable to articulate the space for legitimate politics, but its rupture with the Old Regime was the origin of a new political space that remains to be represented. The concept of the republic that emerged within the French Revolution itself remained a prisoner of the Old Regime's political logic and had to undergo a self-critique. The Republic could stand in the place of the old state; but its form of the fundamental law or constitution had now to be defined immanently, by the rights of "man." Instead, the *Code Civil* came to stand in the place of that constitution, making the democratic republic into a formal *Rechtsstaat*. It is then no surprise that the socialist claim to realize that which began in 1789 defines itself in terms of what it calls real democracy. But its error is symmetrical to that of its enemy; in both cases the autonomy of the political, as defined by the concept of the rights of man, is denied. Both efforts represent an antipolitics that seeks to close off the new space opened by the Revolution's quest for a form of horizontal rather than vertical representation. This is where the rights of man acquire the task of defining a modern politics. The rights of man assume the traditional role of a constitution, making possible and legitimate democratic politics within modern republican institutions.

These last lines have to be read carefully. The claim is not that the legacy of the French Revolution can be reduced to a political recipe familiar to most citizens of the Western world. That would be true only if the rights of man were treated as if they represented a positive catalogue, a more solemn and rhetorical variant of the *Code Civil*. It would be true, further, only if Western democracies were really as stable as their rhetors make it appear, and as easy to erect as is the solution to a problem in formal logic. It would only be true, finally, if the best politics were defined as the end of politics, the return of the philosopher king, in the form of technocrat perhaps, or as the dreamed harmonious community for which conflict and division are unnecessary. These premises cannot be maintained today any more than they could be at the time of the French Revolution. The meandering path that has been followed here, mixing the weight of history and tradition with the force of anecdote and accident, and seeking to grasp the resulting dynamic by means of an abstract and paradoxical logic of the political, should stand as a warning to those who want to transform the legacy of the past into a capital with purchase on the future. The legacy of the French Revolution is its problems, not the solutions proclaimed by those who thought they could bring it to an end.

Notes

1. Recent commentators have attempted to explain the success of this self-affirmation and self-definition of the National Assembly by recourse to Austin's "speech-act" theory. Christine Faure's Présentation of her edition of *Les déclarations des droits de l'homme de 1789* (Paris: Payot, 1989) uses the concept of a "performative speech act" (31ff) to distinguish between two types of constitution-making declarations: those in which the representatives declare (e.g., 1789, 1848, 1948), and those in which the people proclaim (1793, 1795, 1946). Unfortunately, she does not develop this suggestion. Sandy Petrey's *Realism and Revolution. Balzac, Stendhal, Zola and the Performances of History* (Ithaca, N.Y.: Cornell University Press, 1988) uses the concept to present a more substantive analysis of the Assembly's action. Like Faure, he insists that not every linguistic performance is guaranteed success; material conditions cannot be simply ignored. Although Petrey's goal is to analyze the success of literary realism, his subtle analyses of nineteenth-century French literature (and his refutation of Marxist or deconstructivist simplisms) has broader implications. See my review in *Philosophy and Social Criticism* 16, no. 1 (1990): 55–59.

2. This trajectory was defined most clearly by François Furet's *Penser la Révolution française* (Paris: Gallimard, 1978); his numerous publications since then have developed the argument. The most detailed study of a nineteenth-century predecessor from this point of view is Pierre Rosanvallon's *Le Moment Guizot* (Paris: Gallimard, 1985). The most important theoretical justification of the return is provided by Claude Lefort's *Essais sur le politique* (Paris: Editions du Seuil, 1986). See also Lefort's "Guizot: le libéralisme politique," in *Ecrire. A l'épreuve du politique* (Paris: Calmann-Lévy, 1992).

3. We remain haunted by Robespierre's distinction in "Sur les principes du gouvernement révolutionnaire" (5 nivose, an II): "The goal of constitutional government is to preserve the Republic; that of revolutionary government is to found the Republic. The Revolution is the war of freedom against its enemies; the Constitution is the social reign (*régime*) of victorious and peaceful freedom." Our temptation is to side with the Revolution and to denigrate the Constitution as long as there remains but one unhappy citizen, one unjust

relation, any exploitation. I will return to the grounds of this temptation in part 4. Suffice it for now to indicate that I reject the "two revolutions" thesis, which, in its various forms, suggests that a bourgeois, liberal, or merely political revolution has to be followed or completed by a proletarian or popular, social or truly democratic revolution. The path that is followed here is critical in the Kantian sense suggested already in the nineteenth century by Edgar Quinet: I am proposing a "critique of the Revolution" in which the Revolution is both the subject that undertakes the critique and supplies its standards, and the object to which the critique is applied, immanently. Thus, for example, in the next paragraph I point to the fact that the Constituent Assembly was both the subject and the object of its political initiative.

4. On what basis was it to end? The timing and political emphasis could differ, but the logic of the position remained constant. The phrases through which the Revolution passed can be read as successive attempts to find a noncontradictory end. At the one extreme lies Robespierre's definition of a constitution (fn. 3, above); other gradations had appeared already during the Constituent Assembly, beginning with the departure of Mounier and the Monarchiens and including Mirabeau's attempt to convince the king that the Revolution actually worked to his advantage by eliminating not only the resistance of the nobles but also the parlements, whom his grandfather and Maupeou had failed to defeat. As this latter point will be treated in the text, two other instances can be cited here. Before the flight of the royal family, the noble "triumvar" Adrien Duport opposed revision of the not-yet completed constitution on 17 May 1791: "The Revolution has ended. We must fix it, preserve it by combatting its own excesses. Equality must be restrained, liberty must be reduced, and opinion must be fixed. The government must be strong, solid and stable." After the fleeing king was captured at Varennes, this need for stability became more important. Seeking to justify the constitutional compromise, Duport's bourgeois colleague, Barnave, insisted on a more material foundation on 15 July: "Are we going to finish the Revolution? Are we going to begin it again? You have made all men equal before the law; you have consecrated civil and political freedom, you have taken for the State all that had been taken away from the sovereignty of the people. One step more would be threatening and dangerous; one step further in the direction of equality and the result will be the destruction of property." (Citations are from Jean-Denis Bredin, *Sieyès. La clé de la Révolution française* [Paris: Editions de Fallois, 1988], 204 and 200. See also, note 33 below concerning the Le Chapelier proposal to forbid political associations.)

The thesis that reads the Revolution in terms of the attempt to give it a legitimate end runs throughout the pages of Furet and Ozouf's *Dictionnaire critique de la Révolution française* (Paris: Flammerion, 1989). A somewhat different picture is offered by Bronislaw Baczko's fascinating *Comment Sortir de la Terreur. Thermidor et la Révolution* (Paris: Gallimard, 1989), which begins from the often neglected fact that, for many of its authors, the overthrow of Robespierre on the ninth of Thermidor was the continuation and the defense of the Revolution against the "tyranny" of one man who had come to exercise a monopoly of power exactly as had the despots of the Old Regime. Thermidor was thus an immanent "critique of the revolution" before it acquired a different and ultimately uncritical sense in the jargon of Marxism.

5. The *Code Civil* was not an unexpected result of a political decision by the Legislative Assembly. The Constitution of 3 September 1791, produced by the Constituant Assembly, had concluded its Title I by affirming, "A code of civil laws common to the entire Kingdom will be elaborated." The process proved more difficult than had been anticipated. The most complete study remains Philippe Sagnac, *La législation civile de la Révolution française (1789-1804)* (Paris: Librairie Hachette, 1898), which argues that the code that finally emerged in 1804 had abandoned the philosophical spirit that had been dominant in 1789 in favor of a compromise with tradition, authority, and the interests of the state. The opposition of the philosophical perspective in the work of 1789–1795 to the juridical perspective that came to prevail is clearly demonstrated; but Sagnac fails to integrate the properly political dimension, which he reduces to conflicts of interest. He does not see the dilemmas involved in finding a political-legal structure that could provide unity to the new individualist society whose foundation is the quest for the equality that is the underlying principle of its individualism.

6. Roland Mousnier, *Les institutions de la France sous la monarchie absolue*, 2 vols. (Paris: Presses Universitaires de France, 1974), vol. I, 499. I will rely here on Mousnier's presentation of the basic structural features of the Old Regime all the more because the description of an "institution" that he offers in his introduction takes seriously the theoretical demands while making clear their historically variable structure. Mousnier's basic definition is worth citing: "An institution is first of all a guiding idea (*idée directrice*), the idea of a determined end which the public good should realize by predetermined procedures that are imposed according to an obligatory mode of behavior. That idea has been accepted by a group of men who have taken the responsibility for putting into practice these procedures and reaching this end. It is the guiding idea and the procedures which make this group of men into an institution." As such, Mousnier goes on, these men show commonalities in behavior, attitude, and relations to others such that the institution becomes continuous over time regardless of the temporary occupants of positions within it (vol. I, 5).

7. The theological foundation of this external legitimation is presented in Ernest H. Kantorowicz's eloquent and evocative, *The King's Two Bodies* (Princeton: Princeton University Press, 1957). The contradictory task of the Constituant Assembly implied that the New Order had to define itself from within, immanently, without changing the notion of the state that it inherited from the Old Regime. This will be developed in detail below.

8. The political implications of this latter example will be discussed below.

9. Mousnier, *Les Institutions*, vol. I, 505. Mousnier notes five other funda-

mental laws, including the oaths of the sacré, the age of majority, the fact that the successor to the throne is legitimate as soon as his predecessor dies (such that there is no interregnum and the old ordinances remain in effect: "the king is dead, long live the king!"), the inalienability of the royal domain, and the Catholic religion.

10. Mousnier points out that the traditional interpretation assumed that the king possessed the kingdom mediately from God, that is, by the intermediary of the people. After two kings had been assassinated in twenty-one years, and the failure of the Estates General of 1614–15, the notion of an immediate relation to God was established and with it the strong formulation of the divine right of the king.

11. This is the explanation for the so-called *lit de justice* when the monarch can overrule the parlements; it explains also why the king is not bound by the majority wishes of the Estates General. We will see Louis XVI try to apply this procedure at the 23 June 1789 meeting of the Estates General. His failure consecrates the end of the Old Regime.

12. Loyseau distinguishes between *souveraineté* and *suzeraineté* in this context. He also adds another set of limits by enumerating the rights that are the public domain: making laws, creating officers, deciding war and peace, final recourse in justice, creating money. Interestingly, Loyseau considers a sixth limit, the raising of taxes, of which he says it is an "*entreprise et pouvoir déréglé*" (Mousnier, *Les Institutions*, vol. I, 512).

13. Cited in Mousnier, *Les Institutions*, vol. II, 571. Mousnier's description of the ensuing battle that culminates in the Revolution is titled " 'The Three Hundred Years Trial': The Battle of the Officers [i.e., the parlements] against the Commissaries."

14. Since the politics of the Fronde included a revolt by the princes, the argument could be extended here to suggest that since the princes belong to France by nature or bloodline, they should have a role in government during the minority of the king or in his absence. The politics of the duc d'Orléans, later Philippe Egalité, have to be seen in this light. See George Armstrong Kelly, *Victims, Authority, and Terror: The Parallel Deaths of d'Orléans, Custine, Bailly, and Malesherbes* (Chapel Hill: University of North Carolina Press, 1982).

15. We will see in a moment that the parlements made the same error in the period immediately preceding the Revolution. But the status of the Estates General had changed in the interval.

16. Mousnier points out that during the last forty-two years of his long reign, Louis XIV permitted no remonstrances from the parlements and refused their right to interpret texts or to appeal to equity or the public good to moderate edicts, which they had to register immediately. Also worth noting is Mousnier's observation that the calling of an Estates General during the height of the Fronde would have led to a solution like the German *Ständestaat* (supported at the time by Claude Joly). Louis XIV saw this possibility and

justified his own absolute rule by pointing to the disastrous results of the Thirty-Years' War in Germany, which implied that *Ständestaaten* became second rate powers in a Europe where war demands absolutism's command by recourse to a *raison d'état*, which stands above all positive law. The Revolution would follow in his footsteps.

17. Mousnier suggests that this climate made it difficult for France to get foreign loans during the Seven Years' War, such that the parlements bear a heavy responsibility for France's loss of its colonial empire at this time (*Les Institutions*, vol. II, 615).

18. As we saw in note 4, Mirabeau recognized that the Revolution had achieved what Maupeou and Louis XV could not. But Louis XVI persisted in his support for the old institutions. Maupeou, who was exiled, lived to see his prophecy verified: "The King wants to lose his crown; after all, he is its master." He died a natural death at home in Paris on 29 July 1792, six months before Louis XVI was guillotined (cited in Mousnier, *Les Institutions*, vol. II, 627).

19. Tocqueville recognized this situation when he proposed as a title for chapter 3 of volume 2 of his *L'Ancien Régime et la Révolution*, "How the Parlement, thinking that it was making a traditional opposition, made a revolution without precedent" (Paris: Gallimard, 1953), 53 note a.

20. Mousnier, *Les Institutions*, vol. II, 631, 635.

21. Tocqueville stresses the role played by public opinion toward the end of the Old Regime, citing a passage from Necker in 1784, "The majority of foreigners have difficulty understanding the authority that public opinion has in France today; they have difficulty understanding the nature of that invisible power which rules even in the palace of the king" (*L'Ancien Régime*, vol. I, 222). This insight is elaborated in a recent manuscript by Keith M. Baker, "Public Opinion as Political Invention," which notes that at the time of the *Encyclopedia*, "opinion" was the opposite of "truth." Little more than a decade later, public opinion had taken on a rather different force. Baker's manuscript develops arguments from his earlier essay, "Politics and Public Opinion under the Old Regime: Some Reflections," in *Press and Politics*, edited by Jack R. Censer and Jeremy D. Popkin (Berkeley: University of California Press, 1987), 204–46. Further historiographical and conceptual reflections can be found in Roger Chartier's *The Cultural Origins of the French Revolution* (Durham: Duke University Press, 1991), especially chapter 2, "The Public Sphere and Public Opinion."

22. I have already suggested that the notion of the monarch as representative in the sense that he is the "first servant of the state" should not be interpreted as a modern notion (see pp. 103–4.). We will see in the following how the Old Regime's constitutional conception of the monarchy is at once preserved and transformed by the Revolution, which was constrained by the traditional logic even while struggling to overcome it. This argument is developed by Marcel Gauchet, *La Révolution des droits de l'homme* (Paris: Gallimard, 1989), whose approach I have adopted and adapted in the following.

23. Although the Estates General was an old institution, it had not met since 1614. It was not a part of the fundamental law, or constitution, of the Old Regime. Its role was to serve as a counsellor to the king in the same way that Calonne wanted the Assembly of Notables to function in 1787. Its more-important function, as Mousnier notes, was social: it assured each of the orders of its solidity and corporate character within a classical theory of mixed government (*Les Institutions,* vol. I, 40, 94). This element of a "social caste" made problematic the status of the Estates General of 1789.

24. As we will see, attempts were made to conceive the new situation in the old representative logic. The tendentially egalitarian society could be conceived as the unitary Nation that one hoped to represent. It would then function analogously to the universality of the old state. Or it could be taken as founded by the rights of the individual "man" whose universality serves the same function, as the revolutionary Declaration of 1789 would show.

25. I am following Tocqueville's *L'Ancien Régime et la Révolution,* vol. II, here; the reference to Montesquieu and Rousseau is at p. 107. Tocqueville explains the domination of general speculative ideas by the logic of egalitarian democracy. A different interpretation is suggested by Augustin Cochin, whose arguments are presented by Ran Halévi's article on the Estates General and by Patrice Gueniffey's article on elections in the *Dictionnaire critique* cited above. The suggestion is that because the deliberative assemblies had to produce a unitary opinion, opposition was excluded, debate was limited, and those with prior experience in the manufacture of unity—the participants in the sociétés de pensée and the local clubs—could dominate the proceedings. Roger Chartier points out that this model of the politicization of public opinion (which he calls the "Cochin-Furet model") differs from what he calls the "Kant-Habermas model." In the latter case, rather than stress the role of private voluntary associations, the emphasis is placed on the developing *public* exercise of critical opinion in the social quest for enlightenment (see *The Cultural Origins of the French Revolution,* 16–17).

26. The hatred of all privilege that characterized the French Revolution explains why even the moderate Monarchien, Mounier, supported the radical claims of the Estates General against the king, proposing the Tennis Court Oath and insisting—along with Sieyès and Mirabeau on 23 June—that the Estates meet together. Mounier felt that the debris of privilege had to be swept away radically before a balanced government modeled on the English system as theorized by Montesquieu could be established.

27. It is worth noting that this is an appeal to number and not to the "nation," which, in the modified logic of the Old Regime, stood in the place of the state. This first appearance of a problem that would return—representation of a numerical majority or representation of the Nation as a unity?—was not noticed at this time. Sieyès was to prove himself the most devout adherent to the new logic, suggesting that this was perhaps a tactical ploy. On the other hand, Keith Michael Baker tries to show that there are two

approaches that coexist in Sieyès's theory: one of them privileges the social, which is analyzed in terms of Adam Smith's notion of the division of labor, suggesting that representation is simply a form of this fundamental social fact; the other is political, leaning heavily on Rousseau's notion of a homogeneous republic. The latter was dominant during the first phase of the Revolution; but after the experience of the Terror, Sieyès returned to the priority of the social in his speech of 2 Thermidor year III, which elaborated his new constitutional theory that sought to limit absolute sovereignty by means of a special "constitutional jury" that would avoid the degeneration of the republic into what Sieyès calls a "ré-totale," a sort of totalitarianism (see *Dictionnaire critique*, especially 339ff and 343ff).

28. The active role of the public in the development of the style of political deliberation of the National Assembly is stressed in François Furet and Ran Halévi's introduction to their *Orateurs de la Révolution française, I, Les Constituants* (Paris: Gallimard, 1989). Architecture again played a role by leaving open tribunes from which the public could regard the new political spectacle. The contemporary English traveler, Arthur Young, was astonished that such public intervention would be permitted in the work of an assembly. The pressure of the crowd affected the votes of the deputies, who did not dare risk falling into popular disfavor. When some did protest, the reply brought out the ambiguity of the new representative politics: after all, "those are our masters who are seated there, we are but their workers and they have the right to censure and to applaud us," answered a typical deputy, Volney. For Furet and Halévi, this situation poses "a central dilemma of the French Revolution and especially of Jacobinism: how to celebrate the people while at the same time imposing the factual predominance of its representatives?" (See the discussion on pp. xxx–xxxvii, as well as the later debate concerning the work of the legislative commissions, pp. lv–lvii. See also in this regard my discussion of the American confrontation with a similar problem in chapter 5.)

29. I have capitalized Nation when referring to the general concept while leaving the lower case when speaking of the reality of the nation. The use of this distinction will become clear in the following; its explicit usefulness is presented at the end of part 3, in Sieyès's reply to Lally-Tollendal and in the debates on the royal veto. See also note 41 below.

30. We will see (in part 3) that the role of the Declaration of the Rights of Man involves the inverse identical contradiction. This is why the French Revolution, rather than the American, is the *locus classicus* of what has usually been called revolutionary political thought. The French had to constitute their new order and to define the universal rights and liberties it would guarantee. The American Constitution was written in order to protect already existing rights of the particular citizen. The results of the two different starting points have had fundamental importance in the history of the past two centuries of political theory.

31. This destruction of the Old Order was only symbolic; real inequality

would persist, and not only because the Assembly decided to buy back the old privileges, including a payment of 3.3 percent interest to their former holders. But the interplay of the symbolic and the real is more complicated. The abolition of the tithe (the *dîme*) made necessary the civil constitution of the clergy, who now depended on a state that could, and would, seek to strip the church of its power, an action whose consequences for the further course of the Revolution need not be elaborated further.

32. This suggestion by Michelet is cited by Bredin (*Sieyès*, 156), who adds that he thinks Mirabeau's choice had already been made. Tocqueville sees the invasion of the National Assembly by the Paris women as the beginning of the excesses that were to characterize the subsequent path of the Revolution. That was Mounier's reason for abandoning the National Assembly. We will see in a moment how Le Chapelier tried to justify seizing the opportunity provided by the events of 5–6 October that returned the court to Paris, while recognizing the dangers it entailed and attempting to ban such intervention once the constitution had been established (see note 33).

33. Le Chapelier's measure was directed at the Jacobins. He had already introduced a proposal to forbid "coalitions" of workers on 14 June. Both are reprinted in Furet and Halévi, *Les Orateurs*, 428ff and 432ff. Le Chapelier argued that the clubs had been useful in making the revolution but became dangerous when the revolution had ended and the Constitution had to be applied. He added that the sovereignty established by the new constitution implied that there could be no intermediary bodies between the citizen as individual and the sovereign Assembly to which the nation has delegated its power. Furet and Halévi compare the clubs with a modern notion of political parties, which the French Revolution could never admit because of the relation of its own immanent logic to the Old Regime corporate society and its political structure (1355). As for the coalitions, they were criticized as bearing the "corporative" status typical of the Old Order (1351ff).

34. Article 3 was in fact first voted on 23 September 1789 as the first article of the proposed constitution. The political events in the intervening period explain in part the precautions of the final document. Theoretical difficulties explain the rest. For example, although the Declaration of the Rights of Man was placed at its head, the actual constitution begins with a paragraph negating the particularisms of the Old Order; and its first title repeats those rights as constitutionally guaranteed—and adds to them, including provision for "*Public aid* for raising abandoned children, caring for poor invalids and giving work to the healthy poor who have not been able to find any." After Title 2 defines the departmental, district, and cantonal geography of the unitary country, and the conditions that make the individual a citizen, Title 3 insists that "Sovereignty is one, indivisible and imprescriptible. It belongs to the Nation; no section of the people, nor any individual can claim to exercise it." Rather, "The Nation, from which alone emanate all the Powers, can only exercise them by delegation . . . the representatives are the Legislative Body and the king." The precau-

tions, in other words, were made necessary by the unresolved representative relation between the Nation and the public authorities. (See *Les constitutions de la France depuis 1789* [Paris: Flammerion, 1970] for a convenient reference to the constitutional issues referred to here.)

35. Voted on 26 August 1789, the Declaration was adopted as the preamble to the Constitution of 1791. It was modified by the Constitution of 1793, but taken up again by the Constitutions of October 1946 and that of October 1958. As opposed to the American Bill of Rights, which is in effect the first ten amendments to an existing constitution, the Declaration is the premise or presupposition of which the Constitution is the particular incarnation.

36. Both Michelet and Quinet point repeatedly to the ironic fact that the most radical measures of the Revolution, in the face of external threat, domestic troubles, or material problems like famine, were justified by a logic typical of the Old Regime's appeal to necessities of state. The *Dictionnaire critique* points out in its article on coups d'état that this concept was developed in the Old Regime to justify extraordinary measures taken by the crown to assure public safety; even in 1823, the term had still not taken on its modern meaning. More important, the measures taken by the Committee on Public Safety, including those that are usually interpreted as showing its progressive socioeconomic concerns, were in fact an imitation of measures typical of the Old Regime.

37. This point is stressed by Claude Lefort's brilliant critique of the Marxist reading of the Declaration (based on Marx's "On the Jewish Question") as simply "bourgeois." See "Droits de l'homme et politique" in *L'invention démocratique. Les limites de la domination totalitaire* (Paris: Fayard, 1981), and his "Les droits de l'homme et l'Etat-Providence" in *Essais sur le politique. XIXe-XXe siècles* (Paris: Editions du Seuil, 1986).

38. This would indeed become the goal of the Revolution, and the Nation would seek to constitute itself as a republic. But a "Société républicaine" was founded only in June 1792 by Condorcet and Paine. After the failed flight of the king, this republican demand began to be heard in the broader public sphere. Condorcet published "De la République, ou un Roi est-il nécessaire à l'établissement de la liberté" in July. During the polemic that he and Paine engaged against Sieyès on this issue in the course of the same month, it was clear that like the Assembly, Sieyès rejected a republic because he saw it as identical with direct democracy (see Bredin, *Sieyès*, 201ff). The pressure of events, beginning 17 July with the massacre at the Champ-de-Mars would transform the abstract debate about the future of a republican—or at least nonmonarchical—France.

39. I have not mentioned article 17 of the Declaration, which guarantees property rights. Enough Marxist ink has been spilled on this issue. It may suffice here to note that the Assembly suspended its debate on the Declaration on 26 August, and that attempts were made to add further articles. For the grounds of their failure, and the most subtle account of the Declaration to

date, see Marcel Gauchet's *La Révolution des droits de l'homme*, cited in note 22. I should express once again my debt to Gauchet's subtle reading of the interrelation between practical political necessity and theoretical developments.

40. The concept of "slippage" (*dérapages*) was introduced in Furet and Richet's *La Révolution* (Paris: Hachette, 1965), which broke new conceptual ground in the study of the French Revolution.

41. The speeches to which I refer here are reprinted in Furet and Halévi, *Les Orateurs*, which gives helpful contextual documents as well. To say that Sieyès's position is based on the concept of the real nation rather than the abstract Nation is problematic, but justifiable insofar as we have seen that at least one variant of Sieyès's theory of representation is based on the political application of the concept of the division of labor as well as a recognition of real differences among the citizens that determine their capacity to take part in the representative process. See the article by Keith Michael Baker in the *Dictionnaire critique*, cited above, note 27.

42. The concept of "originary politics" can be understood in commonsense terms; its theoretical foundation is explained in my book *From Marx to Kant*, which I have published in revised form with a lengthy introduction (London: Macmillan, and Minneapolis: University of Minnesota Press, 1992). See also chapter 3 above, "Origins of Revolution."

43. See Claude Lefort, "Reversibility," in *Telos*, No. 63 (spring 1985): 106–20, originally published in *Passé-Présent*, no. 1, 1982, and reprinted in Lefort, *Essais*.

Part III

Political Theory or Theory of the Political?

7

Politics of Modernism:
From Marx to Kant

Avant-Gardes and Vanguards

The torch of avant-garde art passed to America at the beginning of the
1950s, at the very moment when political repression and massified
pluralist conformism were at their height. By the end of the decade,
the relation was inverted. The avant-garde was materially integrated
into the expanding university; its product entered the curriculum of
the liberal imagination or joined the market for what Harold Rosenberg
labeled "The Tradition of the New." Lionel Trilling rejected the
"adversary culture," while repentant drummers like Leslie Fiedler set
out in search of the "real" America, which an elitist alienation from
mass life supposedly denied. But then again, the "end of ideology"
and the "lonely crowd" gave way to a political renewal with the sit-ins
in the South, the emergence of Fidel and Che—and what Irving Howe
called the Goldwaterite "crusaders from the barbecue pits."

The 1960s seem to have been the decade of the vanguard; at the
same time, avant-garde modernism was bent on demonstrating the
action-prophecy of Tinguely's self-destroying machine sculpture at the
Museum of Modern Art. Pop glorification and serialization of the
banal had as its materialist counterpoint the stress on the immediate
materiality of the art-object, its reduction in status to Clement Greenberg's "decorative" or Harold Rosenberg's "anxious object." The
symmetry at the end of this decade is not so clear as its beginning. The
vanguardism that remained when the New Left acquired a Third World
tinted Marxist orthodoxy had become nothing but an avant-garde
object of contemplation. The avant-garde, on the other hand, in its

search for the New, had in a sense introjected the political painting of the vanguard-art 1930s, creating a variety of new realisms as it turned again toward representation.

Avant-gardes and vanguards claim to be representatives of something; they are the delegates or forerunners of a mighty mass, of history itself. Although their lives bear a charm, their hour on stage must be short and fretful. Their history is neither the cyclical natural revolution of the seasons, nor the eschatological leap to a city of God. It is a history that, precisely because of its dogged and dogmatic secular character, becomes in its own eyes the only deity left on the calendar. The politically minded historians tell us that this history came into its own when capitalism finally effaced the remnants of the traditionalist cultures toward the end of the nineteenth century. When this history passes, so will its avant-gardes and vanguards. Indeed, their task is precisely to bring about their own demise—a paradox that bears reflection, for while an exploited proletariat may define its goal as its own elimination as an exploited, alienated class, this Hegelian dialectical figure of thought is harder to conceive in the case of the art object or artist. This paradox is also the basis of various theories of intellectuals as a new dominating class, articulated from the Left (represented by Alvin Gouldner) or the Right (represented by neoconservatives such as Irving Kristol). That, however, is another issue.

An always-present danger is that avant-gardes become *ersatz* vanguards, and vice versa. Whatever the relation of art and politics, we know that the two are not identical. One can see, however, why the substitution or confusion might take place in specific conditions. Once it became impossible to deny that the proletariat was not playing its designated role in transforming the Russian Revolution into a world revolution, or when the deformed and deforming character of the society instituted in the name of that proletariat could not be ignored, then those who placed their bets on history could turn to culture and art as the new midwife and spiritual guide. If the cultural revolution is said only to prepare the ground for the political one, this transfer may not be too dangerous. The more frequent case, however, finds the one serving rather as a substitute gratification that drives the other from the stage.

Two souls, alas, seem to dwell in the breast of modern history. Were we premoderns, we would try to unify them into one subject, transcending the tension between art and politics. As secular moderns, we have to remain earthbound to history. The Frankfurt School and, in the context just sketched, particularly Herbert Marcuse illustrate some of the structures of the modernist project. Marcuse knew that Marx's proletariat is not the agent of history (although in his 1958 treatment of this theme, Marcuse was cautiously optimistic that a rational political negation of this negation might yet be possible). What Marcuse never abandoned was his faith in the negative power of art sketched already in his brilliant essay of 1937 criticizing affirmative culture and returning as the theme of his last published book whose German title, significantly, is *The Permanence of Art*.[1]

The premoderns are not the only ones to attempt to reduce the two souls to one—to one dimension, we might well say here. A few illustrations from Marcuse will show the parallel reductions of Soviet and advanced Western society. For example, in *Soviet Marxism*, Marcuse talks about the repetition of linguistic "rituals":

> The value of these statements is pragmatic rather than logical, as is clearly suggested by their syntactical structure. They are unqualified, inflexible, formulas calling for an unqualified, inflexible response. In endless repetition, the same noun is always accompanied by the same adjectives and participles; the noun "governs" them immediately and directly so that whenever it occurs they follow "automatically" in their proper place. The same verb always "moves" the proposition in the same direction, and those addressed by the proposition are supposed to move in the same way. These statements do not attribute a predicate to a subject (in the sense of formal or of dialectical logic); they do not develop the subject in its specific relations.[2]

The Soviet situation turns out, on Marcuse's account, to have family resemblances to our own social relations in the capitalist West. For example, *One-Dimensional Man* criticizes the pragmatic insistence on speech as designation, finding it to be magical, authoritarian, the ritual denial of mediation. There is an "abridgement of the concept in fixed images; arrested development in self-validating, hypnotic formulas; immunity against contradiction, identification of the thing (and of the person) with its function."[3] In each case, one finds the rejection of transcendence, of development or change, and of contradiction or negation. It is not that art is reduced to politics, or vice versa; rather, Marcuse sees a general leveling in all spheres of life to the common denominator of production for its own sake.

The productivist reductionism does, however, affect the soul, and thence politics and art. In *One-Dimensional Man*, as earlier in *Eros and Civilization*, Marcuse presents an incisive criticism of the therapeutic goals of contemporary social science, psychology, and philosophy. Each specialty, for apparently humane and even socially critical reasons, seeks a cure for an "unhappy consciousness," which, like the Hegelian model from which Marcuse takes this concept, cannot be so easily trivialized. The same problem is addressed in *Soviet Marxism*, with some of the same examples: "If Tristan and Isolde, Romeo and Juliet, and their like are unimaginable as healthy married couples engaged in productive work, it is because their (socially-conditioned) 'unproductiveness' is the essential quality of what they stand for and die for—values that can be realized only in an existence outside and against the repressive social group and its rule."[4] The problem is not merely artistic or cultural; it is also political. For example, in the context of the Russian Revolution: "Kollontai, who is considered as the representative spokesman of revolutionary sexual morality, sees in childbearing and child raising a mode of 'productive labor,' and brands the prostitute as a 'deserter from the ranks of productive labor.' "[5] Soviet and modern Western society appear to Marcuse to share this productivism and its logic, although his 1958 analysis of Russia envisages the possibility of a (dialectical) revolt from within the logic of the system whereas the Great Refusal of his 1964 *One-Dimensional Man* is explicitly the product of the outsider, and is nondialectical.

When he turns to the place and role of art in *Soviet Marxism*, however, the optimistic dialectical logic gives way to a description that is interestingly close to that of *One-Dimensional Man*.

> But art as a political force is art only insofar as it preserves the images of liberation; in a society which is in its totality the negation of these images, art can preserve them only by total refusal, that is, by not succumbing to the standards of the unfree reality, either in style, or in form, or in substance. The more totalitarian these standards become, the more reality controls all language and all communication, the more irrealistic and surrealistic will art tend to be, the more will it be driven from the concrete to the abstract, from harmony to dissonance, from content to form.[6]

These terms—irrealistic and surrealistic, abstract, dissonant, formalist—that characterize the "total refusal" of the administered Soviet society could also describe the succession of avant-gardes that have arisen within the capitalist historical order. Both social forms— capitalism and Soviet Marxism—seem to be equivalent in Marcuse's eyes, and only art can in fact criticize them validly. The implication seems to be that art replaces politics, so that the avant-garde art, becomes the *ersatz*-vanguard. The politicization of avant-grade art, in turn, should then explain the various forms of "anti-art" that arose during the 1960s as well as a certain aestheticization of politics in the West. But especially this latter development recalls images like Marinetti's description of the battlefield as art, or the notion of Hitler's Nuremberg Rallies as a "communication system." Marcuse had to draw back from any association of this type. He saw that the negation carried nondialectically by art had not been legitimated immanently. The avant-garde's claim to be the vanguard of history was based only on external criticism.

Marcuse's last two books defend the performance of art *as art* while at the same time they confront its relation to politics. *Counter-Revolution and Revolt* emphatically rejects modernist anti-art claims to replace politics: "The abolition of the aesthetic form the notion that art could become a component part of the revolutionary (and pre-revolutionary) *praxis*, until under fully developed socialism, it would be adequately translated into reality (or absorbed by 'science')—this notion is false and oppressive: it would mean the end of art."[7] Similarly, in *The Permanence of Art*, he insists that "the discourse of the end of art belongs today (differently than with Hegel) to the ideological arsenal and to the possibilities of counterrevolution.[8] Marcuse sympathizes with the instinctive anti-elitism and the activist pragmatism that wants to democratize creativity by putting an end to the split of art and life. Yet he is insistent on art as art: "To interpret this irredeemable alienation of art as a mark of bourgeois (or any other) class society is nonsense."[9] Indeed, he is willing to admit that: "Revolutionary art can very well become the *enemy of the people*."[10]

Marcuse's political argument for the permanence of art is that anti-art makes the artist unnecessary without thereby making creativity something general and shared by all members of society. To declare or decree that daily life is art is not to change daily life. Not only is this anti-art naive; it is potentially dangerous. "The truth of art," Marcuse insists, "lies in breaking through the monopoly on reality as it is exercised in the existing society."[11] By denying itself as art, by becoming reality, art opens itself to cooptation and to control. The dialectical Marcuse of the Frankfurt School returns here. The denial of form and creativity as something elitist is only an "abstract negation" of domination.[12] As part of reality and no longer its critical transcendence, art is no more a protest against but rather a part of the established order. The avant-garde that takes itself for a vanguard becomes simply a commodity, part of what the Situationist, Guy Debord, wisely called the society of the spectacle.

Marcuse's arguments are nearly convincing. The shadow of doubt is cast by the immanence of secular modernist history, which poses the problem of vanguards and avant-gardes. The most wily and reflective participant-commentator on modern art, Harold Rosenberg, had criticized Marcuse as "an instance of the intrinsic conservation [*sic*: should be conservatism] of the contemporary Marxist outlook on art. In the name of a future new society, it rejects the changing imaginative substance of the present."[13] More specifically, Rosenberg notes that "Marcuse is committed to the art object; modernist notions of art as action, event, process, communication seem to him distortions of the inherent nature of art."[14] This criticism predates Marcuse's last books, which clarify his position on the latter point. Before accepting his defense, however, the first charge needs amplification. Rosenberg's article, from which the above citations are taken, is titled "Set out for Clayton!" Clayton is the fictional town described in Kafka's *Amerika* where everyone is an actor in a "nature theater." Karl Rossmann's rather good-natured escapades on our shores move toward the happy end of departure toward Clayton when Kafka's manuscript breaks off. Marcuse would no doubt condemn the naturalism of Kafka's prose as destroying the possibility of negation, of integrating the revolt (of Karl, and the unemployed and exploited) into a seamless web of sameness. However, the significant point about Clayton (and perhaps about Kafka's relentless modernism, his world without transcendence or appeal) is that there are no spectators in Clayton's "nature theater" and, hence, no spectacle. Modern art, it seems, is more complicated than its vanguardist translators will admit.

Marcuse's disposition of the territorial claims of art and politics, like the debates of the avant-garde with the vanguard, is not sufficiently radical. It accepts the terms in which the claimants pose their demands, forgetting that these are the inherited traditional titles from the Old Regime. Rosenberg's criticisms stand scrutiny. The "permanence" of the modern—not that of art or the art-object—should be the focus. Because the modern explicitly rejects external and traditional norms and values, it can only be studied on its own terms and with its own tools. Framing the issue in terms of avant-gardes and vanguards at first suggests Marxism as the appropriate method for critical evaluation. In fact, the adequate tools of analysis will turn out to be those of Kant, as another great protagonist of American modernism, Clement Greenberg, has suggested. Since "the essence of Modernism lies . . .

in the use of the characteristic methods of a discipline to criticize the discipline itself,'' Greenberg concludes that the beginnings of this immanently self-critical tendency are found "with the philosopher Kant."[15] This assertion of the priority of the Kantian philosophical critique over Marxist politics may shock both the philosopher and the historian of modernism who were brought up with a distant admiration for a Kant whose stature as a classic stripped him of any but antiquarian or textbook interest. To justify the central place of Kant, a self-criticism of our representation of modernism will have to follow an arc from Marx to Kant.

Revolution and Revolutionaries

Harold Rosenberg drew the modernist implications of Marx's theorizing over thirty years ago. In "The Resurrected Romans," he begins from Marx's famous depiction of the revolutionaries of 1789 who, blinded by the immensity of their undertaking and incapable of conceiving that their action was creating a world-historical *novum*, costumed themselves as the Roman heroes that their literature and painting had taught them to venerate.[16] Marx applies what is in effect an Aristotelian dramatic theory to these bourgeois-as-Romans: through their action and its results they, like the tragic hero, will come to learn who they are and what their disguised passions have made of them. The actors of 1789 could not consciously undertake the project of creating a capitalist order; they had neither the knowledge nor the courage to look such a task in the eye. Masking themselves in the dramatic personae of antiquity kept their passions kindled until finally—in the tragic defeat of the revolution they thought they were making—they could recognize themselves for what their everyday reality in fact had made of them: a bourgeoisie reproducing itself and its society. Such, broadly speaking, is the Marxist political ideology. The Marxian philosophy, however, puts into question this political schema.

The self-deceiving bourgeois travestied in Roman robes is not the modernist revolutionary. Marx thought of himself, and of his revolutionary proletariat, as the great debunker, the clear-eyed realist whose broad shoulders could support the weight of history, come what may. But when the author of *Capital* came to describe revolutionary practice, his approach shifted. The *Eighteenth Brumaire* describes bourgeois revolutions as a theater on whose stage actions "storm swiftly from success to success; their dramatic effects outdo each other; men and things seem set in sparkling brilliants; ecstasy is the everyday spirit."[17] In contrast, proletarian revolutions "criticize themselves constantly, interrupt themselves continually in their own course, come back to the apparently accomplished in order to begin it afresh . . . recoil ever and anon from the indefinite prodigiousness of their own aims, until a situation has been created which makes all turning back impossible, and the conditions themselves cry out: *Hic Rhodus, hic salta!*" This contrast is consistent but troubling. For the proletariat to act, it is the situation that makes all turning back impossible, and the conditions that cry out for action. On the other hand, although it had to disguise the fact from itself, the bourgeoisie actually creates a historical *novum*, breaks the historical continuum, ruptures time, and transforms conditions and situations. The clear-eyed and realistic proletariat, for its part, only brings to fruition what history already placed in the cards. This recalls the caricature of Hegel for whom freedom is the recognition of necessity. It calls to mind the resigned preface to his *Philosophy of Right*, which argues for the rationality of the actual while insisting on the impotence of theory that can only paint its (modernist?) "grey on grey" after the fact. Or, at the practical level, this picture of proletarian revolution invokes Hegel's world historical individuals whose short-run conscious reaction to immediate conditions makes them the unconscious tools of history's plan. The proletarian revolutionary is not modernist.

The question of the modernist revolutionary returns thematically in a lecture Rosenberg delivered at the height of the political/aesthetic confusion of vanguards and avant-gardes at the end of the 1960s.[18] He begins from the famous repetition, again in the *Eighteenth Brumaire*, of events in history, first as tragedy then as farce. Marx had shown how each class on the French stage is impotent, so that the field is left free to the "theatrics of revolutionary revivals" by Louis Bonaparte the Nephew. The farce occurs because the motor of history, class struggle, has been stilled. The farce is a farce because it is played on a stage somehow above or apart from the ongoing rush of historical progress. One could say—as Engels did later and as our contemporaries groping vainly for some sort of Marxist theory of state and politics try to maintain—that this proves *a contrario* that class struggle is the real motor of history, since precisely its absence permits such a farce. But that is category-juggling in the minor tradition of negative theology. The situation described by Marx in fact depicts the limits of the Marxist theory of history; or, at best, it shows the limits of what

Marx means when he talks about history. The conclusion of the *Eighteenth Brumaire* supports this assertion. The pamphlet predicts that the fall of the imperial mantle from the shoulders of the Nephew will also demolish the stature of Napoleon, his uncle, at the Place Vendôme. The meaning seems to be that the farce of the Nephew's lumpen regime will debunk the Napoleonic myth that prevented the French proletariat from examining lucidly its own situation and courageously acting as material conditions demand. Then, the demystification accomplished, the historical drama will progress as its vanguard completes its assigned role.

Modernist revolutionary avant-gardes and vanguards apparently act at the service of history. Yet the very nature of modernism demands rejection of any transcendent or external justification, including justification by appeal to history. Rosenberg's conclusion is rather pessimistic. Granted, the first time may be tragedy and the second farce; what about the third, the fourth and the fifth? How long until that situation, those material conditions, bring the *Hic Rhodus, hic salta*?

Marshall Berman's more recent reading of the problem provides a counterpoint of Rosenberg. He summarizes his results:

> I have tried to read Marx as a modernist writer, to bring out the vividness and richness of his language, the depth and complexity of his imagery—clothes and nakedness, veils, halos, heat, cold, etc.—and to show how brilliantly he develops the themes by which modernism will later define itself: the glory of modern energy and dynamism, the ravages of modern disintegration and nihilism, the strange intimacy between them; the sense of being caught in a vortex in which all facts and values are whirled, exploded, decomposed, recombined; a basic uncertainty about what is basic, what is valuable, what is meaningful, even what is real; a flaring up of the most radical hopes in the midst of their radical negations.[19]

Berman's theoretical premise is that "modernism [is] the realism of our time." But his political conclusion is based on a forced and self-contradictory syncretism. On the one hand, he sees Marx's "great gift" as "not a way out of the contradictions of modern life, but a surer and deeper way into these contradictions." On the other hand, these contradictions are such that "people's lives are going to keep falling apart" until "radical social and economic changes come about." That, he adds, "could be a while." The difficulty is that Berman's radical social and economic changes don't come about from the "surer and deeper way into these contradictions" of his modernism. The changes, the solution, are to come from a different sphere—the social-economic—than the modernism that poses the problem in the first place.

That Marx wrote a book called *Capital* instead of a compendium under the heading "socialism" testifies to the modernism of his self-understanding. That he also wrote *Communist Manifesto* indicates that he was caught in the dilemma of the avant-gardes and vanguards. *Capital* portrays a radical uprooting of traditions and transcendences; it shows the constitution of a new temporal rhythm, a new history. No more natural cycles or transcendent values hinder the M-C-M', the money exchanged for (materially indifferent) commodities whose processing brings the cycle to a qualitatively identical but quantitatively increased close. Capitalism's M-C-M' is continual expansion, dynamism, and change in a paradoxical expanded reproduction of the same. It is value begetting new value, self-reproduction, and expansion; everything and anything become food for its voracious process. Opposition or criticism must therefore be immanent to this structural reproduction of the same. Vanguards and avant-gardes are caught in the capitalist cycle however much they may wish or even imagine themselves apart from it. The *Communist Manifesto*'s description of capitalism's "stripping the halo" from professionals and intellectuals through the commodification process that profanes "all that is holy" shows Marx to be aware of their problematic position. Yet the *Manifesto* does appeal to history: like Berman, it mixes its media syncretically. It does this most tellingly in its central argument: the definition of the communist.

By realizing history's immanent goal, the avant-garde or vanguard servant of history paradoxically eliminates the preconditions of his or her own existence. The consequences of this paradox can be seen in the theoretical self-definition and the practical behavior of Marx's communist. The communist is defined in the *Manifesto* as having "the theoretical advantage over the rest of the proletariat of an insight into the conditions, the path and the general results of the proletarian movement." The *hubris* expressed here is stunning. Theoretically, it flies in the face of Marx's own account of the modernist temporality of capitalism. It supposes that the communist is both inside and outside, both participant and transcendent observer in capitalism's reproduction of the same. The practical consequences are seen in assertions such as this one, from *Class Struggles in France*, that the 1848 revolution could not possibly have been socialist because "the state of economic development on the continent at that time was not ripe enough for the elimination of capitalist production.'' The same stance justifies Marx's warning in the *Neue Rheinische Zeitung* that one must beware of ''moving ahead of the revolutionary process of development, pushing it artificially to a crisis, pulling a revolution out of one's pocket without making the conditions for that revolution.'' In a word, this caricature of the Hegelian secretary to the World Spirit can become the secretary general of the party. The foreknowledge of the vanguard impels it to impose itself as the ''selfless servant''[20] of truth whose conservator it is.

Part of the *hubris* of the communist is an apparent modesty and selflessness, a parental or pedagogical concern for those still caught in history's wheel, and even what at first glance might be confused with a democratic faith. This behavior by the communist vanguard, shared with the artistic avant-garde, fits the immanence of modernism and modernity. The revolutionary is not guided by ideas, utopias, or classical models. His or her critique is nothing but the self-critique of capitalism; revolution is inexorable; no force can dam its flow since—as in the case for capitalism's self-reproduction—nothing can maintain itself outside of it. Revolution is the actualization of an essential truth, a pregiven potential brought to actuality by the catalyst of revolutionary praxis. The revolutionary doesn't debate in order to convince; he or she only presents the ''facts'' as revealed by revolutionary science; as with Plato, to know the good is to do the good. There is an appearance of democracy here, as Plato had already seen, since the truth is that one good that we can all share without its possession implying monopoly. But it is a democracy whose results are pregiven, like the democracy of the community of scientists whose methods and problems are redefined, and whose apparently free action in fact ensues with algorithmic necessity. The parental or pedagogical revolutionary will be the Socratic midwife bringing the slave to actualize the innate idea. It is not for nothing that Marx's writings abound in midwife imagery, womb-and-birth metaphors, seeds, and germinations.

The *hubris* and modesty are simply two sides of the same coin. Choose your passage from Marx. Either side can be more than amply illustrated. His *German Ideology* appears modest in asserting, ''Communism for us is not a *state of affairs* (*Zustand*) that must be established, an *Ideal* according to which reality must be formed. We call communism the *actual* movement which eliminates the present state of affairs.'' Here the revolutionary would be but the modest ''speaking part,'' as Rosa Luxemburg put it in her polemic against Lenin's views on the role of the party.[21] A year later, in Marx's *Poverty of Philosophy*, the revolutionary gets more latitude: "The economic relations first of all change the mass of people into workers. The domination of capital has created for this mass a common situation, common interests. Thus this mass is already a class over against capital, but not yet for itself." The revolutionary now has to bring to actuality (to its self-consciousness or "for itselfness") what is only implicit in the class situation. This was to become the theoretical justification of Leninism and its later Stalinist form. Yet, speaking of an actual movement that he came to see as a model, Marx wrote of the Paris Commune that "the working class has no fixed and pre-given utopias to introduce through popular referendum. . . . It has no ideals to realize; it has only to free the elements that have already developed in the womb of the collapsing bourgeois society." The only consolation this paradoxical back-and-forth can offer is that anything and everything can find textual justification. The proletariat, in Castoriadis's image, is the constitutional monarch of history: it takes credit when all goes well and blames its ministers for deviations from the true path.

The coin whose symmetrical sides are *hubris* and modesty is drawn from the treasures of capitalism. The revolutionary is the agent of the proletariat, which, according to Marx, incarnates the "solution to the riddle of history." But this is the riddle of capitalism, not that of all human history. Capitalism creates the proletariat, and capitalism's continual process defines its possibilities at any given moment. Its self-actualization or "for-itselfness" is therefore only the realization of the immanent logic of capitalism. This is not the creation of radically new social relations in the way that, with the French Revolution, capitalism's temporality was said to introduce modernity in the place of feudalism. Marx's revolution, and his revolutionary, are caught in the paradoxes immanent to the dilemmas of modernism and modernity. While the modest or "reformist" Marxist fought it out with the *hubris* of the "revolutionary": within the Second International, capitalism careened toward the first modern world war. The reformist argued, with Bernstein, that "the movement" is more important than prescriptive goals assigned by theory. His revolutionary opponent, especially Lenin's Bolshevik, insisted on the final goal that the party must bring from without to a class preoccupied by mere economic demands. After the terrible few years' hiatus of war, they renewed their opposition.

The paradoxes confronted by the revolutionary vanguard have the same structure as those faced by the modernist avant-garde. The philosophical categories, genesis and validity (or normativity), permit a clearer formulation of this paradoxical structure. In the case of the vanguard, the reformist is suggesting that genesis—"the movement"— determines the eventual normative success of the result. The revolutionary, on the other hand, is opting for normativity because only a knowledge of the ends permits a correct choice of the means that will generate revolution. Similarly for the avant-garde, a genetic approach stressed the act-aspect of the creative process while the normative orientation moves from the end sought to the means for its achievement. The case of the art-work suggests the path toward a reformulation of the paradox. The successful modernist creation preserves the tension of genesis and normativity whereas the work becomes stilted, either pedantic or childish, when one or the other side dominates. Think of Jackson Pollock on the one hand, Mark Rothko on the other. If the act, the genetic, were dominant, or if the normative pictorial suppressed the painter altogether, the canvas would fail as its constitutive tension collapses. A similar structure prevails in modern capitalism.

Genesis and Validity: The Problem of Ideology

The tension between an approach built on genesis and a construction premised on normativity is a modern (although not specifically capitalist) phenomenon. Classical ontology and its worldview took for granted that what was first in the order of being (as norm) also had precedence in the world of becoming (as genetic). The classics knew the dualisms of becoming/being, is/ought, real/rational, particular/universal, and so on; but for them these dualisms were embedded in a single rational cosmos. The classical world was inclusive: a both/and, not an either/ or. The shifts called Renaissance, Reformation, and birth of modern science introduce a tension that necessitates a choice; the dualism becomes exclusive when the external guarantee that held together the world as coherent cosmos is no longer self-evident. This tension reaches theoretical explicitness in Kant, where the two versions of the "transcendental deduction" in the *Critique of Pure Reason* stand sharply as the option for genesis or the orientation to normativity. The remainder of Kant's work can be read as an attempt to hold this tension without fusing it. In politics the same structure peaks in the French Revolution with the conflict between the Jacobin appeal to *le peuple* as genetic source of further action as opposed to the Thermidorian claim to *une légitimité révolutionnaire* as normative ground for setting limits on action.

Marx's analysis of ideology makes implicit use of the problematic tension between genesis and validity. As Claude Lefort points out, Marx did not simply apply the criticism of ideology from outside to the various social representations and individual attitudes in order to refute them by reduction to their supposed material base.[22] It was the Enlightenment that specialized in such reductive debunking, and it was Feuerbach who summed it up in the epigram, "Man is what he eats" (*Man ist was er Ißt*). Marx's notion of ideology was significantly different. He did not criticize from a position outside or above (*de survol*) the object criticized. Marx discovered ideology as the fundamental or immanent structural characteristic of a particular historical form: capitalism. This means that, for the Marxist, religion is not the model or archetype of ideology. Ideology is not simply false consciousness of whatever kind. That is too general an assertion to be useful; it implies also that the critic has a true consciousness. Ideology is only possible when the traditional external, transcendent legitimations give way to capitalism's recklessly self-expanding immanent value-logic. *The German Ideology* is misleading; one does better to take as a model the discussion of reification in the famous first chapter of *Capital*. But even here, the paradox of vanguardism calls for caution and further nuance.

Capitalism's modernism is a reply to the tension that emerged as the classical synthesis began to break down. Capitalism's self-reproduction in the cycle of M-C-M' continually creates the possibility of qualitative difference, a New that must be reduced to quantitative sameness. Capital continually expands, immediately invades new worlds, and creates new needs; yet it can preserve itself only by making certain that what it produces remains immanent to its fundamental logic of sameness. Ideology is that process by which normativity (embodied, for example, in the contractual logic of equivalence exchange) or genesis (embodied, for example, in the new needs and possibilities created by expanded reproduction) serves to legitimate the system of capitalist domination by reducing difference to sameness. The traditional society faced no such problems because its appeal to external justification made all things appear as parts of a hierarchical organism in which each has its proper place. Capitalism no longer has this luxury; it produces difference continually and explicitly, and it must always reduce that difference to identity, by appeal either to normativity or to genesis. Ideology is thus a process structurally homologous to capitalism's M-C-M'; or, to put the point more strongly: capitalism is ideology.

This brief formulation of the process of ideology helps to explain the dual option confronting the vanguard revolutionary. The proletariat is the agent of revolution, the so-called solution of the riddle of capitalism. Marx formulates the logic of its position in Hegelian language: the proletariat is the "nothing that can become everything" because it has "no particular but only general" griefs. Marx also suggests a formulation closer to the terms employed here—namely that the proletariat is, or is supposed to be, the real unity of genesis and normativity. The proletariat is both the product of capitalism and the producer of capitalism. It is, in Lukács's phrase, the subject-object of history. The norms of which it is the bearer are generated by the very capitalist system that it is destined to overthrow. Marx's critique theory unites at one and the same time a genetic theory that explains how capitalism comes into being and reproduces itself, and a normative theory of the revolution that will overthrow it. Genesis and normativity are both incarnate in the proletariat. The problem for the revolutionary is to avoid opting for one side to the exclusion of the other, to avoid reformist trade unionism as privileging genesis, and to avoid revolutionist Leninism as overstressing normativity.

The problem is that this structure of revolution as the successful unification of genesis and validity is the solution to capitalism's own riddle. If capitalism's ideological process integrates difference and avoids the threat of a new that it nonetheless continually produces, it would seem that we face a situation as frustratingly paradoxical and repetitious as modernism's continual devouring of its avant-gardes. The syncretism for which Marshall Berman's "realism of our time" was criticized a moment ago come back to front-stage. This time, however, we have the categorical frame in which to understand it.

Ideology of Real Origins

Marx's claim is that the proletariat is the real unity of genesis and normativity. The proletariat would then be the real origin of revolution, the immanent source of the genetic impulse toward transformation and the immanent, normative justification of the necessity of the change itself. But this claim puts Marx in the situation whose logical contradictions structured the interaction between vanguards and avant-gardes. The typical modernist refusal of any transcendent, suprahistorical justification is coupled with an implicit reliance on history as providing precisely that justification. Explicating the grounds of this paradox will permit avoidance of some of the distortions in the results of revolutions made in Marx's name.

Contemporary philosophers have devoted much effort to deconstructing the myth of real origin. Logically, an origin cannot be real, or realized. If the origin is a real presence generating a series of events as its result, then it is either itself caused by something, or it is a first cause. In the former case, one confronts the problem of a regression to more primary levels; in the latter, the events following the origin are accidents or "appearances" with no independence or reality of their own. No real event or thing can exhaust or satisfy the origin; each measure is a partial realization and determination of it; but were it fulfilled, it would be a cause, not an origin. The origin, rather, must remain absent. But if the origin is taken as a (real) absence—for example, the nothing that can become everything, the proletariat that is not yet "for itself"—then it can never be realized because any satisfaction would destroy the radicality of the origin. Its realization would be its destruction, and thus the elimination of its originary function. In a word: either the origin manifests or realizes itself, in which case it is no longer originary; or it remains an originary but undefined source and goal, in which case there is nothing more that can be said of it. Yet, if not real, the origin still has its effect; it is, Hegel would say, *wirklich*, actual. *Es wirkt*, that is, it has its effects, but its work cannot be conceived in terms of the (Marxist) model of productive labor.

The French Revolution provides a useful illustration of the implications of this notion of origin. The claim made earlier was that it presents a radical choice between the option of genesis (the Jacobin appeal to *le peuple*) and that for normativity (the Thermidorian *légitimité révolutionnaire*). The usual interpretation suggests that it is a bourgeois revolution and, hence, the origin of modern capitalism. A simplified Marxism suggests that the bourgeoisie overthrew a feudal order that was constraining its growing productive capacities; indeed, there are passages in Marx that would justify such a straightforward causal explanation. But that interpretation neglects the role, pointed out by Rosenberg, of "resurrected Romans," while its definition of capitalism reduces a system of social relations to a merely economic structure for material production and reproduction. The discussion of capitalism-as-ideology suggested another angle of vision that integrates but also goes beyond the causal account of origins. The philosopher posed the problem of origins when the breakdown of the classical ontological framework no longer assured identity in time and homogeneity in space. The quest for origins and the search for identity go hand in hand. The same is true, *mutatis mutandis*, in the drama of modern history.

The significant question concerning the French Revolution is not why it came about but what was/is it? This question of identity was posed by the Revolution itself, as it proceeded through phases, temporary halts, debates and self-doubts, coups and restorations. When did it really begin? With the calling of the Estates General? the refusal of the Third Estate to leave the hall? the Bastille? Or did it begin, as Tocqueville provocatively suggests, already in 1787? When did it end? with Thermidor? the Directory? the defeat of Babeuf? the Consulate? the Empire? Or, ought one observe, with François Furet, that

> The history of the French 19th century in its entirety can be considered as the history of a struggle between the Revolution and the Restoration across episodes dated 1815, 1830, 1848, 1851, 1870, the Commune, the 16th of May, 1877. Only the victory of the republicans over the monarchists at the beginning of the Third Republic marks the definitive victory of the Revolution in the depths of the country: the lay teacher of Jules Ferry, that missionary of the values of 89, is the symbol more than the instrument of that long victorious battle.[23]

In its own process, and then again in its effects through the next century, the Revolution acts exactly as did Marx's revolutionary proletariat described in the *Eighteenth Brumaire*: self-critical, interrupting itself in its course, returning to the apparently accomplished to begin it again, recoiling from the prodigiousness of its own aims. Missing only is the *Hic Rhodus, hic salta*.

Furet presents two strands of analysis that need to be integrated in order to understand—to *penser*, as his title insists, with a philosophical overtone—the Revolution. On the one hand, there is Tocqueville's account of a long revolution whose sources predate 1789 or even 1787. This revolution is rooted in the administrative centralization and territorial unification sought by the politics of the absolutist state. These structural changes alone could not make a revolution. To them was added a new mode of political action, analyzed particularly by Augustin Cochin in the functioning of the revolutionary societies, such as the Jacobins. This new mode of action carried by the message of the Enlightenment and institutionalized prior to 1789 in the *sociétés de pensée* was the necessary complement to the long structural revolution. In our conceptual terms, the Tocquevillean analysis concentrates on the question of normativity; that of Cochin centers on the genesis of action. The French Revolution is the simultaneous presence of these two strands. It should not be surprising, therefore, that the Revolution is continually preoccupied with the question of its own identity; that the Revolution sees itself as originary; and that the posterity of the Revolution continually turns back to it in the search for self-understanding. This is why the French Revolution can be called the first modern Revolution, and why it is the model for all the others. It is in this modernist sense that the French Revolution is a capitalist revolution.

The advent of modern capitalism in France also marks the end of the French Revolution in a very specific sense. Capitalism's ideological structure means that the question of origins, the relation of the genetic and the normative legitimation, is eliminated as a problem. Ideology solves the question of origin by stressing one or the other pole. In this sense, capitalism as an economic system is an answer or solution to a question whose roots are social and whose primary form is political. At the same time that capitalism's advent marks the end of the Revolution of 1789, it also preserves the question of revolution itself. Capitalism-as-ideology not only covers up the question of origins by its option for one or the other pole; capitalism also continually reposes that question because its own internal process is also continual creation. This is why there appears a structural isomorphy between the French Revolution and the proletariat portrayed in the *Eighteenth Brumaire*.

The structural analogy between revolution in modern capitalism and the French Revolution should not, however, veil their radical difference. The French Revolution poses a political problem to which modern capitalism can give only a temporary response, which is unstable because it is ideological. Marx's proletarian revolution, in its turn, promises to overcome capitalism's instability. But that Marxian revolution takes the proletariat as the real—if not yet "for-itself"— incarnate unity of the genetic and the normative aspects of the capitalist process. It makes the proletariat a real origin, in terms of which it then elaborates a discourse of identity, which is a form of false consciousness no different from that of the "resurrected Roman" bourgeoisie. This is the theoretical reason that neither capitalism nor the actually existing socialisms have been able successfully to create republican democracies that satisfy at once the demands of society and those of the polity. The French Revolution from this point of view presents the problem haunting our own politics in its most radical form: the normative question of the republican polity arises simultaneously with the genetic question of social (i.e., democratic, not simply economic) justice. Capitalism occluded this questioning, as did the Marxian proletarian revolution. It is returning in practice today, yet we lack the self-critical tools necessary to understand it.

From Marx to Kant

The call for a return to Kant appears peculiar, even on the theoretical grounds set out here, since Kant is usually accused of having presupposed a radical disjunction between genesis and validity—the sensible world and the categories that seek to grasp its conditions of possibility, or more radically, the difference of phenomena and noumena—at the outset of the first *Critique*. This radical disjunction is said to have been widened in Kant's ethics, whose implication is a formal and abstract *Rechtsstaat* on the political plane. What is more, Kant's separation of genesis and validity is based on a transcendental argument that explicitly avoids the question of origins by presupposing the givenness of that synthetic a priori knowledge or that ethical action whose "conditions of possibility" it then sets out to deduce. And one need hardly add that Kant's taste in art is surely not that of the avant-garde, nor was his life that of the vanguard militant.

Kant's writings on history, which have been called a "fourth *Critique*," suggest a somewhat different approach.[24] The fundamental dualism of the first *Critique* is expressed most sharply by the Third Antinomy, which shows the necessity of thinking that everything that occurs has a lawful natural cause, as well as the necessity of thinking a causality that is expressed in free human actions. Without the latter, morality is impossible. Yet Kant's theory in the first *Critique* gives no way of grounding a causality of freedom. The second *Critique* and the *Foundations of the Metaphysics of Morals* attempt to resolve this problem in terms of a "primacy of the practical." Unsatisfied by that too formal solution, Kant's *Critique of Judgement* is then interpreted as a return to the problem, this time invoking implicitly the problematic of genesis/validity and the question of origins. But the solutions Kant apparently offered—the notion of "genius" and the natural "happy chance"—are unsatisfactory precisely because they postulate a *real* origin. Consequently, the historical writings are read as Kant's attempt once again to resolve the dualism of nature/freedom from which his critical enterprise had begun.

Kant's theory of history is also a political theory of a type that at first appears familiar although in fact it will be seen to put into question the vanguardist approach. Kant formulates his approach to history in terms that the Marxist should appreciate: those of the relation of theory to praxis. This is the orientation of the 1784 essay "Cosmopolitan History," and it returns in Kant's last published work, the 1798 "Conflict of the Faculties." In the latter, Kant replies to his own question "How is history *a priori* possible?" with the assertion that "it is possible if the prophet himself occasions and produces the events he predicts."[25] But Kant's prophet and Marx's revolutionary predict and act on quite different theoretical grounds.

The theory of history offered in "Cosmopolitan History" makes implicit use of categories that Kant fully thematized six years later in the *Critique of Judgement*. Within the context of Kant's own struggle with his dualist presuppositions, and in the broader context of modernism that has concerned us, the advances of this third *Critique* are astonishing. The first two *Critiques* were troubled by the ambiguous genitive in their title: a critique "of" pure or practical reason could be a critique from without, in terms of externally given standards; or it could be the self-critique, operating with immanent measures given by pure or practical reason itself. The difference between the two interpretations of the genitive is that between the classical and the modern approaches that has led us back to Kant. The *Critique of Judgement* goes beyond this alternative; it is an explicit self-criticism of "the means of criticism." The crucial distinction between a subsumptive or determinative judgment and a reflective judgment, as well as the notion of a teleological causality present in our judgment of the organisms of nature, permit Kant to go beyond the constraints of his initial dualism. At the same time, although this was not his intention, Kant can be read as formulating a theory of the modern.

Kant's theory of history becomes a political theory because of a particular twist he gives to the familiar introduction of organic analogies and teleological concepts into political and historical explanations. The immanent, self-critical project suggests that an object has a teleological structure when it is self-caused; when it becomes what it is by realizing its own plan; when consideration of the particular always leads to and demands understanding of the whole or the universal. Such a teleological structure is that of the organism that fascinated scientists as well as political theorists in Kant's time. Its implications emerge once Kant asks the critical question: what kind of judgment permits the scientist (or the citizen) to make this teleological claim? Kant distinguishes determinant or subsumptive from reflective judgment. The former asserts, in the manner of causal science, that a real predicate is attached to a real subject. It makes this assertion monologically, like the natural scientist, claiming it to be valid for any particular subject in the same experimental situation. The reflective judgment, on the other hand, does not concern a real object; it is the action of a subject on itself by means of a consideration of the world outside itself. Leaving aside the application of reflective judgment in the science of nature and its extension to the "cosmopolitan" theory of history that Kant had presented in 1784, the crucial problem for the political "prophet" to whom Kant referred in 1798 is the shift from a monological, abstract, and formal individual subject to a public actor capable of producing the growth and novelty that is history. The form of judgment of the prophet making history *a priori* will not be that of either the vanguard or the avant-garde.

Consideration of the aesthetic judgment of beauty, and of the aesthetic experience of sublimity, explains what makes the application of teleological judgment to history both theoretically valid *and* political. The experience of the sublime is an awareness of the overpowering greatness of an object; sublimity is something for which I can hope but that I can never really reach. The result of the experience of sublimity is a feeling of incompleteness, of respect for the object and dissatisfaction with myself. From this experience emerges a new awareness of the ethical task, a new recognition of the humanity in my own person. The subject here is capable of growth, of *Bildung*, of interaction with others. The monological or transcendental subjectivity that makes Kant's first two *Critiques* formal and abstract is thus surpassed. The judgment of beauty, which is Kant's major concern, brings more than just this advance beyond the formal growth or *Bildung*. My judgment of beauty must be able to claim universal assent. That means that it must go beyond the particularity of the object that was its occasion and that of its subject; it must be lawlike and it must be public. The beautiful is neither the natural nor the willful, since those antinomic categories from the first two *Critiques* are redefined by the immanent self-reflection of the third *Critique*. The beautiful is the experience of the immanence of nature and will; it is what Kant calls a "purposeless purposefulness." This means that the experienced object is judged to be beautiful because of properties whose lawful relation cannot be proven by causal science because there is no room for purpose in nature. The reflective judgment of beauty presents, continues Kant, a "lawfulness without law." Proof of such a judgment cannot follow the model of the first *Critique* with its transcendental, abstract "I think" as subject asserting a predicate of a real object; rather, proof must be achieved through a public and intersubjective process of reflection and deliberation whereby agreement comes into being. This kind of "lawfulness" points to the step to politics.

Kant insists that the only philosophically adequate form of political sovereignty is the Republic. He rejects the democratic form of sovereignty (although not the democratic Republic) because it conflates the conditions of genesis with those of validity by making the assumption that *le peuple* (or their hedonistic or utilitarian desires) are a real origin. Although Kant's Republic appears superficially to be merely the formal and abstract *Rechtsstaat*, the self-reflective categories from the third *Critique* suggest the need for a modern reading. Republican law is not like the causal laws of nature; it is structured like the judgment of beauty's lawfulness without law that is justified through a public process of interaction. That is why Kant continually repeats the injunction from the 1784 essay "What Is Enlightenment?" which insists on the "freedom to make public use of one's reason at every point," and rejects "any contract made to shut off all further enlightenment." Enlightenment is not a one-shot unmediated experience; freedom is not simply formal or self-referential autonomy. The experience of the sublime is not yet political; indeed, in its modernist avant-garde forms, it may become antipolitical, the foundation of a vanguardist politics. On the other hand, the judgment that this object occasions an experience of the beautiful does not mean that only this object can do so; beauty is plural; it is not given once-and-for-all but can be created, anew and differently. The Republic preserves without conflating particularity and universality, as does the aesthetic judgment.

Kant's rejection of the democratic form of sovereignty makes clear why his republican argument is not merely formal. The goal cannot be to exclude popular participation since that would exclude the public validation necessary to reflective judgment. "The touchstone of everything that can be concluded as a law for a people," asserts Kant, "lies in the question of whether the people could have imposed such a law on itself." Kant will not accept the enlightened despot's supposedly "realist" argument that, under present conditions, the people are too stupid to govern themselves, noting that " 'as they are' ought to read 'as we have *made* them by unjust coercion, by treacherous designs.' "

His point turns on the rejection of any assertion of a real origin, a final and permanent solution to the political riddle of history. Kant's concern is with the growth of freedom, the creation of the new. He warns against "a contract made to shut off all further enlightenment from the human race," which, he insists, "is absolutely null and void even if confirmed by the supreme power, by parliaments, and by the most ceremonious of peace treaties." The Republic is to be an institutional form guaranteeing that the public political forum remains always open. Like the French Revolution, the Republic preserves the tension of genesis and normativity that defines an origin.

Although Kant's prophet functions well once the Republic exists, he is unable to explain the origin of this originary republican form. In one of the *Lose Blätter* found after his death, reflecting no doubt on the French Revolution, Kant had written, "In order to institute a Republic from a *pactum sociale* there must already be present a Republic. Hence, the Republic cannot be instituted save by *force* (*Gewalt*), not through *agreement*." This recourse to providential nature to justify a political path that Kant thinks both prudent and right could be said to entail a leap of faith that is wholly unmodern. But the organic teleology Kant has in view is clearly not an appeal to an external, traditional form of justification. The precondition for this teleological assertion is the originary tension of the genetic and the normative entailed in the reflective judgment. Since reflective judgment of just this type is characteristic of a republican public, the implication is that the task of Kant's "prophet" is to bring to the public agenda precisely this originary question. That is why, in "Perpetual Peace," he asserts that "all maxims which stand in need of publicity in order not to fail [to achieve] their end agree with politics and right combined." This is why Marx's revolutionary who supplies answers based on the dictates of scientific necessity has to be replaced by the Kantian prophet who poses the questions that thematize the origins of a modernity that is not simply the product of causal, mechanical, or technical necessity.

The republican solution is usually criticized for its neglect of the problems of social—usually meaning economic—justice. This objection, however, presupposes the logic of capitalism (and Marxism) based on a division between the domain of civil (or economic) society and that of the political state. Enough has been said about the dead ends of vanguardist logic to put the objection into doubt. Moreover, the analysis of capitalism-as-ideology suggests that opting for either the political state or the civil society is just the kind of false resolution immanent to the one-dimensional logic of domination in modern society. Social or economic justice is a political problem, not something that the predicative logic of natural science can solve. The same is true for the problems of politics: they cannot be addressed without the democratic quest for social justice.

The danger is the separation and privileging of the one or the other pole—a danger that is the omnipresent structural pull of capitalism itself, and to which the reformist or revolutionary Marxist position corresponds. The Kantian prophet who recognizes the "permanence of the modern" and avoids the temptation really to solve the riddle of history by ending history, is forced, as a republican democrat, to deal with social (and economic) justice. Because of the type of reflective and, therefore, public judgment that such a prophet applies to material as well as to aesthetic problems, his or her solution, itself continually put into question, opens up rather than closes off the public stage of history. Setting off for Clayton, the prophet lives in a republican democracy without spectators.

Notes

1. See "The Affirmative Character of Culture," in Herbert Marcuse, *Negations* (Boston: Beacon Press, 1968) and Herbert Marcuse, *Die Permanenz der Kunst. Wider eine bestimmte marxistische Aesthetik. Ein Essay* (Munich: Carl Hanser Verlag, 1977), 37. The subtitle of Marcuse's essay, "An Essay Opposing a Certain Marxist Aesthetic," should be stressed. It is also interesting to note that Marcuse wrote this volume in German, after years of publishing in English. The English translation was published a year later under the title *The Aesthetic Dimension* (Boston: Beacon Press, 1978). The following discussion of Marcuse relies on a paper that I presented at the New York Marxist School at a meeting to commemorate Marcuse's death. That previously unpublished text is reprinted as delivered in *Defining the Political* (London: Macmillan, and Minneapolis: University of Minnesota Press, 1989).

2. Herbert Marcuse, *Soviet Marxism* (New York: Vintage Books, 1961), 71–72. I will return to the last aspect of this argument later, since the development (*Bildung*) of the subject is crucial to my thesis.

3. Herbert Marcuse, *One-Dimensional Man* (Boston: Beacon Press, 1964), 96–97.

4. Marcuse, *Soviet Marxism*, 229.

5. Ibid., 233.

6. Ibid., 117–18

7. Herbert Marcuse, *Counter-Revolution and Revolt* (Boston: Beacon Press, 1972), 107.

8. Marcuse, *Die Permanenz der Kunst*, 37.

9. Marcuse, *Counter-Revolution and Revolt*, 108.

10. Marcuse, *Die Permanenz der Kunst*, 43.

11. Ibid., conclusion and 18.

12. Marcuse, *Counter-Revolution and Revolt*, 93.

13. Harold Rosenberg, *The De-Definition of Art* (New York: Horizon Press, 1972), 249.

14. Ibid., 248.

15. Clement Greenberg, "Modernist Painting," in *The New Art: A Critical Anthology*, edited by Gregory Battock (New York, 1966), 101. Cited in Donald B. Kuspit, *Clement Greenberg, Art Critic* (Madison: University of Wisconsin Press, 1979), 136. Marcellin Playnet cites Greenberg as saying (in my translation): "Because he was the first to criticize the very means of criticism, I call this philosopher the first true modernist" (*Paris-New York* catalog, 122).

16. Reprinted in Harold Rosenberg, *The Tradition of the New* (New York: McGraw-Hill, 1965).

17. As I am citing the well-known passages from Marx and indicating their source in the text, I have not pinpointed any of the passages from Marx to one or another of the editions or translations of his work.

18. Harold Rosenberg, "Politics of Illusion," in *Discovering the Present* (Chicago: University of Chicago Press, 1973).

19. Marshall Berman, "All That Is Solid Melts into Air," *25 Years of Dissent*, comp. by I. Howe (New York: Methuen, 1979), 370ff.

20. The term is from S. Wolin, *Politics and Vision* (Boston: Little, Brown and Co., 1960). It is first used with reference to Plato, whose political theory is structured by the same paradox to which I have pointed: it is a politics whose goal is the elimination of the political. The "selfless servant" politician reappears frequently; his most recent avatar is the technocrat (liberal, conservative, or Marxist) in power. See Claude Lefort's notion, taken from Solzhenitsyn, of the *bien-pensant*, in chapter 5 above.

21. Rosa Luxemburg, "Organizational Questions of Russian Social Democracy," *Selected Political Writings*, edited by Dick Howard (New York: Monthly Review Press, 1971).

22. See "Marx: d'une vision de l'histoire a l'autre," and "Esquisse d'une genese de l'idéologie dans les sociétés modernes," reprinted in Lefort, *Les Formes de l'histoire* (Paris: Gallimard, 1978).

23. François Furet, *Penser la révolution francaise* (Paris: Gallimard, 1978), 16–17. See "Origins of Revolution," above, chapter 3.

24. The editor of Kant's writings *On History* (Indianapolis: Bobbs-Merrill, 1963), Lewis White Beck, notes that this suggestion was made by Renato Composto in *La quarta critica kantiana* (Palermo: 1954), xviii, no. 14.

25. As with citations from Marx, I have not specified the edition or page (and the translations are usually my own). The source is clearly given in the text, and can be found either in the above Beck edition, or in Reiss's edition, *Kant's Political Writings* (Cambridge: Cambridge University Press, 1970).

8

Hermeneutics and Critical Theory: Enlightenment as Political

The Problem: Founding Politics

In a letter printed as an appendix to Richard Bernstein's *Beyond Objectivism and Relativism*, Hans-Georg Gadamer describes the central difference between himself and Jürgen Habermas as political. "Political" here does not refer simply to *Weltanschauungen* or party politics; it does refer to different conceptions of the practical role of philosophy. As Gadamer describes it, Bernstein and Habermas deny that truly modern societies share the *Ethos* or community of normative consciousness that made possible Aristotle's linkage of his *Ethics* to his *Politics*. Modern conditions are said to demand instead the move from practical philosophy to social science. Gadamer rejects the *hubris* of this claim; he insists that social solidarities do exist, and that we are not living in a society "constituted only by social engineers or tyrants."[1] "Plato," he continues, "saw this very well: there is no city so corrupted that it does not realize something of the true city." This "something" shared by the community founds the *phronesis* that is, for Gadamer, the philosophically adequate form of practice.[2] The question is how to found the demonstration of its presence or absence.

Bernstein's book is a remarkable effort to draw together the disparate threads of contemporary philosophy around the structure of a modernity that he epitomizes as the "Cartesian Anxiety." The reader familiar with the "Critical Theory" elaborated by the first generation of the Frankfurt School will recognize in Bernstein's study the attempt to ground immanently the distinction between

159

critical and traditional theory that Max Horkheimer brought to a head in his 1937 article "Traditional and Critical Theory." Although Horkheimer's method differs from Bernstein's, their political goals are the same: in Bernstein's words, without sharing "Marx's theoretical certainty or revolutionary self-confidence," nonetheless to "dedicate ourselves to the practical task of furthering the type of solidarity, participation and mutual recognition" that will in fact "move us beyond objectivism and relativism."[3] Unfortunately, neither Horkheimer nor Bernstein succeeds in founding this political imperative as philosophical.

It would be wrong to oppose critical to hermeneutic theory as if the former were resolutely modern whereas the latter's appeal to authority or prejudice is a dogmatic, external, and ultimately traditional foundation. Gadamer's reply to such criticisms refers explicitly to Horkheimer and Adorno's *Dialectic of Enlightenment* as well as to Lukács's *History and Class Consciousness*.[4] He attempts to show the specifically historical character of a philosophically founded hermeneutics that goes beyond the naivetes of nineteenth-century historicism. "Truly historical thinking must think simultaneously its own historicity. . . . The true historical object is no object; it is . . . a relation in which the actuality of history as well as the actuality of historical understanding are co-present. An adequate hermeneutics would have to demonstrate the actuality of history in understanding itself."[5] This immanence of historical understanding and the historically given object refuses to appeal to external norms to explain either the genesis or the validity of hermeneutic knowledge. This leaves the philosopher confronted with the need to found his or her arguments.[6] The refutation of the claim that hermeneutics is premodern makes explicit a theoretical dilemma that the definition of hermeneutics as "ontology" tends to obscure. Gadamer's hermeneutics, like the politics of the Frankfurt School's critical theory, must be founded philosophically.

From the point of view of political theory, Gadamer's description of an "adequate (*sachgemessene*) hermeneutics" recalls unintentionally Hegel's insistence that true history can only be the history of states.[7] Critical theory and hermeneutics share an origin in German Idealism. Kant's critical theory was built on an ambiguous premise, expressed in the very title of the *Critique of Pure Reason*. Kant never explained the ambiguous genitive: is it reason doing the criticizing, but under what warrant? Is reason being criticized, but by whom or what? Or is it the claim to purity that is at issue? But why then go on, in the second *Critique*, to admit practical reason? Kant's *Critique* can claim either to show the conditions of the possibility of experience or to ground the conditions of the possibility of knowledge—or, as Hegel noted, it can do both, becoming an ontology. But then, asks Hegel in the *Science of Logic*, with what must philosophy begin? This suggests that the question of foundations and the question of beginnings imply each other. The result of this ontological philosophy apparently excludes political practice.[8] Thus, at the end of the *Philosophy of Right*, Hegel's state is dissolved into the flow of history, which is "the Court of the Last Judgment." Exit Hegel—enter Marx.

The Critical Theory of the 1930s was simply a code name for Marxism. Horkheimer's Inaugural Lecture as director of the Frankfurt Institut für Sozialforschung in 1931, "The Present Situation of Social Philosophy and the Tasks of an Institute for Social Research," explains the birth of social philosophy from German Idealism without mentioning Marx. Yet, his definition of the "tasks" of social research is perfectly orthodox.[9] Marx did not worry about beginnings or foundations. His doctoral dissertation accepted the Hegelian realization of philosophy as philosophy; the next task, he argued, was to "make worldly" that realized philosophy. Two years later Marx found the locus or beginning of realized philosophy in civil society, in the essay "On the Jewish Question" and then its agent and foundation in the proletariat in "Toward a Critique of Hegel's *Philosophy of Right*." Nearly a century later fascism's seizure of power and the deformations of the Russian experience made it difficult to accept either the locus or the agent postulated by Marx. Without Marxism's foundational guarantee—whether as proletarian praxis or as a structural logic of historical or economic necessity articulated in civil society—Critical Theory is in the same position as modern hermeneutics. It retains from Marxism a theory that political crisis must be immanent in capitalist society but its political choices cannot be justified either by material or by theoretical necessity. The result for its contemporary heirs is the tendency to conflate empirical research with metaphysical claims in the vain effort to conjure forth a new "revolutionary subject" in the guise of a new working class, a rainbow coalition of the oppressed, or perhaps the Third World or the periphery. Each of these efforts is condemned to fail, and this, for theoretical reasons. The crisis is presupposed by its theory as "always-already" there, but the practical political solution is nowhere guaranteed. Critical Theory is no better off than Gadamer's assumed *phronesis* based on an undemonstrable but taken-for-granted communal solidarity.

Politics of Theory

In their foundational essays of the 1930s, Horkheimer and Marcuse seek to explain not only the "conditions of the possibility" of their critical theory, but also the conditions of its necessity.[10] This philosophical demand for objective foundation as well as subjective beginning means that the hermeneutic quest for understanding is incorporated along with the revolutionary concern that, as Marx famously put it, "the point is not to understand . . . but to change" the world. This double imperative makes explicit the sense in which, philosophically, Marx goes beyond the ontological tradition of transcendental philosophy's *quid juris*. Although Horkheimer is aware of this philosophical demand, he is unable to satisfy it. For example, his second contribution moves toward an almost pathetic conclusion: "But when its concepts, which are rooted in social movements, today seem vain because nothing stands behind them but their enemies in pursuit, the truth will nevertheless emerge—for the goal of a rational society, which today appears to exist only in the imagination, is of necessity in every human."[11] The only ground given for what is otherwise a statement of faith in the human power to resist is sociological. Horkheimer claims to justify his "existential judgment" by a comparison of the difference between stable feudalism's categorical judgments and modernizing capitalism's hypothetical or disjunctive judgments. But this attempt to found necessity in external material conditions is one of the often-stressed criteria that were said to define a theory as "traditional." It is correlative to the other major criterion of traditional theory, its Cartesian subjectivism.[12] A better case for Critical Theory can be made . . . hermeneutically.

Whereas Horkheimer spoke of social theory, Marcuse begins his argument from the imbrication of philosophy with the very definition of humanity. "Philosophy wanted to discover the ultimate and most general grounds of Being. Under the name of reason it conceived the idea of an authentic Being in which all significant antitheses (of subject and object, essence and appearance, thought and being) were reconciled. Connected with this idea was the conviction that what exists is not immediately and already rational but must be brought to reason. Reason must represent the highest potentiality of man and of existence. Both go together."[13] While this idealism designates philosophy's inherently critical nature, it does not make philosophy itself into social or political theory. The realization of reason is not supposed to be left to philosophy itself. Marxism expected the proletariat to perform the task that would eliminate (or *aufheben*) philosophy. When this expectation was falsified historically, the nature of philosophy as critical is reaffirmed; philosophy acquires a social role for the philosopher. This grounds the subjective possibility of philosophical critique; its objective necessity remains to be demonstrated.

Critical philosophy without the proletariat must develop a specific technique that combines demystifying criticism with positive critique. Marcuse wrote "The Concept of Essence" because "so much of men's real struggles and desires went into the metaphysical quest for an ultimate unity, truth and universality of Being" that analysis of such concepts reveals concretely the "phantasy" and "desire" for "material happiness" that animate humanity. Thus, for example, Marcuse asks why Descartes accompanies his mechanistic philosophy, analytic geometry, and treatise on machines with a philosophy based on the *ego cogito*. Marcuse does not interpret this as the original sin of modern philosophy's abstract subjectivism and dualism that lead to the Cartesian "anxiety" diagnosed by Bernstein. In his reading, Descartes was seeking to preserve a domain of human freedom and autonomy in the face of the new mechanical-rational external world. The famous admonition to conquer one's self rather than fortune is thus seen not as the abandonment of freedom, but, rather, as the paradoxical attempt to preserve it. Similarly, what Marcuse analyzes elsewhere as the "affirmative character of culture" is not only or simply an escape from hard reality. Culture contains also that Stendhalian *promesse de bonheur* that preserves the real-dream and existential phantasy of freedom even when material conditions do not allow its realization. The aim of such a critical philosophy can be said to be to provide a "hermeneutic" demonstration of the phantasy and existential judgment to which Horkheimer appealed by showing how philosophy's imbrication in the human world makes it a material force.

The difficulty with this solution is that, like Marx's proletariat or Hegel's Spirit, it remains within the confines of a "philosophy of the subject." There is no demonstration of the necessary receptivity of the external world to the deliverance of the existential judgment and phantasy, just as Kant can be accused of incompleteness in the

Transcendental Deduction of the first *Critique* because he does not show why the sensible manifold should be in fact receptive to the imposition of the categories of the understanding.[14] Hegel's assumption of the rationality of the actual at least recognized this imperative. Marx's *Capital*, or the logic of alienation in the *1844 Manuscripts*, provided the concrete demonstration of what Hegel and Kant could only postulate. The next move was suggested by Lukács's 1923 *History and Class Consciousness*. The logic of alienation, or the commodity logic with which Marx introduces the fetish character of capitalism, explain what Lukács described as "second nature." But in 1923 Lukács could still appeal to the class-conscious proletariat as the agent of revolution. A decade later, the Frankfurt School's Critical Theory had to try to transform Marx's "Critique of Political Economy" into a critique of instrumental reason. "False consciousness" expresses the general structure of the modern world within which the apparently autonomous and affirmative subject becomes either the analytic *Verstand*, which Sartre describes as a "passive activity" whose social relations are those of powerless "seriality,"[15] or the passive receptive subject hiding its dependence in the illusory affirmative culture that substitutes dreams for happiness. In this way, the analysis of the modern world as shaped by instrumental reason claims to overcome the dualism that vitiates a philosophy of the subject; because philosophy and social reality have the same structure, critical theory can claim both subjective and objective necessity.

The Missing Theory of the Political

The Frankfurt School's critique of instrumental reason is based on a significant paradox. As philosophy, its Critical Theory was able to explain the conditions of its own possibility. It was unable, however, to demonstrate its necessity. The attempt to resolve this difficulty by showing the receptivity of the world to the deliverances of theory demanded the transition to critical theory as social theory, followed by the analysis of modern society as dominated by the principle of instrumental reason. Leaving aside the immanent difficulties in this proposal,[16] it fails for the symmetrically inverse reason: it is unable to explain the conditions of the possibility of that critical philosophy from which the entire quest began. The practical consequences of this circle of paradoxes emerged starkly in Herbert Marcuse's *One-Dimensional Man*: Marcuse was left with recourse to notions like a qualitative physics, the revolt of the outsider, or the Great Refusal. The move to the critique of instrumental reason was too powerful; it destroyed the very question from which it emerged.

Marcuse's radical posture was the result of his violation of one of the cardinal premises of Critical Theory. If one-dimensional society were the totality, there would be no place from which that totality could be criticized, and no fulcrum from which it could be moved. As with Adorno's aphorism "the whole is the untrue," this assumes the validity of the theory of instrumental reason. Its difficulties suggest problems for that theory. The quest for an Archimedean point makes an illicit assumption. It introduces an externality, something or somewhere freed from the spell of instrumental or one-dimensional reason. This reintroduces the philosophy of the subject. It neglects the concept of totality that founded Lukács's attempt to transcend the theoretical and practical consequences of capitalist-modernity's world of reified forms. Lukács's Hegelian Marxism, however, assumes that the proletariat as the subject-object of history represents the modern totality. As we have seen, the Frankfurters' Critical Theory could not accept this presupposition, even in the 1930s.

Marcuse recognizes that the standpoint of totality has to be reintroduced. The analysis of instrumental reason describes an atomistic world of abstract individuals striving to maintain their mere existence. The result is an increasingly incoherent, crisis-ridden process of social reproduction. As the whole grows more irrational, rationality is flung to the outside and to the outsiders who refuse to submit. But if the totality is truly total, these outsiders are insiders, needed to keep the system functioning through what Paul Piccone calls a "dialectics of negativity."[17] Either the instrumental reification is total, in which case critique is at best immanent and therefore ultimately affirmative despite its own expressed critical intentions; or the critique is external to the totality it criticizes, in which case there is no guarantee that its intended addressees will be receptive to the results of the critique. In the one case, the possibility of critical theory excludes its intended political results; in the other, the intended political results cannot be grounded theoretically.

The source of the dilemma is the overly narrow conception of civil society that Critical Theory inherited from Marx. Hegel knew that the structures of modern civil society pose a problem that has to be resolved at the level of the political state. Marx took this problem to be a solution. By equating modern civil society with capitalist society, Marx developed a theory of political economy that claimed to show why and how capitalist society creates the subjective and objective conditions of the possibility of its own overcoming. However, Marx could not demonstrate the necessity that this possibility be realized. The theoretical consequence of this incompleteness is drawn in the first sentence of Adorno's *Negative Dialectics*: "Philosophy, which once seemed obsolete, lives on because the moment to realize it was missed."[18] The political consequence, however, need not be the pessimism of Horkheimer and Adorno's *Dialectic of Enlightenment*.

A conception of modern civil society that does not equate it with the capitalist economy permits the reintroduction of the standpoint of totality. Horkheimer and Adorno treat the Enlightenment from the point of view of a philosophy of the subject. Conceptualization of the Enlightenment as political was suggested already by Kant, for whom the creation of a lawful civil society was *the* problem of modernity.[19] Kant's solution turned around what historians, conscious of the conceptual paradox, call Enlightened Despotism. The circle is familiar, but it is not hermeneutic; it is political. The equation of modern societies with capitalist (or socialist) economic formations is erroneous. The classical question of the Good Life in the City that is so important for Gadamer has not disappeared. On the contrary, modernity has made it more acute by robbing society of its traditional political institutions. The turn to economics or to social science, to subjective reason or to objective instrumental reason obscures this fundamental fact.

Hermeneutics and Critical Theory as Methodology

The necessity of both a subjective and an objective foundation for a modern philosophy results in a paradoxical dialectic in which either one or the other, but not both, demands can be met. Without a demonstration of the conditions of the possibility of philosophy, the adventure loses its rational seal. Modernity introduces self-doubt into philosophy, thrusting it toward the subjective pole. When the doubt becomes anxiety, philosophy seeks an objective anchor in the positive world. With this, it sacrifices its self in order to maintain itself. The other option is the ontological "identity philosophy," which subsumes the particularity of the world under the lawfulness of philosophical reason. The resulting monism veers toward solipsism when it avoids schizophrenia. This paradoxical structure is the result of a philosophy of subjectivity that cannot ground itself without losing the world, or ground the world without losing itself.

If modern society is conceived as political, the dispute between Bernstein's critical theory and Gadamer's hermeneutic can be resolved by showing each to be correct—but for the wrong reasons. The immanence of the political as a question to modern society means that Gadamer's insistence on the possibility of political judgment and practical *phronesis* is justified. The difficulty, however, is to show when and how this *phronesis* functions. That demands a theory of those particulars that make necessary political reflection; and it demands a theory of judgment that avoids the subsumption by which identity philosophy reduces otherness to mere appearance. This is where a Frankfurt School type of critical theory enters, following the model suggested by the relation between Adorno's *Negative Dialectics* and his aesthetic theory. The existential judgment, mimesis, and fantasy to which it appeals are grounded in the immanence of the political question within the modern. But this is only the first step. The goals Bernstein and Horkheimer postulated as the *telos,* or totality, guiding the critical theory could not be grounded because the Marxian tendency to equate civil society with the capitalist economic form neglects the political question of the theoretical and institutional foundation of the being-together of society. This question emerges when particular events or institutions release practical energies whose repression constitutes social injustice. The result is that possibility is completed by necessity, and particularity is completed by totality, without their conflation or their irreparable separation.

In this way, hermeneutics explains the conditions of receptivity that ground the necessity of the particular assertions whose possibility is designated by the Critical Theory. Critical Theory stands as the political pole whose task is the articulation of particularity; hermeneutics provides the philosophical complement whose universality assures that this politics is grounded. Their relation is thus one of inclusion; excluded is only the economistic Marxism—accepted by the first generation of Critical Theory—which denies the immanence of the political question to civil society. But inclusion is not identity. Each approach has its legitimate place and domain. This limitation transforms the nature of both hermeneutics and Critical Theory. Neither can make the totalizing claims that their philosophical formulation suggests. Each, rather, becomes a methodological moment within a theory of modernity that transforms both. In this context, Bernstein's political critique of Gadamer is perfectly correct. Gadamer is a political *naïf*, but there is no need to treat him as a political philosopher. The political philosophy of a noneconomistic Critical Theory shows hermeneutics its proper limits and place, just as hermeneutics shows the Frankfurt Critical Theory its own.

Notes

1. Hans-Georg Gadamer to Richard Bernstein, 1 July 1982, trans. James Bohman, Appendix to *Beyond Objectivism and Relativism: Science, Hermeneutics and Praxis*, by Richard Bernstein (Philadelphia: University of Pennsylvania Press, 1983), 262.
2. Ibid., 264.
3. Ibid., 231.
4. Hans-Georg Gadamer, *Wahrheit und Methode*, vierte Auflage (Tübingen: J. C. B. Mohr, Paul Siebeck, 1975), 258, 259. Gadamer criticizes Horkheimer and Adorno's extension of the notion of enlightenment to the *Odyssey*, implicitly rejecting the notion of "instrumental reason" to which we will return below.
5. Gadamer, *Wahrheit*, 283.
6. The modern hermeneutics that distinguishes itself from the "philosophy of consciousness" typical of nineteenth-century historicism, Diltheyian *Einfühlungsphilosophie*, or methodological *Verstehen*, makes a virtue of necessity—it literally ontologizes its own embarrassment. It explains that we cannot pose the question of foundations because these foundations found our very being-as-questioning. We cannot pose the question of beginning because we have always already begun. Whether the hermeneutic circle is conceived ontologically, as with Gadamer, or linguistically, as with Apel, the dilemma remains. Philosophy cannot rule out the question of foundations without risking the accusation of irrationalism. A modern philosophy cannot invoke foundations whose normative character it cannot justify immanently.
7. Hegel argues, for example, that "peoples without a state may have passed a long life before arriving at this their destination. And during these periods, they may have attained considerable development in some dimensions." He continues more explicitly

> It is the state which first presents subject matter that is not only adapted to the prose of history, but involves the production of such history in its very being. Instead of government issuing merely subjective mandates sufficing for the needs of the moment, a community that is acquiring a stable existence as a state requires formal commands and laws, comprehensive and universally binding prescriptions. It thus produces a record as well as an interest in understandable, definite transactions and occurrences which have results that are lasting. (G. W. F. Hegel, *Werke*, vol.

12: *Vorlesungen über die Philosophie der Geschichte*, edited by Eva Moldenhauer and Karl Markus Michel [Frankfurt am Main: Suhrkamp Verlag, 1970], 83)

8. This is argued explicitly by Hegel in the resigned tones of his preface to the *Philosophy of Right*, trans. T. M. Knox (Oxford: Oxford University Press, 1967), for which philosophy can only "paint its grey on grey" after the fact, when "the Owl of Minerva" has taken flight. For a theoretical argument making this point from the perspective of Critical Theory, see Jürgen Habermas, "Hegel's Critique of the French Revolution," in *Theory and Practice*, trans. John Viertel (Boston: Beacon Press, 1973), 121–42.

9. Max Horkheimer, *Sozialphilosophische Studien*, edited by W. von Brede (Frankfurt am Main: Fisher, 1972), 33–46. The research proposed for the Institute asks why the working class has not fulfilled its designated function. The changed economic, psychological, cultural, legal, and religious conditions of modern capitalism are to be examined empirically and integrated theoretically by the renewal of that "social philosophy" whose inadequate foundation in German Idealism will be completed by the equivalent of a modern Marxism. Nowhere does the lecture put into question the adequacy of the Marxist manner of posing the questions. It questions only the nineteenth-century solutions offered by orthodox Marxism.

10. Max Horkheimer, "Traditionelle und Kritische Theorie," *Zeitschrift für Sozialforschung* 6 (1937): 245–92; Max Horkheimer and Herbert Marcuse, "Philosophie und Kritische Theorie," *Zeitschrift für Sozialforschung* 6 (1937): 624–31 (Horkheimer), 631–47 (Marcuse). Marcuse's contribution to the essay is translated as "Philosophy and Critical Theory," in *Negations*, trans. Jeremy J. Schapiro (Boston: Beacon Press, 1968), 135ff.

11. Horkheimer, "Traditionelle und Kritische Theorie," 630.

12. Marcuse's interpretation of Descartes, like Marx's presentation of Epicurus in his *Dissertation*, sees a different implication in this subjectivism. Horkheimer's argument is concerned with the methodology of the social sciences whereas Marcuse's concern is to ground Critical Theory in conditions where it can no longer appeal to the proletariat (Marcuse, "The Concept of Essence," in *Negations*, 50).

13. Marcuse, "Philosophy and Critical Theory," 135–36. (I have changed the translation of the penultimate sentence to stress that both *must* [*soll*] be brought together, i.e., that this imperative is an active task.)

14. See the brilliant argument of George Schrader, "The Status of Teleological Judgment in the Critical Philosophy," *Kantstudien* 45 (1953–1954): 204–35. I have developed this argument in a broader context in my *From Marx to Kant* whose fifth chapter is "The Logic of Receptivity."

15. Jean-Paul Sartre, *Critique de la raison dialectique* (Paris: Gallimard, 1960), passim.

16. Jürgen Habermas has pointed to some of the major problems of this argument in the concluding chapter to his *Theory of Communicative Action*,

vol. 1: *Reason and the Rationalization of Society*, trans. Thomas McCarthy (Boston: Beacon Press, 1984), 339–403. To summarize Habermas's point, it is not possible to reduce a social totality to one form of reason. Communicative (and emancipatory) reason must always function alongside instrumental reason if the society is not to be pulled apart by the centrifugal weight of the individual atoms seeking self-preservation at the cost of destroying the mechanisms of social reproduction.

17. Paul Piccone has argued this position in numerous essays in the journal *Telos* of which he is the editor. Its political consequences can be quite problematic, as for example in the assertion that the feminist movement is simply necessary for the expanded reproduction of a blocked capitalist society. Indeed, I might add from the perspective of 1995, the positions of *Telos* have become increasingly irresponsible, to put it gently.

Two other positions are possible within the framework of the political goals of Critical Theory taken more generally. Along the lines of Walter Benjamin or Theodor Adorno, one could attempt to recover an intimation of the suppressed totality through the "lightning" of a mimetically based critique founded either in art or in the structures of the everyday. Or, along the lines of Ernst Bloch, one could propose a kind of "anticipatory hermeneutics" that develops the immanent futurity that traditional hermeneutics covers over through its classical orientation. On the former see Habermas, *The Theory of Communicative Action* 1: 339–403; on the latter, see Burghardt Schmidt, *Ernst Bloch* (Stuttgart: G. B. Metzler Verlag, 1985).

18. Theodor W. Adorno, *Negative Dialectics*, trans. E. B. Ashton (New York: The Seabury Press, 1973), 3. Habermas's earlier reconstruction of Marx's philosophical debt to German Idealism expresses this difficulty by speaking of the need for a "Fichtean moment": since ego is itself only in the act of relating to the world, there must be a moment of intersubjectivity that transcends the subject philosophy of the Kantian "I think" and unifies and makes my representations mine. This Fichtean moment is translated as the phenomenon of class consciousness in Marx's reconstruction of the capitalist civil society. This provocative argument, developed in *Knowledge and Human Interests*, would appear to Habermas today as depending on a "philosophy of the subject," which he has since rejected.

19. This is most explicitly stated in Kant's theses on the idea of history from a cosmopolitan point of view. For an interpretation of Kant from the perspective to which I can only allude here, see my essay "Kant's System and (Its) Politics," *Man and World* 18 (1985): 79–98.

9

Law and Political Culture

Those who had slipped into the habit of talking about the project that Habermas announced a decade ago in his *Theory of Communicative Action* as his *Rechtsphilosophie* may be surprised by the sobriety of his choice for the book's title. The foreword to *Faktizität und Geltung* rejects any comparison with Hegel's systematic *Grundlinien der Philosophie des Rechts*. Habermas contrasts his "methodical-pluralistic" proposals to the idealistic concepts of *Geist* and *Sittlichkeit*, which are unable to account for complex modern societies. The apparent modesty of Habermas's claims is underlined by his subtitle, "Contributions to the Discourse Theory of Law and of the Democratic Constitutional State." Habermas's goal is to replace the old, unitary notion of practical reason, according to which the organization of the state and political life provided for the unification of society, such that individuals belong to society like the parts to a whole, by a communicative reason whose normative orientation to validity claims entails no commitment to any specific institutional structure. At the same time, by means of a systematic reconstruction of the nature and the sociopolitical place of law in complex modern societies, Habermas seeks to reclaim the democratic legacy of the political project that began with the French Revolution. Sober in appearance, Habermas's reach is in fact remarkable.

Although Habermas has philosophical reasons for rejecting Hegelian conceptual tools, the structural parallels between the two projects are nonetheless worth remarking.[1] Hegel's system begins from the structure of the Will, which must express itself in the factual world in order to actually exist as will, but whose temporary empirical existence then contradicts its validity claim to be self-related and autonomous. This simple dialectical structure becomes the machinery by which Hegel

171

constructs first the theory of law, then the theory of morality. But these two parallel domains presuppose (rather than constitute) what Hegel calls *Sittlichkeit*, the sphere of concrete sociocultural relations, whose structure Hegel reconstructs in the institutions of the family, civil society, and the state. The question that has troubled Hegel's interpreters is how to understand the relation between the theories of law and morality on the one hand, and the institutions of *Sittlichkeit* on the other. Habermas's democratic theory, whose foundation is not the unitary practical reason that Hegel calls Will, can be interpreted as offering a solution to this Hegelian dilemma. I will try to indicate the nature and implications of Habermas's solution by stressing the notion of political culture. Following the parallel with Hegel, I will analyze first Habermas's Legal Project, proceed to his Social Project, and then go on to his Political Project, before asking, finally, what is democratic culture?

A further parallel between Hegel and Habermas suggests that his arguments have a political premise. In his preface to the *Philosophy of Right*, Hegel defined philosophy as "its time grasped in thought." Habermas could accept this claim even though he rejects its idealist premise that "the rational is the actual and the actual is the rational." His foreword to *Faktizität und Geltung* situates his project concretely at the historical moment when the Marxist project has collapsed, and when the capitalist (or welfare state) alternative has apparently succeeded in providing economic betterment and social peace—but at the cost of ignoring ecological risks, disparities between North and South, streams of immigration and renewed ethnic, national, and religious wars, all within the horizon of nuclear threat. In such a context, Habermas asserts, "politics today in the constitutional and democratic societies of the West has lost its orientation and self-consciousness. . . . I suspect that under conditions of a completely secularized politics, the constitutional state cannot exist or be maintained without radical democracy. To make this suspicion into an insight is the goal of the present study."[2] After 525 pages of systematic analysis, Habermas concludes that he has shown that this goal is not utopian. To reconstruct his reasoning, our analysis will therefore have to take into account also the passage from Hegel to Marx. This will permit a clarification of two concepts that Habermas often uses as if they were synonymous and self-evident: liberal culture and democratic culture.

The notion of a radical democracy, based on solidarity, is the legacy that Habermas wants to inherit from the socialist project. He points out in the foreword that he had criticized Marx's sociological reduction of Hegel's philosophy and the theory of natural law already in 1962. The error of Marx's followers was to confuse socialism with a specific, concrete life form, to be imposed upon society. On the other hand, for a communicative theory of the type Habermas is seeking, socialism is "the essence [*Inbegriff*] of the necessary conditions for emancipated life forms concerning which the participants *themselves* must come to agreement" such that "the democratic self-organization of a legal community is the normative kernel of this process."[3] Habermas hastens to add that this does not mean that a concrete politics can be developed on the basis of that theory alone; indeed, the temptation to conflate philosophy and politics is avoided by clarifying the unique place of the law in a modern, democratic society.[4] That is why my reconstruction of *Faktizität und Geltung* will begin from the political even though Habermas's presentation takes its departure from philosophy. This procedure is justified also by Habermas's essay "Popular Sovereignty as Procedural," which is republished as an appendix to *Faktizität und Geltung* and which begins from the actuality of the French Revolution and concludes with his own synthetic project. This approach will permit me to reformulate the philosophical challenge of Habermas's system, as well as its implications for contemporary politics.

Revolutionary Project

While working on *Faktizität und Geltung*, Habermas published in 1990 a small volume of his political essays under the curious title, *Die nachholende Revolution*. The title essay attempted to put into perspective the transformations under way in Eastern Europe—which Habermas does call "revolutions." The perspective sought is double: what is the place of these revolutions in the two centuries of Western history that began symbolically in 1789? What does the collapse of this self-proclaimed socialism mean for the contemporary left? Habermas's answer to the first question is contained in the idea of "catching up" (*nachholende*) in his title; the East is said to be seeking to rejoin the modern history that began with the Enlightenment and the French Revolution.[5] His answer to the second is suggested by the full title of the essay, "Nachholende Revolution und linker Revisionsbedarf. Was heißt Sozialismus heute?" ("The Catching Up Revolution and the Left's Need for Revision: What Does Socialism Mean Today?"). For

Habermas, the project of the Left remains what it always was: the self-critical critique of reified systems that impose their imperatives on the life-world of the individuals whose autonomy was first asserted by the French Revolution's Declaration of the Rights of Man and of the Citizen.[6]

Habermas's reconstruction of two centuries of self-critical left politics sets the stage for his systematic and normative political theory. He first shows the inadequacy of three attempts to maintain the socialist ideal—the Stalinist, the Leninist, and the reform-communist variants; but he then goes on to criticize three antisocialist proposals—the postmodernist, the anticommunist, and the liberal positions. The best interpretation, he argues, was offered already by the *Communist Manifesto*'s "hymn" to the revolutionary role of the bourgeoisie, which

> by the rapid improvement of all instruments of production, by the immensely facilitated means of communication, draws all nations, even the most barbarian, into civilization. The cheap prices of its commodities are the heavy artillery with which it batters down all Chinese walls, with which it forces the barbarians' intensely obstinate hatred of foreigners to capitulate. It compels all nations, on pain of extinction, to adopt the bourgeois mode of production; it compels them to introduce what it calls civilization into their midst, i.e., to become bourgeois themselves. In a word, it creates a world after its own image.

Of course, adds Habermas, that heroic bourgeoisie has today been replaced by an anonymous and worldwide economic system; and the "social [or welfare] state compromise" has provided an answer to the old forms of class struggle.[7] Yet the irony suggested by Marx's stress on "what it calls civilization" points to the critical wedge. Marx's critique was directed at an economic system that has closed itself off to any but economic values, whose self-expansion is its only political or "steering" imperative, and that for this reason carries the seed of its own self-destruction. That is why Marxism as critique retains its actuality.[8]

The factual demise of "really existing socialism" does not mean that the socialist goal exists only as an ideal. The tradition called "Western Marxism" in which Habermas situates himself was able to learn from the changing modern society; it has been resolutely self-critical, and critical of the founder. It recognized that the model of liberation through labor and the notion that technology is inherently progressive have been refuted by the absence of worker solidarity and by the environmental impact of industrial progress. It saw that the holistic view of a society that would regain its solidarity once the imperatives of capitalism were eliminated blinded its adherents to the need for autonomous economic and administrative steering functions in modern, pluralist societies. It admitted that the theory of classes as unified social actors no longer makes sense in complex and differentiated societies; and that none of the many corollaries added to the reductionist theory of the state can save it. It learned that the functionalist interpretation of the democratic state and the criticism of "merely formal" democracy, along with the Saint-Simonist illusion of the possibility of a neutral "administration of things," left no room for the preservation of freedom in institutions that permit the social debate and deliberation needed to resolve conflicts. It concluded that the teleological interpretation of history, which hides its normative presuppositions under a naturalistic theory of evolution, covers over the space of contingency in which decisions guided by theory are necessary. Finally, it rejected the vanguardism that pretends to govern the entirety of the life-world on the basis of a theory whose presuppositions are ultimately idealist.

Although he defends the "socialist goal," Habermas is a social *democrat*. Social democracy assumed the neutrality of the state whose intervention was supposed to permit the universalization of the rights of man. It did not realize that it became increasingly caught up in the state machinery as its political party became integral to the state's need to provide legitimation for administrative decisions within a manipulated mass democracy. That is why a noncommunist Left *to the left* of social democracy emerged in the late 1960s, even though this new Left found it difficult to abandon the holistic concept of society and to accept the autonomy of the market. That new Left was still caught up in a romantic vision of the end of alienation, the complete emancipation of the human senses, the resurrection of nature and the overcoming of the opposition of freedom and necessity. Habermas's social *democracy* remains, however, in sympathy with this Left (and with Marx) insofar as its politics is founded on the critique of any structural blockage of the communication among free and equal citizens that forms the basis of a social solidarity. He insists, however, that this communicative solidarity cannot be manifested in any concrete social subject; it is, as we shall see, a "self-organization" without a self, be it that of a class or a nation. Habermas describes his ideal in terms that he will develop systematically in *Faktizität und*

Geltung: "A popular sovereignty that is in this way intersubjectively dissolved and anonymous withdraws into the democratic procedure and the demanding communicative presuppositions of its implementation. It finds its placeless place [*ortlosen Ort*] in the interactions between constitutionally [*rechtsstaatlich*] institutionalized will formation and culturally mobilized publics." But, continues Habermas, whether this vision can be realized cannot be answered by theory; it is a "practical-political question."[9]

If Habermas were to leave the matter here, admitting the separation of theory and practice, his social-*democratic* theory would have only that abstract or ideal status that he refused to accept for the socialist ideal. While the concluding section of his essay does address what seem to be empirical practical-political problems, Habermas's fundamental thesis—that the revolutions of 1989 are only catching up with the history that began in 1789—suggests that there is a more systematic theoretical claim behind his political argument. The fact that he did not republish his 1989 essay on the French Revolution in *Die nachholende Revolution* but did include it as an appendix to *Faktizität und Geltung* provides the theoretical and political link to the revolutionary project that is the premise of the systematic theory of radical democracy.

Rejecting the postmodernist critics, for whom (as, ironically, for Hegel) 1789 was only the most powerful expression of Reason's attempt to submit all and everything to its systematic imperatives, as well as the self-righteous former communists who spit in the ideological soup that once nourished them, Habermas sees the French Revolution as a living legacy whose testament has not been exhausted. However, if the Revolution is seen simply as inaugurating the conditions of capitalist transformation—or its final overthrow by the associated producers—its originality would be put into question by the fact that other nations became capitalist without a revolution. If it is seen as creating the preconditions for the modern bureaucratic state, the same observation holds. And, if it is seen as inaugurating the modern nation-state whose citizens are united by a republican patriotism, its uniqueness might be maintained but at the price of its irrelevance in our increasingly multinational and multicultural societies. What remains alive today, insists Habermas, are the ideas of democracy and human rights that form the universalistic kernel of the constitutional state.[10] This universalistic goal, or theory, could be formulated because of the emergence of a new mentality that incorporated three new things: a new time-consciousness breaking with the continuity of tradition; a new concept of political praxis based on self-determination and self-realization; and a new notion of political legitimation based on the idea of a rational discourse. In this way, concludes Habermas, there emerged "a radical inner-worldly, post-metaphysical concept of the political."[11]

The legacy of the French Revolution is the modern concept of the political. We need not follow Habermas's reconstruction of two-centuries' attempts to inherit this legacy. Some of the pitfalls are obvious. The idea of autonomy as self-realization clashes with the recognition that society is plural and that in modern societies domination is exercised by the impersonal forces of the economy and the political administration. A politics based on reason encounters resistance from singular and collective wills pursuing their own paths, and may be tempted to impose its dictates, abandoning the distinction between morality and tactics and allocating to intellectuals the role of a vanguard. The dynamic spread of culture brings urbanization, individualized life-spheres, and the clash between culture and commerce. At another level, liberalism competes with radical democracy and with socialism's attempt to expand the concept of the political to include the economic even at the cost of formal constitutional rights. Socialism, in turn, confronts the anarchist stress on horizontal relations and nonfunctionalist orientations in a society whose growing complexity renders this dream utopian. The result, concludes Habermas, is the need to recognize a division of the concept of the political between communicatively produced and administratively applied power.[12]

Although Habermas insists that the question of which of these forms of the political will dominate is an empirical one, he offers a normative account of the concept of sovereignty. The communicative praxis of the public sphere, the forms of democratic will formation, and the institutions of public freedom produce a form of popular sovereignty that is desubstantialized and whose seat must remain vacant. But the division of the political changes the sense of this normative account by giving it a rival: the administrative form of political power. Communicative power now becomes a form of political action, which Habermas describes by a significant metaphor: the "siege modality." It does not have the goal of external conquest; its aim is to speak to the besieged in their own language in order to bring them to recognize its demands and to act upon them. Two criteria must be met for the siege to succeed. The first falls to what Habermas calls, without further specification, the "political culture" of a people whose tradition and socialization have accustomed them to freedom. This is necessary because there is "no rational political will-formation without the cooperation of a rationalized life-world."[13] More concretely, representatives will vote as the public wishes because of "the emergence, the reproduction and the influence of . . . a network of associations [that] depends on a liberal political culture which is egalitarian, sensitive to problems concerning the whole society, nervously vibrating and thus capable of receiving its signals."[14] But Habermas does not specify the origin or the nature of this "liberal political culture," despite its obvious relation to the new mentality born with the French Revolution.

This notion of a siege imposed by communicative power on administrative power was present also in Habermas's description of the tasks posed to the Revolutions of 1989. In that case, however, it was not possible to appeal to an already existing liberal political culture. Instead, Habermas spoke about "problems concerning the whole society," illustrating them with examples such as underdeveloped continents or ecological damage that remains latent like time bombs. "Such problems can be brought to a head only by means of a moralization of the themes across a more or less discursively undertaken universalization of interests in non-institutionalized publics of a liberal political culture."[15] This "moralization" is described as a mass transformation of values that, while remaining latent, strips the state of the basis of its legitimacy. The political problem is to complete the task of destruction and to begin the rebuilding. But Habermas offers no hints for this next stage. Instead, he argues that a similar task faced the revolutionaries of 1789; and he adds that the same problems confronted the West German Left after its fight against the Reagan rearmament program. He writes that "this example illustrates a process of circulation in which actual conditions bring together a latent change of values with processes of public communication, changes in the parameters of the institutionalized democratic will-formation, and initiatives to disarmament which, from their side, react back on the changed value orientation."[16] Even if this description of the Western Left of the 1980s rings empirically true, Habermas has not given the "moralization" and "value orientation" the kind of normative foundation that is needed if they are to replace or complement what he called liberal political culture and a rationalized life-world.

This is where the second criterion for the successful siege has to be introduced. The difficulty is that the concept of political culture was not related explicitly to the modern concept of the political or to the two forms into which Habermas showed it to have split. Rather than begin from the concept of political culture, Habermas's second option starts from the democratic nature of communicative power. "Communicative power can only become effective indirectly, as a sort of limitation on the execution of the administrative power that is actually applied. And such a siege function can be fulfilled by the non-institutionalized public opinion only by means of a decision process which is organized by and responsible to democratic procedure."[17] To be effective, as we saw, the besiegers must translate their demands into the language of the besieged: the system of administrative power. This is where the law will enter Habermas's argument. Its place and role can be suggested by a final passage from Habermas's essay on the French Revolution.

> The democratic constitutional state becomes a project, at one and the same time the result and the catalytic accelerator of a rationalization of the life-world *that goes far beyond the political.* The only content of the project is the step-by-step amelioration of the institutionalization of the procedure of rational collective will formation. . . . Every step on this path has an effect on the political culture and the life forms without whose cooperation—a cooperation that cannot be produced voluntarily—forms of communication that are adequate to practical reason cannot emerge.[18]

This suggests that there is a complement to the revolutionary project inaugurated in 1789 that produced the modern concept of the political and then divided it into administratively and communicatively produced power. The rationalization of the life-world is political, but it is not *only* political. The law will provide a mediation between the domains of politics and the life-world while permitting each to retain its autonomy, thereby insuring each its own place in the revolutionary legacy of 1789.

Legal Project

The French Revolution consecrated a society of individuals as bearers of rights whose legitimation was not based on any transcendent grounds. These were rights of reason, whose justification could be only immanent. *Faktizität und Geltung* illustrates the genesis of this modern imperative of immanence in the history of philosophy and by sociohistorical analysis. It is this imperative of immanence that, already, makes of the distinction of fact and validity a problem: in a world of immanence, what makes one fact more valid than another? What is the source, and the justification of the source, of validity? The problem becomes the more acute if the fact in question is the individual conceived of as a bearer of rights. How are such individuals to live together? How are they to coordinate their expectations and behavior? Habermas refers to this as the problem of *horizontal* socialization. It is a well-known difficulty, whose proposed solutions by Weber and Durkheim form contrasting poles. Habermas's earlier proposal in the *Theory of Communicative Action* appealed to the normative foundation of intersubjective behavior. The difficulty, however, was that this can be provided only from the standpoint of the participant in this horizontal exchange. Its account of validity comes at the cost of facticity as seen from the standpoint of the observer. That is why Habermas was led to propose a dualist theory of law in that earlier formulation of his legal theory.[19]

The modernity inaugurated by the French Revolution that destroyed external legitimation also set free the systems of regulation of social behavior that had previously been organized in one, hierarchical and organic unity. The economy and the state administration could now specialize, develop their own experts, delimited domains of action, and linguistic codes for autonomous communication. The problem of the self-government of autonomous individuals or nations could be transferred to these systems, which could develop, in turn, their own forms of rationality. Since the end sought by such systems is simply their own self-reproduction, their rationality differs from the reasoned deliberation among participants in a communicatively regulated relation in which the question of ends must also be posed, and where goals in principle are open to revision. The result is that systems-rationality is strategically oriented to choosing the best means to achieve a pregiven goal, self-reproduction. In this case, facticity is prized over validity; and the standpoint adopted is that of the observer. Systems rationality tends to grow rapidly because of this specialization. Further domains can split off from it, developing their own specific expertise, their own logic and forms of communication. The result is a further decentering of a society composed solely of individuals—and the challenge to find a political form through which the participating citizens can replace the old absolutist, hierarchical and organic, externally imposed unity that 1789 had destroyed.

The temptation is to use the rationality of strategic or systemic action to solve the problems of action coordination among the autonomous participants in the new society of individuals. Not all relations are, or ought to be, governed communicatively. Strategic action by individuals is not necessarily wrong or immoral; and it can be quite efficacious. Indeed, strategic action contributes to the complexification, differentiation, and decentering that permits and encourages the individual autonomy characteristic of modern society. The question is, when is strategic action appropriate and legitimate? Conversely, when does strategic action expand its reach to the point that, in Habermas's metaphor, it "colonizes" the life-world such that the resources of communicative action—which is still necessary in some spheres—are dried up? This was the problem posed by Habermas's *Theory of Communicative Action*. His response was ultimately political.[20] However, his politics were defined negatively, as the resistance of the life-world to the expansion of systemic imperatives. Although Habermas supported the new social movements of the time, he tended to see them more as protecting the life-world than as positive forces for the rebuilding of new and democratic institutions. Politics became "a defensively formulated task," but, added Habermas, "this defensive redirection of the steering process will not be able to succeed without a radical and broadly based democratization."[21] How this democratization was to occur was not explained. At best, Habermas offered a more subtle reformulation of his notion of a "crisis of legitimacy."[22]

The difficulty encountered by Habermas's earlier approach may be explained in part by the fact that his analysis remained at the horizontal level of interaction among participants. *Faktizität und Geltung* adds a vertical dimension. This is consonant with Habermas's reflections on the French Revolution and its legacy. In addition to the philosophical account of the advent of the modern imperative of immanence, Habermas now stresses the role of the absolutist state in a manner that often recalls Tocqueville's *Ancien Régime* (which, curiously, he does not cite).[23] The overthrow of the absolutist state left a void that, for all their efforts, could not be filled by society or its subsystems, let alone by the people whose sovereignty was proclaimed by the Revolution. The presence of this absence—what Habermas called a "placeless place" that is "intersubjectively dissolved and anonymous"[24]—and the constant attempts to replace the royal body, constitute the political space of modern societies. As we saw, the modern concept of the political divides into forms of power exercised administratively and communicatively. This division can be understood by recalling the justification of absolutism in terms of the theory of the king's two bodies. The absolute monarch was at one and the same time the incarnation of the Kingdom and yet also an individual ruler. He was, so to speak, fact and value at once; that is why, on his death, his subjects could cry, *Le roi est mort, vive le roi.* The continuity of the Kingdom was affirmed beyond the mortal body of the king. In the same way, the modern form of the political has both a factual, administrative function and a normative role in legitimating the continuity of communicative socialization processes.

The absence of a vertical unification of the liberated and rights-bearing individuals of a modern society opens up the first parameter for the development of law.[25] The division of the political into its administrative and communicative spheres then points to the need for a second parameter. In the first instance, the law will have to replace the absent center by taking on an administrative-political role. In this way, the political *system* takes the responsibility for the functioning of the society as a whole. The individuals whose increasingly complex and differentiated interactions it regulates can now relate to it as if it thereby also gave sense to their actions and interactions. However, they may also relate to it strategically, taking advantage of its universal form in order to reduce the complexity of their individual decisions. This is where the second parameter enters. The law is not a fact that is imposed by force; it must be understood to be legitimate. To be legitimate, law must be based on consent, which, in the conditions of modernity, means that it has rational or normative validity. This is where the communicative parameter enters. These two parameters are not separate from one another, any more than were the two bodies of the king; but they are not fused immutably: the Law does not succumb when new laws are legislated, any more than the Kingdom dies with the king. The question is that of their proper, which is also to say, legitimate relation.

Habermas stresses from the outset the bifunctionality or duality of the law. The tension or "interlacing" (*Verschränkung*) between facticity and validity, and the double perspective on law or right that this implies is introduced in the first chapter. The second chapter develops the "hinge" metaphor for the function of law as making possible the relation between the self-steering of social systems and the communicatively reproduced life-world. When he begins to explicate the system of rights in chapter 3, the tension becomes a paradox:

> It is paradoxical for this reason, that the rights of the citizen as subjective rights on the one hand have the same structure as all rights: they create for the individual spheres in which he can express his free will [*Willkür*]. In spite of the distinctions in the modalities of the use of these rights, political rights must be able to be interpreted as subjective freedoms to

act which make only legal behavior a duty; that is, they *liberate* motives for rule-following behavior. On the other hand, the democratic process of legislation must confront its participants with the normative expectations of an orientation to the common good because this process itself can draw its legitimating force only from the process of an agreement [*Verständigung*] of the citizens about the rules of their common life. In modern societies, law can only fulfill the function of stabilizing expectations when it preserves an internal connection with the social-integrative force of communicative action.[26]

When he turns to the reconstruction of the principles of the constitutional state in chapter 4, Habermas brings in the vertical dimension of political power—a dimension that, he insists, was "*already presupposed*" by the horizontal system of rights.[27] In this way, the paradox from chapter 3 can be again treated as an interlacing.

The most simple form of the bifunctional duality of law appears as the opposition between the private freedoms that the law is to guarantee and the public good that it must be perceived to be seeking if its legitimacy is to be assured without the imposition of force. This was the paradox stressed by Habermas in the above passage from chapter 3. It cannot be escaped by basing legal legitimacy on morality. Law has to provide both norms for action and the institutional framework within which that action must occur. As purely rational, morality provides norms or maxims permitting the evaluation of action, but it does not thereby motivate those actions.[28] The universality of morality is not sufficiently selective; it cannot discern conditions of fair compromise, legitimate negotiation or changes in the will of the partners. Legal institutions can serve morality insofar as they reduce complexity by providing experts who can evaluate conditions that the individual alone cannot understand, or insofar as they create institutions that permit action in complex situations—Habermas's example is giving aid to alleviate famine in Africa—where the action of the individual alone could not fulfill a moral obligation. Legal institutions also insure the motivation to act insofar as they insure that others will also act in conformity with them. In each of these instances, legal institutions perform a systemic function; but their bifunctionality—based on the tension of fact and validity—remains. "As opposed to morality, law does not regulate contexts of interaction *in general* but serves as the medium for the self-organization of legal communities which assert themselves under given historical conditions in their social environment."[29] This self-organization points to the communicative element that must also be present if law is to be legitimate.

The paradoxical relation of private freedom and the public good cannot be avoided by the liberal insistence on the primacy of the "rights of man." The criticism of liberalism's individualist premises is well known. Habermas develops, for example, Michelman's argument that the concept of subjective rights already implies a relation to others, optimally in the form of cooperation and reciprocal recognition. He underlines Young's insistence that rights are not some "thing" that we can "have" on our own.[30] More important, he sees that the implication of his paradox is that a complete legal codification of the rights of man is not possible. Since the legitimacy of rights depends on the "process of agreement among the citizens about the rules of their common life," whatever rights are agreed upon can always be put into question or expanded. This explains a further error of liberalism that appears when the court confuses individual rights with normative values, a procedure that conflates the distinction of fact and validity. As norms, laws are valid whereas values have always to be evaluated; normative laws form a system whereas values compete and are flexible; normative laws are imperative whereas values only recommend a course of action. The result of the conflation of value with rights or laws is an activist judiciary that cannot justify the validity of its own interventions. It extends the function of law beyond its paradoxical and bifunctional role.[31]

The quest for an activist solution to the tension between fact and validity can also take the form of an immanent critique of legal liberalism. In this case, the tension is retained, as is the paradox that expresses the "hinge" function of the law. The immanent critique does not simply oppose social rights to individual rights, as if they were external to each other rather than being bound together by the tension of fact and validity. The immanent critique notes that in order to insure the legitimacy of law, individuals need to have the capacity to exercise their rights as equal citizens in formulating that law; but legal equality (*Gleichheit*) is not the same as factual equality (*Gleichstellung*). From this point of view, the paradox becomes a "dialectic of legal and factual freedom" in which factual equality depends on the social results of legal provisions, whereas legal equality is the competence to decide freely the laws by which the society will be governed.[32] This produces the space for a competition among alternative legal paradigms, in which the liberal and the welfare-state models each seek to offer the framework for the establishment of the legitimacy of the law. The problem, however, is that both of these paradigms share a functionalist interpretation of the law according to which rights serve as a mechanism for horizontal social integration within a society of individuals. By neglecting the vertical dimension—the political dimension of law—they ignore both the negative consequences of legal institutions—the juridification of individual rights or the perverse effects of the new dependencies created by the bureaucratic welfare-state—and the positive role of solidarity that can emerge from political participation.

Habermas's dialectical reformulation of the paradox that preserves the tension of fact and validity leads him to propose a *procedural paradigm* of law. The legitimacy of law depends, first, on the fact that the procedures for its positing are legally institutionalized. This implies, second, that the process of its positing and application is rational. By rational, Habermas means that the legal norms treat all as free and equal members of the society, protecting their personal integrity. This implies, third, that *in the relevant conditions*, equal will be treated equally and unequal treated unequally. Habermas illustrates his argument with a brief history of feminism via a number of paradigms. It passed through the liberal paradigm in which women demanded to be included as citizens, to the welfare-state paradigm that demanded basic social rights necessary for participation, to a procedural paradigm that is able to reflect upon the potential perverse effects of earlier victories, and on the fact that women do not exist as a single collective subject but are affected by specific situations such as age, ethnic origin, sexual orientation, or social conditions of life. The upshot of this "two hundred years of learning" is the recognition that rights are neither individual nor social but rather the means permitting an autonomous individual life-formation *and* participation as a citizen. Its result is the feminist challenge to the notion that equality can be defined within an already existing institutional space and in a culture that have been defined and dominated by men.

The procedural paradigm is not the *Aufhebung* or elimination of the law and its institutions. It provides the criterion for understanding (or criticizing) the legitimacy of these institutions. In this way, the procedural paradigm points to another aspect of the "hinge" function of the law. How, we may ask, did feminism—or any of the other social movements described by Habermas—succeed in institutionalizing their new demands? What makes their successes legitimate? It is one thing for members of the movement, as those who are potentially concerned by the measures taken, to define for themselves what Habermas calls "the relevant aspects" that determine equality. It is another thing for these measures to find a receptive polity that accepts their validity.

That is why some legal theorists seek to broaden the community of legal interpreters beyond the legal profession by expanding the public discussion about "the relevant aspects" and the rights that correspond to them. Habermas takes a different tack by returning to the basic structure of legitimate right as at one and the same time a system of legitimate administrative power and the communicative production of power. Insofar as the law is rooted in the communicative conditions of its production, it must be and remain open to the movement of society, including the demands of the excluded who cannot make strategic use of the already existing legal structures. By translating these demands of society into the language of law—as was suggested by the siege metaphor used in describing the revolutionary project—legal institutions serve to make their demands comprehensible to the administrative power, whose subsequent formulation of them within its own systematic framework as political makes them into laws that are legitimate for the entire society.

Legal institutions thus serve as the medium through which the society and the state can communicate. They permit the self-referential legal and political systems to remain open to impulses from the lifeworld that is their environment. Legal institutions serve to bring together rights-bearing individuals in a society that can know that its rules are legitimate; they serve, in Habermas's metaphor, also to make protests from within that society "audible" to the legally constituted system that administers these rules. But this is only the first step in Habermas's argument. In addition to this discourse-theory of right, which explains how and why a democratic constitutional state institutionalizes procedures and communicative presuppositions permitting a discursive formation of will and opinion through the medium of the law, Habermas presents a communication theory of society, which conceives of the political system instituted by the constitutional state as one of many systems of social action. In the first case, law is said to be legitimate insofar as it preserves the private autonomy of those who, in the exercise of their autonomy, understand themselves as positing the law and thereby assuring its legitimacy. In other words, for the discourse theory of right, private and political autonomy are equiprimordial and mutually entail one another. For the communication theory of society, the political system acquires its specificity from the fact that it is responsible for problems of social integration. It achieves this by means of the interplay between the institutionalized process of will and opinion formation assured by the discourse theory of right and the informal public communication that occurs within a civil society embedded in a life-world.[33] The analysis of this social project is thus a continuation as well as an extension of the legal project.

Social Project

The tasks of the political state increase as society becomes more complex and differentiated. Legal institutions will have to help steer the modern society. They can do so because the "hinge" function of the law opens it to strategic action. However, this strategic use threatens to destroy the tension between fact and validity; and it can produce dysfunctional side effects, for example, by a bureaucracy that is insensitive to the need for individual self-determination by its clients, or by an activist legalism that is blind to the need for receptive social conditions. While such a strategic use of the law may produce results in the short run, it can also threaten the legitimacy of the political state over the longer term. Its error is to neglect the fact that while the law can be used strategically, it alone can define the conditions for its use. The communication theory of society is not independent from the discourse theory of right; the latter showed that the legitimacy of the law that the administration tries to use strategically depends ultimately on the preservation of that autonomy that permits the individual to be also a citizen. In this sense, the imperative that the administration can act legitimately only within the framework of the law implies also the recognition of a self-limitation of the law—what Habermas calls a "counter-steering" that restricts administrative arbitrariness. The communication theory of society will now add to that criterion of legal legitimacy an explanation of the manner in which civil society, and the informal movements within it, can achieve legitimate representation.

True to his own method, Habermas proceeds in his reconstruction of the theory of modern society through a dialogue with its contemporary theorists, seeking to draw out the normative presuppositions on which social integration depends. These normative premises, as communicatively produced, point to the source of the power that empirical analyses take for granted. Social scientists, for example, tend to assume that there exists something called "social power," which is translated directly into politics. In so doing, the analyst takes the standpoint of the observer rather than that of the participant, assuming that the goal of social institutions is to achieve stability by means of a presupposed belief in their legitimacy rather than by analyzing the roots of that legitimacy itself.[34] Pluralism, for example, has an instrumental notion of power as simply the manifestation of social power, which it in turn defines as the ability of organized interests to use the existing legal institutions to achieve their goals. Its only normative assumption is that there exists in fact a more or less equal and justified sharing of social power. When this assumption is empirically falsified, pluralism has recourse to something like Schumpeter's notion of a legitimacy that is acquired as a result of competition among elites for the support of the masses. This, however, leaves unanswered the question of why the nonelites accept the political choices offered by the elites. The only plausible answer is that these offers are rational, but that ignores the further question of how this rational elite becomes sensitive to social interests (other than its own).

The failure of social scientists to explain the legitimacy of the social relations they describe has led to the idea that we are facing a crisis in which the state is overwhelmed by the demands that emanate from society. Neoconservatives claim that democracy must be restricted in order to save democracy (as in Samuel Huntington and the Trilateral Commission Report). In this picture, the state is assumed no longer to be capable of planning rationally for the good of society; the state either simply reacts to crises or intervenes only to avoid them. The administrative state thus shows its own limits and is incapable of drawing new support from the population, which is decreasingly loyal to the established political parties. At this point, systems theory or decision theory can be invoked to explain what remains of the old image of the state's tasks. In this vein, the idea of a "supervisory state" that works on a corporatist society by offering means of incitation or avoidance of action by groups within society can be proposed (as Habermas shows in the work of Wilke). Or the juridical nature of the state's intervention can be interpreted as inciting social actors to reflexively reevaluate their preferences (as analyzed in the work of Peters). Aside from the immanent difficulties in these approaches, Habermas notes that they forget that the supervisory state can become paternalistic, that experts disagree among themselves, and that public opinion does play a role in the redefinition of social goals. More importantly, these positions make a normative assumption about historical progress; they assume that since the increased complexity of the capitalist economy and the administrative state were previously accompanied by an increased inclusion of the citizen, this progressive course will continue. But that, replies Habermas, is contingent; indeed, the world of today seems marked by the increasing marginalization of ever-greater portions of the globe, and of strata or groups within the nation.

To talk of a crisis makes sense only from the standpoint of the participants. If there is a crisis of the political state, its analysis must begin from the society, which finds that its relevant needs, interests, or problems cannot get a hearing in the established system. Society, in its plurality, expresses itself in what Habermas calls the public sphere. This public space reproduces itself by means of communicative action. Because it is not a system, public space remains open to the exterior; it does not seek solutions to specific problems, since these problems can emerge only within an already existing public space. Specialized knowledge and the codes of experts are of no use in this space, which is without strategic goals. Freed from the need to act because its function is to permit problems to emerge rather than to (dis)solve them, the public sphere becomes increasingly intellectualized and highly reflexive. Of course, actors can try to use the public sphere to achieve their own goals strategically, by the application of organizational power or through the expenditure of money. This manipulation may succeed, but to do so they will ultimately have to use arguments to justify their cause—and these arguments can always, in principle, be reopened to criticism. In this way, all become participants in the public space and in its reproduction through communication. However, the problem is that this participatory structure remains latent most of the time; its presence is felt only at moments of mobilization.[35]

Rather than attempt to account for an objective crisis of the apparatus of the state system, one must focus attention on the society and the question of its mobilization as a public. The public sphere concerns all those who are potentially affected by a given measure, even when they are affected only in their private lives. That is why, says Habermas, art, religion, and literature can have a political import; the line between the public and the private spheres is not fixed but depends on the communication among "private persons who have come together as a public."[36] The experience of totalitarianism shows the importance of the preservation of the autonomy of the private sphere from which, when necessary, the public space can be rejuvenated; its attempt to destroy the communicative structures of the private sphere, the family, school, neighborhood, professional organizations, and the like proved to be self-defeating in the end. But, continues Habermas, the guarantee of basic rights cannot by itself preserve the public sphere and the autonomy of civil society. This is where social movements play their role, alongside of what Nancy Fraser calls "weak publics."[37]

The latter constitute subcultures that emerge spontaneously, whose boundaries remain fluid, and that remain open to new identities, needs, and problems. Such weak publics are not as effective as institutionalized publics, organized around specific causes; and they can be easily repressed or ignored. They may, however, crystallize in the form of social movements.

Habermas's account of social movements clarifies his communication theory of society and points toward its political implications. These movements are situated at the hinge where the systematic imperatives of constitutionally institutionalized opinion formation meet with communicatively engendered power. The movements emerge from society; they create a public space in which their demands or needs can be articulated and debated. In this sense, the social movements are agents of cultural modernity, which prevent the freezing of social patterns and expectations. But their communicatively engendered power cannot as such be transformed directly into political power. Their action has to be interpreted in terms of the metaphor of the siege. It is only when their demands are adapted and reformulated by the political system that they can begin to be institutionalized. This may appear to imply a compromise on their part; but such negotiation is justified as long as the conditions of the compromise meet the legitimation criteria presented by the discourse theory of right.[38] That is why the social movements pursue a double strategy; besides their explicit goal, they must be concerned constantly to preserve and to reproduce the public space within which their power could emerge in the first place. The social movements are "self-limited" with regard to the political system precisely because their complete inclusion within that system would destroy the public space from which they emerged. That is why social movements must be constantly on the alert for any threat that may appear anywhere—even concerning movements different from themselves—that would deny the autonomy and plurality of public life.

This theorization of social movements confirms the argument for radical democracy as the legacy of the revolutionary movements. Social movements, and the civil society in which they are embedded, can never become an autonomous, self-managing unity. Civil society can immediately transform only itself; it can have an impact on the political system only mediately. It can produce only what Talcott Parsons called "influence," not political power, and even this influence must be filtered through the institutionalized procedure of democratic will formation, for only then can it be examined and judged legitimate.

That is why Habermas distinguishes between social actors who are pre-identified by their issues and groups and those that must first produce their identity and constantly reassert it, as well as between actors using an existing public space and the excluded or minorities that must first constitute a public space. This distinction permits him to point to the danger of a populism that makes use of the modern phenomenon of a public sphere to propound premodern themes and demands. As opposed to such populist atavism, Habermas's social movements are modern. By bringing up new themes, questioning the traditional lines between the public and private, raising new issues, and thematizing new problems, they pursue the decentering that began with the overthrow of absolutism and contribute to maintaining the democratic process.

As a social project, radical democracy is not an end in itself; its existence presupposes the democratic constitutional state within which it functions and to whose function it, in turn, contributes. Radical democracy is not itself a politics; it can realize its political goals only by means of the hinge function that turns it at once toward the legal institutions of the political system (which also preserve the autonomy of the individuals who become actors in social movements or civil society) and toward the public space whose openness its actions regenerate (even while they are directed also to the political system). In this way, the social movements prevent the political system from neglecting the normative perspective of the participants, which was seen to lead to a dysfunctional or insensitive administration or judiciary, if not to a political crisis.

At the same time, these social movements can be seen as defining the political. Habermas recurs repeatedly to theatrical metaphors in this context, speaking of a "dramatization" (*Inszenierung*) or a theatrical *mise en scène* to designate the manner in which, as he puts it elsewhere, "cases become cases of conflict."[39] This permits the public debate about "the relevant aspects" of equality, which was raised, for example, by feminism. A similar process is illustrated by movements of civil disobedience, whose analysis has the added benefit of making clear why Habermas insists on the self-limiting character of social movements and their need to lay siege to and ultimately to affect the political system.

Social movements (and civil society) thus articulate the two moments into which the autonomy of the political that emerged with the overthrow of absolutism has divided. The problem is that the self-steering political system defines its own goal as the reproduction of existing social relations; this permits it to be constantly active whereas the public sphere can fall into a state of quiescence.[40] Yet Habermas claims that this public sphere can be mobilized, and that at the moment of mobilization the power relations between civil society and the political system are changed. This mobilization appears when a perceived crisis leads the public to intervene in "the critical moments of an accelerated history."[41] History is said to show that social movements perceive difficulties before the state becomes aware of them. In so doing, they actuate a "lawfulness which otherwise remains latent."[42] This is possible because the political system would not be legitimate (for the participants) if it did not draw its legitimacy from its rootedness in the communicatively produced power of civil society and its autonomous actors. Once these private individuals come together as an autonomous public, the political system can be forced to transform itself. Habermas's political project is thus rooted in, and depends on, his social project—just as his social project (as formulated by the communications theory of society) depended ultimately on the legal project (as formulated in the discourse theory of right).

Political Project

The interweaving of analytical domains continues at the level of the political. Although modernity was inaugurated by the overthrow of absolutism, the individual autonomy and systemic complexity that it makes possible were seen to presuppose the vertical dimension whose concretization appears as the political state.[43] The legitimacy of this political state depends not only on its ability to act for the whole of society but also on its embeddedness in the communicative society of autonomous (public and private) individuals. For this reason, the political state can be controlled, its programs put into question, and its relation to the individual modified. The result is a double limitation that corresponds to the "division of the concept of the political" that we saw Habermas describe as emerging in the wake of the French Revolution: "Politics as a whole cannot be identified with the praxis of those who talk with one another in order to act as politically autonomous. . . . The concept of the political is legitimately extended *also* to the application of administrative power in, and the competition for access to, the political system."[44] This reciprocal limitation exercised by each of the moments into which the modern notion of the political divides has a further implication. To the vertical dimension of the political, whose presence above the relations among autonomous individuals makes for their stability corresponds another vertical dimension that, so to speak, lies "below" them, and that also serves to insure their stability. This is what Habermas calls the "life-world," a concept that now is given an articulated political place.

The emergence of the life-world is a further characteristic of modernity. Habermas shows how premodern societies made use of custom and ritual in order to regulate their social relations from without. The overcoming of such external forms of societal legitimation leaves autonomous individuals with the task of finding new regulatory forms, of which the law is the most evident illustration. But not all behavior is, or should be, legally regulated; the danger of a "colonization" that restricts individual freedom is always present.[45] This is where the life-world acquires its role. It is a kind of background consensus that permits individuals to stabilize, or to make less risky, their expectations about the behavior of others. Because its function is to reduce complexity, the life-world can be understood to function analogously to the systems of the economy or the political administration. This systemic character explains how it can further differentiate itself into an increasingly complex structure. The legal system is only one illustration of such a process, of which the system of scientific knowledge, the educational system, or the family are other examples. As autonomous systems, each of these can specialize and develop its own codes, experts, and logic. In this sense, one might be tempted to speak of the rationalization of the life-world; but the problem is more complex.

The rationalization of the life-world is not a systemic project; its logic is political. Insofar as the life-world serves to regulate relations among autonomous individuals, its tasks are the formation of personal identity, the socialization of that individual, and the provision of a culture within which these processes can occur. Each of these tasks, which presuppose the others, can become the province of a specialized system or systems. As systems, each of these is similar to the economic and administrative systems; but each differs in one fundamental respect: the medium by which it organizes itself and expresses its goals. The economy is organized by money, the administration by power, whereas the systems of the life-world depend on communication for the articulation of their goals and the organization of their institutions. This fundamental difference among the organizing media poses problems of coordination; at its extreme, it can lead to the phenomenon of colonization insofar as relations that should be governed by processes of communicative decision become subject to the organizational logic of the economy (money) or the administration (power). This distortion—and its democratic correction—is made possible by the hinge function of the medium of the law.[46] Insofar as the discourse theory of law has shown that legitimate law is rooted in the communicative interaction of autonomous individuals, that law must be receptive to the signals emitted by the systems of identity formation, socialization, and culture; but insofar as its formal character is compatible with the imperatives of the economic and administrative system, it is receptive also to the signals emitted by these systems. Habermas's social project sought to show how the law can serve the communicative process by which "private persons constitute themselves as a public"; his political project has to show why law's legitimacy depends on its actually playing that role.

The concept of the life-world and of its rationalization can be easily misinterpreted. As a taken-for-granted background consensus, the life-world can never be thematized as such; that would contradict its very nature and destroy its function. It is not a "macro-organization to which members can belong, nor an association to which individuals can adhere, nor a collective composed of those who belong to it." The life-world is not "a whole emerging from parts," even though "socialized individuals could not assert themselves as subjects if they did not find support in the stabilized relations articulated in the cultural tradition and the legitimate orders of reciprocal recognition—and vice-versa." Habermas speaks, in italics, of an *equi-primordiality* of communicative everyday praxis (which he says is "certainly" centered in the life-world) and the interactions of cultural reproduction, social integration, and socialization.[47] These latter were seen to be organizable also as systems; in that way, they could serve to reduce complexity and stabilize behavioral expectations. This does not mean, however, that the rationalization of the life-world would be its totalization as an all-encompassing system—although it does point to that possibility. Its implication is that Habermas's political project will have to articulate the relation between system and life-world. The political project is thus the culmination and specification of the legal and social project in the form of a communicative rationalization of the life-world.[48]

Because systems belong to the life-world—rather than being a part of it—its rationalization affects them as well. This is why the modern form of the political was said to present the division of the administrative state and the communicatively produced power that emerges from the life-world. Habermas turns to the regulatory dilemmas of the contemporary social state to illustrate the problems posed by the relation of system to life-world. The state may suffer either from irrelevance, failed steering, or its own self-destructive attempts to use the legal medium in a manner that deprives it of its normative validity in the eyes of those concerned. In each case, the source of the failure lies in the separation of the administrative decision making from the communicative power engendered by the life-world. The state becomes irrelevant when the measures it proposes do not find a receptive public attuned to carrying them out; its steering failures arise when it cannot "hear" the particular public or private demands of its citizens; its normative deficit comes from its neglect of the need to assure legitimacy to its proposals. However, the problem does not lie solely on the side of the administrative system. The life-world may lack the resources necessary to formulate and transmit its demands; its demands may themselves be distorted by strategic interests or produced by forms of public communication whose means corrupt the ends its seeks; or, in the inverse movement to the self-destructive state, it may take itself as both means and end in the quest for complete self-transparency in the ideal of self-management. Any of these cases can produce a crisis.

The political rationalization of the life-world does not seek a kind of functional equilibrium between system and life-world. That would imply that the two domains can be separated from one another by impermeable barriers and that their relation is external rather than immanent to one another. The liberal image of a state relating to a self-governing economic society in whose functions it intervenes only to protect the freedoms necessary for that (economic) self-government cannot be justified. The contemporary state no longer simply reacts to problems; it must plan, deal with risks, and try to reduce complexity. This future-orientation means that it formulates its measures in general terms that must then be interpreted by administrative or judicial agencies. The old functional division of powers is put into question in this process, as judges or quasi-judicial agencies assume legislative functions. The legislator, in turn, is marginalized by the administrator, who enters into negotiations with social systems that can often resist its steering. In the process, state and society meet on one horizontal plane. Political parties abandon their role in the formation of public opinion to become a part of the state machinery, charged with reproducing its elites and producing mass loyalty. Common to all of these functionalist successors to the classical liberal account is the stress on the media of money, information, or expert knowledge rather than on the normative means offered by the law. As the system responsible for social integration, politics has to be able to communicate with these other domains; yet it can do so legitimately only through the legal medium.

The political function of the law is not limited to steering the other social systems. Because the law is also engendered by the communicative power of the life-world, its intervention in the political system affects that life-world as well. Habermas speaks here of a "counter-steering" by which the law forces the life-world to reflect on itself (in the practical form of social movements, and most explicitly in the form of civil disobedience).[49] The role of the law is not simply to represent or incarnate the communicative power of the life-world; its bifunctionality means that it serves also to preserve the tension between fact and validity that makes the life-world dynamic and open to the new. This leads Habermas to propose a reformulation of the classical concept of the division of powers. The articulation of the legislative, executive, and judicial is not explained by the functional role of each: the division of powers insures, rather, that administration is bound by democratically posited law. Further, this division should not be seen simply as a protection of the individual from the state. It guarantees, moreover, that politics does not become a separate system functioning according to its own rules and colonizing the life-world. Only in this way can the administration retain its legitimacy. That is, the legal hinge opens the administration itself so that it can hear the input of the life-world; and the life-world, in turn, is led (by the counter-steering) to reflect upon itself because it must formulate its demands in the language of law if it wants to be heard.

The law is thus not a neutral medium parceled out to the distinct and divided functions of law giving, law application, and law realization. Because the law is embedded in the communicative structures of the life-world, the distinction among the political powers depends on the kind of argumentative ground that each can offer to justify its measures. Some problems need concrete solutions, others can be resolved through the protection of rights, while yet others are clarified by communication about their grounds.[50] The legislator must ask, for example, should I decide this matter, and if not, who will? She must ask who will realize the proposed law—the citizens or the courts? Similarly, the administration cannot hide behind neutral procedures or the possession of expertise. Its measures gain both legitimacy and efficacity not only by protecting citizens' rights by remaining within legal forms but also by public participation in administrative processes. In both cases, the justice of the choices made depends on the protection of the procedural conditions that insure the continuation of the democratic process as it is defined by the twin programs of a discourse theory of right (which explains the kind of grounds that are required and the procedures for their validity), and the communications theory of society (which insures the autonomy of both the system and the life-world). This implies that the political project is defined neither by the classical notion of representation nor by that of a plebiscitary democracy. Both of those models assume the prior existence of the popular will, whereas Habermas's procedural democracy is concerned with the conditions under which such a will can be produced, legitimated, and eventually changed.

Habermas's political project and the process of the rationalization of the life-world are thus one and the same. The political project began with the revolutionary overthrow of absolutism and the advent of modernity. The life-world emerged from the same movement. With it came the autonomous individual who had to invent the implicit and explicit conventions by which its relations with others would be governed. The systems of the economy and of political administration began to evolve their own special codes, reducing the complexity of the life-world and insuring the stability of behavioral expectations. Because these systems could also come to threaten the autonomy of the life-world, it had to develop another system by which to protect itself (and to reduce the complexity of its own relations): this new system is the law. In its system character, the law can be abused as well as used for strategic ends. To avoid this, more than just a constitution is needed; and more is entailed in the very nature of the law, whose openness to the life-world contains the potential for its democratic legitimation. Such a democracy, however, is not identical with the life-world, which, because it is not a real subject, cannot as such act as if it were a unified agent. The life-world expresses itself through plural social movements, whose efficacy depends on their ability to articulate themselves in the language of the law. Although only the political system can act on society, the life-world can act on itself through this plural democratic political process. As a result, it transforms itself, increasing its own rationality by generalizing this form of self-reflexion that is able to put discursively into questions its taken-for-granted norms.

What Is Democratic Culture?

Habermas's communications theory of society is often taken to propose simply the social concretization of the linguistic model of "discourse," with its counterfactual assumptions about the equality of the participants, their right to demand grounds for all opinions or measures, and their common quest for normative validity in all domains. *Faktizität und Geltung* shows the inadequacy of such an interpretation.[51] Habermas insists that no complex society presents a pure model of democratic institutions; and he knows too that individuals are fallible, weak willed, lacking competence, or forced to operate under pressure. One of the functions of law is to correct these weaknesses and to compensate for the inadequacy of morality. But law is more than just a functional system. It also provides counter-steering, which serves to maintain complexity. "This poses the question of how far the normative counter-steering of constitutional state institutions can compensate for those communicative, cognitive and motivational limitations which are presupposed by a deliberative politics and the translation of communicative into administrative power."[52] This question provides Habermas's transition to chapter 8, which elaborates the kernel of his social project under the heading "The Role of Civil Society and the Political Public Sphere." We have seen that, for Habermas, social movements and political publics take part in the modernization and rationalization of the life-world. That demonstration, however, runs the risk of presupposing what it wanted to prove: the existence of a democratic political culture.

Habermas's addition to not just one but two vertical dimensions was central to his formulation of the communication theory of society and to its distinction from the discourse theory of law. Neither of these vertical dimensions—the political system and the life-world—can exist without the other, just as the private and the public are equiprimordial and depend on each other. This was the implication of the previously cited paradox, which is worth repeating here.

It is paradoxical for this reason, that the rights of the citizen as subjective rights on the one hand have the same structure as all rights: they create for the individual spheres in which he can express his free will [*Willkür*]. In spite of the distinctions in the modalities of the use of these rights, political rights must be able to be interpreted as subjective freedoms to act which make only legal behavior a duty; that is, they *liberate* motives for rule-following behavior. On the other hand, the democratic process of legislation must confront its participants with the normative expectations of an orientation to the common good because this process itself can draw its legitimating force only from the process of an agreement [*Verständigung*] of the citizens about the rules of their common life. In modern societies, law can only fulfill the function of stabilizing expectations when it preserves an internal connection with the social-integrative force of communicative action.[53]

But at the conclusion to chapter 4, which begins from this paradox, Habermas admits that legal institutions cannot exist "without the initiatives of a population *habituated* to freedom. Its spontaneity cannot be forced by law; it regenerates itself from traditions of freedom and maintains itself in the associative relations of a liberal political culture."[54]

Although Habermas describes various aspects of this liberal political culture, which presumably belongs to the life-world as one of its (communicatively reproduced) systems, he does not explain its origin. Yet its presence is crucial to the political success of his social project. Without it, as we saw, social movements might well take the negative form of atavistic populism using modern forms for regressive ends. This liberal culture formed the "lawfulness that otherwise remains latent," which is mobilized by social movements. It is the precondition for the existence of a public of spectators who will be moved by the "theatrical" politics that transforms "cases into cases of conflict" as well as for the success of movements of civil disobedience.[55] Habermas seems to equate it with a rationalized life-world, but that either simply restates the problem or forgets that the rationalized life-world entails the existence of social systems as well.[56] The implication seems to be that the liberal culture required for the success of Habermas's system can exist only insofar as his system exists (or else his theory would be historically relative). That ignores the claim that Habermas's project itself contributes also to the rationalization of the life-world (and that it can claim universal validity). It ignores also the counter-steering function that maintains the complexity of the life-world by constraining it to admit its own self-limitation and its need to appeal to the political (and legal) systems in order to maintain and to reproduce itself.

The problem can be posed more clearly if we escape finally from the immanent constraints of Habermas's own argument to return the question of the revolutionary legacy that we saw him seeking to inherit. At the same time, we can return to the question of the relation of his variant of a *Rechtsphilosophie* to the Hegelian edifice. The democratic project seeks to replace the quest for "the" revolution, while the intersubjective and participatory discourse theory of right and communication theory of society are to replace the monological unfolding of the Hegelian Spirit in the form of Will. Common to both of these projects is the notion of solidarity. At the level of the communication theory of society, solidarity is defined as a "resource" needed by the administrative political state in order to insure the legitimacy of its measures. It is a scarce resource that cannot be reproduced by any system or drawn by force from the life-world. The democratic procedural model proposed by the discourse theory of law showed how this legitimacy could be produced by means of a democratically articulated legal structure. The paradoxical preservation of individual private autonomy in the process and through the results of the making, administering, and actualizing of law insured a *de jure* solidarity among equals. The social project represented by the self-limiting social movements that must always insure the preservation of the public space can be seen as its *de facto* existence, and as the catalyst that prevents the distortions that produce colonization.

The unrealized legacy of the revolutionary movement is that emblematic *fraternité* that it inscribed on its banner. For two centuries, individualism has been the paradigm in terms of which modern political and legal systems have been constructed and construed. Even the arguments for the welfare state have had to appeal to this principle of individualism to justify the demand for social equality. The attempt to invert that paradigm by stressing equality even at the cost of liberty was no more successful in inventing new forms of fraternity. The dilemma is that fraternity cannot be conceived of as producing a sort of macrosubject, a whole that dissolves the parts within itself. Although Habermas does not make this point explicitly, his critique of subject philosophy implies it. The result is thus a defense of liberalism not for its own sake but as the precondition for the democratic process that, as process, makes possible the movement of fraternity. Fraternity cannot be presupposed as the principle of politics, any more than culture can assume that role. Politics is concerned, as system, with specific actions and choices; democratic procedures serve to legitimate, or criticize or alter, these actions and choices. This is why Habermas criticized Rawls's notion of an "overlapping consensus," which, as cultural, explains why individuals would accept laws but does not accomplish the other function incumbent on legal institutions: to mediate institutionally the particular relations between the systems of the economy and administration and the life-world.[57]

Conceived in this manner, the interrelation among Habermas's legal, social, and political projects is articulated by the concept of a democratic culture. As in the case of Hegel's *Sittlichkeit*, which is both presupposed and preserved by the domains of Abstract Right and Morality, Habermas's concept of a democratic culture is the precondition and yet the result of his systematic theory. But Hegel's *Sittlichkeit* was modeled on the classical Greek notion of a unified polity, and it clashes with the modern social relations that he described, such that his political state seems often to be in contradiction with itself (putting for example the monarch as the first moment of immediacy instead of having the system culminate in the monarchical individuality). Habermas, on the other hand, by starting from the revolutionary project can situate his theory within the continuity of that project, such that his legal project culminates in the social project, which in turn culminates in the political project, which finally points toward the further rationalization of the life-world as its implication. The concluding moment, the quest for a rational life-world, restates what was implicit at the outset, making it explicit and self-reflexive in the procedural paradigm with which the book concludes.

The conclusion of Habermas's system does not remain static; self-reflexivity is not stasis. This is the implication of Habermas's citation of Ingeborg Maus in his final arguments. The "kernel of the proceduralistic paradigm of right, according to a formulation of I. Maus, is the 'thorough combination and reciprocal mediation of legally institutionalized and non-institutionalized popular sovereignty.' ''[58] This has implications for the question posed by, and to, the catching-up revolutions of 1989. The challenge is not simply to introduce constitutional protections and procedures to replace the arbitrary and bureaucratic forms of totalitarianism. Indeed, that attempt may well present a danger insofar as the legal institutions have been seen to carry with them the possibility of the colonization of the non-institutional life-world. It is not liberal institutions that are needed to catch up to the West, but rather the culture of democracy that Ingeborg Maus calls, significantly, "non-institutionalized popular sovereignty." The concept cannot mean simply the protection of private or corporate autonomy; Habermas's paradox has shown that such autonomy cannot perdure without the autonomy of the public sphere. Noninstitutionalized popular sovereignty is not simply the always-present background consensus provided by the life-world; for, as we have seen, the life-world alone cannot act. Nor does it suffice to call for—or to wait for—social movements, popular associations, or nonpolitical citizen actions; these can only have resonance if the liberal culture that they are supposed to produce already exists.

The realization of the revolutions of 1989 depends on their ability to reflect on themselves as revolutions. This self-reflexivity, which is also the culmination of Habermas's system, results from the interplay of steering by the communicative power of the public sphere and counter-steering by the imperatives of the political system on that public sphere. The danger is double: that the political system in fact be replaced by the world market on which influence cannot be exerted; and that this will result in the inability of the public sphere to rational-ize itself. In this sense, the revolutions of 1989 have to catch up with the Western model of the nation-state just at the moment when, according to Habermas's own notion of "constitutional patriotism," that traditional model has supposedly lost its hold. The solidarity that Habermas hopes to make possible is not the mute coexistence of individuals in a prereflexive life-world; but it cannot be reduced either to the background knowledge that permits me to regulate my expecta-tions about the behavior of others. Solidarity can be expressed only through the political system, whose imperatives only apparently stand opposed to that life-world. The catching-up of the East calls, in this sense, on the West to catch up to its own principles by redefining the political rather than seeking to avoid its paradoxes by appeal to economic, administrative, or judicial necessity. In this sense, liberal culture and radical democratic politics mutually imply one another.[59]

Notes

1. There are many further parallels as well. Both enterprises are qualified by their subtitles. Hegel's *Grundlinien der Philosophie des Rechts* offers an apparently modest "Naturrecht und Staatswissenschaft in Grundrisse." In fact, Hegel, like Habermas, seeks to account for philosophical questions, such as the relations of ethics and law, of state and society, or the nature of legitimate law, as well as institutional questions, such as the division of powers or the structure and justification of legal proceedings, and sociological questions, such as how to account for the changes that a complex society has delegated to its legal and political institutions, the limits and self-limitations on the spheres of justice and politics, and the problem of the sociological media-

tions necessary to preserve the unity of a society whose foundation is the rights-bearing individual. As does Habermas, Hegel explains the logic behind well-intentioned contemporary political proposals before tellingly criticizing their misunderstanding—for example, the effects of overproduction or the marginalization of the laboring class. The power of both theories, however, lies in their systematic claims. Their difference is not explained by historical conditions, as Habermas's treatment of Hegel's near-contemporaries, the German liberals, indicates. More important, in Habermas's eyes, Hegel is a conservative, seeking to eliminate the democratic implications of the French Revolution on whose positive legacy Habermas insists. See, on this latter point, Habermas's early essay "Hegels Kritik der Französischen Revolution," in *Theorie und Praxis* (Neuwied: Luchterhand Verlag, 1963), 89–107. For a different reading of Hegel, see Dick Howard, "Revolution as the Foundation of Political Philosophy," in *Hegel and Transcendental Philosophy: Essays in Honor of Klaus Hartmann*, edited by H. T. Engelhart and Terry Pinkard (Dordrecht: Kluwer, 1993).

2. Jürgen Habermas, *Faktizität und Geltung* (Frankfurt am Main: Suhrkamp Verlag, 1992), 13. Hereafter, I will cite this volume as *FG*.

3. Ibid., 12. A similar argument returns on the final page (537) of the book.

4. Although this issue will be addressed in detail below, it should be noted at the outset that Habermas's account explicitly revises the dualistic notion of law—as institution and as medium—that he had proposed at the end of his *Theory of Communicative Action*. The social-integrative function of legal norms and the legal forms that are used for steering the political process cannot be so simply distinguished. See *FG*, 502n for this self-critique.

5. Habermas's brief foreword to the volume, written in March of 1990, can be cited in its entirety. "The revolutionary processes in the GDR and in East-Central Europe maintain their hold on our passions, even though the original enthusiasm has given place to fear and skepticism. Events are changing the international and the inter-German scene nearly daily. But the catching-up revolution throws no new light on our *old* problems. These, as Adorno would have said, negative constants in the midst of an accelerated history may justify a certain continuity in my positions during the past years" (*Die nachholende Revolution* [Frankfurt am Main: Suhrkamp Verlag, 1990], 7).

6. I have suggested a somewhat different interpretation of the import of this historical period in "The Marxian Legacy and the Problem of Democracy," chapter 2 of this volume. My claim is that the problems raised by the French Revolution's overthrow of absolutism and invention of the individual as a bearer of rights, posed a problem that liberalism on the one hand and socialism on the other constantly sought to avoid. The revolutions of 1989, I argue, have returned this problem to the forefront of political theory and practice. My analysis of 1789 and its legacy is consonant with that of Habermas. Our difference lies only in our interpretation of the significance of 1989. That is another reason why I begin this discussion with his account of 1989,

whose uniqueness I would underline more than does Habermas. His depiction of a continuity in leftist politics is more of a self-description than it is, alas, an account of general tendencies—a point that honors his own self-critical rigor.

7. That is why Habermas adds another citation from the *Manifesto*: "And as in material, so also in intellectual production. The intellectual creations of individual nations become common property. National one-sidedness and narrow-mindedness become more and more impossible, and from the numerous national and local literatures there arises a world literature."

8. As Habermas notes, "Marxism as Critique" was the title of his first systematic confrontation with Marxism, published in 1960 and reprinted in *Theorie und Praxis*, cited above. The problem that Habermas addresses here—that of self-referential systems separated from the life-world over which they exercise control—was at that time more usually formulated in the Hegelian-Marxist language of alienation. Habermas gave it a first systems-theoretical formulation in *Legitimation Problems of Late Capitalism* (1973), but he finds an adequate solution, as we shall see, only in the present work.

9. Habermas, *Die nachholende Revolution*, 196. With regard to Habermas's description of the 1960s New Left, see chapter 11 of this volume for a contrast of the American and European perspectives.

10. I will use the term "constitutional state" as the equivalent of the German *Rechtsstaat*. There is an ambiguity involved in the German term. The explicit goal of the French Revolution was the creation of a republic, a concept that could be equated with the German term *Rechtsstaat* insofar as it implies that the law is universal and applied impartially to all. Only under republican conditions does democratic participation become both possible and necessary. In Germany, however, the *Rechtsstaat* took the nondemocratic form of an *Obrigkeitsstaat* until the Weimar Republic. Because Habermas does not consider the French case in *Faktizität und Geltung*, his critique of republicanism is directed against the American form of communitarian legal theories most forcefully articulated by Frank Michelman. The result can be an at times misleading appeal to democracy as a kind of autonomous or protean political form, as if the self-management of society in the form of a basis democracy were the goal. Habermas explicitly rejects this conclusion, for example in his critique of Joshua Cohen (*FG*, 369ff). He generally speaks about a *verfaßte* (i.e., constitutionalized) democracy, and insists that it must be embedded in a "liberal political culture." The problems presented by this latter notion will concern us later. For the moment, it should be noted that when Habermas does, on occasion, make use of the French concept of the republic, he also sees its radical democratic implications for the notion of popular sovereignty. On this latter point, see *FG*, 364ff, which, however, follows a critical discussion of the American-communitarian variant of republicanism from which Habermas does not demarcate this more specific usage, to which I will return in part 2's discussion of what he calls the "vertical dimension" of social unity.

11. "Ist der Herzschlag der Revolution zum Stillstand gekommen? Volks-

souveränität als Verfahren. Ein normativer Begriff der Öffentlichkeit," in *Die Ideen von 1789 in der deutschen Rezeption*, edited by Forum für Philosophie Bad Homburg (Frankfurt am Main: Suhrkamp Verlag, 1989), 11. This essay is reprinted as "Volkssouveränität als Verfahren" in *Faktizität und Geltung*, 600–631. I will cite from the original publication.

12. Habermas had proposed this distinction already in his critique of Hannah Arendt ("H. Arendts Begriff der Macht," in *Philosophisch-politische Profile* [Frankfurt am Main: Suhrkamp Verlag, 1981], 228–48).

13. *FG*, 31.

14. Ibid., 32–33.

15. Habermas, *Die nachholende Revolution*, 201.

16. Ibid., 202

17. Forum für Philosophie Bad Homburg, ed., *Die Ideen von 1789*, 34.

18. Ibid., 34 (emphasis added).

19. See note 4 above regarding Habermas's self-critique on this point.

20. I have tried to justify this claim in the afterword to the second edition of *The Marxian Legacy* (Minneapolis: University of Minnesota Press, and London: Macmillan, 1988), 286–97. On the earlier evolution of Habermas's conception of the political, see 80–114.

21. In "Entgegnung," in *Kommunikatives Handeln. Beiträge zu Jürgen Habermas' Theorie des kommunikativen Handelns*, edited by Axel Honneth and Hans Joas (Frankfurt am Main: Suhrkamp Verlag, 1986), 393. My argument with Habermas in the afterword to *The Marxian Legacy* was that his stress on the state as a *Steuerstaat* (both steering and taxing) led to difficulties that could be corrected by concentration on the notion of a *Rechtsstaat*, and that the law could serve the kind of "hinge" function that Habermas gives it in *Faktizität und Geltung*.

22. See *Legitimationsprobleme im Spätkapitalismus* (Frankfurt am Main: Suhrkamp Verlag, 1973). For a commentary, see *The Marxian Legacy*, especially 80–89 and 108–14.

23. This neglect, which is typical of Marxists since Marx, is criticized by Claude Lefort, who calls attention as well to the work of Ernst Kantorowicz, *The King's Two Bodies*, to which I will refer in a moment. That Habermas avoids the category of the theologicopolitical is no doubt due to the fact that its influence in Germany was owed to its use by Carl Schmitt (and the Young Conservatives, with whom Kantorowicz was at one time associated) as a weapon against the Weimar Republic. See, on Schmitt, "Die Schrecken der Autonomie," in *Eine Art Schadensabwicklung* (Frankfurt am Main: Suhrkamp Verlag, 1987), 103–14. On the Young Conservatives, see "Die Kulturkritik der Neokonservativen in den USA und in der Bundesrepublik," in *Die neue Unübersichtlichkeit* (Frankfurt am Main: Suhrkamp Verlag, 1985), 30–56.

24. See the citations at footnote 9 above.

25. It opens as well the space for the development of Habermas's radical democratic political theory, to which I return in more detail in part 4. For the

moment, attention should be called to the discussion of republicanism at note 10. The French use of that concept at *FG*, 364, leads Habermas to insist that the quest to embody the absent sovereign must fail, but that what he calls liberalism's more "realist" attempt to formulate a representative democracy is also unsatisfactory since it, too, presupposes the notion of a whole that, although divided, seeks to "express" itself in its plurality. Habermas proposes instead of these subject-centered conceptions a discourse theory of democracy within a decentered society where sovereignty exists neither in the republican people nor in the liberal rules of constitutionalism but in the communicative power that emerges from the self-organization of a legally constituted community. He insists, once again, that this does not imply that all of society should be organized in this way. The political remains a specific system whose structural logic must also be studied for its own sake.

26. *FG*, 110–11.

27. Chapters 5 and 6 deal with questions immanent to legal theory per se and are dealt with here only insofar as they concern the broader questions with which I am concerned. Chapters 7 and 8 present Habermas's procedural concept of democracy and his account of the role of civil society and of the political public sphere. Chapter 9 returns to the bifunctional duality of law by means of the notion of a competition among legal paradigms in which the legal "hinge" of chapter 1 takes the form of a dialectic of legal and factual equality.

28. This is also Habermas's objection to Rawls's notion of an "overlapping consensus" (*FG*, 80ff). In order to insure the motivational aspect of law, which cannot be based on force, Habermas turns in chapter 3 to the immanent perspective that treats law as a system of action rather than just a system of rules.

29. *FG*, 188.

30. On Michelman, see *FG*, 116ff; on Young, see 505.

31. Although I have presented the critique of judicial activism from the side of liberalism, a similar criticism is addressed to the "republicanism" defended, for example, by Michelman. There too the normative and the evaluative dimensions are conflated in the attempt to realize social solidarity against the impersonal systemic imperatives of the economy and the administrative state. Similarly, Ackerman's extension of Thomas Kuhn's model to argue that special cases like the New Deal testify to a latent popular will that, by extension, decisions of the Supreme Court are supposed to represent is criticized for a "vitalism" that presupposes what it wants to prove. What is more, the result of this argument contradicts its own goal by justifying a judicial activism that would be unnecessary if the republican polity—which this vitalism presupposes—in fact existed (*FG*, 337–48).

32. Ibid., 493ff and 501. Habermas offers a detailed account of the competition between the liberal and the welfare-state paradigm whose upshot is depicted in a graphic comparison of the methodological presuppositions of each. The result shows a shift in the observer perspective from the primacy of

action to that of system, while the actor perspective shifts from the image of a spontaneously formed society to that of society as a kind of "second nature" into which intervention is possible (Ibid., 489).

33. Habermas returns to and underlines this distinction between the discourse theory of right and the communication theory of society, and its importance, at the end of *FG* (527ff). It might be noted in this context that, even while reprinting the essay "Volkssouveränität als Verfahrung" in the same volume with *FG*, Habermas notes that his "picture of the state administration as a democratically 'besieged' fortress" could be misleading if it neglects the fact that administrative measures must also at least claim to meet normative criteria. Insofar as this claim is made by the state administration, one can demand that communicative procedures be introduced within that administration—for example, in the form of ombudsmen or public hearings concerning proposed regulations. Habermas insists that these procedures must take place *ex ante* as part of the process by which administrative measures acquire their legitimacy (Ibid., 531).

34. The clearest formulation of this argument is found in Habermas's presentation and critique of Werner Becker, in *FG*, 352ff.

35. On the last point, see *FG*, 441. This assumption of a moment of mobilization seems to presuppose what it wants to prove in the same way that Michelman's or Ackerman's republicanism was to realize a latent communal spirit when awakened by a court decision (see note 31 above). Habermas has to show that the mobilization is more than simply the kind of defensive reaction of a life-world to the threat of colonization that he described in the *Theory of Communicative Action*. I will return to this issue in part 5's discussion of democratic political culture (p. 198). That Habermas is aware of the difficulty is indicated by his critique of Dahl's empirical argument for the emergence of democratic resistance. Dahl's introduction of variables like income levels, growth of the social product, decreasing infant mortality, and increased life expectancy neglects the normative dimension of such forms of social mobilization (see, especially *FG*, 385ff.).

36. Ibid., 442. This definition is a reaffirmation of the equiprimordiality of private and public autonomy on which we saw Habermas insist in his discourse theory of law.

37. Ibid., 373.

38. Successful compromise can have negative effects if the social movements themselves become institutionalized by the political system. Habermas cites Simitis's argument concerning the trade union movement whose success against the capitalists has come at the price of a normalization or "colonization of the behavior of the worker." Simitis makes a similar argument concerning progress in family law (*FG*, 498, 501). The point is that there is no single correct relation between factual and legal equality; that relation can be legitimate, however, when it is decided by autonomous individuals participating in their self-determination as citizens.

39. For the last citation (*Fälle zu Konfliktfällen zu machen*), see *FG*, 433. For the theatrical metaphors, see, among others, 382 (*Inszenierungen*), 434 *mise en scene* (*in Szene zu setzen*), 435 (*dramatisieren*), 461ff (actors playing to a gallery). I can only note in passing the parallels here with the radical democratic political theory of Claude Lefort, whose foundation, like that of Habermas, is the demise of the absolutist state and the dilemmas that ensue for the project of social integration. Habermas cites Lefort only once (534), and in that case he refers to a passage from Dubiel, Frankenberg, and Rödel's *Die demokratische Frage*. Nonetheless, the parallels in the two projects—if not in their methods—are worth remarking.

40. Habermas speaks in italics of an *Öffentlichkeit im Ruhezustand* at *FG*, 458.

41. Ibid., 460.

42. Ibid., 461.

43. That is why, after reconstructing the system of rights in chapter 3, Habermas turned in chapter 4 to the principles of the constitutional state. In his introductory remarks, he notes that

> the self-referential act of the legal institutionalization of the autonomy of the citizens is in essential aspects incomplete; it cannot stabilize itself. The moment of the reciprocal recognition of rights remains a metaphorical event; it can perhaps be remembered or ritualized, however it cannot be durable without the construction or the functional use of a state power. . . .
> [There exists] a political power that is *already presupposed* by the legal medium, to which both the positing of law and its actualization owe their actual binding force (*FG*, 166).

44. Ibid., 185ff. Habermas's critique here is directed at Hannah Arendt's communicative theorization of the political (see footnote 12 above).

45. Habermas points out, for example, that institutions like the family or the school usually function without the need for legal intervention; however, in exceptional circumstances, such legal intervention may show itself to be necessary. To be justified, such intervention depends on agreements among those concerned as to "the relevant aspects" of the problem.

46. Habermas uses also the image of a "transformer" in this context. For example, at the end of chapter 2, he writes that "the language of the law, as opposed to the moral communication which is limited to the sphere of the life-world, can function as a transformer in the total social communication process between system and life-world" (*FG*, 108).

47. All citations are from *FG*, 107.

48. This points to the Hegelian logic that underlies Habermas's project. But it leaves open the foundation of that logic, to which I will return in part 5 below.

49. See *FG*, 463ff, 535. Habermas also adopts Preuß's argument that a constitution should be understood as a fallible learning process permitting

society to overcome its incapacity for normative self-thematization. As procedural, a constitution is not simply formal but serves as a reference point permitting democratic processes to play a new role, namely the production of that ultimate scarce resource: social solidarity (535). I will return below to the notion of counter-steering (discussed for example at *FG*, 398).

50. See *FG*, 236, 521ff. See also Habermas's discussion of Peters's attempt to explain social integration in terms of the validity aspects of truth, normative correctness and authenticity that stresses that the moral regulation of conflicts and the ethical protection of identities demand different sorts of grounds than do technical and economic rationality.

51. See, for example, Habermas's critique of K-O Apel, whose position is much closer to such an interpretation (*FG*, 391ff). See also his concluding remarks, which insist that his theory "does not aim at indoctrination and has nothing totalitarian" about it (*FG*, 536). He describes his own position as follows:

> to the degree that it would affect the horizon of a pre-understanding within which all take part in the interpretation of the constitution according to a division of labor, each in his own way, every perceived historical change in the social context would have to be understood as the challenge for each to re-examine the paradigmatic understanding of law. This assertion certainly has, like the constitutional state itself, its dogmatic kernel: the idea of autonomy according to which men act as free subjects only to the degree that they obey precisely the laws that they give themselves according to their intersubjectively acquired insights. (*FG*, 537)

52. *FG*, 398.
53. Cited above, at note 24, ibid., 110.
54. Ibid., 165.
55. See, for example, ibid., 461, 462, 463.
56. This is not to deny that, as with other aspects of the life-world, there can be a systemic aspect of liberal political culture. Thus, for example, at *FG*, 434, Habermas notes that "autonomous publics capable of resonating in this way are however [*wiederum*] dependent on a social anchoring in liberal modes of political culture and socialization, in a word: on the reciprocity [*Entgegenkommen*] of a rationalized life-world."
57. See *FG*, 89. This is simply another formulation of the above-noted (n. 28) criticism of the overlapping consensus notion for its inability to motivate action.
58. See *FG*, 532. Since the publication of Habermas's *FG*, Ingeborg Maus has published her arguments in *Zur Aufklärung der Demokratietheorie* (Frankfurt am Main: Suhrkamp Verlag, 1992). Her critique of the premodern presuppositions of those who would defend the autonomy of civil society as if it were a substantial entity—like the traditional corporations that were typical of absolutist society—is useful, as is her radicalization of the concept of popular

sovereignty that, she shows, can exist only as democratic and processual. It is to these two arguments that Habermas is pointing in the cited passage. For an overview of Ingeborg Maus, see Dick Howard, "Just Democracy," in *Constellations* 2, no. 3 (winter 1996).

59. As a concluding note to this reconstruction, I should refer to a concrete illustration of the twin problems facing East and West. As I was completing this chapter, German democrats had begun to take to the streets in symbolic "candle chains" (*Lichterketten*) to demonstrate against the outbreaks of violence against foreigners and the rise of a radical right wing. Norbert Kostede's "Erleuchtung für die Politik" presents an insightful analysis of these demonstrations in *Die Zeit* (no. 5, 5 February 1993). While agreeing with the need for symbolism in politics ("There is no politics without symbolic action."), Kostede points to the danger of reducing politics to mere theatrical demonstrations. This danger is all the greater as the "political class" has increasingly been seen as irrelevant to actual problems (if not simply corrupt). But silent marchers holding candles, however impressive their numbers, cannot on their own bring about change. "And in parliaments it is not a holy fire that burns but rather the democratic struggle for power." For that reason, "citizen initiatives cannot replace institutional politics but only broaden it." Therefore, concludes Kostede, "We should not call for candle-chains *instead of* parties, but rather bring the spirit of the candle-chains *into* the parties." With this, I think, Habermas would agree.

10

From Marx to Kant:
The Return of the Political

Capitalism and Modernity

The contemporary crisis of capitalism, which should bring hope to the political Left, is accompanied by theoretical difficulties that the Left would be foolish to deny. Neither liberalism, welfarism, nor Marxism can offer grounds for an eventual collapse of capitalism, nor can they identify the elements of a new economic system that would replace it. No one believes any more that the breakdown of capitalist relations of production will give birth to a new socialist mode of production carried in the womb of the Old Order. The conceptual crisis is manifested in lame labels like neo- or late-capitalism, and in the Bahro's widely accepted euphemism "really-existing socialism." The theoretical difficulty has practical consequences. The nature and locus of the so-called "revolutionary subject" is as uncertain as the goal for which it is supposed to strive. Evaluation of the "new social movements" is as difficult as judgment of the popular component of the Polish Solidarity. Only with regard to the Third World is an ironic advantage gained: the conceptual crisis makes recognition of complexity inevitable; friend/foe Manichaeanism is no longer tenable. The rediscovery of democracy as a positive force by many Latin American Lefts is emblematic of the new situation.

How have we come to conceive of our common social life as dominated by the economy? Of course, the capitalist looks at the world from the point of view of her personal interest; Marx was not the first to denounce the resulting "Robinsonnades." When the children of peasants accustomed to living in customary societies had to be

211

transformed into workers, capitalism had to teach them this new world outlook. But the capitalists are not the only preachers of economism; the bureaucrats in really-existing socialism legitimate themselves by a similar economic logic. But too many revolts, open and collective as well as silent and individual, witness the irreducibility of humans to machines, of reason to a means-ends rationality. Might not a Copernican Revolution ask the preliminary question: what are the conditions that make possible the reduction of social to economic life? Might not such a proposal lead us, as it did Kant, to pass beyond a critique of the laws of nature and morality to a critique of our faculty of judgment? The result may reawaken the radical imagination, making possible a move beyond the present conceptual crisis.

The proposed Copernican Revolution suggests that the economic logic presupposed by both liberal and Marxist representations of civil society cannot be maintained (if it ever really existed). The priority of economic life is not the solution but the problem. The conditions of the possibility of its temporary dominance must be explained. The explanation will have the philosophical structure suggested by the Kantian critique. It will be presuppositionless and self-reflexive. It will be both a positive demonstration and a negative (or "dialectical") presentation of the antinomies that account for the illusory priority of the economic. The result will be neither a system of philosophy (as with Hegel) nor its end (as claimed by Marx). If philosophy is returned to its throne (as Kant hoped), politics becomes not only possible but necessary. This interdependence of philosophy and politics is incarnated in Kant's notion of the republic, which puts the political nature of society back on the radical agenda.

Marx also entitled his work a "critique." This is not the place for comparative philology. My claim is not to restore a true Marx nor to reconstruct Kant's actual intentions. My guiding question is defined by the double crisis: of capitalism and of its conceptual representation. The description of capitalism in *The Communist Manifesto* suggests an empirical and theoretical starting point for the analysis. Marx describes a "constant revolutionizing of production, uninterrupted disturbance of all social conditions, everlasting uncertainty and agitation" that distinguish the capitalist epoch from all others. "All fixed and fast-frozen relations with their train of ancient and venerable prejudices and opinions are swept away, all new-formed ones become antiquated before they can ossify. All that is solid melts into air, all that is holy is profaned." The result is that "man is at last compelled to face with sober senses his real conditions of life, and his relations to his kind."

This critique, which the *philosophes* of the Enlightenment had sought to deliver down to the people, is said to be capitalism's own self-critique. It has a reflexive structure, and, like the Kantian model, it is presuppositionless. Marx's reconstruction of its conditions of possibility can be accepted or rejected. His replacement of Kant's negative version of the dialectic by a positive revolutionary politics has more important implications.

Capitalism is defined by its specific difference from other social formations. This difference is articulated in its self-critical secular process. Such a self-critical character exemplifies the structure of modernity. A modern formation is defined by its presuppositionless procedure that can only be legitimated immanently. The resulting structure is characterized by a conceptual antinomy that can be described by the concepts of genesis and normativity. Illustrations of this antinomic structure are found in modern art as in modern capitalism, modern philosophy as in modern politics. Modern society cannot be reduced to its mode of production; the economic base demands a normative political legitimation. The contemporary crisis cannot be overcome only within the economy; praxis is not identical to production, political judgment cannot be reduced to tactics. Even if political norms are called "ideological," they are nonetheless a reality that modern societies must constantly reproduce. The constant change in the political norms adopted by capitalist societies cannot be reduced simply to an effect of economic reality (although they cannot be neatly separated from it). The interdependence of genesis and normativity provides a guideline for the formulation of a political Copernican Revolution.

The specificity of modernity, and the categories useful for its description, can be illustrated from the sphere of art.[1] Four artists, two from the beginnings of modern times and two contemporaries, serve as models. The paintings of Joseph Mallord William Turner and Jackson Pollock stress the formation of the work of art; their orientation can be called *genetic*. The brush of Caspar David Friedrich and Mark Rothko affects the viewer by means of an aesthetic of totality; their art can be called *normative*. These generalizations ignore the substantive differences among the works of each artist. Successful paintings are characterized by the fact that neither the genetic nor the normative aspect dominates. The genetic artist fails if he forgets that he is truly painting an artwork; similarly, the normative artist fails if his creation petrifies into an eternal presence. The successful work unites the tension of the genetic and the normative. This tension that is the life of the work can also overpower it; it will then appear as a crisis that threatens the work from within. Modern art is defined by the attempt to fight off the seductive "perpetual peace" that would overcome the internal crisis that defines the modern. The temptation is omnipresent, in the artwork as in the modern society defined by the *Manifesto*, because there exists no preconceived or external norm that would define once and for all the good work or society. Legitimation can only be immanent.

The Kantian thread guiding this argument will be seen to explain why the analogy to art succeeds in describing a more general structure. In the history of philosophy, Kant discovered and articulated the structure of modernity. The Transcendental Dialectic of each of his *Critiques* illustrates the temptations inherent in the modern tension of the genetic and the normative that confront the philosopher Kant, for example, in the forms of empiricism and rationalism. Kant's goal was to unite the genetic and the normative orientations without eliminating their respective truths. Hegel and Marx confronted the same difficulties. Hegel's genetic *Phenomenology* demands as its counterpart the normative *Logic*; Marx presents at once a genetic theory of the revolutionary proletariat and a description of the paradoxical reproductive logic of the capitalist mode of production. Between Kant and Hegel/Marx, the world had changed in one fundamental aspect: civil society emerged, and its development tended to be dominated by the economy. Kant, too, spoke of civil society. His "Idea of World History from a Cosmopolitan Point of View" defined its creation as "the crucial problem for the human race"; it is also, he says, "the most difficult" and "will be the last to be resolved." This is the political ground for the Copernican Revolution. Hegel and Marx presupposed the existence of civil society; Kant wanted to create it. Such a project demands a political analysis. Although his republican theory is not fully elaborated, Kant's philosophy respects the immanence of modernity; this makes it possible to propose a new understanding of modern politics, its relation to civil society and its supposed economic foundation.[2]

Marx and Modern Philosophy

The modern imperative of immanent self-critical justification and the categories of genesis and normativity permit a global interpretation of Marx's theoretical development. A note appended to his philosophy dissertation summarizes his project. The editor of Marx's writings gave this note the apt title, "On the World's Becoming Philosophical as Philosophy's Becoming Worldly." This relation of mutual implication entails a double difficulty. Marx speaks of a "psychological law" that explains why "philosophy as will turns against the phenomenal world." However, a psychological hypothesis does not provide an adequate philosophical foundation; a modern philosophy demands immanent legitimation. To this problem on the side of the subject is added another from the side of the object. The world must be shown to be receptive to the philosophy that sacrifices its purity to engage with the world. Philosophy cannot be applied to a world that is different from it and indifferent to it; the world must itself possess the normative structures of philosophy. These two difficulties arise from the young Marx's attempt to confront the imperatives of modernity. His first solution is unsatisfactory because it treats philosophy as at once normative and genetic in the process of changing itself and the world. Marx's further development can be seen as the articulation of the structural necessities created by the paradoxical unity of genesis and normativity in a modern philosophy.

The premise of Marx's second strategy is the inverse of the first. He had left the university, worked as a critical journalist, and now returned to philosophy in order to criticize the external and artificial relation of the state to civil society. Marx is aware of the danger of a premodern reductionism, which would be only the inverse of the application of the psychological law. His working notes for "Critique of the Hegelian State" were never completed because the simple application of Feuerbach's materialist "invertive method" was not sufficient. The "Contribution to the Critique of Hegel's *Philosophy of Right*," which he wrote a few months later, was more nuanced. The critique of religion that he proposes is followed by an "irreligious" critique whose foundation is that "Man makes religion." This genetic human activity is not psychological; Marx insists that a man is not a "being squatting outside the world," he is "the world of man." This completes the first systematic requirement by explaining *receptivity*; the human world is open to human action because it is made by humans. Marx then elaborates the *genetic* argument to explain the necessity of this possible action within the human world. The "world of man" is an inverted world that produces the "inverted consciousness" of religion. Religion, however, is not only an opiate, but also an act of "protest against actual suffering." This active character provides the genetic completion of the argument that the earlier psychological law could only suggest.

The result of Marx's second strategy is the thematization of the revolutionary proletariat at the conclusion of "Towards a Critique of Hegel's *Philosopy of Right. Introduction.*" Marx's argument can be interpreted by the framework of genesis and normativity. Marx asks whether "theoretical needs will become immediate practical needs." He replies that "it is not sufficient that thought should seek its actualization; actuality must itself strive toward thought." This theory of the receptivity of the world to the *normative* demands of philosophy is elaborated in the notion of radical needs. The *genetic* component then returns. The proletariat is the particular that can and must make universal claims; it is the nothing that can become everything, a praxis with theoretical consequences. Marx's argument is familiar, logical, and rhetorically satisfying. Two difficulties recognized at the conclusion of this demonstration point to the further development of his theory. They point as well to contemporary difficulties. (1) Marx speaks of the formation (*Bildung*, implying a reflective education and not simple material causality) of a proletariat, which he says is an artificial (*künstlich*) process. This distinguishes the proletariat from any naturally given agent (such as the poor who "are always with ye," or women, oppressed races, or any naturally given substratum). It poses the contemporary problem of the "revolutionary subject." (2) When he asks how the structural possibilities that define the proletarian position will be actualized, Marx has recourse to the metaphor of the "lightning of thought" (*Blitz des Gedankens*). This has come to imply "class consciousness." Little more precise has been said about its nature and source since Marx's metaphorical expectation.

The *1844 Manuscripts* can be read as the unity of the two strategies and the attempt to solve the twin difficulties in actualizing the revolutionary proletariat. (1) The first Manuscript accounts for the formation of the proletariat by means of lengthy citations from the classical political economists. This is a *normative* economic presentation of the logic of receptivity; it is completed by the theory of alienated labor that provides a normative explanation of the class consciousness that would explain the *genetic* action that completes the systematic circle.[3] The implication of this first strategy is that Marx has not fully abandoned the temptation to derive genesis from normativity. The *Poverty of Philosophy* and the causal-structural crisis-theory (*Zusammenbruchstheorie*) of *Capital* can be understood as the continuation of this orientation within Marx's later work. (2) The *genetic* concern with class consciousness is elaborated in the third Manuscript. Marx develops the implications of "the greatness of Hegel's *Phenomenology*" in his theory of objectivation through labor. This process leads to "a completed humanism = naturalism and a completed naturalism = humanism." The movement toward communism shows how the senses "in their praxis" become "theoricians." Its result is that "the eye has become a human eye, just as its object has become a social, human object derived from and for man." The result of the genetic process of labor is shown here to have *normative* consequences. This second orientation is elaborated in *The German Ideology* and in those aspects of *Capital* (such as the transition from absolute to relative surplus-value) where class struggle is the crucial factor.

Sometimes Marx appears to combine the two orientations, as for example in the first parts of the *Communist Manifesto* where the logic of capitalism is not presented simply as structural and objective but also as practical and subjective insofar as the object described is the unification and development of the consciousness of the proletariat as the subject-object of history. Such unifications appear more frequently in the historical writings, expressing what Merleau-Ponty called that "*sublime point* where reality and values, the subject and the object, judgement and discipline, the individual and the totality, the present and the future, rather than colliding came gradually to work subtly together."[4] These unifying moments recall Kant's attempt to bridge his dualism by the introduction of a natural genius that creates "lawfulness without law" by the happy chance of an action defined as "purposive purposelessness." The Marxist would denounce this conceptual trick as ideology. That accusation permits a further development of the structure of modernity. Its insufficiency makes clear that Marx's difficulties arose from his awareness of the demands of a modern philosophy.

Modern Philosophy and Ideology

The concept of ideology and its critique are often introduced in order to avoid the difficulties entailed by the two strategies that appear to present two Marxes. The critique of ideology is perhaps too familiar. It seems to be based on the application of the notion of "false consciousness" developed on the model of the Feuerbachian critique of religion (if not on the simple reductionism of the Enlightenment *philosophes*). This procedure can be criticized doubly. Religion is premodern; it expresses a relation of externality between ideas and their material foundation. Religion is not the model for a modern ideology. More important, as Claude Lefort has shown convincingly, Marx does not *apply* the critique of ideology. He does not stand outside the world, pretending to know the structures of the really real and to enlighten the Platonic cave-dwellers about their misperceptions. Marx's discovery, Lefort insists, is that capitalism itself is structured ideologically. This is the true sense of the Marxian notion of "critique." It will permit us to see more clearly why economic capitalism could become a paradigm of modernity.[5]

Two complementary illustrations of the material reality of modern capitalist ideology illustrate the normative and the genetic strategies. (1) Marx describes the normative structure of capitalism in the formula M-C-M': money is invested in commodities whose combination in turn produces the return of more money. The labor theory of value is the genetic component of this structure. A peculiarity within the normative formula itself is more important. The process continually produces difference, inequality, the new. The constant production of novelty is necessary for the process of capitalist reproduction. At the same time, the novelty must always and again be reduced to identity, sameness, repetition. Capitalism is (in one word) the-continual-production-and-reduction-of-the-new, the unequal, the different. Crises are moments when this reduction cannot be achieved. Since capitalism has destroyed all traditional forms of life, it can only legitimate itself immanently. Either the genetic process of the production and satisfaction of needs or the normative logic of free and equal contractual exchange can be invoked. This situation becomes an active crisis only when a genetic component is added. The labor theory of value, which in this model provides that genetic moment, is not sufficient to explain a political intervention that would actualize and overcome the latent crisis. (2) The genetic structure is analogous to the normative picture. The worker is formally "freed" from tradition and from ownership of his own means of production. He is a commodity whose value is determined on the neutral free market. Formally free, the worker is really dependent. Yet, although he is a commodity, he knows full well that his value is determined in a struggle with the capitalist (for higher wages or better work conditions, against speed-ups. . .). Thus, the worker has daily experience of the contradiction of personal freedom and social dependence. This experience is ramified in the production process itself. The worker enters the factory as an individual, works as a member of a collective, and returns home from work as an individual. He experiences the social nature of the capitalist production process. He knows that inequality has no objective or personal basis to justify its existence. Further, the continual application of science to the productive technology shows the worker that the difference among products is only a remake of the old in new wrappings. The worker can share the knowledge of possible technical advances because he is not caught up in the competitive imperatives of capitalist survival. His place in the hierarchy does not depend on political relations or wealth inherited from elsewhere. The worker can thus look soberly at reality, uniting with comrades while the capitalists compete with one another and hide reality from themselves. This genetic potential, like the possibility demonstrated by the normative logic of capitalism, needs its complement to become actual.

Ideology is produced only in modern societies (of which capitalism is only one of the possible forms). Ideology is the constantly renewed attempt to unify the process whereby the new is necessarily and continually produced. It can take three forms: (1) the primacy of the genetic determines the normative; (2) the normative is treated as an essence of which the genetic is simply a mode of appearance; (3) the difference between the two is denied by an identity-logic whose forms were discovered and criticized in the Hegelian-Marxist tradition from Lukács to the Frankfurt School. Ideological illusion is not found only within the ruling class or its politicians. Insofar as capitalism is defined by the formula M-C-M', the profit (designated by M') characterizes the ideological nature of this mode of production. The new (i.e., the commodity produced) is reduced to the homogeneous monetary form from which the process began. The revolutionary who wants only to abolish the old relations of property, to give labor freedom and dignity, commits an ideological error. The goal is not to redistribute what already exists; that would not be the negation but the affirmation of the primacy of the economic that defines modernity as capitalist.

The structure of ideology explains the constant reappearance on the left of debates between reform and revolution. From the *genetic* point of view, a reformist tactic is legitimated by the premise of an immature proletariat whose political education can take place only through experience. Yet, Rosa Luxemburg—who was hardly a reformist— argues from the same genetic premises that only active democratic participation in direct struggles can bring about that political education. Lenin counters this position from the *normative* point of view, claiming that in its immediate struggles the proletariat can develop only a trade-unionist consciousness; it needs the help of the party and its theory to become a revolutionary agent. But that putative normative certainty incarnate in the party is separated from the empirical everyday world; in the hands of a Kautsky, it could become the justification of a conservatism within the party and the society it rules. The hope of uniting the two poles of modern ideology motivates the different political practices that claim to derive their legitimation from Marx.

Two political conclusions follow from the concept of modern ideology. (1) The Marxist politics, which attempts to avoid contradiction, seeks to do exactly what the capitalist attempts vainly. However different their rhetoric, both seek to put an end to history as qualitatively new. This Marxist version of politics does not understand the implications of the notion of ideology as capitalist reality. This assertion is valid also for the position that begins from the proletariat as the revolutionary unity of genesis and validity. The glorification of labor is, after all, coterminous with the ethic of capitalism; neither Greek nor Christian societies glorified it. Both the Marxist and the capitalist reduce modernity to the economic logic of civil society. (2a) The theoretical justification of this politics can be itself explained by the structure of ideology. Theory can understand itself as genetic or as normative. As *normative* it claims to present the truth about things; this truth is to be put in the service of revolution. Empirical sociological studies can claim to serve the revolution when parties use their results tactically. This presupposes, however, that the parties know the correct strategic direction. This separation of the truth about things from the things repeats the ideological paradigm. The normative truth about things applied by this type of theory *for* revolution is necessarily inadequate to the contradictory ideological structure of modernity. (2b) The other option is to treat theory as *genetic*. Marx's notion of his theory as a theory *of* the proletariat is the best illustration. Its difficulty is apparent when the second part of the *Communist Manifesto* explains the role of the communist. He claims to represent the interests of the proletariat as a whole because he understands "the line of march, the conditions and the ultimate general results of the proletarian movement." The result is a metaphysics of history that does away with the particularity of proletarian conditions. Genesis has determined a normative necessity that is separated from the proletarian actors and incarnated in the communist or the Communist Party.

If Kant were a Marxist . . .

The Marxist thinks according to an economic, not a political logic. He imagines an actor, and asks himself how that actor produces a society and a history. He supposes that this production takes place within specific limits defined by the given physical and social conditions. But the fact that these limits and conditions are produced by humans is made into a virtue, since it implies that these same humans are capable of understanding and, eventually, changing them. Such a theory is *genetic* in its orientation toward history; but it is transformed, without admitting it, into a *normative* approach. The History that has been produced becomes the measure of a history that is being made. It becomes that knowledge that justifies the *hubris* of Marx's communist who becomes the bureaucrat of History applauding his own speech at the party congress because, after all, he is merely the accidental organ by which reality expresses its truth. But one must be careful. The grounds of the development by which the Marxist becomes a totalitarian are not found in the ideological *Gestalten* that express the paradoxical structure of modernity. A further philosophical ingredient is necessary. The Marxist Kant makes clear that additional step by revealing what I will call the constitutive temptation.

The Marxist Kant was presented for the first time in Lukács's *History and Class Consciousness*.[6] Lukács claims that Kant's dualism reproduces the actual dilemmas of the really existing bourgeois subject. This subject is monological; it is unable to know anything but appearances; and it is troubled by a moral will that can be sure only of its intentions, not of their actual results. This subject is portrayed as attempting to bridge the dualism that is presented positively in the Transcendental Analytic of the first *Critique*. The Third Antinomy of the Transcendental Dialectic illustrates the difficulties of Kant's solution. Free will and determinism appear to contradict one another; Kant's demonstration of their noncontradiction is not sufficient because it shows only the possibility, not the necessity of moral action. The *Foundations of the Metaphysics of Morals* develops the three forms of the categorical imperative as the basis of Kant's ethics; but Kant's argument is still incomplete because it presupposes the existence of the free will. Recognizing the difficulty that this entails, the *Critique of Practical Reason* attempts to found the free will through the Postulates of Practical Reason. The existence of God, freedom, and immortality are supposed to guarantee that the will knows that its intention can in fact be realized. This certainty apparently makes necessary the merely possible morality of the Third Antinomy and of the *Foundations*. These Postulates are, however, only postulates. Kant therefore adds a further argument in the *Critique of Judgement*. The genius who produces disinterestedly a purposeful purposelessness and a lawfulness without law is combined with the happy chance (*glück-licher Zufall*) that gives nature a teleological structure. This intuition produced a flourishing post-Kantian philosophical industry headed by Schelling. It is, however, hardly satisfactory systematically. A fourth *Critique* seems necessary to solve the problem of Kantian (or bourgeois) dualism. Its possibility is apparently suggested by Kant's historical writings.

Kant's historical essays articulate concretely the dualism that was the premise of his philosophical system. The short text, "What Is Enlightenment?" presents only a formal answer. The enlightened consciousness whose development Kant portrays is autonomous but empty of content. Its *sapere aude* leaves no room for education (*Bildung*). "The Idea of History from a Cosmopolitan Point of View," written also in 1784, attempts to give a concrete content to this formally autonomous consciousness. In the process, the movement beyond the monological subject begins. Kant's fourth thesis suggests that "the means used by nature in order to bring all human capacities to full development is the *antagonism* of men in society." Kant introduces here the concept of human nature as "unsocial sociability." The fifth thesis goes a step further in giving social form to this antinomic structure. "The greatest problem for the human species, to whose solution nature forces him, is the achievement (*Erreichung*) of a *civil society* under law." Kant poses immediately the classical question that has become identified with Marx's "Theses on Feuerbach": "Man is an animal which, when it lives among others of its species, needs a master. . . . But where is he to find this master?" The seventh thesis avoids the question by turning to relations among states as central to the formation of the lawful civil society. This is a genetic development of the notion of "unsocial sociability" from the fourth thesis. Kant appears to reason in terms of a social learning through catastrophe; the costs of war will bring people to recognize the need to regulate lawfully their relations. However, Kant does not follow through the implications of this genetic argument. His eighth thesis adds a postulated normative complement in the form of a natural teleology that is to justify the hope that nature's goals will indeed be realized. Since such a hope is not realizable without praxis, Kant concludes with a ninth thesis, which (anachronistically) recalls Marx. A philosophical attempt of the kind he has proposed is seen as "contributing to this end of Nature."

The essay "The Idea of History from a Cosmopolitan Point of View" thus brings together the genetic and the normative orientations only syncretically; the philosophical attempt of the ninth thesis has no real institutional place. The dualism remains in the form of a teleological Nature that coexists with the "crooked wood" of unsociably social humans. These humans are only apparently part of the natural teleology. The ideological structure of modernity is repeated in the illusory unity whose poles are in fact external to each other. At times, genetic human action explains the normative natural teleology; at others, the normative teleology founds the postulated hope that genetic action will succeed and therefore should be undertaken. The mediation is unsuccessful because one or the other moment is treated as constituting a unitary structure. This constitutive orientation is another attempt to escape from the dilemmas of modernity that fall into the ideological distortion. It can function *normatively*, as an essentialism that treats history as a natural teleology overdetermining particular acts. It can also function *genetically*, as in the phenomenological labor of Marx's *German Ideology*. It is inadequate because it is a premodern structure in which externality replaces the immanent self-critical structure of the modern. Kant himself goes beyond it after 1784.

. . . he would not have written the *Critique of Judgement*

The interpretation of Kant as the philosopher of modernity has textual justification. In the first edition of the *Critique of Pure Reason* (1781), Kant insists that his era is "the particular epoch of critique to which all must be subjected." The second edition (1787) adds the need to struggle against every "dogmatism which pretends to philosophize without first undertaking a critique of its own capacities." These are only external signs, which could be multiplied. More important is an ambiguity in the title of the critical project itself. What is meant by the genitive "of" in the title of the *Critiques*? Who does the critique? on whom? on what? from what grounds? Is it the supposed purity that is questioned? Is it its rationality that is doubted? Or, conversely, is pure reason the subject or actor of the critique? In this case, whence comes the object that is criticized? What is its nature? Why does it call for a critique?

These questions are unanswerable from a modern perspective. Neither reason nor its object can be presupposed as a given. Subject and object emerge together (as we saw with the young Marx's philosophy and world). They are not, however, identitical with one another. The question of their interrelation appears explicitly only in the *Critique of*

Judgement. Its introduction insists on the systematic place and role of this third *Critique*. Kant begins from "the divisions of philosophy" and from the "domains of Philosophy in general." He describes his work as "a mediator (*Verbindungsmittel*) of the two parts of philosophy into a whole." After considering the results of the first two *Critiques*, he concludes with the proposal for the "unification of the legislation of the Understanding [i.e., of the first *Critique*] and that of Reason [i.e., of the second *Critique*] through the faculty of judgement." The object of the *Critique of Judgement* is thus also its subject. In this sense, the work is explicitly modern.

The systematic content of the *Critique of Judgement* suggests an interpretation of the antinomic unity of the Kantian project as a whole. The table of contents shows already its difference from the other Kantian *Critiques*. The copresence of the Analytic of the Beautiful and the Analytic of the Sublime corresponds to the copresence of a critique of aesthetic judgment with the judgment of teleology in nature. The normative natural teleology that functioned constitutively in the "Marxist" Kant's theory of "Cosmopolitan History" is given a new status. The function of nature within the account of the sublime suggests that the *genetic* role assumed by judgment differs from the *normative* rational imperatives that motivate moral action. This structural peculiarity is given further weight by a comment in the preface. Kant announces that this book marks the "end of my entire critical business (*Geschäft*). I will now immediately pass on to the doctrinal." Kant does not explain what he means by the "doctrinal." He speaks of a metaphysics of nature and another of morals (*Sitten*). The 1797 completion of the *Metaphysics of Morals* does not make use of the new concept. It could be suspected that, parallel to the transformed status of nature in the third *Critique*, the new doctrinal philosophy will provide a new interpretation of the unsocial sociability that was so crucial to the "Marxist" Kant.

The systematic (Marxian) Kant helps to interpret the systematic structure of the *Critique of Judgement*. Its central conceptual innovation is the distinction between reflective and determinative (or subsumptive) judgment. Science and morality proceed according to the determinative judgment; a critically justified law proposes universally valid predicates under which any particular can be subsumed. "Critique" is the method by which the validity of this universal predication is justified. Such critique cannot exist in isolation; its categories cannot be imposed externally on an experienced world that has not been shown to be receptive to them. This is the addition that the third

Critique makes to the Transcendental Analytic of the first.[7] The systematic concerns of the young Marx suggest the place of the doctrinal in the Kantian project. Kant must show *which* particulars call for the reflective judgment that moves from the particular to a universal that cannot be presupposed as valid. Determination of these particulars permits the transition to a political theory.

The need for a political complement to critical philosophy was apparent in the formalism of "What Is Enlightenment?" The abstract autonomous consciousness needed content; it had to be able to learn, grow, and develop. Kant's rejection of any "contract made to shut off further enlightenment" expresses this concern. A remark in *Religion within the Limits of Reason Alone* suggests the implications of Kant's new orientation.[8] Kant comments that even if the necessity and the success of a revolution could be demonstrated scientifically and morally, that revolution would still not be justified. Its demonstrated necessity would be based on a determinative, subsumptive judgment whose results would entail the end of history and of enlightenment. This suggests that politics differs from morality because of the form of its judgments. The key to a theory of politics is the reflective judgment that proceeds from the particular to the universal. From this point of view, the *Critique of Judgement* constitutes a "prolegomenon" to any modern politics. But it is not itself a political theory.

The Analytic in the third *Critique* provides more than the formal structure of political argumentation. The first two moments of the Analytic of the Beautiful reproduce the copresence of the genetic and the normative moments. Kant insists that reflective judgments proceed without interest in their object. Correlatively, they do not presuppose a universally valid concept or law. In this way, judgment is not legitimated by appeal to genetic interest; nor does conceptual universality guarantee its normative certitude. After these preliminaries, the third moment of the Analytic proposes a new move from the genetic orientation, while the fourth moment adds to it a normative component. The third moment postulates a "lawfulness without law" or "purposeless purposiveness," which unifies the first two moments from the side of genesis. This unification functions differently from the constitutive proposal that we saw in the ninth Cosmopolitan Thesis. But Kant's genius, like Schiller's concept of "play," reify this unification ideologically. Its practical function in fact serves only to designate those particulars that call for reflective judgment. As he develops its implications, Kant says that this moment presents the "exemplary" nature of the beautiful; he treats it as a symbol of morality; and he analyzes it as the culture that permits humans to postulate goals that are more than natural.[9] Kant's fourth moment in the Analytic moves from the opposite direction in order to account for the normative receptivity to the reflective judgment. He begins from the need to postulate a "common sense" that makes the subjective reflection of each individual communicable and acceptable to all. This common sense is described at first in quite physical terms. As the analysis continues, the accent turns toward its common or shared character, which is guaranteed by the imperative to "think in the place of the other." Finally, Kant argues that this common sense can only take the form of a "communal" (*gemeinschaftlichen*) sense.

These elements of the theory of reflective judgment—to which must be added for completeness the account of natural teleology, which not only explains the particularity of the third moment but also avoids the temptation of a "convivial" voluntarism—permit the construction of a Kantian political edifice. The political can be said to be the doctrinal complement to the critique within a systematic unity. The political serves to determine which particulars make necessary the reflective judgment; the critique serves to explain the receptivity of the world to the categories proposed by the doctrine. The systematic unity of doctrine and critique explains Kant's option for a republican politics. Kant's description of republican institutions is faithful to the imperatives of modernity. It suggests the political implications of the proposed Copernican Revolution at the same time that it explains why the model of aesthetic judgment served to define the structures of modernity, as was suggested at the outset by the illustrations from modern art.

Modern Republican Politics

The systematic structure that I have attributed to Kant on the basis of the interpretation of the Marxist Kant is present in the decisive essay "Perpetual Peace."[10] This philosophical project of 1796, which sums up Kant's political thinking, is apparently naive, unsystematic, and confused. It begins in a pseudo-diplomatic form, with Preliminary Articles that are neither simply moral nor openly pragmatic. Their order is not logical, and their relation to the three Definitive Articles that follow is not explained. The Definitive Articles are of such generality as to discourage the practical politician. The text concludes with four supplements, of which a Secret Article (added to the second

edition) guarantees the place of the philosopher. After several reread-
ings, these supplementary materials seem to provide the negative
demonstration—or deconstruction—of the systematic role of the
essay. They repeat, in a nonexplicit irony, the path that took the
"Marxist" Kant through the *Critiques* toward the discovery of history.
The final supplement can be read as a reflection on the systematic
structure of the whole. Kant presents first a "critical" theory of what
he calls the "transcendental concept of public right." Its formulation
is negative: "All actions relating to the right of other men whose
maxim is not compatible with publicity are unjust." This analytical
argument is then joined by a "dialectical" remark that points out that
a powerful prince could let his injustices be known without danger.
This comment ends the critical phase of the argument. Kant concludes
it now with a "doctrinal" proposal: "All maxims which need publicity
(in order not to fail to achieve their goal) agree with right and politics
together." This relation of the critical and doctrinal philosophical
moments can be spelled out institutionally in the republican form.

Politics is the art—the *mise en scène* or representation—that presents that particularity that makes necessary a public, reflective judgment. The first consequence of this broad definition is negative. Technocratic–bureaucratic institutions or procedures that function by
predicative subsumption are antipolitical. A second negative implication needs to be underlined in our postmodern epoch. Not all particulars lend themselves to this form of judgment. Not all God's creation
lends itself to the experience of the beautiful. Not every issue belongs
to the political arena. The institutional stage of political particularity is
the Republic. It is the doctrinal complement to the critical system that
shapes the framework that permits the transformation of unsocial
sociability from a natural postulate to a communal achievement of
shared meaning.

Kant's republic is opposed explicitly to what he calls "democracy."
His reasoning parallels the forms of ideology that we derived from the
Marxist account of modern capitalism. As a form of sovereignty, the
democratic polity provides normative legitimation of the type "my
country right or wrong." As a form of self-government, democratic
decisions are the basis of a genetic proceduralist legitimation that is a
threat to minority interests (like the philosopher, whose place the
Secret Article appended to "Perpetual Peace" explicitly guaranteed).
In the form of a small-scale self-managing utopia, democracy would
unite the genetic and the normative in a unity that implies the end of
history. Each of these *Gestalten* is defined by the attempt to put an

end to the political. Such a politics is paradoxical. The republican alternative does not advocate the return to a premodern aristocratic formation based on an antiquated ideal of civic virtue and self-denying individuality. A modern republican civil religion would articulate the communal sense of which Kant's theory spoke, and whose contribution to reflective judgment gives it its historical form. The modern republican institutional frame serves the doctrinal purpose of defining (and delimiting) the objects of political action, providing the guarantee of minority rights that democracy endangers.[11]

The process of representation is the foundation of republican politics. Its philosophical structure is defined by the modern imperative of immanence and by the centrality of reflective judgment in politics. One contemporary interpretation develops the distinction between needs and interests.[12] Needs cannot be represented; interests can. It seems to follow that one seeks to replace the politics of capitalist and economic interest by the attempt to realize directly radical and human needs. The difficulty, however, is not only that a modern politics cannot assume the (prepolitical) existence of needs prior to the process of their representation. This is why Kant's republican politics of representation excludes any "contract made to shut off further enlightenment." The republic is explicitly and necessarily historical; the lack of fixed traditional and thus prepolitical forms makes politics not only possible but necessary. Representative politics does not exclude democratic participation. It succeeds precisely when the particularities it articulates make necessary what Kant meant by a communal process of reflective judgment. Conversely, the theory that is the inverse identical to the refusal to represent radical needs fails for the same structural reason. It conceives of the state as a "court" that judges among the competing interests represented before it. This violates the modern imperative of immanence because it treats political judgment as subsumptive. As opposed to this perspective, the institutional basis of republican politics is not fixed; its Constitution defines basic rights—the right to have rights, as Arendt puts it—which cannot be violated; but it does not preclude thereby the expansion of these rights. The only requirement philosophy imposes on this structure is that it contain the possibility of its own revision; modernity takes care of the necessity that actualizes this possibility.

This republican conception of politics has to be able to defend itself against the Marxist accusation that its formal structures provide the framework within which the capitalist economy can become predominant. The Copernican Revolution suggests that both the republic and the capitalist civil society are forms of the basic structure of modernity. This does not yet explain why the capitalist form has been dominant. Although it was not his question, Kant's concern with the problem of a revolution that would institute the republic suggests the direction in which an answer might be proposed. His seventh Cosmopolitan Thesis proposed that a "civil society under law," that is, a republic, would result from international relations among states. The citizens would learn from the relation of their state to others what kind of domestic relations were desirable. Kant's intuition was concretized in an essay by Otto Hintze on the "origins of the representative constitution."[13] The relations among the Italian states of the Renaissance, at a time when world empire was no longer possible, made it necessary for each state to be represented to the others by ambassadors. These states did not give up the idea of growth or change. Their relations acquired new spatial and temporal possibilities. This led to a new conception of representation, which was transformed in domestic relations among competing groups.

World politics today suggests a similar structure to the one intuited by Kant. The relations among states, and the "war" that was to lead individuals to a form a liberal social contract can be compared. The difference is that in relations among modern states, individuals are involved doubly, as individuals and as citizens, whereas it was the simple relations of individuals among themselves that grounded the classical idea of the social contract. The implication is that interstate relations form a republican or doctrinal framework that determines which particulars are in fact capable of, and in need of, political representation. This determination is not one-sided. The relation of a state to the international environment has the same immanent, modern structure as did the relation of civil society and the state in the classical model of liberal society. The two poles stand in a (reversible) relation of genesis and normativity. The danger, in both cases, is the separation of the one or the other moment. This second implication of the Copernican Revolution should not be confused with the kind of neo-Marxism (e.g., that of Immanuel Wallerstein) that treats the world economy as the basic unit of analysis of which domestic politics can be only the dependent variable. The republican relation among states defines a political, not an economic, structure.

Return of the Political

The proposed move from Marx to Kant does not assume that Kant provides the answers that some still try to extract or distill from Marx.

The Copernican Revolution instead reformulates the questions in a way that may be compatible with the concerns that animate contemporary radical politics. It suggests reading Marx from the point of view of the problem of modernity, of which capitalist civil society is simply one possible manifestation. Kant proves a more adequate guide to that structure because his problem, the formation of a "civil society under law," became for Marx instead the source of a solution that became antipolitical. Insofar as the capitalist form of civil society has entered a period of crisis, Marx's optimism can no longer be accepted. Kant's problem returns. If the goal were to save Marx, the means would have to be Kantian. But philosophy confronts its own internal limit here. The emergence of capitalist civil society cannot be explained simply by the structure of modernity. Capitalist civil society is the attempted answer to a properly political problem. Its crisis returns the political problem to the agenda.

The return of the political is not the kind of historicist solution against which Hannah Arendt cautioned in the passage cited earlier. The political was present all along; the economic is but one of its forms. It returns now in its own name. Philosophical reflection is necessary for its articulation. Conversely, its presence makes philosophy a modern necessity. Modern philosophy is inevitably political; modern politics is inevitably philosophical. The poles are united by that fundamental tension that defines modernity. Politics today can lead only to the kind of philosophical reflection typified by the Copernican Revolution and concluding with new questions. Philosophy today cannot neglect the question of its realization that animated the young Marx. The danger would be to treat either of these necessary modern adventures as simply ideological.

Notes

1. I am borrowing the following example from Robert Rosenberg, *Modern Painting and the Northern Romantic Tradition* (New York: Harper and Row, 1975). The relation between modern art and Marx's theory is suggested by Harold Rosenberg. See for example, "Set Out for Clayton," in *The De-Definition of Art* (New York: Horizon Press, 1972), and "The Resurrected Romans," in *The Tradition of the New* (New York: McGraw Hill, 1965), as well as "The Politics of Illusion," in *Discovering the Present* (Chicago: University of Chicago Press, 1973). Another approach is suggested by Marshall Berman, "All That Is Solid Melts Into Air," in *25 Years of Dissent* (New

York: Methuen, 1979). The argument proposed here is developed somewhat differently in chapter 7, "Politics of Modernism: From Marx to Kant."

2. I will be suggesting a somewhat idiosyncratic reading of Kant, justified in more detail in my *From Marx to Kant*. The more typical view is the one suggested in this chapter under the subhead, "If Kant were a Marxist . . ." That is the Kant criticized by Hannah Arendt in an otherwise cogent argument that concludes, "each time the modern age has had reason to hope for a new political philosophy, it received a philosophy of history instead" (*The Human Condition* [Chicago: University of Chicago Press, 1958], 298n). The Kant who wrote the third *Critique* presents the materials for the "new political philosophy" sought by Arendt. However, this does not mean that the third *Critique* is itself to be read politically, or as politics, as some disciples of Arendt have proposed.

3. The mostly lost second manuscript suggested a similar normative strategy to explain the genetic action by the proletariat. It offers an economic argument that demonstrates the "necessary" collision of capital and labor.

4. *Les aventures de la dialectique* (Paris: Gallimard, 1955), 12.

5. Lefort's argument is developed in "Marx: D'une vision de l'histoire à l'autre," and in "Esquisse d'une genèse de l'idéologie dans les sociétés modernes," in *Les Formes de l'histoire* (Paris: Gallimard, 1978). The relation of Lefort's analysis of modernity and the Frankfurt School's notion of "immanent critique" needs to be developed, particularly with regard to Habermas's reformulation in his *Theorie des kommunikativen Handelns* (Frankfurt am Main: Suhrkamp Verlag, 1982). The crucial point turns around the ability of each approach to move beyond social analysis to political theory. (See the afterword to the second edition of *The Marxian Legacy* on this point.)

6. The Second International had tried to assimilate Kant to Marx, but its results were always syncretic. Kant was treated as an ethical thinker; Marx was the scientific sociologist. The unity of Kant and Marx was then easily defined by the relation of the first to the second *Critique*. What that relation might imply in fact remained unexamined until Lukács. A representative selection of the Second International positions is found in Sandkühler and de la Vega, *Marxismus und Ethik* (Frankfurt am Main: Suhrkamp Verlag, 1970). For a discussion, see my "Kant's Political Theory: The Virtue of his Vices," in *Review of Metaphysics* 34 (December 1980): 325–50.

7. The details of this argument were first presented by George Schrader, "The Status of Teleological Judgement in the Critical Philosophy," *Kantstudien* 45 (1953–54): 204–55. I have elaborated them in *From Marx to Kant*.

8. Kant, *Werke (AKA)*, vol. 6, 122.

9. Marx's radically needy proletariat is also a particular that can make universal claims. Marx's error is to treat these claims as scientific and determinative rather than reflective judgments. I will return to this problem in a moment. See also "Law and Political Culture," chapter 9 above.

10. I can only sketch here what is argued in detail in *From Marx to Kant*, and in "Kant's System and (its) Politics," in *Man and World* 18 (1985): 79–98.

11. The republican form proposed by Kant introduces a curious distinction between the functions of executive and legislature that needs explication. Kant's structures show remarkable parallels to the institutional reforms proposed by the French revolutionary Abbé Sièyes. The function of the executive was to present to the legislative body those materials with which it was to deal. In Kantian terms, the legislative function was "critical"; it worked by subsuming under universal forms the particulars that the executive judges reflectively. This executive is not a bureaucracy—although Napoleon's later deformation of Sièyes's proposals under the Tribunat did in fact lead to the domination by the emperor. A modern formulation of this structure would argue that politics is the competition for the *mise en scène* of particular relations that demand to be represented. Politics in this sense can have a *democratic form* within the republican structure.

12. The best discussion of these arguments remains Jean L. Cohen's review of Agnes Heller's *The Theory of Need in Marx*, which was published in *Telos* 33 (Fall 1977): 170–85. In recent years, this discussion has fallen unjustly from favor, save perhaps for its modified presentation by André Gorz.

13. Otto Hintze, *Weltgeschichtliche Bedingungen der Repräsentativverfassung* (1931), in *Gesammelte Abhandlungen zur allgemeinen Verfassungsgeschichte* (Göttingen: Vandenhoeck & Ruprecht, 1962). For an attempt to actualize this observation, written at the time I was working on this essay, see "France, Germany and the Problem of Europe" and "The Republic and the International Order," both reprinted in *Defining the Political*. In the meanwhile, rereading Hintze in the light of the movements of civil society that led to the fall of the totalitarian empire, the other aspect of his argument—the role of the Estates in the emergence of Western modernity—appears more important than it did when I wrote this chapter. The jury remains out; but Hintze is an historian still worth pondering.

Part IV

Political Judgments

11

European Left, American Left: The Same Struggle?

It appears that the market, capital, and free enterprise have triumphed.[1] If there is any opposition, it appeals to atavistic grounds such as nationalism or integrist religiosity rather than to the values of a Left whose dominant characteristic has always been its belief in a radiant future and a necessary historical progress, if not a voluntarist utopia. The decisive defeat of what some called euphemistically, apologetically, or ironically "really existing socialism" seems in retrospect to have been inevitable. There may have been a time when (as Adorno put it) theory and the hope that it was supposed to incarnate remained valid even though, or because, practice was not up to its level. That dream has turned into a nightmare. The problem is not that the leaders have failed, or that conditions were not ripe, or that the imperialist enemy had forced a revolution that had been good and honest at its origin to follow a defensive and costly path. The very nature and possibility of leftist politics has been put into question. "What's left?" asked a series of articles in the not particularly left-wing daily newspaper, the *Frankfurter Allgemeine Zeitung*.[2]

New Left or Postmodern Left?

New contexts should not be interpreted by categories inherited from the Old Order. If the Cold War has ended, then both sides have lost their *raison d'être*: the Left and the Right, after all, defined each other reciprocally, and the disappearance of the one implies that the other too must vanish. The result, for some, is that we have come to "the

235

end of history.'' The idea of an end of history is paradoxically an idea shared by leftist visions, be they Marxist or not, and a Right whose most pregnant characteristic is its refusal of modernity. Does that mean, as Fukuyama and others claim, that we are experiencing the triumph of liberalism and, along with it, the end of ideologies?

Some want to make a virtue out of what they take to be a necessity; for them, we have entered into a postmodern world. This rhetorical turn of phrase is not as liberating as it appears. Western postmodernism can be interpreted as a theory invented by worn-out activists trying to justify their retreat from the political stage. Inverting their old beliefs without changing them, they assert that history has no sense and that it is therefore wrong to think that choices of action can be justified by the inevitable logic of a human progress or some other *grand récit*. For them, the old theory-praxis problem is just a vain mental exercise that attracts only immature minds that have not yet understood how old-fashioned and vain it is to take oneself seriously and to want to have a good conscience. The postmodernists, who claim to know better, praise themselves for having understood that the theory of historically necessary progress had served to justify a praxis that contradicted the goals that it wanted to achieve. In this sense, although it rejects its past, postmodernism now claims to be radical just because it rejects the idols of progress and humanity.[3]

The postmodernists cannot, however, simply forget history; indeed, they remain modernists in spite of their proclaimed intentions. Their radicalism forces them to remain militants, fighting against the ''old error'' that they know all the better because they were willing accomplices in its perpetuation. As a result, they still take a stance and have to confront its paradoxical implications: they are militants of antimilitantism. They refuse the idea that there is a progress in history precisely in order to be able to understand the true sense of history. They have replaced a theory that justifies practice by a theory that claims that praxis justifies itself. The irony is that this rejection of activist theory is based on the very same logic that, previously, had justified their activism: in the postmodern world, one must act within the logical framework of a postmodernist vision of history, and in so doing, one preserves the old modernist insistence on autonomous individual creation, which, however, is now justified by an external necessity rather than claiming to be the logical conclusion of an immanent development. The transparent relation of means and ends, theory and praxis, or practice and theory is thus retained in this inversely identical formulation.

In this way, postmodernism is founded on a paradox that it pro-duces. Its practical origins lay in the protest against a dehumanized functionalist architecture that claimed the label modernist and—as its immediate political corollary—promised literally to incarnate a future. Once the unified modernist theory was replaced by an eclectic, "Las Vegas" architecture based on the notion that "anything goes," a new theory was needed. Postmodernism was there with its offer. The difficulty, however, is that modernism was more than a theory, and to succeed in replacing the politics implied by modernism, postmodern-ism has to be more than a simple abstract negation of modernism. If it does not show its ability to cope with the political problems that the modernists were incapable of mastering, if postmodernism is not itself a politics, politics will impose itself on postmodernism. It is possible that the politics that will be imposed will not be what the radical postmodernists expect or what these still-militant ex-militants desired.

The new ex-militants who call themselves postmodernists not only retain their old worldview in their attitude toward politics, they have also maintained an attitude that is based on a moral Manichaeanism that refuses to accept the same bourgeois and philistine society hated and opposed by the traditional leftist militants. This leads to another move in their posture. Adopting Hegel and Marx's modern concept of *bürgerliche Gesellschaft*, they no longer translate *bürgerlich* as bourgeois; it now appears as a concept called "civil society" that is supposed to represent the opposition to a centralizing state and to the logical imperatives of impersonal technology. This ability to invert relations of power by conceptual reinterpretation has had a concrete correlate in Eastern Europe, where the domination of the Soviet empire seemed to rule out liberation of the nation-state but left open the possibility of playing off society against the state. This tactic, which the Hungarian György Konrad defined as "antipolitics," be-came a common metaphor for the processes that accelerated so rapidly in 1989. Why was it able to have this effect? Was it also postmodern in its understanding of the nature and limits of the political? What role can it play now that 1989 has come and gone? What does this East-West conceptual overlap imply?

The new ex-militants of the West had borrowed another lesson from Eastern Europe and another concept as well: the rights of man, which in the totalitarian East had obvious and direct political implications. The idea of a politics of human rights began to take shape; its claims were explicitly universalist and rationalist, and they laid claim to the modern tradition of the Enlightenment.[4] How could the new postmodernists deny the validity of historical universals at the same time that they used human rights as a justification of their own politics? The claim that the affirmation of human rights was a *de facto* redefinition of the nature of the political as such only covered over the basic problem. The dilemma remained hidden as long as there was a common enemy whose presence covered over the absence of a positive postmodernist politics.

After 1989, the incoherence could no longer be hidden. The Western postmodernist theory of "antipolitics" was transformed, nolens volens, into a *nonpolitics*. Ironically, for a time—even though no one asked its opinion—History had served to give a political sense to postmodernism. Today, that irony is no longer relevant. But morality and the spirit of revolt—which are essential to a Left politics—do not yet constitute a politics. This is all the more clear in the East, where those who were the vanguard of the revolutions of 1989 are disappearing from the political stage as normal political life asserts itself. One has the impression that the qualities needed for the antitotalitarian struggle have proven useless, if not frankly harmful, in the newly democratic societies. Postmodernism gains no support from that source. How, then, is one to find new criteria for critical judgment?

Before going further, let me make an autobiographical remark. The idea of a triumphal liberalism and the notion that modernity was identical to the "end of ideology" were common coin when I was a student in the United States in the 1960s. It was my generation that attempted in practice to refute those notions by inventing what was called a New Left. I will return to this experience, but it is important to underline from the outset the distinction between a Left that claims to be new and a Left that seeks to realize the ideals and the dreams of its ancestors. To give but one example, the American New Left did not attempt to realize and complete the timid beginnings of a welfare state whose task was to take charge of the life of those who were disfavored. It did not understand itself as *social*-democratic but rather as social-*democratic*. The distinction is important, although its implications were not clear at the time because the Cold War still deformed the perception of both the participants in the movement and external analysts. What was, on the other hand, clear, was that the New Left identified itself with the idea of civil rights, and that, a quarter of a century later, the idea of a *civil society* would find echos in that earlier experience.

In order to understand the present situation, I propose to return toward that recent past and to rediscover a world that was not yet deformed by political Manichaeanism. By recovering one of the moments marking the birth of modern politics, it will become possible to see that democracy is not defined as the opposite of socialism. Democracy is rather the practical critique of claims of all absolutism to unite in one institutional hand the moments of power, of law, and of the legitimate interpretation of the limits and applicability of power and law. In this sense, democracy is not a completed system that can be opposed to another system; it is rather the challenge to a hierarchical society inherited from a rigid and fixed past.

To understand the recent past, it is also necessary to see why the American, the West European, and the East European variants of a New Left differ in their own self-understandings, and why the illusion of a shared postmodern world is indeed an illusion. That requires a fuller historical detour—to the origin of democracy at the time of the French and American revolutions, which marks not only the beginnings of modern politics but also the moment when the distinction between the Left and the Right appeared. That historical reflection will explain why one has to talk today of the existence and the projects of a Left that is better called "posttotalitarian" than postmodern—but whose origins were present in outline within the New Left.

Between Determinism and Idealism

Don't worry: I'm not going to review two hundred years of comparative history in the course of this discussion. A couple of historical and even philosophical remarks will, however, cast some light on the contemporary problems that we face.

Leaving aside the context of the Cold War, the Left was defined traditionally by its modernizing project, which is itself based on a philosophy of history. That philosophy of history sees politics as a domain where the interaction of individual wills leads (in various ways) to the creation of a common will. The reality of the individualist and capitalist society that was born from the Revolution of 1789, however, was just the opposite of that optimistic image: and so the democratic Left had to redefine itself as *social*-democratic. Its politics had to be the expression either of a truly unified subject or at least of a subject whose political unification would realize the *telos* of history. That subject was then called the revolutionary agent; in Hegelian-Marxist language, it would be transformed from what it was "in itself" to become "for-itself," that is, self-consciously, the actor capable of giving a direction to the historical process. But this idealist and activist philosophy of history appealed also to materialist foundations in order to explain not just the real possibility but, in the last resort, the necessity of the appearance and realization of such a will. Thus, the direction given to history would be said to be, in fact, only the immanent direction of history itself. The arbitrariness of domination was thus, rhetorically, avoided.

We therefore have a picture of modernity as the *telos* of world history. Modernity will be realized by the intervention of (1) a subject that itself is conceived of as (2) an object produced by (3) a necessity inscribed in the very materiality of the world. On the basis of this trinitarian assumption, two possibilities can be distinguished: either the subjective will of the historical actors is made secondary to the search in the real world for a so-called principal contradiction that insures historical development; or else that principal contradiction is assumed to be found in the relations between the subject (including the rights that guarantee to that subject its individuality) and a material world that tends to deny it the autonomy that some continue to call "bourgeois."

In the first case, the result is a determinist materialism; in the second case, an idealism with a strongly voluntarist flavor emerges. It is worth noting that the first option, which came to be called "structuralist" in the 1960s, is compatible with the postmodernist theory insofar as they both deny the subject as a volitional entity.[5] The second option could appear during the same period as the existentialist critique of an ontological alienation with Sartre and those whom he influenced. The second option carries also other possibilites if one underlines—as I suggested a moment ago—the rights that make it possible for the subject to exist as an autonomous individual. The reason that I stressed that aspect was that I wanted to return to the American and the French Revolutions in order now to begin the comparative analysis of the contemporary Lefts.

History and Its Exception

America and France share an attitude toward their own history: each insists on the exceptional nature of its national story. Despite this similarity, their histories can be seen as polar forms of the relation that can exist between the political and the social. Whereas the Americans separate the two domains and tend to concentrate their energies on the social, the French seek to unify the two in a movement that starts from the political and incorporates the social. It is not necessary to develop here these two well-known schemas: American democracy is rooted in its social experience whereas the French variant tends to take a political form. Americans are said to be pragmatic, materialist, and ready to work with their neighbors to resolve problems that concern them all, whereas the French are said to be statists and idealists, waiting for solutions from an external agency that defines what is permitted. The American is said to believe that history ended with his revolution, which he takes as a model valid for the entire world, as long as that world is willing and able to look to it ("the City on the Hill" of the Puritans); whereas the French historical project carries a vision of a future that is not simply national but international (the Grande Nation). These two so-called exceptional histories suggest an approach to our question of the two Lefts today, and the lesson to be learned for 1989.

The American Left is caught in a political context where everything pushes toward a depoliticization. This takes the form of a pluralism of interests and movements that act and compete in society in a way that insures that none of them can have a long-term and direct impact on the whole. This was the vision of the most political of the Framers of the Constitution, James Madison, who explained it clearly in the tenth *Federalist Paper*. The pluralist system excludes any radical challenge—not by censoring or banning opposition, but by coopting, integrating, and assimilating it. An American Left therefore cannot present a fundamental oppostion, a radical or moral denial of the entire system. Such total and totalizing critique would appear to be "un-American"—as was seen in the 1950s, when the congressional committee that attempted to repress social movements that took a political form was called the House Un-American Activities Committee (HUAC). It should perhaps be no surprise that one of the first appearances of the New Left was at a demonstration against this committee when it came to San Francisco to hold a hearing at the beginning of the 1960s.

The French Left, on the other hand, could understand itself as being part of the national project; even more, it could claim to be the legitimate heir of an historical project that was either betrayed by the Right, or which the right was incapable of realizing. Thus, in France—as elsewhere in Europe in the nineteenth century—nationalism could be a left-wing project. After the Second World War, the European Left tried to reclaim its own national history, most clearly in the case of the French Communist Party, which claimed to be the party of the victimized heros (the *parti des fusillés*). But the rival Gaullists also claimed the legacy of the nation. For the same reason, the French and the European Lefts concerned themselves with the completion of their welfare states, and managed to assure to their citizens some of the basic forms of social solidarity that are necessary to the existence of a unified nation. This meant that the Right could not fall back on a kind of free-market individualism; and so the dividing line of Left and Right was, in Europe, far to the "Left" of the American division.

The European Left was thus rooted in a tradition of which it was the highest point and culmination; it was part of a history of which it could legitimately consider itself the heir. For its part, the American Left faced a choice that wasn't a real choice: either try to create a European Left at home, or else redefine the political parameters that denied the Left a legitimate place in the national story in order then to develop its own program and action. That is why the American Left returned to the campuses, where research concerning social history and popular culture could give it access to the national tradition, and to the idea that its own project was not totally foreign to the nation.

But the European Left lost its self-assuredness at the time of decolonization. It had to ask whether to interpret each of the individual histories of the colonies as part of that progressive history that supposedly included them all in a project of liberation. Should support for autonomist movements be based simply on autonomy as the ultimate value in our modern world, such that anyone who asserts it deserves to have it? This question can be posed in terms of the theoretical choice between a structural-materialist analysis or a politics founded in the autonomy of the political will. The victory of the latter option had important consequences for the development of the European Left (which became Third Worldist and lost its simple identity with the history of the nation). Meanwhile, the American disaster in Vietnam could be seen to have liberated its Left from the impossible task of imitating the European model. The result was that the American Left had to take on the project of creating a New Left that could renew its relations to the democratic roots of the American polity that were founded by its Revolution and by its refusal of a static and hierarchical society. We will see the implications of that new approach to the political when we return to the political choices that emerged in 1989.[6]

Old and New Left

We need now to retrace some of the stages of the evolution from an Old toward a New Left. To do so, it will be helpful to recall some well-known events but without claiming to present an exhaustive interpretation of them. Not only events in the directly political arena count here; intellectual reflection on political life and its transformations can also be part of the kind of political change that concerns us in the present context.

A: 1956

The Kruschev Secret Report on Stalinism, the Polish reforms in October, followed by the Hungarian Revolution and the Russian intervention were one side of a picture that was counterbalanced by the Franco-British-Israeli intervention in Suez, to which the American refusal to participate put an end.

The first serious challenge to the socialist nature of the Soviet Union was thus relativized by the imperialist aims of what proved to be dying empires. The wave of decolonization now had to be taken seriously. The United States, which was not contaminated by Suez, could easily imagine that decolonization represented a confirmation of its political values since there did not exist anything like an American Left after McCarthyism. Indeed, those who maintained honorably the cause of the Left took as the title of the journal they founded in 1956 *Dissent*. This was the moment of the apotheosis of liberalism among historians, even those who had previously been politically engaged, such as Louis Hartz or Richard Hofstadter. Another political veteran, Daniel Bell, published the book that retrospectively described an epoch, *The End of Ideology*, at the end of the decade.

Meanwhile, decolonization gave birth to two tendencies: (1) Sartre's "Fanon" had a resonance in the United States, particularly among the many who became admirers of Fidel Castro, and then took as models the moral purity of Che and his voluntarist politics of revolution carried across the Third World; (2) geopolitical theories that claimed to show that anti-imperialism was the only way to make a revolution *within* the imperialist nations. The theoretical translation of this orientation was found in the pamphlet of the (temporary and failed) successor to Mao, Lin Piao, whose proposal to "create one, two, many Vietnams" was less voluntarist and more structuralist than it at first appeared. The point is that the Left responses to the apparent solidity of the First World once again follow the pattern of division into the poles of voluntarism and a quest for structural necessity.

The successes in decolonization forced a re-evalutation on the domestic front. The creative trade unionist activities in Italy, and their translation (and reformulation) in France by Serge Mallet and André Gorz were significant contributions to the new mood. Although he was perhaps better known for his concept of the "new working class," Mallet posed the crucial challenge in *Le Gaullisme et la Gauche* (1965): has capitalism entered a new stage of development, to which the old theories and politics are no longer adequate? In *La nouvelle classe ouvrière* (1963), Mallet had explained that his new analysis emerged from his experience as a communist union organizer: each time he would visit a new factory, the local militants—trying, apparently, to rationalize their own failures, would explain: "comrade, you must realize that things are different here." Mallet came to realize that they were right; there were distinctions among categories of workers; there is no unified revolutionary subject. But Mallet, who was an active participant in the May 1968 events in France, was killed in an automobile accident before he could unite a new structural account of a differentiated society with a politics that would avoid the danger of voluntarism.

In the case of André Gorz, a member of the editorial board of *Les Temps Modernes*, the Italian trade union experience led to the idea that one had to invent "revolutionary reforms" aimed not only at the working class but also at the growing population of students and technical workers in a modernizing Europe (proposing, for example, wages for students who in the modern mode of production are only glorified apprentices). Despite its reformist novelty, this proposal still reflected the presence of a Marxist, productivist paradigm as its premise; Old Left presuppositions limited the search for new questions. Gorz would go further in the 1980s, in *Adieux au prolétariat* (1980) and then in *Les chemins du paradis* (1983), before publishing in 1988 his remarkable *Métamorphes du travail. Quête du sens. Critique de la raison économique*—where the Marxian paradigm is finally consigned to the wastebasket. But this gets us ahead of our story.[7]

B: The Birth of a New Left in the USA

The Civil Rights movement, and in its wake, the emergence of the first forms of feminism represented the birth of a New Left. What is important here is the public character of the demands being made; the quest is not for what some called bourgeois reforms. One has to bear in mind the pioneering function of the Free Speech Movement at Berkeley, and recall as well that the American SDS was an abbreviation for Students for a Democratic Society unlike the German SDS, which as the radicalized and then expelled youth section of the Socialist Party was the *Sozialistischer Deutscher Studentenbund*. I will return to this point in a moment. First, May 1968 should be introduced into the discussion in order to underline above all the international character of the sensibility that was being expressed, which the term anti-authoritarian summarizes well. Not only should one not forget the influence of the occupation of Columbia University on the militants of the 22 March movement at Nanterre; equally important was the sense of an international effervescence and a commonality of rebellious sensibilities that, for example, I encountered on leaving Paris in June 1968 to travel to England, Germany, and Italy. Even in Switzerland, one encountered kindred spirits.

I alluded to the German SDS a moment ago because in a certain sense they were the ones who mediated between the new political forms of action that the Americans were trying out and the European tradition. Raised in a postwar society that some of them disdainfully called "the dictated or imposed democracy" (*die oktroyierte Demokratie*), their Social-Democratic Party had been reformed at the Bad Godesberg Congress of 1961 where all references to the Marxist-Socialist project were eliminated. This party appeared now as a sort of imitation of the American Democratic Party and called itself a "people's party" (*Volkspartei*). At the same time, because of the American influence on their educational system after the war, the younger Germans had not been exposed to the works of Marx and the Marxist tradition, and could therefore believe that there existed a true socialist thought that someone was hiding from them. They thus became at once hypertheoretical, sometimes nearly scholastic in their Marxism; and at the same time, they were militant activists suspicious of any compromise. The passion of their activism was rendered the more fierce because of their hatred for the complicity of their fathers with the Nazi regime (which some take to be one reason for some of them to have been tempted later by terrorism—a choice that is the opposite of any Left politics).

The importance of the German SDS is also explained by the geographical proximity of Germany to Eastern Europe. But—and this is a crucial point—despite a common anti-authoritarian sensibility, there was no meeting of minds. Typical was a meeting in Prague in 1967 between the Berlin SDS led by Rudi Dutschke and a group of Czech student dissidents. As some of the latter explained to me when I visited that year, the Germans wanted to realize the socialism that they imagined without understanding the good fortune of their own political situation, whereas the Czechs dreamed of freedoms whose only foundation and only content was a radical autonomy. The two poles were again separated. This single meeting symbolizes one of the reasons why, when German unification took place twenty-two years later, the Left (i.e., the Greens, the left wing of the SPD, and parts of the intelligentsia) was ill prepared. It suggests as well why a theory like that of Rudolf Bahro describing what he called "really existing socialism" could be so explosive in the 1980s, when the choice seemed to be between a turn to terrorism or the privatization of the political. It was also the reason that the *Ostpolitik* of Willy Brandt's Social Demo-cratic Party, which sought a change through rapprochement (*Wandel durch Annäherung*), could be criticized by the Right after 1989 as proposing "change through brown-nosing" (*Wandel durch Anbieder-ung*). In a word, the German Left had been Americanized; it offered no model for a New Left.

If we return to France after this encounter with Eastern Europe, we see the emergence of a serious reflection on totalitarianism and, in particular, in the journal *Esprit* and in the writings of its editor, Paul Thibaud, the attempt to translate the notion of human rights into a politics. This represented a radical shift from the statist images of politics that the still Stalinist French Communist Party could use in its own behalf. At its most extreme, this would take the form of a speaker—say against the American war in Vietnam—joining with the public in applause—since, after all, the speaker was only the mouth-piece through which universal truth was being expressed. This new orientation returns us to the early American SDS's stress on civil rights. What is important also in this new French politics more gener-ally is that antitotalitarianism is not so much a rupture with a previous political engagement; rather, it is a way of adjusting one's goals and thinking anew the relation between ends and means.[8]

C: Toward a Posttotalitarian Left

While the French were reflecting on totalitarianism and its effects on leftist politics, madness fought with realism among those who were trying to reinvent a left-wing politics ("realos" vs. "fundis" among the Greens, identity politics among minorities, and among the intellectuals, first in the United States, then in Europe too, and the rejection of the "subject" for ex-structuralists who had become postmodernists). On the other side, the political class continued a practice that was apparently the opposite of that of the Left but that showed itself in fact to be identical with it: the Cold War intensified, Reagan thought he could destroy the welfare state by running a deficit so large that no new spending would be possible; at the same time he sought the destruction of communism by means of an accelerated arms race (well designated by the German term, *totrusten*: arm them to death). On the other side, the pacificist movement claimed to be the realist alternative to a Cold War that national politicians constantly rekindled because they lacked any other legitimations for their actions. What was one to think of the surprising propositions at the Reykjavik Summit? Did Gorbie know already what awaited him?

At this point, I have to take up a point that has been only referred to briefly thus far: the Eastern European Left. When I speak of an Eastern European Left, I am not referring to the kind of intraparty opposition that was able to triumph in Poland in 1956, for example. Granted, we cannot know what would have happened to the Czech reforms undertaken when Dubcek replaced Novotony and the old guard: could socialism with a human face have been stabilized or were the oppositions to the Dubcek-led party (such as the famous "5000 Words" or the attempts by certain autonomous students to join with young factory workers during the summer of 1968) the first sign of a crumbling that would take place even more rapidly in 1989, once the fraternal aid of the Soviet Union was no longer a threat. Perhaps twenty-five years ago a reform was possible—but I doubt it. In all events, Soviet tanks (and those of the allies in the Warsaw pact—save Romania) put an end to the experiment.

The spirit of Prague was seen by some in the West as that of a New Left that refused all forms of paternalism and external control. Some claimed that this represented the emergence of youth as a class or as a political subject; for others, it was only a reflection of a postproductivist society that replaced the old competitive model. The Western attempts at theorizing the new forms of life and of political action after 1968 came from different groups—from the Situationists to feminists and homosexuals, each claimed a right to autonomy. Whether the accent was put on autonomy or on rights, what was behind all of the demands of these new movements was the idea that politics had to be redefined.[9] That was the idea behind the American slogan "the personal is the political," just as it motivated the Prague students who came under fire when, in 1967, they organized an autonomous demonstration against the war in Vietnam (which of course their party also opposed): it was not the content of political slogans but rather the *autonomy* behind political decisions and the *right* to public debate that the party leaders feared. This same spirit would give birth later to initiatives like Charter 77, whose political thinking should not be identified only with the existential moralism of Vàclav Havel.

The problem is that the transformation of the existential and individualist concept of autonomy into political terms is not self-evident or immediate. The missing link was the notion of rights and laws, and their relation to the political. Without that link, the years following 1968 saw a series of excesses and exaggerations often based on a voluntarism seeking to legitimate particular causes by appeal to the sacrosanct idea of autonomy. Democracy gradually came to mean anything goes.[10] This is where Eastern Europe presented the inspiration for the conceptual renewal of left-wing politics by the way that it managed to give political content to the Third Basket of the Helsinki Accords (which guaranteed the protection of human rights). From Charter 77 to KOR and on to Solidarity and then to the Bulgarian Ecoglasnost, the path passed each time by the question: how to make human rights into a politics? The answer depended on rethinking the political.

The Left after 1989

After this sketchy and impressionistic historical excursus, we find ourselves after 1989 face-to-face with a history that has once again shown itself to be open. The question now is not what is new about the New Left but what is the Left in this new world?

A: Two Hundred Years Later

Recall the historical point from which we began: the American and French Revolutions that marked out two distinct paths for left politics. At the same time, both revolutions put into question the established hierarchical order and posed the problem of an open history and that of the subjects—or the conditions—that make that history. In this light, the "events"—to speak like the French in 1968—of 1989 constitute a revolution, and the Left has to support that revolution. The Left cannot hope for a return to a (reformed) Old Order, nor even for the chimera of a Third Way. But does 1989 only repeat 1789? Will 1993 bring modern versions of Robespierre and the other members of the revolutionary portrait gallery? Will there emerge the kind of divisions seen in 1793, when a leadership that was unable to lead the nation to safe harbors justified its remaining in power by denouncing all those who wanted to form some sort of compromise with the established order as counterrevolutionary? It would be naive to doubt that something like that could occur—but that is not the only possible path.

B: Constitutional or Economic Solutions?

Should one hope for an American-style solution, characterized by the creation of a constitutional space that protects the rights of individuals so that they can seek the good as they see fit?[11] Once again, it would be naive to refuse, especially to people who are emerging from forty years of deprivation, the right to live the life of a privatized consumer. But it would also be naive to think that such a life suffices and that people are ready once and for all to give themselves over to such a life. As a kind of empirical proof, recall that the political invention of a New Left took place in the United States at the end of the 1950s in just those years that, retrospectively, are called the best years of our economic lives. Does that imply that a Left is born only in a stable, productive, and prosperous society? If that is the case, what can one hope for in the ex-Soviet empire? Will developments in that part of the world affect our own possibilities—just as it did when the antitotalitarian analysis led to the invention of a politics of the rights of people?

C: Defining Necessity

The problem that confronts the newly liberated Eastern Europeans is that of defining necessity. It seems to all of them—and they are not wrong at this level of generalization—that the free market with its implacable logic and its imperative of efficiency that will not surrender to moralizing appeals and that rejects advancement by personal favor or bribery—is the *sine qua non* of any attempt to reorganize their societies and their personal lives as well. In this, they are still antiauthoritarians in being opposed to arbitrariness, even while accepting the impersonal and supposedly neutral authority of the market. The problem is knowing how far this market necessity should penetrate into the lives of the society and the individual. What are the limits of its application? What are the unintended consequences that will come forward when, for example, market logic penetrates into academic relations, or personal health, or social conviviality?

This problem of the political meaning of "necessity" leads to three final questions:

1. Does the Left define itself as a political formation capable of looking reality in the face and of making the hard decisions that are necessary? That is what the French Socialists wanted people to think when, in 1983, after the failure of their attempt to pursue *social*-democratic policies of redistribution, they opted for an austerity politics (which they nonetheless called a "politics of rigor" for fear of shocking the sensibility of their socialist foot soldiers). That is also the politics of a large part of the former opposition in Eastern Europe, where it is justified by contrast to the voluntarism and the irrealism of the former communist regimes. But, once again, how can one define the domain of that which is necessary? Is this not precisely the task of the political? One should recall the American Framers who, in Philadelphia in 1787, said that they were not giving their fellow citizens the best constitution but the best one that they could accept. But how does one find out what is acceptable?[12]

2. I said at the outset that the Left that emerged from the French Revolution could understand itself as part of a continuous national history, and I suggested that the structural conflict of the American Left with its own history forced it to take positions that were incapable of gaining public support. The Revolutions in Eastern Europe seem to present a third possibility for understanding the relation of the Left to its own national history (since, despite national differences, each experienced the common thread of Soviet external domination and communist control domestically). Each of these countries has to find a way to make sense of and to integrate forty years of nonsense, of political repression and economic sloppiness that also had their effects in the private sphere. This poses the question: how can the Left be conceived within an historical continuity? Or is the Left defined by certain universal ideals that transcend history?

3. This is where an element that I have not mentioned until now finds its place within any left-wing politics: morality. The appeal to historical necessity or to material structures too often leads one to forget this dimension—which should not be reduced to individual behavior or private relations. The question that is implicit in the quest for a definition of the Left is precisely that of the relation between the

behavior of the individual and his or her social responsibility. In the present context, the ethical question appears concretely as that of the responsibility of each of us for our actions, inactions, or compromises. The situation was clearer for those who lived in the old totalitarian societies—and by implication, for those in the West who stood on their side.[13] Today as well, there will be an impact in the West of the solutions proposed in the East. The attitude to be adopted toward the world of business, the reform of health care, or the limits and rights of the private sphere cannot be decided in terms of individual behavior alone. A broader sense of our responsibilities comes about when the challenge of reconstituting democracy defines the frame in which questions of morality as well as those of necessity and authority are posed. That is, when we recognize that we can only affirm our own autonomy if, at the same time, by the same action, we actively solicit and encourage that of others. This is the final criterion, the one that can avoid any temptation for the Left to return to the kind of paternalism, do-goodism, and self-satisfied sacrifice in the service of the victim that were just what tended to define—sometimes for the best, but usually for the worse, the Old Left.

Post Scriptum (1995)

Two issues should be mentioned here in conclusion. The remarks concerning the immanent contradictions of postmodernism were intended as a warning—to the reader, but also to myself. The idea of "defining the political" can lead to arbitrariness, a perverse kind of voluntarism that makes a virtue out of the inability of the Left to formulate practical political proposals. The reason for this was seen to lie in the need to find a space between idealism and materialism. Once that problem has been seen, then the postmodernist temptation gives way, and one can follow the European and American attempts over some forty years to find a political solution in the form of a New Left. That is why, finally, a discussion that began by trying to learn from the postmoderns concludes by pointing to the need, instead, to learn from the experience of the antitotalitarian experience taking place still in Eastern Europe.

Notes

1. This is the revision of a talk given in January 1992 at the Fondation de l'Ecole Polytechnique in Paris. Earlier versions were published in *Autres*

Temps, in *M*, and in *Aesthetik und Kommunikation*. The present version was reworked for the Canadian journal *Possibles* and is translated by the author from that version. Although the spoken styles in English and French are different, in translating this paper I have tried to preserve the oral cadance.

2. See *What's Left? Prognosen zur Linken* (Berlin: Rorbuch Verlag, 1993).

3. The category "postmodernist" does not refer to any single individual, although the reader may recognize aspects of the arguments developed by Jean-François Lyotard or those of André Glucksmann. The category is certainly exemplified most clearly in France, where this paper was first presented. Despite this geographical-historical specificity, I think that the type of attitude that is described here is also present in other postmodernists—although more often implicitly, since the category was, after all, originally coined in France.

4. The most important contributions to this debate are to be found in the journal *Esprit*, which published the work of Claude Lefort, Jean-Marc Ferry, Luc Ferry, Pierre Hassner, and Paul Thibaud. The idea of a politics of human rights posed problems for conservatives, for whom individualism and secularism are of course the original sins of modernity. These problems are seen in the writings of Pierre Manent, published in the journal *Commentaire*. For an analysis, see the reply to Manent by Claude Lefort, "Les droits de l'homme et l'Etat-providence," *Esprit*, November 1985, reprinted in *Essais sur le politique* (Paris: Editions du Seuil, 1986).

5. It was no accident, as one used to say, that Althusser and Derrida were colleagues at the Ecole normale for so many years; or in more postmodernist terms, their cohabitation had to leave "traces."

6. Third Worldist voluntarism and its political consequences were also present in the United States. But the difference between the historical-cultural traditions meant that the ideals of the militants, who expected that certain "exemplary actions" or militarized-militant organizations would be capable of overthrowing the state and taking power, were totally irrealist. Nonetheless, there is no need to go to the other extreme, which asserts that the lack of a European-style state in the United States implies that a revolution would only take place there when daily life itself is radically transformed. "Change Life" (*changer la vie*) is only a political slogan; the challenge is that of *rethinking the political*. The personal is not the political, as I will argue in a moment.

7. On Gorz and Mallet's early work, see my "New Situation, New Strategy: Serge Mallet and Andre Gorz" in *The Unknown Dimension: European Marxism Since Lenin*, edited by Dick Howard and Karl E. Klare (New York: Basic Books, 1972), and my preface to Serge Mallet, *Essays on the New Working Class* (St. Louis: Telos Press, 1975). On Gorz's later work, see the afterword to *The Marxian Legacy*.

8. Like all generalizations, this one exaggerates: it neglects those who would in fact become liberals in the American sense of the term, and also others who would become neoconservatives. Nonetheless, it seems to me that those who worked through (in a quasi-Freudian sense of this term) the critique

of totalitarianism think differently about politics than those who simply chose to work in one or another traditional political direction or organization.

9. Some of the reasoning behind this demand appears in the essays collected in *Defining the Political* and in *The Politics of Critique*.

10. Thus, for example, it seemed to me that the failure of May 1968 could be dated to the moment when, toward the end of May, during a general assembly at the University of Nanterre, some students came into the room with cans of paint that they threw onto the walls. That was supposed to incarnate free or liberated art. But spontaneity is not identical either to politics or to creativity in itself.

11. I have considered this view, and the arguments particularly of Bruce Ackerman and Ulrich Preuss, in the introduction to the German translation of *The Birth of American Political Thought*. See *Die Grundlegung der amerikanischen Demokratie* (Frankfurt am Main: Suhrkamp Verlag, 1996).

12. See, in this regard, the discussion of "The Politics of Sacrifice or the Sacrifice of Politics," chapter 12 of this volume.

13. See "Guilt and the Birth of Democracy," chapter 13 of this volume.

12

The Politics of Sacrifice or the Sacrifice of Politics?

The budget that President Clinton proposed on 17 February 1993 sought to mark out a new political course after twelve years of Republican faith in the wisdom of unregulated markets and unleashed acquisitiveness. The budget that Congress approved nearly six months later, by the narrowest possible margin, seemed little different from the deficit cutting "deal" reached by President Bush and Congress in 1990—a deal that some said cost Bush his reelection. Along the way, step-by-step, the new president constantly lost his footing, gave ground and grounds to his opponents who united against him while his own supporters quarreled, complained, and broke ranks. Sometimes his problems were cosmetic or bad staff work (such as a two-hundred dollar haircut by a coiffeur named Pierre while the presidential plane was blocking the runways of Los Angeles airport, or the "Nannie-gate" problems of his first two nominees for attorney general); sometimes they showed an apparent lack of principle (as in the withdrawal of the contested appointment for a black woman as assistant attorney general for Civil Rights, or the compromise on gays in the military); and sometimes the two combined to produce the image of a president unwilling to take strong positions or unable to make them stick by rallying representatives or appealing over their heads to the public (as in the withdrawal of increased fees for the use of public lands in the West in the face of opposition from the region's senators, which led implacably to retreat from the ecologically progressive and economically vital energy tax that would produce the revenue to fund urban and educational reform). But the budget did pass, and the president could claim that it was a necessary, though limited, first step. Still, the margin of victory was narrow, public opinion is divided evenly about its significance, and the popular disillusion with politics that defeated President Bush has returned.

Various reasons could be advanced to explain the present unhappy state of American politics. On the one side, there are structural problems built into American political institutions, which tend to produce "gridlock" between a president elected nationally for a four-year term, a Senate chosen for six years and composed of two representatives from each state (regardless of population), and a House of Representatives whose members serve for two years for districts of equal population. On the other side, there are conjunctural problems, the greatest of which is the ominous deficit accumulated under the Republicans who, at the same time, let enormous social pressures build by reducing the funding available to cities and states. In between lie the political parties, economic interests, and associations of a still-vibrant, though frayed, civil society that compete for influence and prizes. Can a president—especially one elected by a minority of the voters, 19 percent of whom preferred the nostrums of the "antipolitician" Ross Perot—govern in such conditions? Ronald Reagan did.[1] Can Bill Clinton?

The unhappy state is not unique to American politics. Western Europe, which seemed well on its way to new unity with the signing of the Maastricht Accord, faces similar dilemmas. The final ratification of the Maastricht Treaty by the Danes (who rejected it the first time) and the British seems almost as anticlimactic as does the passage of Clinton's budget. Structural problems lame the institutions of the European Community while conjunctural difficulties rip at its social fabric. Its inability to act in the former Yugoslavia and the *de facto* destruction of the European Monetary System (EMS) that was to unify its monies and lead to fiscal harmonization have left Europe without a political project. The widely felt "democratic deficit" is visible in the fact that, were Europe a state, it would not meet the democratic criteria required for admission to the European Community (EC). Meanwhile, the Oder-Neisse line that now divides it from East Europe has become a sort of Rio Grande, protecting the EC from unwanted immigrants. The national political parties are in disarray, an international civil society scarcely exists, and economic interest produces only an unstoppable growth of unemployment. How can independent states, or the citizens of independent states, form a community? The old philosophical question of the source of the solidarity that is presupposed by the social contract acquires here a modern form.

Without that solidarity, the contract is only formal and will break at the first challenge.

More concretely, what is common to the unhappy state in Europe and America is the need for sacrifice. Individuals must be brought to recognize the priority of the collective good. But how can modern individual*ists* come to accept—to participate in—a politics of sacrifice that puts others first? One solution to the problem was suggested by the process of European unification, which culminated in the Maastricht Treaty. As we shall see, the problem is that this type of politics of sacrifice is bought at the price of a *sacrifice of politics*. A similar temptation faces President Clinton, who can appeal to the implacable "necessities" imposed by the budget deficit in order to get his way. The danger is that this tactic becomes a strategy, that the reduction of the deficit becomes not a means to political renewal but an end in itself. This is what seems to have happened, as the president gave up his progressive energy tax, abandoned his stimulative investment program, put off the reform of the welfare system, and scaled back his volunteer community services project. By appealing only to economic necessity, the president appears weak; with no positive programs, he can neither rally his own supporters nor divide and conquer his enemies.[2] The victim is politics itself, whose dignity is debased when, for example, a senator, worried about reelection, says, in public, to the president: I will vote for your budget if it has a gas tax of 4.3 cents but not if the tax is 5 cents. The antipolitician, Ross Perot, will surely reappear on such a political stage.

A politics of sacrifice that does not sacrifice politics depends on the solidarity of citizens. Sacrifice is not charity; its foundation is more than human compassion, which is ultimately private, not political. That is why the polls that say that Americans are ready to sacrifice in order to reduce the budget deficit are deceptive. Those who demand that the president stand on principle and appeal to "the nation" over the heads of its representatives neglect this distinction. By the same token, raising revenues by imposing levies on gasoline, cigarettes, or liquor—or, as is occasionally suggested, imposing a value-added tax (VAT)—is an excuse to avoid the political challenge. Even the fact that Clinton's budget draws 80 percent of its new revenues by taxing the wealthy and the corporations can produce at best the unity of populist resentment against "the interests" but not political solidarity among autonomous individuals. The missing link lies in that wide and amorphous middle class to whom Clinton's campaign appealed; but what is a middle-class politics? If it is to be more than an oxymoron, the possibility of political renewal must be shown—and the temptations of antipolitics need to be illustrated. The parallel hopes and illusions raised by Clinton's election and by the Maastricht Treaty pose the classical question of political philosophy—how to form a community of free individuals—in the contemporary form of a middle-class politics.

Return of the Political?

At first glance, it appears that the American elections and Maastricht process point in the same direction: to a renewal of politics after a period during which the market and its ironclad necessities formed the basis of an antipolitics. In the United States, this trend, which began in the later Carter years, became a new religion with the triumph of Ronald Reagan. In Europe, the French Socialists' 1983 refusal of neo-Jacobin calls to withdraw from the European monetary "snake" seemed to confirm the wisdom of Thatcher-Reaganism. More dramatically than the replacement of Helmut Schmitt by Helmut Kohl, it implied not just the dominance of the market but also that no nation could go it alone; the nation-state seemed a remnant of the nineteenth century with the function of providing symbolic satisfaction to its citizens while insuring that the market provides neutral ground for the pursuit of private happiness. Problems that formerly would have been dealt with politically were left to a moral rhetoric whose function was to insure loyalty and gain mass support from private individuals. A temporary economic boom made it unnecessary to worry about the fact that this devaluation of politics permitted the emergence of virulent social problems (abortion and multiculturalism in the United States, immigrants and racism in Europe), which could become explosive if they did not find a place in the political arena. By 1992 it had become necessary to look for a new political initiative, from Washington, and outside the rule-making Eurocracy of Brussels.

From this perspective, candidate Clinton's "the economy, stupid" was not just an electoral slogan recalling the New Deal Keynesian idea that politics must intervene to direct and correct the anonymous forces of the market; it meant also that the social issues that had divided Americans had become problems that could be healed only by political action.[3] (This is perhaps the reason Clinton did not stress the usual liberal argument that, were Bush reelected, the right wing would dominate the Supreme Court and impose its social and cultural agenda; he implied that these issues had to be solved by political means, reversing the antipolitical temptation to solve social problems by leaving them to the supposed neutrality of the courts that had proved so pernicious to the Democratic Party.[4]) In this sense, Clinton's so-called waffling on issues rather than taking univocal stands is not a character weakness, since character becomes important only when politics as a process no longer integrates society and the only thing that guides the privatized elector is TV images. Waffling could be a recognition that politics is the art of confronting difficult choices and of finding legitimate compromises based on reasoned adherence rather than symbolic loyalty. Similarly, the use of "town meetings" and talk shows that the press criticized for avoiding its "expert" questions about issues could show a concern for the problems of real people—and a recognition that politics *is* an art of appearances, not a science of economic tinkering.[5]

From this same perspective, Maastricht would be a reply to the "democratic deficit" of the European nations whose political class was discredited not only by scandal (including the scandal of its own self-reproduction and self-protection) but also by its irrelevance to the tasks at hand. This irrelevance was of course of its own making, once it had yielded to the imperatives of the market. Maastricht appeared to point beyond the Treaty of Rome's creation of a common economic market by promising a new form of political integration, a community entailing eventually a social charter and perhaps even a common foreign policy. Limited as sovereign nations, Europe needed to invent a larger framework for political action to be possible. Lacking a political project at home, their self-unification would provide a new one. This political space could englobe and restrain the savage market forces, putting the economy in its proper place and defining its boundaries. Eventually, the new Europe might even re-create the structure that apparantly had become antiquated: a supranational state would emerge in which the market, culture, and politics function as a unified whole, taming the forces of the global economy and commodified culture while encouraging new types of regional cooperation and environmentally sound development. Above all, it would provide the sense or *telos* without which no political project can emerge and acquire legitimacy.

Although this rediscovery of the virtues of the political was apparently given wings by the end of the Cold War and the triumph of democracy, in fact, the results of 1989 are more ambiguous. In America, they encouraged the traditional reflex to withdraw from the secretive and opaque world of diplomacy and to focus on the social problems neglected by Reagan and his unlucky heir. In a paradoxical sense, George Bush's great moment, Desert Storm, made possible Clinton's new politics; and Bush's inability to project a vision of a New World Order meant that American foreign policy would be limited to clear-cut, legally defined forms of power projection in a world otherwise left to its own devices. This legalism entailed an orientation toward multilateral action for the common interest rather than unilateral projection of a way of life against the enemy. Renewal at home was thought to be compatible with legalism abroad; but political choice could not be so easily avoided. Candidate Clinton attacked President Bush's inaction in Bosnia, while President-elect Clinton agreed with the defeated George Bush's intervention in Somalia, and President Clinton found himself caught in an imbroglio in Somalia and unable to lead his allies in Bosnia. Foreign politics can no more be left to the antipolitical realm of international law than domestic politics can be reduced to economic imperatives.[6]

The new political vision guiding Europe appeared more comprehensive. The rule of the global economy had limited the reach of the state, and had made domestic politics sterile while consecrating egoism in the name of the entrepreneur. After the revolutions of 1989, when Warsaw was closer to Berlin than Bonn to Lisbon, the political dimension of economics could not be ignored. Silent in 1987, when Serbian advances into Kosovo prefigured the present Yugoslav confusion, Europe had to find mechanisms of collective decision. It could not simply repeat historical patterns—although that is what it ultimately did: German recognition of Croatia opposed by French Serbophilia proving British wisdom in keeping distant from a continent whose division was traditionally quite acceptable to it. Still, the demise of the Warsaw Pact confirmed the anachronism of the political ideologies that had made domestic divisions into issues rather than problems. This meant that the debate over a European political vision might become the basis for not only a realignment of the political parties but also for a rejuvenation of political life. This new political project would be accompanied by the expansion of regional alliances cutting across artificial state frontiers and bringing the citizenry closer to politics. At the same time, the lesson learned from Eastern European opposition to totalitarianism was that only the autonomy of civil society can prevent the antipolitical illusion of a technocratic state above the realities of daily life.

This picture of a return of the political in the Western democracies can be accused of idealism. Clinton is not FDR nor is he JFK; the

America of 1992 inherited burdens undreamt of in 1932 or 1960. The weight of the deficit prevents a social policy directed at the unemployed and underemployed who have been excluded from the market; it rules out also the kind of fiscal boost offered by Kennedy's 1962 tax cut. Worse, as opposed to 1932, the nation is divided, its social fabric torn, its cultural ethos weakened; as opposed to 1960, its industrial base is not adapted to job creation, its workers are ill prepared, its educational system is anemic, and ethnicity has replaced civil rights as the tie that binds. A voluntarist politics from Washington in these conditions could discredit the political, reinforcing the notion that only the law of the market can save us.[7] The same voluntarism could sink the Maastricht process. Europe has been incapable of formulating a foreign policy even as suffering comes closer to its borders (and onto its TV screens); its open frontiers have provided no solution for its unemployed and excluded, while its immigrant problem has become not only a political but a social—and moral—dilemma. The members of the "community" congratulate themselves on preserving a unity that they can maintain only by doing nothing. Conceived on the model of a nation-state, Europe plays the role that socialism once played: it is a *telos*, constantly put off to the future, yet supposedly giving meaning to the present. When this idealism loses its halo, deception could turn into bitterness.[8]

There are, of course, counterarguments. The American can point to the traditional theory of political realignments (developed first by Arthur Schlesinger, Jr.), and note that just as in 1896, 1932, and 1968, so in 1992 the party in power lost some 16 percent of its electorate, that a third party with populist rhetoric appeared on the horizon to push the electorate in a new direction, and that the rhetoric of class conflict became more salient.[9] He can point out that while JFK was hardly a man of the Left, his election carried a message of the need for a change that had been prevented by an older generation caught in the theories and the institutional strictures of a now-revolved past. This message transcended the new man and his programs. So it was that the Kennedy era made possible the Civil Rights movement, the War on Poverty, and the quest for the Great Society, none of which were issues in the 1960 campaign that brought the Democrats to power.[10] Similar unintended consequences could also arise from the Maastricht process, which has revivified political debate at least in some countries (but not in Germany, where the issue has been turned over to the High Court). Europe may not become a nation-state; but it can force its constituents to rethink their own autonomy within the anonymous forces of the global economy. Even those who stubbornly hold on to the concept of national "sovereignty" have to answer the question: what do you want to *do* with that sovereignty? So, too, do those for whom political renewal itself provides a new *telos*: neither socialism nor the market but democratic participation is what they must defend.

Sacrifice of Politics: The Logic of Maastricht

Our modern world is founded on the assertion of the self-evident rights of the individual. This individualism was the result of a political victory over the world of absolutism in whose organic and hierarchical network each and all had a prescribed place. The modern individual was set free to form new social bonds and to create an autonomous culture. But these supra-individual creations had nonetheless to preserve the individuality of the individuals who are their foundation. As early as the seventeenth century, philosophers sought in vain to square the circle of individualism. The emergence of the market and the consumer seemed to realize this "virtuous circle." The principles of neutrality and of the free choice among goods that are qualitatively equal (as goods) and quantitatively comparable (in monetary terms) are premised on and preserve the modern individual. These economic institutions appear to present a framework that achieves justice.[11] Arbitrariness exercised by one person on another is excluded in principle; economic law is neutral and results from the free choice by autonomous individuals seeking rational satisfaction of self-defined needs. In this way, the economic replaces the political, which becomes (at best) subordinated to it. Private vices are to become public virtues, as Mandeville put it in *The Fable of the Bees*. Modern societies are (at least) market societies.

The antipolitical individualism of this worldview is implicit in the behavior of our political classes. In the United States, the "new Democrat" Clinton sought to avoid the rhetoric of solidarity with one or another group of the excluded, which had been so harmful to the Democratic Party over the years.[12] In identifying himself with the middle-class wage earner, Clinton took care to distinguish himself not only from ethnic, racial, or social categories of the population, but also from labor organizations, which have been perceived as a special interest since the Mondale campaign of 1984.[13] In the case of Europe, the French Socialists' 1983 decision to accept the discipline of the market rather than the "diktat of the Mark" was only the most remarkable of many attempts to make a virtue out of necessity and to cover over political weakness with the rhetoric of European unification. As Paul Thibaud points out, the beneficiary of the freedoms that have accompanied the falling of national frontiers is not the citizen but the consumer, the traveler, the entrepreneur—a private individual seeking constant novelty while insisting on protection by familiar rules and guarantees of legal security. This Europe, implied by Maastricht, would be only a better functioning welfare state.

For all of their differences, Americans and Europeans face the same, classical problem: how to generate solidarity among individuals who seek to conserve their individuality at all costs, including costs to others? The European case illustrates the contemporary difficulties better than does the American heritage. The solidarity among individuals depends on the solidarity among sovereign states, whose quest for a European "solution" was made necessary by the inability of national politics to produce social cohesion domestically. But those who assume that the global economy has made the sovereign state a relic of the past confuse sovereignty with invulnerability.[14] They assume that because modern individualist culture is transnational, politics must also take place in that dimension. Thus, they propose a single monetary system followed by unification of budgetary and fiscal policy; but this neglects particularities among and within nations, as well as the possibility of a crisis affecting one or the other of them for specific reasons. Theirs is an antipolitical solution that assumes either that history does not exist or that the realization of Europe would entail the end of history.[15] A similar antipolitics was already explicit in the method by which Jean Monnet sought European unity. He wanted to create a series of *faits accomplis* such that unity would result from quantitative accumulation rather than a qualitative leap. Politics, he thought, was too much a matter of passions, rhetoric, and fallible people who, he assumed, would be happy to be freed of the need to make decisions by the work of experts and planners. But Monnet's model was commercial negotiation; it presupposes the existence of common values, goals, and identities, which are just what is lacking today and which are the premises for solidarity. That is why Paul Thibaud argues that it is no accident that the growth of Europe has accompanied the decline of politics.[16]

The danger that threatens contemporary political life can be seen in the steps that led toward Maastricht. The so-called crisis of governability in modern democracy exploded worldwide in 1968. The disciplinary underside of the welfare state that reproduces traditional values of school, work, and family was rejected. The traditionalists sought to reimpose values; the radicals called for self-management in participatory institutions. The cunning of reason imposed a different path. The economic crisis that followed the 1973 oil shock brought a different kind of constraint. All that remained for politics were human rights, which—at least in the West—became a new moralism rather than a new politics, leaving the private individual free to seek happiness and rules for its guarantee. Unable to inspire a citizenry, politicians found the decrees from Brussels a relief, as Monnet had predicted.[17] Agreement among experts, outside the public eye, can be attained easily; international treaties and laws override domestic parliaments, where debate is no longer necessary. "One can thus say," writes Thibaud, "that Europe fulfills at once the desire for emancipation on the part of individuals and the need for legitimacy among administrators by creating between them a divorce by mutual consent from which common life, political life, disappears."[18] The European project is thus antipolitical.[19] Because they could not produce solidarity by political means, European politicians seek to enforce obedience by appeal to external laws of necessity. They create a modern form of the traditional hierarchical world, undermining the democratic autonomy of the individual they claim to protect.

By conflating politics with the quest for stability, predictability, and rigor in business and administration, the European solution to the problem of solidarity confuses loyalty with legitimacy. The assent of the private individual, based on satisfaction of personal needs, is as easily lost as it is won. While it is easier to rule such private persons, it is difficult to mobilize them for a common project. Without the political space for public debate, their private passions can burst out in ethnic or identitary furor when their fears are aroused. The attempt to defuse this threat by transcending the national framework is an ostrichlike denial that individuals need to feel themselves part of a collective project. It misunderstands such phenomena as Lombard or Catalan nationalism, which are more movements of economic exclusion by wealthy regions than they are traditional nationalisms. It is blind to the development of client mentalities in regions like the Mezzogiorno, Corsica, or Andalusia. Unification by the neutral force of the market permits, or encourages, the flourishing of symbolic differences and aggressiveness that cannot be dissolved in common action. Private loyalty does not create public legitimacy; the iron laws of necessity conflict with the self-determination of individuals.

Another variant of the European solution is suggested by the notion of "subsidiarity," which is the basis for the attempt to create manageable dimensions of regional administration. Subsidiarity assumes that society is a stable, organic unity, each element of which can manage itself if left alone. It is difficult to imagine that such a premodern concept could apply to the diversity of modern individualist society. At most, subsidiarity would further reduce the function of the political without offering the individual new modes of relation and new projects encouraging solidarity. The same criticism applies to the attempt to induce common action by decentralization: it is another form of antipolitics. Its goal, like that of self-management, is to find a unity of action that would be so homogeneous that it would not need to be governed at all. It reflects a fear of political passions that arise from the clash of differences, and the rejection of any decision in which my will is not directly involved. It implies that allegiance to my territory is based on private interest—which of course can change; or it makes membership a romantic or prerational identification, which can become a dangerous atavism in a world of anonymous rules. The idea that direct interpersonal relations can replace politics, or that politics should be simply their expression, misunderstands what Thibaud calls the "civilizing" function of the political.[20]

The European need to invent a politics adequate to the transnational individualism of contemporary society while avoiding the identitary passions that emerge when individualism becomes uprootedness casts light on the challenge facing the new American government. Solidarity is a scarce resource, and the temptation of antipolitics is present on both sides of the Atlantic. Dreams of the America of the 1950s, when social pluralism seemed to produce what Almond and Verba called a "civic culture" echoed in Clinton's appeals to middle-class virtues. It is not enough that the political scientists have demolished that mythical America.[21] In a time of fiscal need, the temptation to transfer political responsibility to the market or to subsidiary associations is great (as is suggested, for example, by Clinton's choice of the "managed care" competitive option for medical insurance, or by the role of those new Democrats who want to make the states into "laboratories for democracy" in order to "reinvent government").[22] On the other hand, the democratic deficit that produced so many "Perotistas" could encourage an activism that uses the televised town meeting to produce popular support outside of the arena of deliberative political debate. Conditions demand a politics of sacrifice; the question is whether this can be done without the sacrifice of politics. Populism is as antipolitical as is the market—and Ross Perot appeals to both of them in his challenge to politics as usual.[23]

Politics of Sacrifice: Clinton's Challenge

Although his inaugural address spoke of the need for "sacrifice" to renew America, the president's rhetoric shifted in the days leading up to the presentation of his economic program to the Congress on 17 February 1993. Now, his aides insisted, the proper word was "contribution," understood as giving to a common fund.[24] Sacrifice was felt to carry too much of a religious connotation whereas contribution suggests participation in a common enterprise. This may be why Clinton had stopped talking about the "new convenant" by which he originally defined his candidacy one year earlier. Yet the address to Congress did propose a vision. The president concentrated on the economy, and his justification was a political appeal to go beyond immediate satisfactions: "It has been too long—at least three decades—since a president has challenged Americans." His purpose was also economic; the challenge was reformulated as the need "not merely to consume the bounty of today but to invest for a much greater one tomorrow." As the president went on to explain his program, he moved effortlessly between economic and political justifications of his choices. Ultimately, he concluded, "the test of our program cannot simply be: What's in it for me? The question must be: What's in it for us?" This was an appeal for political renewal and solidarity that goes beyond the private desires of each individual. However, insofar as the economic program did not demand a sacrifice of benefits but rather a contribution of taxes (rationalized as an investment in the future), it may be seen as contradicting its political goal.[25]

The overriding reality of American politics, said Clinton, was the deficit. He recalled that when Ronald Reagan presented his economic program in 1981, he described the deficit as a stack of dollar bills 67 miles high; now, Clinton noted, it would reach 267 miles into the air. Interest payments on the debt were nearly as large as the entire military budget. The space for politics was limited by this economic reality: taxes could be raised, benefits limited or cut, or the economy stimulated. In all three cases, politics seemed reduced to picking economic winners and losers—and then convincing the losers that they were nonetheless the winners of tomorrow. The best way, apparently, to succeed in this game was by appealing to the rational self-interest of the individual. Thus, health care reform, including provision for the thirty million Americans without health insurance, was justified in economic terms: "For every dollar we invest today," he said, "we save three tomorrow." The private individual may understand perfectly this calculation. But does her willingness to "contribute" express solidarity in a common venture? Or does she expect, as she did before Clinton's political challenge, to reap the benefits as a private person? In the latter case, the notorious fickleness of opinion could leave the president with little support for the next phases of the reforms that are necessary to confront other tasks.

It is too easy simply to denounce the utilitarianism of the politicians (and the citizens) of an individualistic society. Interest and self-interest cannot be—and should not be—divorced from politics, at least not from democratic politics. The rhetoric of sacrifice can be easily abused. As Samuel Johnson noted at the beginning of the democratic era, "patriotism is the last refuge of a scoundrel."[26] Democratic peoples are rightly suspicious of those who call them to great crusades. Bill Clinton certainly remembered the mockery heaped on a previous Democratic president, Jimmy Carter, who tried to garner support for his energy policy by calling it "the moral equivalent of war." Such exhortations have little effect on the democratic individual. Senator Ted Kennedy may be right to denounce the 1980s as a "me decade" and to demand that it be replaced by a "we decade . . . in which helping others becomes a national priority."[27] But President Clinton better understood the kind of individualism that underlies the democratic spirit when he insisted on the need to end welfare as we know it, because "no one wants to change the welfare system as much as those who are trapped by the welfare system." Clinton wants to help others to help themselves. But how can such individualism provide the basis for a politics, or for a renewal of the political? What kind of solidarity is premised on individualism?

The American political class is caught in a double bind: each representative has to satisfy particular constituencies in order to be reelected while the product of their collective work must be accepted by all. This has led to the present fiscal dilemma and to the discrediting of the political class. The price of compromise among interests is growing government spending coupled with the inability seriously to cut the budget. Some hoped that the election of a Democratic president, who could work with a Democratic Congress, would ameliorate this situation; others feared that it would only strengthen the utilitarian calculus that commands politicians to give (benefits) in order to get (reelected). In fact, the situation is more complicated. The American people elected not only a new president who called for change, but also a changed House of Representatives and Senate. Moreover, the elections took place in a newly reapportioned electoral map that gave advantages to minorities, and in a political climate labeled "the Year of the Woman."[28] But the mood of the public is volatile; although California seemed to have left the Republican camp for good in 1992, Los Angeles ended twenty years of Democratic domination by electing a Republican mayor in 1993. And Ross Perot's "United We Stand America" remains an active presence that could help the Democrats by dividing the Republicans (as it did in Clinton's election) or help the Republicans if they can coopt its themes (with which, however, many Republicans disagree).[29]

The months of debate that led to the narrow adoption of Clinton's revised economic plan seemed to hesitate between two possibilities. The first can be called "populist," although the concept is too general. It appeals to the traditional American egalitarianism, which is revolted by the existence of special interests of any kind. Its classical twentieth-century expression was FDR's attack on the "economic royalists" who opposed the New Deal. But this egalitarianism is also individualistic; it sees government as another "interest" whose interference is to be resisted by the self-reliant American free to "pursue happiness" as he or she sees fit. This variant of populism led to support for the Reagan Republicans against the so-called tax-and-spend Democrats. The political instability of American populism is due to its antipolitical nature, but antipolitics has its own political effects. Despite the tendency of those who take the trouble to call to be the most opinionated and least open to argument, the weight of talk shows in contemporary political choices cannot be underestimated. On the other hand, the success of candidate Clinton's appeals to the middle class is also an expression of this American populism. The challenge is to give this middle class a political project that can unite it for a common action rather than leave it to coalesce as a series of negative reactions. This was the political justification that the president's address to Congress called the "test" of his program: "What's in it for us?"

The second possibility that emerged during the long debate on the budget can also claim a populist root: the reinvigoration of the party system whose decline, begun under the New Deal and completed by the Great Society, coincided with the growth of the welfare state.[30] The cries for campaign finance reform have grown louder; many newly elected representatives made this demand a basis of their campaign.

For the moment, the new members have not been able to affect the hierarchy of Congress; they will need the help of the president, who in turn needs their support. Public funding of campaigns would not only weaken the dependence of the representatives on special interests but could break the spiral of government spending that has ruined the fiscal health of the nation as each representative feels that he or she has to deliver the goods back home. The fact that the only noneconomic remark in the president's address concerned campaign finance reform and restrictions on lobbyists suggested that he was considering such a move.[31] For the moment, however, nothing more has come of it, as the president could not afford to alienate supporters of his budget.

The challenge facing the president is to unite populism and party-renewal in the context of a *politics of sacrifice*. Such a politics cannot be justified by interest-calculations on the part of the private individual; but the communitarian ideologies that some (of the Left and the Right) have tried to oppose to the reign of the individual offer little guidance when it becomes necessary to pass from critique to proposition. In a multicultural society, where the right of difference has been driven to the extreme of open hostility among ethnic communities, the need for new forms of solidarity is intense. The urban centers from which, traditionally, political culture has drawn its energies are seats of dispair. The associative texture of civil society that has been the admiration of democrats since Tocqueville's visit to America a century and a half ago is losing its foundations. American society, whose division was once its dynamic strength, seems incapable of giving these divisions a political form that would make their expression a positive force. This explains the president's appeal to the necessities of the economy to motivate individuals to change the old ways. But, as with the Maastricht process, this runs the risk of antipolitics. Nor can the imperious necessity of the economy be mastered by political voluntarism; economic necessity is real, but it need not entail the sacrifice of politics or the sacrifice to antipolitics by a populist simulacrum of immediate communication through talk shows or the staged exchange of opinion calling itself informed debate.

All politics has to work within prior constraints, some of which are self-defined. Bill Clinton won office by an appeal to the middle class. His strategy was to win over the mostly white, ethnic and urban groups who had become ''Reagan Democrats'' out of frustration with the redistributive economic policies and the juridically imposed social policies of a Democratic Party whose liberalism came to be perceived as elitist. Calling himself a "new Democrat," Clinton rejected both the left-wing's attempts to put the party in the service of the excluded, and the traditional Democratic identification with the industrial working class. But the concept of a "middle class" is notably vague; as a political concept, its weakness is that it describes people in their private station; as a social concept, it refers more to life in idealized small towns than to complex and pluralistic urban centers; as a cultural concept, it connotes consumerism rather than creation. The idea of a mobilized middle-class public seems like a contradiction in terms. That is why politicians and intellectuals look to the margins, assuming that it is difference that represents potential political force (be it the Left's exploited and excluded, or the Right's entrepreneurs crushed by bureaucracy or morally righteous victims of liberal elitist tolerance). But the foundation of democracy is equality. That is why Clinton insisted that the welfare recipient "trapped by the welfare system" wants only to become like the rest of us. Politics is not charity; solidarity can exist only among individuals who are equal in their individuality, able to take responsibility for themselves and, thus, to define themselves as part of a public debate. The sociological vagueness of the middle class means that it can only define itself by political choice.

The six months of debate after the president presented his economic program in February 1993 gave grounds for pessimism. The budget deficit had been a looming cloud hovering over the political horizon. It played the same role that Maastricht played in Europe; it became our destiny. Its importance could not be challenged, either by the economic arguments that pointed out that as a percentage of GDP its weight was decreasing, or by the political insistence that a deficit based on investment for the future was not the same as debt incurred, for example, in the arms race. The president argued that even the adulterated budget that Congress finally accepted is "his" budget; his politics have taken "necessity" into account. The opposition appealed to the privatized middle class whose aversion to taxes and hope for a painless solution was the basis of Reaganism. The president blamed his difficulties on poor communications, hired a former Reagan aide (and friend of Perot) to assist him, and created a "war room" in the White House to carry the attack to his opponents. The debate grew stale, bitter, and pointless. As the summer vacation began, Americans saw a president who did not even have a home to which he could retreat for rest and relaxation. Politics had become rootless, abandoned to the ritual rhetoric of sacrifice and the play of interests. It has left only the barren soil on which ethnic and communal particularisms can provide the symbolic sense of belonging that is normally its task. Such atavistic solidarity provides illusory comfort for those who see themselves as victims and who therefore refuse to take responsibility for their fate, let alone express their solidarity with others.

But there is hope as well. The politics whose renewal was the premise of Clinton's election had a civilizing function. If politics is an art, it is the art of the possible; it entails both strategy and tactics, knowing when to attack, where to retreat, and how to enter legitimate compromise. Thus, for example, days after the budget vote, the president issued an Executive Order increasing grazing fees on public lands—the very issue on which his retreat in the budget debate began.[32] Another Executive Order reversed Ronald Reagan's 1981 disqualification of striking members of the air controllers' union (PATCO) from ever serving the government again. Clinton began to speak of the budget as a "partial victory," and to recall the issues on which he would attack in the fall, including campaign reform. He defended his controversial black female nominee for surgeon general rather than withdraw support, as he had done with his nominee for assistant attorney general. The Congress passed his weakened but important program for national service after a Republican filibuster was finally defeated. What was missing in all of this, however, was the *political* explanation of his politics. The same held for his much criticized foreign policy, particularly in the former Yugoslavia. Were he to furnish this political explanation, the series of discrete measures that make up a president's days and works would not be seen as the waffling of a president without principle or character but—a politics. Compromise need not be a sign of weakness, after all.

A politics of sacrifice that does not sacrifice the political has to start by rethinking the concept of the middle class. This will not be easy. Candidate Clinton stressed the need for governmental investment to provide "good jobs at good wages." While President Clinton lost the battle for investment, he did win an important victory in the budget fight. Congress accepted the earned income tax credit (EITC), a negative tax that would permit those working at minimum wage jobs to attain a decent living standard without having to depend on welfare. This implied a recognition that politics must be concerned with the citizen, not simply with the private individual. It is not a measure aimed at creating jobs for their own sake; it is part of the project to end welfare as we know it by giving the individual the dignity needed to be an equal of all others. It is not charity or the expression of compassion but the gesture of solidarity that is the foundation of politics. The problem is that it seems to conflict with the goals of candidate Clinton, who espoused a vision of a postindustrial society. Yet it need not entail the abandonment of that vision; it contributes, rather, to a better understanding of its presuppositions, which are not limited to the economic sphere. The good jobs that candidate Clinton promised were to be meaningful work in which the individual could realize his or her individuality. But that individuality, the president now admits, depends on the social recognition of equality.

The middle class is the class of equals living their individual lives together. The middle class is not composed of consumers making choices in the private sphere. Middle-class virtues like well-done work, curiosity about others, the desire to be informed, to live in harmony with one's neighborhood, community, and environment do not belong to an archaic past.[33] The dominance of middle-class values need not imply a Kojève-Fukuyama vision of the "end of history" and the appearance of Nietzsche's "last man." The undeniable desire of the excluded to become middle class—like the desire to join Europe—points to the need to articulate and legitimate a middle-class politics. The self-conception of the middle class, and its self-confidence, have been destroyed by the modernization that has made the traditional family with a single working parent and a secure industrial job obsolete. This could produce a reflex of self-centeredness whose result would be a populism that is dangerous because it is nourished by fear more than hatred. But such a future is not fore-ordained. After all, the middle class of twentieth-century America was composed largely of industrial workers; and it owed its middle-class status to gains made during the New Deal—to politics and to its own political organization. The new middle class could provide the basis for a renewal of political parties that, aside from the parties' direct representative function, would permit fears to be transformed into arguments, interests into policies, and alienation into solidarities.

Candidate Clinton put the issue of middle-class politics on the table. The new Democrat did not want simply to create an American version of the European welfare state. That is the vision of the intellectual, who looks to politics as a means to integrate difference and whose guilty conscience makes her seek to "serve the people" in the manner of Senator Kennedy or of the Old Left. It is the vision of ever-advancing progress through which history moves toward its destiny, and in which freedom is defined as the recognition of necessity. Such a vision was seen to lie behind the Maastricht process and to be an antipolitical threat to the renewal made possible by Clinton's election. To ask for sacrifice, President Clinton must specify the god to whom it is to be offered. The excesses of the 1980s have disqualified the private individual. Despite its supposed Protestant ethic, the new god needed by Americans cannot be a modern form of the *deus absconditus*, an ominious and arbitrary economic necessity whose grace can be won neither by sacrifice nor by good deeds alone. To what, then, are our sacrifices to "contribute" if not to the renewal of politics itself?[34]

Notes

1. It will be recalled that Ronald Reagan won only 44 percent of the vote in 1980, when he was opposed not only by Jimmy Carter but by the third party candidate, John Anderson. Yet Reagan immediately set to work, and however one evaluates the results of his first term in office (which included a serious recession in 1982, and began the accumulation of today's monster deficit), he did get many programs through Congress. Had conditions changed so greatly after twelve years of Republican rule? One might have thought so after reading some serious political commentators, writing after the victory of Clinton's budget; their only solution was the proposal of constitutional amendments. (See, for example, Christopher Jencks, "Free the Economy from Congress," in *New York Times*, 8 August 1993; or Daniel Bell, "The Old War," in *New Republic*, 23 and 30 August 1993.)

2. It is probable that the combination of social, ecological, and economic interests that will emerge in the debate over the proposed North American Free Trade Association (NAFTA) will divide the at present remarkably united Republican opposition—but they will divide the Democratic Party as well. The original treaty, made in 1991 under President Bush, was supported by 140 Republicans; it passed the House by 231 to 192. The new treaty contains additional clauses concerning ecology and labor protection. Presumably, President Clinton will also add proposals for retraining workers whose jobs are lost to cheaper Mexican labor. How he presents these measures—the political logic he invokes—will be an important clue to the kind of politics he intends to pursue. See part 3 below for my own suggestions. If he only seeks to create divisions in order to get his programs through, one should remember that divisions among the politicians do not of themselves lead to political renewal. The same holds for the health care reform proposals.

3. The distinction between "issues"—which are rhetorical devices designed to divide the public and to label one's opponent—and "problems"—which demand concrete solutions—is stressed by E. J. Dionne, Jr., whose remarkable *Why Americans Hate Politics* (New York: Simon & Schuster, 1991) presents a panorama of the ideologization of American political life, Left

and Right, since 1960. Dionne's book can be read as calling for the appearance of a politician like Clinton.

4. The major ingredient in the Reagan-Bush coalition was the lower-middle class, white ethnic voter who had been a mainstay of the New Deal Democratic Party. The shift of this bloc of voters to the Republican Party can be explained in large part as a reaction to decisions by the courts in matters of racial integration such as busing, welfare rights, affirmative action, and the like. The phenomenon was perceptible as early as the surprisingly strong campaign of George Wallace in 1968, as was noted at the time by Kevin Phillips's *Emerging Republican Majority* (New York: Doubleday / Anchor, 1970). For an overview of the debate, see Dick Howard, "Politics in Review," in *Radical Philosophy Review of Books*, No. 5, 1992, 49–68. For more recent detail, see Thomas Byrne Edsall and Mary Edsall, *Chain Reaction: The Impact of Race, Rights, and Taxes on American Politics* (New York: Simon & Schuster, 1992).

5. I suggested such an optimistic reading immediately after the election in an op-ed, "Clinton, ou la politique réhabilitée," *Libération*, 10 November 1992 (German translation in *Berliner Debatte. Initial*, 1[1993]).

6. Clinton's foreign policy seems to be based on another antipolitical logic as well: that of the military, whose leader, Colin Powell, saw the lesson of Vietnam as dictating that if military means are engaged, they must be massive and must ensure swift victory, for the citizens of a democracy will not tolerate lengthy war. Hence, Somalia was seen as a feasible intervention while Bosnia's complicated terrain ruled out American action. For a critique of the results of this antipolitical logic, see Patrick Glynn, "The 'Doable' War," *New Republic*, 16 August 1993, 15–18.

7. This is precisely the argument of the Republican opposition whose filibuster sank Clinton's investment and jobs program and that has convinced much of the public that the new president is only another tax-and-spend Democrat.

8. This critique of Europe as a self-validating and self-referential process, and the description of the "negative politics" that results, are developed in Paul Thibaud's "L'Europe par les nations (et réciproquement)," in Jean-Marc Ferry and Paul Thibaud, *Discussion sur l'Europe* (Paris: Calmann-Lévy, 1992), on which I will draw frequently in the following discussion.

9. Such is, in part, the argument of Kevin Phillips's recent book, *Boiling Point: Democrats, Republicans and the Decline of Middle-Class Prosperity* (New York: Random House, 1993).

10. This argument is suggested by Maurice Isserman in an article in *Democratic Left*, November–December 1992. Isserman notes as well that when a Democrat is in the White House, leftist movements no longer have to fight defensive battles against reactionary measures; they have then the possibility of developing their own positive agenda, pushing the Democrats to the left and developing forms of social autonomy. On the other hand, Isserman points out that the Kennedy era also produced the war in Vietnam, which was financed

by debt rather than by increased taxes and whose result was the inability to realize the Great Society. The parallel to the dangers that threaten Maastricht because of Germany's insistence on financing its unification by borrowing rather than raising taxes (and thus lowering interest rates, and helping preserve the European Monetary System) is obvious, and ominous.

11. See Albert Hirschmann, *The Passions and the Interests* (Princeton: Princeton University Press, 1977) for an account of the seventeenth-century transformation of the moral theory of humans as beings composed of passions into a global theory of social behavior based upon the one passion that can claim to be "rational": interest. This can be compared, *mutatis mutandis*, with the notion of "justice as fairness," which is claimed to be "political not metaphysical" by John Rawls, whose definition of the concept "political," however, can be challenged insofar as it is based on a kind of rational choice theory that is derived ultimately from economics.

12. For an account, see E. J. Dionne, Jr., *Why Americans Hate Politics*, and Fred Siegel, *Troubled Journey: From Pearl Harbor to Ronald Reagan* (New York: Hill & Wang, 1983). See also note 3.

13. The accusation came from an early new Democrat, Gary Hart, in his 1984 challenge to Walter Mondale. Applying this label was ironic, since only 16 percent of American workers belong to unions, and only 11.8 percent of these are in private industry.

It could be objected that Clinton's careful juggling of his cabinet appointments to include women (four) and ethnic minorities (four Blacks, two Hispanics) contradicts this description of his program. On the other hand, the cynical might note that thirteen of the eighteen cabinet members were lawyers, including four of the top *economic* advisors (see John Judis, "The Old Democrat," *New Republic*, 22 February 1993, 18–21).

14. Paul Thibaud illustrates the distinction by asking whether the fact that I decide to open my umbrella when it rains means that I am not free. I would not be free, he continues, if I had to consult with a commission of my neighbors before making that decision ("L'Europe," 16n).

15. Ibid., 49ff. The stress on the differences within nations is important insofar as the citizenry must have the choice of how to deal with forms of exclusion or inequality, which should not be left to the whims of an impersonal market.

16. Ibid., 36ff. This was the root of Monnet's differences with de Gaulle, for whom politics does not reduce to economic factors alone. Thibaud's point, however, is not to return to a Gaullian politics. "One misunderstands the dynamics of Europe," he writes, "if one doesn't see that it was oriented toward the limitation of those great producers of politics which are the nation-states *infinitely more than to produce another will, to find other sources for politics*" (38, my stress).

17. A French minister of agriculture, for example, unable to convince his domestic constituency of restrictions he knows to be necessary, can happily

justify those measures as imposed by "Brussels." In the process, he confirms his own self-image as a wise administrator who knows best the good of the country—but of course denies his responsibility as a politician, and sets the stage for an eventual back-lash by those whose interests are harmed by the "communal" decision! (See, for example, "L'Europe," 56n.)

18. Ibid., 48.

19. Thibaud denounces "certain statesmen who are in favor of European integration because of their resentment against a people that they have failed to govern" ("L'Europe," 53). How else, he asks, can one explain that the French elites who previously wanted the Community to be structured by a Colbertiste form of planning from above now accept economic liberalism as their gospel?

20. It misunderstands as well, he argues, the nation and its role in a new Europe. I cannot treat here Thibaud's positive arguments for the shape of a new Europe and for its nations. His argument is presented at several levels. After showing the dangers to which the Europe of Maastricht would lead, he proposes several concrete modifications, including a redefinition of the powers of the Commission at Brussels and the creation of national parliamentary committees charged with debate on those issues of sovereignty that must remain with the nation (culture, measures of social solidarity, regional planning, citizenship) but that also concern Europe. At another level, Thibaud presents an historical argument to demonstrate that the progress and uniqueness of Europe have depended always on its diversity; its great moments are the Treaties of Westphalia, Vienna, and Helsinki, not the unification sought by revolution or empire. Finally, Thibaud offers philosophical arguments about the formation of individual identity and the "debt" incurred in this process that, ultimately, is the motivating force that distinguishes ethical moralism from concrete political morality. It is one thing for me to feel ethically responsible, for example, for starvation in the Third World; only through my action as a citizen of my nation can I do something effective about it! On the latter point, see also Paul Thibaud, "Citoyenneté et engagement moral," *Pouvoirs*, No. 65, 1993, 19–30.

21. See Gabriel A. Almond and Sidney Verba, *The Civic Culture: Political Attitudes and Democracy in Five Nations* (Princeton: Princeton University Press, 1963). For a critique, see the still-relevant study by Theodore Lowi, *The End of Liberalism. Ideology, Policy, and the Crisis of Public Authority* (New York: W. W. Norton, 1969).

22. The passages in quotations are from works by David Osborne who, along with the Progressive Policy Institute, was among the leading ideologists of the new Democrats (see *Laboratories of Democracy* [Cambridge: Harvard Business School Press, 1988] and *Reinventing Government: How the Entrepreneurial Spirit is Transforming the Public Sector* [New York: Addison-Wesley, 1992]). At another level, shortly before she was named one of the top economic advisers of the new administration, Alice Rivlin proposed a new federal

distribution of power and responsibility in *Reviving the American Dream: The Economy, the States & the Federal Government* (Washington, D.C.: The Brookings Institution, 1992).

23. The historical roots of American populism, and their deformation by Perot, are well-studied by Sean Wilentz, "Pox Populi: The Corrupt Populist Pedigree of Ross Perot," *New Republic*, 9 August 1993, 29–35. See also note 30 below.

24. See "Throwing 'Sacrifice' to the Winds," *New York Times*, 16 February 1993, A. 14.

25. Critics pointed out that the contributions were to be raised in the first years of the plan, the sacrifice of benefits coming only later. This would give the lobbies and the interest groups time to mobilize and would open the new administration to the reproach of being just like the old tax-and-spend Democrats. This reproach led Clinton to abandon his short-term stimulus program and also to modify his overall plan in ways that made it so similar to the Bush-Congress compromise of 1990.

26. In Boswell's *Life of Doctor Johnson* (1791).

27. Cited in Eric B. Gorham, "The $12 Billion Civics Lesson," *In These Times*, 8 February 1993, 27.

28. There were 122 new members of the House of Representatives elected in 1992; and the Senate had 7 female members, including its first black female senator. But one should note the arrival of the (female) Republican victor in a by-election in 1993 in Texas, who won overwhelmingly on an anti-Clinton platform. The Black Caucus had 38 members, who made their weight felt in the final budget negotiations by fighting for the inclusion of urban reforms.

29. As outlined in his book, *Not for Sale at Any Price: How We Can Save America for Our Children* (New York: Hyperion, 1993), Perot proposes among other recipes, a tax on gasoline, a tax on social security payments, an end to the mortgage deduction, a decrease in the Defense Department budget, a 10 percent across-the-board budget cut, and $140 billion savings (by unspecified means) in health care costs. In addition, Perot tends to be a libertarian on social issues, which clashes with a strong element in Republican politics. When Perot was challenged on his economic figures on the national TV show "Meet the Press," he refused to give any details and, said the liberal *New York Times* (2 August 1993), made himself look silly.

[I should recall to the reader that, as I said in the foreword to this volume, I have not tried to update these political judgments. They would no doubt be dated again soon. Nor will I try to justify my assertions retrospectively, finding bits of evidence that show that, for example, I anticipated aspects of the 1994 Republican victories.]

30. It is ironic that the realization of that political project should have such antipolitical consequences. FDR needed to destroy the old urban political machines in order to press through the New Deal. By weakening the parties, the power of Washington to push through its reforms could be increased.

Although this strategy was probably necessary to the realization of the New Deal, its long-term cost has become apparent as the power of money has grown while the legitimacy of the political class has decreased. For details, see Howard, "Politics in Review." It is tempting to see parallels here with the Maastricht proc ss of depoliticization.

31. Smiling, perhaps ironically, at the applause accorded to this line of his address, the president added an informal remark not prepared by his speech writers to the effect that "the audience at home" was certainly applauding more than were the assembled representatives. This could mean that the president would go over the heads of Congress to make a populist appeal; but serious campaign reform could also have the effect of making possible a renewal of the party, on which the representatives would be more dependent. Parties, in turn, would have to develop political programs for the nation as a whole—ideologies rather than cobbled-together compromises called platforms.

32. While this measure would produce only $30 million of added revenues, its justification was ecological. This suggested that Clinton—and his popular secretary of the interior Bruce Babbit—would not give up on the ecological goals that underlay the original energy tax bill that Congress rejected.

33. As in Europe since Flaubert's Monsieur Homais, there is a long American tradition that makes the middle class the object of mockery, from Sinclair Lewis's Babbit to H. L. Mencken's "bouboisie" to television's Archie Bunker. Its implication is that middle-class politics is a sort of atavistic populism, fearful of modernity and closed to whatever appears alien. A visit to the new Norman Rockwell Museum (in Stockbridge, Massachussetts) suggests that the artist whose idyllic paintings for years graced the front page of the (negatively) archetypical *Saturday Evening Post* had a far more cosmopolitan vision, a hatred of pettiness—and a vigorous brush as well!

34. It goes without saying that the renewal of politics is not without content. Democracy is not merely a formal shell. The old 1960s' slogan, "If voting could change anything they wouldn't let us vote," is historically naive and politically dangerous. One would hope that, in our post-1989 world, this point would not need further emphasis.

13

Guilt and the Birth of Democracy

To say that the events that shook the polities of Eastern Europe in 1989 were a "revolution" poses more questions than it answers.[1] More remarkable than the eviction of the former leaders was the fact that—as in 1789—the Old Regime could not, or did not want to, present a credible or forceful opposition to the forces of the new. But, as in 1848, it quickly became evident that no new society had taken form before the Old Order was driven from the seat of power. The work of destruction must be supplemented by the labor of construction, which makes use of other principles and operates on a different basis. As we know, this is where revolutions confront their critical moment.

Swept away, the Old Order does not disappear in a single instant, leaving no traces. Yet the self-conception of a revolution demands that it represent the radically new, free from a past that it rejects in its entirety. This is where the problem of *guilt* enters the political stage. This concept permits the revolutionaries to justify the elimination of the past, in its institutional forms as well as in its personnel—indeed, as a systematic whole. The concept of guilt is sufficiently ambiguous to be applied in all such contexts, because it does not distinguish between individual, collective, or systematic guilt. Recall the trial of Louis XVI: was he guilty as an individual or as king? Or was it the entirety of a system, or even that of history, that was condemned in his person? In the same way, when the concept of guilt is applied in the fratricidal struggles within the revolution itself, the guilty party need not have followed a conscious intention; guilt is said to be "objective"—or, as a later formulation would have it, it exists in and must be seen from "the eyes of History."

The problem of the politicization of guilt has reappeared in Eastern

279

Europe. No doubt its most extreme manifestation, and its most aber-
rant forms, are found in the former German Democratic Republic
(GDR). There are reasons for this: its incorporation into a Federal
Republic of Germany (FRG) that is still haunted by its own past, and
whose *Ostpolitik* culminated in the official visit (*cum* recognition) of
Erich Honecker in 1987; or a perhaps unconscious need to justify the
wealth of western Germany that, after all, should not be based simply
on the accidental factor of being born in the right place[2]; or even a
conscious politics by the Right to prevent the emergence of a "third
way" that would develop the positive aspects of both systems. On the
other hand, although imposed with the help of the Red Army, the
socialism of the GDR claimed to have indigenous roots—one was
proud to be able to read Marx in the original—and justified its existence
not only by antifascism but also with reference to the failure of the
formal democracy of the Weimar Republic from whose weakness Hitler
could emerge.[3] Whatever the roots of the problem, the accusations of
complicity with the secret police of the Old Regime (the Stasi) not only
have complicated the integration of the five new provinces into the
democratic system but also—and above all—have prevented the emergence of a true citizenship, especially among those who were used to
the need for complicity with the regime or who had simply retreated
into the sanctuary of private life.

The present political problems of the former GDR can be analyzed
in terms of two problems, which are interconnected. The integration
of East Germans into the institutions of a unified Germany has been
made dependent on the proof that one was not "close to the state"
(*Staatsnah*). That is to say: you are guilty until you have proven your
innocence. There is no need to underline the ambiguity of this category
of *Staatsnah*, which lends itself to an indefinite variety of construc-
tions; nor need it be stressed that the only proof is often found in the
archives of the Stasi, which is hardly a source of objective facts
stripped of all political motivations.[4] But if this question has acquired
so great an import, it is also because the only people who seemed free
of suspicion, and who could have taken the lead in formulating a new
politics in the former GDR—the dissidents—have shown themselves
incapable of transforming their refusal of the old order into a construc-
tive democratic politics. With this aspect of the question, we return to
the problem of revolution; and with it is posed the question of the
limits of antitotalitarian politics.

In order to understand the political implications of the present
situation—which are not limited to the German case—I will first

formulate some ideal types of the lives and choices that existed in the former GDR. I will then return to the question of guilt in the terms proposed in 1946, at the end of the war, by the Heidelberg philosopher Karl Jaspers. On that basis, I will try to use one of the fundamental lessons of the critique of totalitarianism—the distinction between politics and the political—in order to suggest a new interpretation to the politics of guilt by treating it in terms of the *corruption of the political.* The usefulness of this reformulation will appear when I turn, finally, to a concrete proposal for confronting the heritage of the ancien régime of the former GDR.

Some Ideal Types

The opposition to the Old Order that captured our imaginations at the time of the denouement and fall of communism can be called moral. These men and women rejected radically a regime that sought to impose itself on society. The basis of their refusal was, ultimately, individual conscience. Such a moral engagement neglects the question of the relation between the individual, who must be assumed to be essentially good, and a society that permitted, if not accepted, the imposition of an unworthy order. The purity required in order to affirm oneself against heterogeneity thus could prove harmful when it came to mobilizing the autonomy of the population. The socialism euphemistically designated—and thus implicitly accepted—as "really existing" was the product of forms of social complicity that could only appear to the pure spirit of opposition as disqualifying compromises: the purity of its refusal prevented it from imagining the political form of the break with a compromised present and the moral autonomy and dignity of which it was the apostle.[5] The opposition could not imagine that space in which individuals whose autonomy depends on that of all others could coexist. In a certain sense, the opposition was monological; its critique was directed at each member of society, but as an individual, and thus abstractly. We will return to this dilemma and to the quest for a dialogue with the past.

At the other extreme of the spectrum are found those men of roughly fifty years of age, living in working-class suburbs, who had managed more or less successfully to carve out lives within an order perhaps perceived as foreign but accepted nonetheless as a certain destiny.[6] They may have shown complicity or compromise, but they betrayed no one by their only too human cowardice. Their new situation is governed by an economy of efficiency whose result is that these men cannot hope to again find productive work. Mature men, who would be normally pillars of stability between the retirees and a younger generation entering into working life in difficult times, find themselves suddenly without function or social status. Worse yet, the new conditions disqualify their very past; they are, literally, worth nothing. Forty years of socialism turns out to have been lost time, effort to no end, a parenthesis that did not even demand a rupture. How can they understand a new order in which they have no place? Who is at fault? Are they? Are we? Or should one blame a destiny that has become a fatality? There is no need to underline the ambiguous potential carried by these people when it comes to establishing a new and pluralist order in the face of populist demagogy.

Between these two extremes, there are those who wanted to be responsible citizens: the "realists." They knew that a lawful social order is necessary for individuals or the group to affirm themselves. They thus joined either the Communist Party or one of the parties allied with it (the *Blockparteien*) whose function was to conserve the pluralist fiction sought by the regime. They knew that this meant constant adjustments and vigilant self-criticism; they knew that they could be effective only at the cost of compromises, which they justified each time by calculations worthy of the best of casuists. Such a position was morally more difficult and less comfortable than that of total opposition.[7] Its premise was that the established order could not be put into question. After 1989, what had been perhaps a realistic attitude could appear to have been a series of abject compromises. What is the value of reforms when the revolution has shown itself to have been possible? As Gorbachev told Honecker, announcing therewith his fall, in politics the person who changes too late will be penalized by life itself.[8] But the temptation of a retrospective—and self-justifying—critique should be avoided. It is no better than the position that uses the weapon of *Staatsnah* to disqualify the realists. There is no justification for playing the *Besser-Wessi*, the one who knows better, perhaps, because of the accident of Western birth.

These three ideal types suggest the way in which the concept of guilt can become a political weapon. Those who do not see a future in which they could have a legitimate place are tempted by a deformed image of a past that they feel has been stolen from them; others may blame that past for their present unhappiness. *Divide et impera* is a slogan from the past that will have a great future. Even if prosperity returns more quickly than expected, this relation to the past is an abscess that must be burst. In the Federal Republic after the war, this labor of society on itself was imposed by the Allies but shunted aside with the return of good times—until a new generation on the Left took up the question again, sometimes fruitfully, but with the always-present risk of excess, as in the case of the terrorist Red Army Fraction (RAF) and its satellite public. If the former GDR is to find a place within a new and democratic Germany, if it is to contribute to that democracy rather than feeling itself the victim of a history with which it refuses to identify itself, and if it does not want to be condemned to live in a society where the only values are money and commodities, then it will have to find the means to open a dialogue with the past. In this context, Karl Jaspers's analysis of the question of guilt at the end of Nazism, *Die Schuldfrage*, can be read profitably, for its philosophical foundation is also a political analysis.[9]

Philosophy of Guilt

Jaspers notes several times that the attitudes of Germans toward the Nazi regime were not homogeneous; there were important differences between the emigré of the first hour and the one who waited until Crystal Night in 1938, between those who maintained their faith in the regime until the moment when defeat seemed probable, in 1942, or when it was certain, in 1943, and those who remained true to the cause until 1945. In the same sense, some were opportunists, others showed only external signs of obedience while retreating into private life, and still others truly believed the Nazi message, whatever they thought of its practical implications. Whatever their attitudes or behavior, Jaspers stresses the fact that twelve years of dictatorship prevented Germans from talking freely among themselves; and that it is precisely this dialogue, which is ultimately political, to which his philosophical essay hopes to provide the introduction. Thus, his introduction concludes with the affirmation that "Germany can only return to itself when we Germans open ourselves to communication with one another. When we learn to truly talk with each other, which means only with the consciousness of our great differences. . . . A common spirit that emerges from truly talking with one another and through understanding leads to a community which can endure."[10]

To communicate, it is necessary first to make distinctions. Jaspers distinguishes four types of guilt, defines the persons to whom these categories refer, and designates those who can judge of guilt in each specific case. There is first of all individual guilt, which applies to criminal acts and is judged by a court of justice. Next is the guilt of the citizen, which is a collective "responsibility" (*Haftung*) for a shared enterprise with specific and defined goals and is judged ultimately in political struggle whose extreme form is war.[11] The third form of guilt is moral; it forbids one to appeal to the adage that "orders are orders" (*Befehl ist Befehl*), and it can only be judged by individual conscience, perhaps with the aid of another who is a friend and who is interested in one's soul. Finally, there is metaphysical guilt that is based on a *solidarity* between men that "makes each co-responsible for all the wrongs and all the injustices of the world, especially for crimes which took place in his presence or of which he was aware."[12] What is interesting about this fourth category is that it is collective, just as is political guilt—although Jaspers speaks of it in theological terms, as if it belonged, he says, to Revelation.[13] This theological element will return.

Jaspers thus distinguishes first of all the forms of guilt that apply to the individual from those that apply to the collectivity, and then those that belong to positive justice from those that belong to morality. That second distinction serves as the basis of a new jurisprudence that he thought he saw taking form at the Nuremberg Trials, and that he hoped would spread to other cases.[14] Thus, Jaspers condemns the Allies for doing nothing in 1933, or at the time when rearmament began, or when the Rhineland was taken. He is suggesting that the legitimacy of a politics is not limited by the "realistic" framework imposed by positive justice. That is why he insists that criminal and moral guilt are individual whereas political and metaphysical guilt are collective. It is not moral guilt—which can be judged only by the individual, perhaps with the aid of a friend—that leads to pardon (*Entschuldigung*) and that prepares what the theologian calls purification (*Reinigung*). To realize this project, it is necessary to move from monologue to dialogue, from the individual to the collective.

The collective responsibility of citizens is not limited to its juridical aspect, as with criminal guilt, nor is it simply moral. Both of these are monological judgments, the reflections of an individual subject. If the Germans accepted their guilt only in this sense, they would not have the possibility of acting together to renew their society. Jaspers's goal is not simply to reject the past but to do so in a manner that permits constructing a common future. That implies the need for a dialogue across their differences by means of that communication for which Jaspers called at the conclusion of his introduction. How can this be achieved? For Jaspers, the citizen who accepts his juridical responsibility recognizes *himself* as responsible. That is "the first sign of an awakening of their political freedom. To know that one is responsible is the beginning of an inner revolution which seeks to realize political freedom."[15] The point is that I can be responsible only toward others. This is not an obligation that is imposed on me; I accept this responsibility in the same way that a member of a family accepts responsibility for the behavior of its members; I am responsible not only for what they are but also for what they can become together. In this way, my responsibility becomes active.

This movement from individual and juridical responsibility toward an active participation in the development of the family of men and women points to the passage toward the political. But, of course, political relations are not the same as familial ones in which the individual properly speaking does not exist.[16] The problem of the identification of the political and the familial is clear when Jaspers speaks of the "family of men," which points toward what he called metaphysical guilt. That form of guilt is at once collective (in that it concerns all of humanity) and individual (in the way in which it is assumed). Thus, beyond a policy of restitution (*Wiedergutmachung*), which is juridicopolitical and collective, Jaspers is seeking to rediscover politics. "Purification," he says, "is also the condition of our political freedom. For the consciousness of solidarity and co-responsibility emerges only from the consciousness of guilt without which freedom is not possible."[17] But such a politics appears far too abstract, as Paul Ricoeur had already argued in his contemporary review of Jaspers's book; it is a thesis that implies the emergence of "a political conscience on the scale of world history," and thus another form of antipolitics. Ricoeur specifies the *locus* of the problem in the fact that Jaspers "invites us on an adventure which expands (*illimite*) the fault or guilt to the point that it demands the absolute. . . . Suddenly sin emerges as if it were at the heart of the fault. This is not a new guilt that appears but the very religious heart of ethics."[18] But this relation between evil and politics is not as abstract as it might seem at first glance.

Corruption of the Political

Although Jaspers criticized the nonintervention of the Allies against Hitler, he did not treat adequately the conditions that gave rise to what he calls simply the Nazi "dictatorship." Paul Ricoeur seeks to explain this lack in his review. He argues that Nazism could take root because of the decline of religious faith "not only as a central spiritual fact, but also as a stable sociological structure."[19] For this reason, politics could become the supreme source and unique value for humanity; freed from all constraints, politics opens—in Ricoeur's words—to the "demonic." When politics is everything and everything is politics, totalitarianism can be born, as Nazism or as its enemy-brother communism. It remains, however, to explain how politics can become that supreme source before becoming finally demonic. How was its true nature corrupted?

The contemporary critique of totalitarianism attempts to explain this development by distinguishing the political from politics. At an abstract level—for example, for deconstructionism or for Horkheimer and Adorno—it analyzes a logic of modernity that has been at work since Descartes, if not since the Greeks, and that must pursue its path until it self-destructs. In a more sociological variant—for example, in Weber or Habermas—modernity is interpreted as a project that, methodically, step by step, autonomizes the separate domains of human existence, permitting them to acquire their own systemic logic, with the result that at a certain moment the autonomization process will have hollowed out the world we share in common (the *Lebenswelt*) such that nothing holds humanity together save a politics that has itself become autonomous and whose goal has become nothing but its own self-realization (or self-preservation). In the end, such arguments can lead to a condemnation of modernity or even to the identification of a "postmodernity" as the proper form for a posttotalitarian democracy.

It is not necessary to accept the entirety of the systematic logic that permits the philosophers and sociologists to explain the birth of totalitarianism without recourse to the political. I speak here of *the* political; that is, of the horizon of sense that permits the articulation of concrete and historically specific politics. More concretely, it is the republican form that articulates the political within which is organized a democratic society that takes part in politics. The danger is the confusion of these two political levels, treating the government as if it were the immediate manifestation of the political. This error, whether they were conscious of it or not, can explain the "realistic" behavior of those who, in Eastern Europe, accepted participation in politics before 1989. They did not see that a government—be it monarchical, parliamentary, or even democratic—seeks always to expand its power. There is no reason to be shocked by this; the argument is classical, and should be familiar to Americans since their own revolution was based on it.[20] The crucial distinction is the different means that a given government uses to achieve this end, which can be simply pragmatic or personal, as well as socioeconomic.

In the present case, the issue is broader; it concerns the corruption of *the* political. If the political is identified with the politics of a given government, that government will be perceived as an actor among other actors rather than as the framework that makes possible democratic debate. In that case, the government is perceived as attempting to impose itself on social actors who, for their part, and in reaction, will seek to take control of the fortress of government. The result is that the political loses its autonomy, just as the society loses its own; the conquest of the administrative machinery becomes an end in itself—and politics will replace the political, which now can be said to be corrupted: it has lost its proper function by being reduced to an object of social competition, the prey to real interests.

This presentation of politics as the corruption of the political should not be understood as the rejection of a politics based on interests. The apparently schematic distinction between the two levels permits the transformation of the question of guilt into the classical political question of corruption. But does that traditional concept apply to totalitarian societies, which, by their very nature, refuse the distinction between the individual and the collective? Were these societies already so corrupted that the concept of political responsibility does not apply to them? The moralists stood up to a corruption that refused the individual his or her moral dignity and his or her rights as a citizen. The realists, on the other hand, did not accept the image of a totally corrupted society; their actions can be located within the domain of collective responsibility, but of the type that Jaspers defined by appeal to the logic of *familial* responsibility. That is why neither the moralists nor the realists can find their place within a democratic society. The moralists cannot understand the logic of collectivity whereas the realists are, at best, paternalists.[21]

From Corruption to the Political

This sketch of the contemporary critique of totalitarianism permits the concretization of Jaspers's categories in the case of the former GDR. The proposition of some former dissidents to create a "Tribunal" that would serve to reactualize their own past does not refer to Jaspers, although it might have.[22] Their *Plaidoyer für ein Tribunal* describes their feelings on opening the archives of the Stasi: "We encounter our own painful and oppressive past. It is an encounter that gives rise to rage and rebellion, mourning and the thirst for vengeance, but also to shame and despair, arrogance and defensive reactions." They explain that this implies the need to "reclaim falsified biographies" as well as the necessity of "re-establishing the criteria of good and evil, of honesty and dignity," which, however, must be understood in the context of the reality of the GDR. That is to say, they recognize that the past cannot be simply rejected in toto; this past must be reappropriated. But how? They underline the difficulty when they say that "he who closes himself off to his own history will not have access either to the past or to the future." The means for avoiding this, they conclude, must take place in the public forum, which gives satisfaction "to the moral right of those who can consider themselves as the victims of the political system of the GDR." The problem is: on what basis can such a tribunal claim legitimacy?

The question may appear tautological, but in fact it is only antinomic.[23] If a normal, and democratic, political life is to come into being, one must face the past; the tribunal seems to offer a means of doing that without confusing the individual and collective categories and without mixing the political, juridical, and moral levels. The legitimacy of such a tribunal can come only at the level of *the* political; yet it is only such a tribunal that, in the context of the ex-GDR, could found a new political legitimacy. This vicious circle can be avoided if one distinguishes the genesis of politics from the norms furnished by the political. The danger is that the political be conflated with positive jurisprudence, and that the reestablishing of right be considered as equivalent to the reestablishment of those (political) rights that make a person a being worthy of coexisting with her peers in a republican polity. Such a republic is in fact nothing but the framework of *the* political whose universality and impartiality permit the confrontation of individual projects and particular claims that are not simply indifferent to each other—as is the case with the neutral relations that exist in the economic market that is called free.

Since what we confront here is an antinomy, the solution must appeal to the master of that philosophical structure: Kant. Two centuries ago, in his "Project for Perpetual Peace," Kant showed first of all how the republican principle of universality provides a negative criterion for the political: it condemns any practice that cannot be presented and debated publicly. But Kant goes further: the republic furnishes also a positive definition of any politics that can claim moral and political legitimacy: any measure that, in order to succeed, must present itself and be debated publicly is *ipso facto* legitimate and just.[24] When we apply these—negative and positive—Kantian principles to the case of the former GDR, they provide the principle of judgment that can make possible a debate that would be at once partisan and yet would conserve a positive tolerance for the rival positions. It is only in this manner, as Jaspers saw in the passages already cited, that a people that has been long oppressed by a dictatorship will finally be able to rediscover itself as a people united above and beyond the real differences of interests that should not and cannot be suppressed nor ignored.

The tribunal that has been proposed would thus not take upon itself to judge facts that could be subsumed under preexisting laws; nor would it deal with individual moral responsibility. In certain cases, that could mean that it consecrates the supposed triumph of one system over another; in other cases—like those of the high-ranking officials of the system—this could give rise to a juridical exculpation, on the grounds of *nulla poena sine leges*, that is, the prohibition against retroactive law. That is why it is necessary to pose the question at the level of the political, in order to avoid a situation in which the inevitable frustrations, incoherences, and probable injustices become the pretext for a moral revolt or for a return to the political passivity that was so well learned in the past. The tribunal would seek to accomplish what Jaspers sought in his way, but without the limits entailed by his familial conception of politics and his theological metaphysics of the political. It will have a better chance to succeed in this task insofar as the former GDR was—even for those who accepted it as their destiny—a regime that was imposed from outside. Such a tribunal may make possible the rehabilitation of the realists, and perhaps also the reappearance on the political stage of the moralists. It could create a public forum where the political can present itself to a public that will be able to participate in the foundation of a Germany capable of uniting itself by itself and as a whole in order to undertake political action.

In the last resort, one might ask whether such a tribunal can serve as a model in other domains? Without falling into the trap of excommunicating each of the systems, as if there were a moral equivalence between them—as if the faults of capitalism in the FRG justified the politics of the Old Order in the GDR—one must hope that the victors will also learn to better know themselves by means of the process that is taking place in the East. There is no place for moralism in the present conditions. Today, when the disintegration of the soviet system is giving way to the excesses of an atavistic nationalism, how can one not debate seriously—as did Jaspers at the end of another dictatorship—the question of an international "right of intervention"? But such a debate can be formulated only in terms of a republican politics whose initiatives, if they are to be efficacious, must show themselves capable not only of being presented before the public but also of being supported by that public if they are to succeed. Such a politics does not consist of simply putting into practice positive laws; it is the creation of a new and radical legality. The task, in a word, is to invent a politics that generates and regenerates the norms of the political. This is perhaps not very realistic—but we have seen also the limits of realism.[25]

Notes

1. This paper was originally written in French for presentation at "Diagonales," sponsored by the College International de Philosophie in Paris in June 1992. It was published in *Autres Temps*, No. 42, summer 1994, 54–66. My translation of it was also presented at the Harriman Institute for Advanced Study of the Soviet Union in October 1992. It was published in *German Politics and Society*, No. 28, spring 1993, 1–15. I have revised it somewhat and brought it up to date for this publication, taking advantage of the comments and criticisms of my audiences. A German version was published in *Berliner Debatte. Initial*, 2 (1993), 3–10.

2. Recall the furor raised when Helmut Kohl, the first German chancellor not to have participated in the Second World War, spoke of the *Gnade des späten Geburts* (grace of being born late) in order to justify his claim that the Federal Republic should not be condemned to remain a diplomatic dwarf simply because of its Nazi heritage. *Mutatis mutandis*, the issue today would turn around a *Gnade des geographischen Geburts* on the part of those who were fortunate enough to be born on the capitalist side of the wall.

3. Is there a typical nation among the former satellites of the former Soviet Union? In all events, the differences are the more striking the further removed from 1989 we become. With regard to the former GDR, see Sigrid Meuschel, *Legitimation und Parteiherrschaft in der DDR* (Frankfurt am Main: Suhrkamp Verlag, 1992), and the interesting research proposal of Rainer Land and Ralf Possekall, "Intellektuelle aus der DDR," in *Berliner Debatte. Initial*, 1 (1992), 86–95. With regard to the FRG and its relation to its own past, the so-called *Historikerstreit* of 1986 provides a wealth of conscious and unconscious detail of which Richard J. Evans's *Im Schatten Hitlers?* (Frankfurt am Main:

Suhrkamp Verlag, 1991) provides a good overview. The issue, it will be recalled, arose when certain German historians seemed to want to relativize the Nazi past by opposing it to Stalinist totalitarianism, as if the one excused the other. That the same questions may be returning in the wake of the difficulties of (re?)-unification is suggested by Volker Ulrich's "Die neue Dreistigkeit," *Die Zeit*, 6 November 1992.

4. Cases have arisen in which Stasi agents kept a dossier on someone without that person having either consented to it or known of it. In other, more frequent cases, Stasi agents seeking to feather their own nests have added to or exaggerated information received. But, one has also to admit that there have been numerous cases in which it has turned out that this or that well-known person was in fact cooperating with the Stasi.

A flagrant illustration of the difficulty in dealing with secret police documents was presented in Czechoslovakia by the case of Jan Kavan, which first arose in the spring of 1991 (see my article in *New York Newsday*, 30 April 1991), and has rebounded once again in the fall of 1992 (see Lawrence Wechsler, "The Velvet Purge: The Trials of Jan Kavan," *New Yorker*, 19 October 1992, 66–96).

5. That this question has wider implications is evident in the east Europe-wide currency of G. Konrad's notion of an "anti-politics" or in Vàclav Havel's insistence on "living in truth." Writing in June of 1990, Adam Michnik weighs the historical evidence in his essay "Ethik und Politik" before coming down on the side of truth in the form of an "ethics of the power of the powerless-ness" (reprinted in *Der lange Abschied vom Kommunismus* [Rheinbek bei Hamburg: Rowholt, 1992]). Michnik assumes that, somehow, or in this way, a true pluralism can emerge. The question, however, is whether one can, or must, live alone to live in truth.

6. Women were found here as well, but their situation was more complicated since they are, in general, the victims of the end of a system that—for reasons that are ideological and often criticizable for their productivist bias—permitted them nonetheless a certain role in active social life, however limited this may have been.

7. Of course, it was also more comfortable at the material level—a fact not to be forgotten when we analyze their behavior from the point of view of the overthrow of a system that most thought was solidly implanted, and for a long time to come.

8. *Wer zu spät kommt, dem straft das Leben*, said Gorbachev at the time of his visit to the GDR in October 1989. The Politburo interpreted this remark as an invitation to overthrow Honecker, which set into motion the process that led quickly to the end. The dilemma of the realists was obvious even before 1989: in order to achieve minor meliorations, they accepted the status quo instituted at Yalta, whereas the moralists—especially after the Helsinki Accords—could appeal to a supposed will of the West to put an end to the divisions sealed in 1945.

9. Karl Jaspers, *Die Schuldfrage. Von der politischen Haftung Deutsch-lands* (Munich: Serie Piper, 1987). The first edition dates from 1946. References to the text will be indicated in parenthesis in the account that follows. I should underline from the outset what will be obvious in the following: I am not in the least claiming that it is possible to identify Nazism with the political regime of the former GDR. That was the tact taken in the *Historikerstreit*, but it has continued to be used after 1989. For a critique, see Herbert Obenaus, "Stasi kommt—Nazi geht?" *Die Zeit*, No. 32, 31 July, 1992, 40.

10. Jaspers, *Die Schuldfrage*, 13ff.

11. The German term *Haftung* refers to the kind of responsibility involved in a joint-stock venture—as in the German term for a publicly owned corpora-tion, a GmbH: *Gemeinschaft mit beschränkter Haftung*. It will be noted that Jaspers uses this term in the subtitle of his essay.

12. Jaspers, *Die Schuldfrage*, 17ff.

13. Ibid., 18.

14. Jaspers admits this goal in the 1962 postface to a republication of his essay, and confesses a certain naiveté with regard to the future of the principles of Nuremberg. In the light of some proposals that have emerged from the sad experience of the former Yugoslavia, one wonders whether the last word has been spoken.

15. Jaspers, *Die Schuldfrage*, 52.

16. The *locus classicus* of this distinction is of course Hegel's *Rechtsphilo-sophie*, which systematically introduces a distinction between the substantive unity that is the Family and Civil Society, which is founded on the individuality of the individual. However, the classical form of civil society was implicitly based on the model of the capitalist economy that tends to destroy that individuality. In this sense, Andrew Arato and Jean Cohen have insisted, in the wake of the experience of totalitarianism as well as that of capitalism, that a modern civil society must preserve the autonomy and privacy of the family as well. This argument is developed also in Jürgen Habermas's *Faktizität und Geltung* (Frankfurt am Main: Suhrkamp Verlag, 1992).

17. Jaspers, *Die Schuldfrage*, 82.

18. Paul Ricoeur, "La culpabilité allemande," published originally in *Esprit* in 1949 and reprinted in *Lectures 1. Autour du politique* (Paris: Editions du Seuil, 1991), 153 and 151ff.

19. Ibid., 153.

20. I am referring to what was called the Old Whig or Commonwealth theory whose role in the events that led from resistance to England in 1763 to a Declaration of Independence in 1776 has been argued by Bernard Bailyn and Gordon Wood. For an overview of its implications, see chapters 4 and 5 in section 2 above.

21. This paternalistic presupposition may explain why some of the realists were willing to work even with the Stasi. They saw the corruption brought on by the domination of the party, but they felt that the Stasi was capable of

overturning, or at least of setting right, the bureaucratic bonzes. They were opposed to the Old Regime, but they were not democrats and understood nothing of democracy's pleasures and dangers. The existence of this category of persons complicates the problem of democratization in Eastern European societies.

22. The proposition seems to have been first formulated by Wolfgang Thierse, who published it under the title "Schuld sind immer die anderen. Ein Pladoyer für die selbstkritische Bewältigung der eigenen Geschichte," *Die Zeit*, 6 September 1991. This essay has been published, along with a series of replies and debates, in *Ein Volk am Pranger? Die Deutschen auf der Such nach einer neuen politischen Kultur* (Berlin: Aufbau Taschenbuch Verlag, 1992). The result of the debate has been a new formulation of the proposition, "Plaidoyer für ein Tribunal" *Frankfurter Allgemeine Zeitung*, 23 January 1992, 29. I am citing from this text in the following.

23. See on this question, Jürgen Habermas, "Bemerkungen zu einer verworrenen Diskussion," whose subtitle is "Was bedeutet 'Aufarbeitung der Vergangenheit' heute," *Die Zeit*, No. 15, 3 April 1992. Habermas makes use of Adorno, who invented the concept "Aufarbeitung der Vergangenheit" (working out the past) and of the Mitscherlichs, who together published a foundational analysis of the problem from the standpoint of psychoanalysis that was heavily debated in the 1960s.

24. For the details of this argument, see *From Marx to Kant*, 2d ed. (London: Macmillan, and New York: St. Martin's Press, 1993).

25. Although that was not my original intention, I have found it necessary to almost "rehabilitate" those whom I call the "realists" because I cannot accept the actual practice in the ex-GDR that treats them as guilty until they have proven themselves innocent. That is why I was led to reflect on their possible motives that, when seen more closely, differ radically from one person to another—even though the criticism of their paternalism and of their lack of understanding of the nature of a democratic pluralism, suggested above, seems to be, alas, a shared attitude.

I should add here that, since this paper was first written, the idea of a "tribunal" has fallen from public debate in the face of more pressing problems of actuality. And the "affair" of Manfred Stolpe, the minister-president of Brandenburg and former mediator between the Evangelical Church and the Old Regime, has been taken into the party-political sphere. Even in that context, the issues raised here retain their relevance, as seen in Richard Schröder's essay on the question, "Am Schnittpunkt von Macht und Ohnmacht," *Die Zeit*, No. 42, 16 October 1992.

14

Toward a Politics of Judgment

It seems so long ago, the fall of the Berlin Wall, which symbolized the division of the modern world. Absent, the Wall recalls a used and useless past that all would rather forget. Even those who have lost the low but solid security that looks more desirable now in the face of an uncertain future can scarcely long for its return. The year 1989 brought an end to the ancien régime; and this time there will be no Restoration. Despite their at times important role, the rebaptized Communist Parties hardly resemble the nobility that fled the Revolution of 1789 with their arms and ideological baggage. They were no more successful at recognizing the need for the new than was Louis XVI; and their most farsighted elements have no more chance of stemming the course of the Revolution than did the Monarchiens in 1790, the Feuillants in 1791, or the Girondins in 1792. It is amusing to speculate about who might be the Mirabeau, the Sieyès, the Danton, or the Robespierre of the new world. One can imagine candidates for the roles—a Walesa, a Klaus, a Meciar or an Illiescu, perhaps. The analogy with 1789 ignores a crucial difference: the new world opened in 1989 is not an uncharted ideal; it is the really existing West. This seems to make the fall of the Wall into a nonevent; and it would imply that there is nothing to learn from the prelapsarian times and the post-1989 attempts to understand and to join the self-confident present. The year 1989 will not have its Babeuf!

The West has had trouble digesting its victory and charting its future. The earlier attempts by Olaf Palme and Willy Brandt to replace the symbolic Wall by the painfully real North-South economic divide have not been renewed, even though political conditions would now seem to make that possible. Disgust with politics, politicians, and political parties has become the common sense of our times. Necessity

295

has replaced invention, but it is an opaque fatality whose meaning is imposed without being understood. War and conflict are endemic, but "history" as a meaningful trajectory and human project seems to have come to an end. The polemics that greeted Francis Fukuyama's interpretation of the end of the Cold War usually neglected to read even the full title of his book: *The End of History and the Last Man.* The allusion to Nietzsche's critique of democracy should have warned the reader. "The decline of community life suggests," writes Fukuyama at the beginning of his concluding chapter, "that in the future, we risk becoming secure and self-absorbed last men, devoid of thymotic striving for higher goals in our pursuit of private comforts." Worse, he continues, "modern thought raises no barriers to a future nihilistic war against liberal democracy on the part of those brought up in its bosom."[1] If the West is the future of the East, its own future remains clouded, as if it lived in an eternal present demarcated only by quantitative measures. Its politicians cannot look to the future because they are blind to the past—a past that has not yet passed.

Politics is not about "who does what to whom"; that is the domain of political science (and Leninism). Politics is concerned with sense; the distinction between living and living well has preoccupied Western political thought since Aristotle. In the modern world, sense emerges in the relation that the present establishes between its past and its future. Undetermined, that sense is not therefore arbitrary. Malleable, the past cannot be manipulated at will; open, the future cannot be produced at will. The remembered past may affect the projected future; the desired future may color the imagined past. Politics can neglect neither dimension. Yet the triumph of liberal democracy seems to exclude any future, and thereby to make politics impossible—or at least to explain its present absence. But the thesis of "the end of history" does not imply a glorification of the present; Fukuyama questions "the goodness of liberal democracy itself, and not only whether it will succeed against its present-day rivals."[2] A disciple of Leo Strauss, he criticizes what he calls "liberal democracy" from the standpoint of classical philosophy. But that classical appeal to a universal natural law provides no orientation for a future any more than it opens to a meaningful past; it produces a curiously unpolitical vision that can imagine a future with "bestial 'first men' engaged in bloody prestige battles, this time with modern weapons."[3]

If one pole of the relation between past and future that provides political sense to the present is blocked, there is no choice but to begin from the other pole. How do we relate to the past? How does it become our past? Because it has passed, the past seems devalued by the present; its intrusion into our present may lame us, blocking action by making us, consciously or unconsciously, incapable of imagining a future. More or less psychoanalytic models of this relation can be suggested, like the Mitscherlich's 1967 book, *Die Unfähigkeit zu Trauen*, or Adorno's 1959 lecture, "Was bedeutet: Aufarbeitung der Vergangenheit?"[4] When the past becomes *our* past, the relation changes; who we are depends on who we were and what we did; we stand now in debt to a past that impels us toward a future; our relation to the past has the possibility of becoming political. The realization of this possibility depends on whether the past to which we accept our debt acquires a positive value, and how it acquires that value. Manipulation and mystification are always possible. Some French may relate to the legacy of 1789 by recalling its demand for liberty, equality, and fraternity; others may remember the wars of the Vendée or the Guillotine. Some Germans may find the legacy of Nazism in the incomparable *Shoah* while others may seek to "normalize" their past.[5] Others, like the Poles, may consider that 1989 brought the "Third Republic," conveniently ignoring nearly a half century during which they lived in a "People's Republic." The past is politically contested territory as well.

Where, then, is one to begin? *Alle Anfänge sind schwer.* In Eastern Europe, the relation to the past has been colored by the question of guilt. The names of the dissidents were known, some in the West (but usually not Western governments) did what they could to support them, a few in the East imitated them. The sudden fall of the Wall revealed a world of compromise, and a compromised world. Guilt, real or supposed, could become a weapon (and a motive) in political struggles. The purity and the unity of the first moments of the Revolution are long gone. Most evident in the former East Germany and Rumania, the phenomenon exists everywhere. I have written elsewhere on how I think the problem might be treated. What struck me most was the ambiguous situation of those who, rather than opt for moral purity, sought a path to and through politics.[6] One may criticize them; but the existence of ambiguity cannot be eliminated from politics. The problem cannot be reduced to juridical categories, although these too have their necessary place.[7] The contemporary antipolitical mood, East and West, suggests the need for a more philosophical and historical return to the question. If the past has truly passed only when it becomes ours, and if our past entails a debt and a legacy, coming to

grips with it opens up the dimension of a future. Only then does
politics become possible.

Politics and Guilt

Why would a Westerner worry about the question of guilt? History
seems to have justified the values by which the West has lived. But one
of those values is the existence of a critical public space in which the
difference between these values and their realization can and must be
questioned, where values can be evaluated. This is where the difference between the Left and the Right first appears. When the Left
challenges the established (dis)order, it appeals to commonly accepted
values that it shows to be inadequately put into practice. It judges its
society guilty of injustice; and it puts itself on the side of the victims.
So it was, in the United States, that the Civil Rights movement
emerged; and so it was that, before his assassination, Martin Luther
King, Jr., was driven to oppose the American war in Vietnam and to
take the side of striking municipal workers. In following this course,
the Left implicitly constructs a past to which it claims that the present
owes a debt—in the American case, to Jefferson's ringing words in the
Declaration of Independence: "We hold these truths to be self-evident,
that all men are created equal . . ." At the same time, it projects a
future in which that past can and must be realized. The problem is that
past and future are thereby identified, and the present is denied its
uniqueness, complexity, and ambiguity.

   In the American case, the leftist feels guilty about the racism,
imperialism, sexism, and more generally all the perceived injustices of
his or her society. Refusing complicity, the leftist takes the side of the
oppressed, the excluded, the discriminated. The guilt of the leftist
comes to outweigh the legacy of values that grounded his critique. By
a simple logic, the oppressed become victims of a system that must be
transformed. The critique becomes an attack on a system because the
values to which the Left appealed lie in the past and the future; the
present cannot be given any depth or complexity of its own. As a
result, the Left puts itself in the service of the victims; as in the
Platonic variant of political philosophy, the politician is a "selfless
servant" of a truth that was and will be but is not yet. But because the
present, the system, has no value of its own, the values of the victim
come to determine concretely the political choices made by the Left.
Thus, many in the New Left in the United States slipped from justified

opposition to the American war in Vietnam to uncritical support for the communist regime in Hanoi. Others accepted the transformation of the Civil Rights movement into an increasingly separatist quest for Black Power; and still others sought to join with the working class, and to remodel themselves into Marxists without reflecting on the nature of "really existing socialism."

Putting politics in the service of others leads not only to mistakes of political judgment; it denies the autonomy and the responsibility of judgment in the formulation of politics. The Left is not alone in this refusal of politics.[8] The Right has, since the French Revolution, appealed to eternal values that transcend the present and devalue its disorderly nature. In its most extreme form, this attitude appears in the German opposition of *Kultur* to the dehumanized technological and atomized world of (democratic) *Zivilisation*. Here, however, the service to values takes an otherworldly form at the same time that it denies the rupture between past and present that opened up the idea of a future and the place of politics. Thus, the Right denies the reality of the modern world that was inaugurated by the French Revolution. Guilt, insofar as it figures in the lexicon of the Right, is that of the others, whose sin is to think that mere human will (or reason) can refashion the present. Insofar as it is a politics, right-wing politics is an antipolitical politics; it denies the autonomy of the political. Since the present is determined by eternal values, the idea that it could be changed is an expression of the error of human *hubris*. Like the Left, the Right denies the ambiguity of the present, and the necessity of political judgment. Both of these two ideal types of "selfless servitude" are antipolitical.

This structural identity of the Left and Right conceptions of politics can be understood by returning to their origins. Left politics was born in the wake of 1789; and so too was the need to reflect on the relation of guilt and politics. Only after the Revolution could the concept of an "ancien régime" emerge; and only then could the past and the future be opposed radically to one another in order to deny the ambiguities of the present. All remnants of the past had to be eliminated; they were guilty of opposing the future. First the monarchy, then the aristocracy, and then in rapid succession any figure or group that sought (or could be accused of trying) to set itself apart by its independence had to be condemned. Amalgamating traits, labeling opponents, accusing one's enemies of treason, or inventing invisible conspiracies, the Revolution gained an imperious momentum. Ultimately, the power that put itself in the service of "the people" was led to institutionalize the Terror as the form of a revolutionary government whose present occupants were merely selfless servants. Seeking to rot out a guilty past, the Terror made politics impossible; because the future was only the negation of the past, no value could be given to the present.

The antipolitics of the Right is at least explicit; but its critique of the Left for identifying politics with will neglects a crucial aspect of politics. The year 1789 liberated two wills that were doomed to clash. Sieyès's claim for the *Tiers Etat* brought the popular will onto the stage of history as the "nothing that can become everything." The "people" became the *volonté générale*, which was valid not only against the *volonté de tous* but also against the *volonté individuelle*. But this latter form of will, individual will, had won its rights in the Declaration of the Rights of Man and of the Citizen. Sieyès tried to harmonize the two by applying the economic notion of a division of labor; and he criticized what he called the *ré-totale*, which could result from the failure to give the rights of the individual their due. Nonetheless, it was the image of politics based on the *volonté générale*, the people as represented by the revolutionary government, which determined the course of the revolution. Even the self-organization of workers' associations was outlawed by the Le Chapelier law because it appeared to imply the constitution of a particular group separate from the unitary whole. The Left, like the philosopher-king, sought to incarnate the whole over against the parts. It would redeem the people, regenerate the victim of a guilty past whose presence was, however, the justification of its actual politics. Victim of the old system, the people could not judge for themselves; revolutionary will had to act for them.

The figure of Napoleon as "king of the Revolution" and its antipolitical culmination is visible in this portrait. But his world-conquering empire was not a Restoration; surviving old revolutionaries found a place in its new "politics" whose denial of political participation permitted the integration of returning emigres as well. But the other side of the revolutionary coin remained present: the rights of the individual, whose codification had begun with the Revolution and was completed in the *Code Napoléon*. These rights were lodged awkwardly between the absolutist dreams of the Right and the totalizing quest of the Left; and the Restoration did not abolish them. Constrained from both sides, individual rights adopted the form of particular interests and found their place, away from politics, in the new sphere of civil society. But these individual rights were not limited to what Marx (in

"On the Jewish Question") denounced as egoistic interests of the bourgeoisie. As Claude Lefort has shown convincingly, Marx did not see that the rights proclaimed in the declaration of 1789 were also rights of association, of communication, of opinion; they were rights that individuals as individuals can realize only together.[9] The new society that emerged from 1789 was not the incarnation of the unitary sovereignty of the will of the people; it was a democratic society, a plural society founded on the rights of the individual. These rights were indebted to no past and to no will external to the individual; the Revolution made possible what Hannah Arendt called "the right to have rights"; and democratic politics is the process through which this revolutionary right acquires its content in a present that owes its essential ambiguity to the preservation of just this right.

The legacy of 1789 remains with us. For some, it is a past that must be realized in a future that was contained implicitly within it but was arrested in its development. Equality and fraternity are the imperatives it has left us. For others, the failure of the totalitarian politics of will, which saw 1917 as the realization of what the revolutionary government failed to achieve in 1793, suggests the need to rethink the revolutionary legacy even while accepting the debt owed to it. My suggestion is that 1789 made possible both modern politics and the antipolitical attempt to overcome it; this paradoxical relation can now be clarified in the light of the experience of totalitarianism and its demise. The ambiguity of the present cannot be overcome by a revolution that will end all revolutions and realize once and for all the unity of true humanity in a future-become-present that redeems the past. Politics is not defined by the representation of the future that determines its action; its place is the present, whose ambiguity demands judgment as it sets itself off from the past and thereby makes possible a future. This judgment does not take place in abstraction, as if one could stand outside the present and gaze down from above it. That was the error of the Right, which sought in the present the eternal unity of past and future. The legacy of 1789 includes the quest for equality and fraternity as well as the individual right to have rights; this constitutes the plurality of the present, which demands the invention of a democratic politics that cannot accept oppression or exclusion any more than it can postulate their overcoming in a final unity.

1989: Revolution or Breakdown?

Four years after the fall of the Wall, faced with political problems that make their social and economic difficulties seem insurmountable, the

East's relation to its past has been put into question. The concept of a breakdown due to technical difficulty rather than revolutionary will has been advanced, often in the West, but as well by those in the East who were not themselves active in the fall. This has the tactical advantage of exculpating the nonparticipants as well as legitimating their post-1989 roles and attitudes. If the system was so totally corrupt that it fell of its own rottenness, what could have been expected of its inhabitants—and what can be expected of them now? Theirs is a past best forgotten, to which no debt is owed, and in which no future can be discerned. Yet that same past remains present after the breakdown, which, because it is seen mechanically, is incapable of introducing the learning process by which the past can be overcome. This would explain not only the emergence of forms of right-wing nationalism and nativism; it would explain as well the return of (reformed and renamed) communist parties to the forefront of the political stage in several countries.[10] But the problem is more complex; its analysis needs to pursue further the historical parallels to 1789 and the philosophical attempts to come to grips with its political legacy today.

The right-wing critique of the revolutionary pretension not only denounces its voluntarism, abstraction, and unfounded claim to speak in the name of the unitary people; it criticizes as well the atomism, egoism, and disorder of democracy. In so doing it appeals to an idealized unity or community. That is why it is not surprising that the Right and the Left could criticize the hedonism of the revolutions of 1989. Thus, for example, the banana came to symbolize the real reason for the East German choice of unification with the prosperous West. This criticism is based on a misunderstanding of democratic rights, which do include the right to seek to live better ("the pursuit of happiness," as Jefferson put it). The problem posed in 1989, as in 1789, is that of the origin of these rights. If they do not simply emerge from the breakdown of an economic system that was incapable of facing up to modern, technological industrial imperatives, are they the result of a moral upsurge by a humiliated population that sought to assert its simple dignity by refusing to play along with its compromised system? If so, how does this moral stance get translated into a political choice? The disappearance of the majority of the leading pre-1989 dissident leaders from the present political scene, and with them the loss of any hope for a Third Way, suggests that morality does not necessarily or easily find an adequate political expression. The difficulty stems from the fact that morality is based on the will. The experience of 1989, like that of 1789, suggests the need to rethink the place of the will in democratic politics.

How does the individual—the bearer and agent of the right to have rights—relate to other such individuals so that they at once constitute a community and yet preserve their individual right to have rights? The French Revolution could not solve this problem; nineteenth-century liberalism tried to avoid it by leaving free the anonymous forces of the market; nineteenth-century nationalism affirmed the priority of the collective over the individual; and twentieth-century communism developed into totalitarian domination before disappearing. Underlying each of these failures is a vision of politics as based on an act of the will, be it individual or collective. While it is true that the will is involved in politics, acts of will cannot create the political sense that permits judging the present as at once indebted to the past and open to a future. In this context, the distinction between politics and the political is helpful. Politics is the willful expression of interest; it is a legitimate manifestation of the right to have rights. But the sense of (individual or collective) expressions of will is given by the political; it provides the horizon within which the expression of interest or demand for a right is communicated to others, becomes an object of debate among them, and is eventually validated or challenged. The process by which this political sense, this sense of the political, becomes present depends on the relation of the past to the future.

Antipolitics denies the democratic character of the political. Dieter Henrich's recent attempt to understand post-1989 Germany illustrates both the emergence of the political and its suppression by antipolitics. Henrich returns to the German Idealists' critique of the French Revolution. Their early enthusiasm gave way to criticism as its course was radicalized and its message of freedom was conveyed by bayonets. The basis of their critique is apparently similar to the antipolitics of the Right: a society of abstractly equal, rights-bearing individuals can never find stability; it will be forced to radicalize internally and to seek expansion externally. The revolution lacked a normative framework of community, custom, and culture, which Henrich calls "pre-political." The German Idealists therefore tried to provide this missing element by appeal to the specificities of German history—to a language rooted in the spontaneity of Luther's translation of the Bible, to communal aspirations seen in Pietism and a "Rousseauvian" sympathy for the common man and his inner light, and to a cultural unity that was expressed in German philosophy (in which Henrich includes Marx). But they had to face the difficulty of living in a divided nation whose unity was cultural not political. The result was a German republicanism for which the demand for national unity was a progressive political imperative, at least until its defeat in 1848. Afterwards, especially after Bismarck chose the *kleindeutsche* solution for national unification, republican (or democratic) politics was no longer a serious option; nationalism and republicanism became mutually exclusive; Weimar democracy was foredoomed.

The conclusion Henrich draws from his philosophical reconstruction is that the newly unified Germany can become a true republic only by inheriting its Eastern legacy.[11] Only a true republic will permit the creation of the political solidarity needed to confront the task of rebuilding the unified nation. Without the sense of belonging to a republican community, the demand for sacrifice will bring only resentment and misunderstanding, egoism and division; life will be privileged over the good life. The contribution of the East is necessary because the two previous German republics were both imposed from outside, on the basis of a defeat, and were the price that had to be paid for German guilt. Those previous republican institutions thus lacked the normative framework necessary to become true republics. Henrich is not always clear whether the East can contribute to the renewal he seeks because its "Marxist" claims and its attempt to identify itself with the "better Germany" kept the legacy of German Idealism alive; or whether it is simply the fact that the Eastern confrontation with Western institutions will make necessary their rethinking and readaptation. What is clear is his refusal to declare the East Germans guilty, to incite them to deny their past, and to force them to integrate themselves into the pre-existing West German institutions. Thus, for example, he challenges the policy of *Abwicklung*, which has emptied Eastern universities of anyone remotely associated with the previous regime, and insists that the Western universities are not above criticism given their own relation to their past and its democratic institutions.[12]

The important point in Henrich's argument is that the "pre-political" or normative bonds that constitute the republican unity of individuals do not depend on an act of will for their foundation. Henrich counts on the intellectual, whom he distinguishes from the propagandist as well as from the dissident insofar as "the figure and the praxis of the intellectual presuppose a republican form of state, its public sphere and its media."[13] But this leads to a circle: the realization of the republic depends on the East; and yet the Eastern intellectual can play this role only if it is assumed that the Western institutions with which he or she has been united—without serious debate on constitutional reform—are indeed truly republican. This makes understandable the bitterness of an Eastern intellectual like Wolfgang Engler, whose "Democracy of and for the Established" describes the attacks to which Easterners are subject when they dare criticize the (generally admitted, even by President von Weizäcker) desolate situation of parliamentary- and party-political life in Germany.[14] Engler cites the Hungarian dissident leader Janos Kis, who asks whether "it is the case that we are joining the democratic community at a moment when it is already in a process of erosion."[15] Engler's diagnosis adds the element that was lacking in Henrich; citing Plato and Aristotle, he explains the Western criticism as due to their understanding of politics as seen by a single, onlooking "eye," or by the appeal to a unique will rather than what Engler calls an "exchange of perspectives" that is the condition of the possibility of democratic politics.

The inadequacy of a politics of will becomes clear in the light of the question, 1989: revolution or breakdown? To call it a revolution seems to imply that the popular will was the active agent that drove out the Old Order; but that leaves unanswered the identity of that ancien régime and opens the question of guilt that we saw emerge with the French Revolution. If these difficulties lead to the adoption of the claim of a breakdown, the problem of guilt remains; the new has come into being, and now all are potentially guilty and political life is poisoned by the corruption of the political. The politics of will, which is ultimately a moralism, calls forth inevitably the question of guilt, which can be made into a weapon in a political struggle for power waged in the name of a unified people, whatever the particular interests it veils. To avoid the political dead end of moralism, one must, like Tocqueville, analyze together l'ancien régime et la Révolution. The sense of the new politics, of the political, can be understood only in the light of the specific social formation that made it possible; the presence of that past makes intelligible the lines of the future. Most of the Western Left, like Americans, never took the concept of totalitarianism seriously; it was seen as simply a weapon in the Cold War.[16] The result was a policy of "anti-anticommunism" which, after 1989, opened its supporters to the reproach of having been complicit with the Old

Order. The Eastern experience with the totalitarian form of the political—not the legacy of German Idealism—can insure that the republic that remains to be established is a democratic one.

Totalitarianism as a Political Concept

The critique of a politics of will can lead to its inverse identical: the projection of a system so total that individual choice is impossible. The move from an intentionalist thesis to a structuralist variant in the analysis of totalitarianism is not due to the inability to imagine a middle point, but because no other axis of analysis can be constructed. The moral muster is defined by sins of commission and sins of omission, as if social action could be measured and comprehended within such binary indices. Because the action of the will takes place only in an immediate present, the dimensions of the past and the future are blended out. The act of will condenses in itself the power to edict its own law on the basis of its own self-certitude. It produces that unity and identity of the body politic that Wolfgang Engler saw to be the defect that Western parliamentary politics inherited from Plato and Aristotle. Yet, though it denies the place of the past, like the French Revolution its action produces or invents a past, which becomes its guilty predecessor and constantly manipulable enemy. Such a total system leaves no place of politics; its agents are caught in its web, and only a moral heroism can oppose it. Such heroes are by definition few, and their heroism is of little use once the Goliath has disappeared. The paradox is that an action that emerged in opposition to a politics of will conceives of itself in the last analysis in terms of a politics of will.

Totalitarianism becomes possible only within the context of democracy. That is what distinguishes it from the forms of dictatorship or tyranny described by political philosophers since Plato and Aristotle. They saw the popular recourse to a tyrant as a rejection of the chaos of democracy, whereas the contemporary totalitarian claim is that their system is the true realization of democracy. The totalitarian argues that merely formal democracy preserves the oligarchic rule of the bourgeoisie; in its extreme form, this formal democracy becomes what the Third International called "the openly terroristic dictatorship of the most reactionary, most chauvinistic and most imperialistic elements of Finance Capital." Real democracy, realized democracy, demands the completion of the revolutionary movement inaugurated in 1789 and aborted by Thermidor; it overcomes the past and puts an end to prehistory. This project is only possible in modern democracies because only with their advent does the individual as the bearer of the right to have rights—a right that is nowhere guaranteed, as were the corporate rights of the ancien régime—become a political actor who feels the need to find a material anchor fixing these rights. Although communism may have come to eastern Europe on the bayonets of the Red Army, another empire builder—Bonaparte—was correct to say that "you can do anything with bayonets except sit on them." What Czeslaw Milosz described forty-five years ago as "the captive mind" was complicit in its own captivity.

The paradox of totalitarianism is that it admits its goal, repeats itself continually and monotonously, attempts to convince itself that it has realized its project (and justified its staying in power) even when it knows that it has not and cannot. Constantly active, working on its society in order to mould it, it claims at the same time to be the immanent expression of that society's true nature. Its invention of what Claude Lefort calls a new political figure, the militant, bears witness to the paradoxical nature of its politics of will. Part of society, the militant is nonetheless separate from it, able to use his single eye to look on it from above (*survoler*), invoking the vision of the unitary whole toward which it must be driven. The very existence of the militant, and the party of which he is an organ, expresses the incompleteness to which totalitarianism is condemned and explains its need to repeat like a mantra the totalizing project. The militant is the future made present whose combat is directed at a past whose presentness his action paradoxically summons forth. The militant is, to use another of Lefort's phrases, the *bien-pensant* who, even when he disagrees with the practice of the party—even in the gulag or at the purge trials—thinks correctly, goes along for the sake of a future and against a past that, together, destroy his ability to judge the present. Without the militant and the constitutionally inscribed "leading role of the party," the system is doomed.

The crucial figures of the militant and the *bien-pensant*, as well as the silent complicity of the population in their project, cannot be reduced to the simple portrait of Vàclav Havel's green-grocer who fears "living in truth." Existentialism is a moralism of the will, not a politics. The militant is, in her way, a philosopher, a Marxist, the incarnation of the tradition of German Idealism invoked by Dieter Henrich. Already in the Note appended to his doctoral dissertation, Marx had defined his totalizing project: to make the world philosophical and to make philosophy worldly. As had the exiled poet, Heinrich

Heine, Marx saw that the constative verb in Hegel's dictum—the actual is the rational and the rational is the actual—had to be read as an imperative: should. But Marx was not a simple moralist; he had read Hegel's critique of the voluntarism of abstract reason in the French Revolution. He therefore sought an immanent critique of the present to demonstrate in it the existence of a future with which it was pregnant; in this way, the critique of the weapons was to join the weapon of critique. The theory of alienation of 1844, the historical materialism that refuted German ideology, and finally the structural theory of capitalism were systematic attempts to avoid the reproach of abstract moralism. But the "lightning of thought" whose necessity Marx invoked when he first theorized the revolutionary moment that would change the proletariat from an object of history into its subject remained mysterious. *The Communist Manifesto* replaced it with the theoretical knowledge that guarantees the superiority of the Communist Party.

A proper analysis of totalitarianism remains important even after 1989. The conditions that made possible its emergence have not been abolished—material inequality, political demands to protect and increase democratic rights, and the philosophical temptation of the quest to make the rational real remain. The project of the militant may be criticized; but the image of (anti-)politics that he or she incarnates has not disappeared. The militant was not wrong in the way that one errs in a mathematical calculation; politics is of a different nature. The temptation remains to say that, yes, "really existing socialism" was bad but so too is really existing capitalism; therefore, by a return to theory or by the change of political actors, a Third Way must be sought. But this again misunderstands the specificity of the political; and that is what the critique of totalitarianism should have made clear. Totalitarianism emerged from, and within, democracy; it could do so when that democracy misunderstood its own political nature and reduced itself to precisely that formal institutional structure that was denounced—rightly!—by totalitarianism. The problem is not the (more or less) capitalist nature of democracy; the difficulty lies in the inherently self-revolutionizing nature of democracy and its rights-bearing citizenry. The revolutionary nature of democracy, rather than *The Communist Manifesto*'s identification of modernity with the self-revolutionizing nature of capital, is the crucial lesson to be learned from the totalitarian experience.

Democracy as Question

Totalitarianism's attempt to realize democracy assumed that the inherently unstable coexistence of rights-bearing individuals could be given a final solution. It assumed that the unified people could express its sovereignty in a single will. Its distrust of private interest led its militant to adopt the Platonic posture of a "selfless servant" of the eternally present *telos* of history. Its *bien-pensants* assumed that knowledge, power, and the law that guarantees rights had to be united in a single will. The result was not simply antidemocratic; it was antipolitical, destroying the sense of the present. The challenge facing the posttotalitarian world is to restore (or to create) the meaning of citizenship. This will not be easy.[17] The citizen belongs at once to the whole of which he or she is a member, and at the same time she or he belongs to her- or himself. Economic modernization can perhaps account for the latter; but the solidarity that explains the former has different roots. It is not enough to appeal to the strategic necessities imposed by a shared socioeconomic world; normative legitimacy is also necessary. Only a politics that can transform a guilty past into a future-oriented debt can offer direction in a pluralistic present. Its premise is the critique of the totalitarian temptation; its condition of possibility is the revolutionary nature of democracy.

Totalitarianism seeks to close the historical adventure of individualism that began with the French and American Revolutions; it rejects the pluralism and diversity that characterize democratic life. Its nearly Platonic quest for unity and its distaste for anarchy blind it to the fact that democracy is organized around a sort of empty center—the people—which no interest, group, or institution can claim to incarnate. As a result, as in the French Revolution, any expression of autonomy appears as opposition that must be eliminated. But as opposed to the French Revolution, which was animated also by the principle of individualism, the totalitarian project articulates an organic vision that may seek to coopt opposition (in so-called oppositional parties like the GDR's *Blockparteien*), or may permit it to exist in cozy niches outside of the political life of the nation. With the demise of totalitarianism and the ruthless introduction of capitalist individualism (often in the person of former regime officials), the niche-communities may appear as a desirable alternative while the coopted, and the Old Regime, furnish apt scapegoats. The problem of guilt reemerges, but it has to be posed in a different light. Totalitarianism destroyed the political space opened

by the democratic revolution; more precisely, it corrupted political
life, and an aspect of that corruption consisted in both the cooptation
and in the encouragement of the apolitical niche-communities. To
reclaim a past that opens to a future, one must come to grips with this
phenomenon; it is not enough simply to project the niche-communities
as a unitary communal future.

The democratic institutions of the West cannot be imported *en bloc*.
The democratic revolutions that gave these institutions their sense
were not defined by constitutional or legislative language and forms;
the spirit of these institutions comes from the experience and struggle
that helped form them. The impossibility for any interest, group,
or institution to incarnate the sovereignty of the inherently plural
people—composed of rights-bearing individuals—has been violated
often in the two hundred years since the democratic revolution. The
interests of capital, the representatives of one social class, or the
institutions established by the constitution have at various times
claimed to incarnate the popular will. Beneath what appears to some
as the anarchy of individualist pluralism, politicians have claimed to
find and to give voice to that sovereign will. Among those politicians
have been, of course, the totalitarians. But they are not alone; democracy is a fragile experience. This was illustrated recently by the
outraged reaction of right-wing German politicians to the philosopher
Manfred Frank's speech at the annual Commemoration of *Kristall-
nacht* at the Frankfurt Paulskirche in 1992. Frank's denunciation of
the changes made in Germany's asylum laws on the grounds that this
was what the "popular will" desired, was greeted with howls of rage
and vituperation. But Frank's point is important. The revolutionary
essence of democracy is its protection of rights, of the right to
have rights, and the public debate that they make possible—and
necessary—for a society of autonomous individuals to hold together
not on the constantly changing basis of strategic necessities but on that
of normative legitimacy. The howls of the politicians were based on a
misunderstanding of this legitimacy: they thought they were being
democratic by expressing the popular will.[18]

It is in the context suggested by this German experience that one
can see the potential contribution of the East to Western democracy.
The East must come to grips with its totalitarian past, and it can do so
only if it understands the corruption of politics *·* t made it possible.
Three decades ago, trying to understand Nazi tot ..tarianism, Hannah
Arendt introduced the concept of "the banality of evil." Her insight

into the experience that was expressed by the character of Adolf Eichmann retains its validity. Without the public space where *judgment* is necessary and responsibility is assumed, all that remains is the place of will, the orders of the *Führer* or those of the party. When Eichmann denies moral guilt by claiming to understand only "bureaucratic language," and refuses responsibility because he was "only carrying out orders," Arendt sees the incarnation of the totalitarian. She points out that this mentality refuses to recognize the novelty of the new, fitting it into already given categories. It is, she says, a literally thoughtless behavior, a comportment that—we might add—recalls the communist militant or the *bien-pensant*. But Arendt goes further; she asks what kind of a society could produce such a figure? Her answer turns to the place of judgment and the need for the public exchange of democratic politics. Thirty years later, in a climate where politics has become stale while the population turns from it to the promise of instant remedies, to the reemergence of populism, atavistic nationalism, or to promises of free-market miracles and crash cures, one has to wonder whether evil is not about to be banalized once again. Democracy is not a permanent achievement; it puts itself into question, and must be conquered again and again if it is to be maintained.

Politics of Judgment

Reflection on the experience of totalitarianism warns against the quest for an hypostatized unity; and it suggests that this temptation emerges when the capacity for judgment is absent or inoperative. It also makes apparent that the conflict between the rights-bearing individual and the community in which he participates, to which he belongs, and from which he cannot be separated, constitutes the framework within which democracy must thread its path. Neither pole can be neglected; both are equally necessary; emerging simultaneously, they are equiprimordial. Contrary to the Marxist criticism of democracy as bourgeois—as if the bourgeoisie had ever led a movement for democracy, rather than giving in, little by little, and grudgingly, to popular demands—this democratic polarity is inherently revolutionary. The interplay between individual rights and communal norms can be stabilized for a time; but the norms are never the actualization of an individual will, and the movement can begin anew. There is no *telos* to this democratic history; there is only a *nemesis*, constantly present, which is the totalitarian denial of the political space as such. It would be an exaggeration to apply the category "totalitarian" to the stagnant liberalism and conservatism that dominate our political life; but the category of antipolitical describes the sense of their political project quite well.

It may appear that this structural description of democracy, based on the rejection of a politics of will, ignores the political actor; and the picture it paints seems to assume that, sooner or later, the history will begin anew. But democracy cannot live without democrats. In *On Revolution*, Hannah Arendt described their periodic emergence and self-organization as "the lost treasure" of the revolutionary movement. But this is no more satisfactory than the young Marx's invocation of the lightning of thought that will make the proletariat into a truly revolutionary subject. Arendt returned to the question at the end of her life in an incomplete lecture series on judgment, which was to open the way to a Kantian theory of the political. We have already seen the role of judgment in Arendt's evaluation of Nazi totalitarianism. The challenge now is to evaluate its place and its formation within democracy. Because the emergence of democracy poses at the same time the question of the Old Regime, and that of its guilt, the theme of judgment cannot be separated from the question of the sense of the political. The challenge is to pose this political question without politicizing the institutions of justice and without making it into a moral issue concerned with the will of the actors or with the effects of their wills. The French Revolution illustrated the dangers of politicized judgment of the past; contemporary debate in the East shows the dilemmas of a morality of the will.

The democratic individual judges and takes responsibility for that judgment. There are analogies between this action and Kant's *Critique of Judgement*. The judgment of taste, for Kant, poses a problem for the philosopher because it can appeal to no pregiven and universal concepts; it is subjective, the expression of a feeling; yet, like judgments based on concepts, it claims universal validity. This poses two questions. Why do we judge in this way? Why, and to whom, do we seek to communicate the validity of our feeling? The answer to the first question is that we encounter a new situation, one that cannot be subsumed under already-given laws or rules. It is as if we were living after a revolution; we seek to understand the sense of the particular, the new conditions in which we find ourselves. We reflect on them, seeking to find a concept adequate to our experience. We, and only we, take responsibility for what we affirm. But to take responsibility is to assume the existence of others without whom the idea of responsibility makes no sense. They too find themselves in the new, revolutionary situation. If we seek their assent to our reflective judgment, it is because we recognize them as autonomous individuals different from ourselves. We accept thereby the existence of an undeniable plurality of the social matrix. At the same time, because our judgment claims universality, we assume also our unity, our commonality, our communality. In this way, judgments of taste appear to bring together the two structural elements that define the character of democracy. It would, however, be too great a leap to argue that this structure constitutes, by itself, a theory of the political.

The novelty of the situation, the need to judge without preexisting concepts, the necessity of assuming my responsibility and at the same time seeking assent from my fellow citizens whose diversity and autonomy I accept, all characterize the post-1989 world. Codes of universal morality or juridical concepts (retroactively taken over from the codes of Western liberalism) only reduce the properly political dimension of the problem. They do not help to form a democratic citizenry capable of judging on its own, and especially of accepting the coexistence of multiple standpoints. They do not, to adopt another Kantian phrase of which Arendt makes much, teach us "an enlarged mentality" based on the imperative of learning to "think in the place of the other." Worse, they do not permit the transformation of the past into a debt that opens toward a future; they eliminate (Kant would say, "subsume") the past, rather than teach us to understand the novelty of our experience in order to judge it in a plural present. That is the task of political judgment that, insofar as it seeks to communicate my experience of the plurality of others, is an action among them and with them rather than an affirmation about them delivered by someone (like the militant) standing outside or above them. In this sense, the judgment is that of the democratic individual among democratic individuals who are, together, affirming the value and normative validity of their democracy.

The totalitarian experience can hardly be compared to that provoked by a work of art; but that experience can be formulated in political terms by reflecting on another of Kant's attempted political syntheses. In his essay "Perpetual Peace," Kant tries to explain the "harmony that the transcendental concept of public right establishes between morality and politics." "All maxims," he asserts, "that *stand in need* of publicity in order not to fail their end, agree with politics and right combined." Coming to grips with *our* past, sharing that past in a present that, because of this past, is open to the future, is possible only in a public space that, because it is shared, belongs to none of us. This empty center was seen to be the condition of the possibility of democratic politics. The need for publicity in the realization of this debate about the past is obvious—indeed, public debate will be necessary even to put it on the agenda in the East. But Kant's formula concerns also the Western democracies into whose fellowship the formerly totalitarian societies are entering. The past of the East casts a shadow on the West, whose democratic spirit the example of the reaction to Manfred Frank's speech showed not to be naturally given or divinely protected. The experience of totalitarianism uncovers the political structure—the structure of the political—which is at once the foundation of and the threat to democracy. A public debate shared by East and West would not only permit the East to assert the autonomy and dignity of its own experience; it would also confront the West with an Other who is not so foreign as some would like to believe. Western liberalism and conservatism are not totalitarian; they are, however, antipolitical.

The politics of judgment replaces the liberal version of democracy whose theoretical foundation is the idea of a contract between two abstract wills. It implies the rejection of the increasing juridification of political life, which seeks formal answers to fundamental questions on which difference of opinion is legitimate and where compromise must be based on the strength of argument rather than the argument of strength. At the same time, the replacement of a politics of the will by a politics of judgment avoids the philosophically fashionable critique of the "subject" because it stresses the responsibility that the individual accepts when asserting the claims of his or her experience of the new and seeking to establish its communicability in a shared public space inhabited by plural subjects. Morality (as opposed to personal ethics) does not depend on the will or the result of its actions; morality lies in the acceptance of responsibility, including responsibility for one's past and for the future to which it opens a shared present. Politics, the other pole of Kant's "transcendental concept of public right," has as its task the preservation of the public space in which difference can become manifest, legitimate itself, and challenge the claims of interests, groups, or institutions to incarnate the popular will.

From the standpoint of a politics of judgment, 1989 was a revolution not a breakdown; the challenge is to assume its consequences— including its past—and to preserve the vitality of the democracy that is indeed revolution's lost treasure. The question of the origin of the rights of the individual, which remained in suspense after 1789 and which led to the antipolitics whose extreme form was the totalitarian corruption of the political, is posed anew. The postmodernist would say that these rights are affirmed only by the will of those whose action demands and affirms them. But the politics of judgment implies a more communitarian interpretation. The claim of rights makes sense only as a demand, debate, and dialogue with others, whom I assume as my equals even while accepting their autonomy and their difference. Demanding rights alone, like the singular expression of my will, is the expression of what Kant, following Aristotle, called insanity. I can only assert my rights by seeking the assent of others whose autonomy and plurality is implied by my very quest. My rights depend on our rights—our right to disagree as much as our need to enter debate on why we should agree. Political action and critical reflection complement one another; rather than the end of prehistory, the revolutions of 1989 have made history reflect on itself. Fukuyama's classical end of history is thus replaced by a democratic modernity that relegates to a past that has finally passed the revolutionary dream of a second revolution in which formal liberty is replaced by material equality. Only in the democratic present is the struggle for a better future possible.

Notes

1. Francis Fukuyama, *The End of History and the Last Man* (New York: Avon Books, 1992), 328, 332. Fukuyama is no less tender about communism. Citing Vàclav Havel, he notes that "Communism *humiliated* ordinary people by forcing them to make a myriad of petty, and sometimes not so petty, moral compromises with their better natures" (168).

2. Ibid., xxi.

3. Ibid., xxiii.

4. Jürgen Habermas takes up Adorno's theme in the contemporary context in "Bemerkungen zu einer verworrenen Diskussion. Was bedeutet 'Aufarbeitung der Vergangenheit' heute?" *Die Zeit*, No. 15, 3 April 1992.

5. The most recent example of this latter phenomenon is the *Historikerstreit* of 1987. The normalizers attitude is, strictly speaking, antipolitical; they simply wanted to be freed of the past to live in the present, with little imagination of a future. On the other hand, some participants in the *Historikerstreit* went beyond the normalizers to produce a positive legacy for Nazism. Jürgen Habermas, whose polemic against the normalizers began the *Histori-*

kerstreit, returns to the temptation of normalization in "Bemerkungen," note 4.

6. See chapter 13, "Guilt and the Birth of Democracy." The shift in my attitude toward the reformers can be explained by the fact that prior to 1989—for example, in the common platform elaborated in 1988 by the West German SPD and the ruling East German SED—the attempts by the Western Left to work with these reformers inside the party put peace above human rights—living above living well, as Aristotle would say—and were therefore willing to ignore the demands for rights and democracy that were coming from the dissidents. It also assumed that no change was possible, save from within the party itself. (On this latter error, see Michael Schmitz, "Wie die Linke sich verrannte," *Die Zeit*, No. 8, 14 February 1992; on the former, Robert Leicht, "Trübungen auf der Netzhaut," *Die Zeit*, No. 13, 20 March 1992.) I maintain my critical attitude. But now that 1989 has occurred, the question is how to translate the demand for human rights into a politics. This does not, on the other hand, imply that those on the Right who opposed the various forms of pre-1989 *Ostpolitik* were correct.

7. For an overview, see Reinhard Merkel's provocative essay "Politik und Kriminalität" in *Politik ohne Projekt? Nachdenken über Deutschland*, edited by Siegfried Unseld (Frankfurt am Main: Suhrkamp Verlag, 1993). More interesting in the present political context is Helmut Dubiel's contribution to the same volume, "Deutsche Vergangenheiten," which compares the attitudes toward the Nazi past in West and East Germany, and their implication for the role of intellectuals in each system. East German antifascism bound the critical mind to its regime in a way that differed also from that of the other East European regimes where nationalism could become the basis of a critique of communism (248). But the West German Left critique of fascism had its own political limits, as was apparent in its attitude toward the Gulf War of 1991 (249). See also the subtle analysis in Antonia Grunenberg, *Antifaschismus—ein deutscher Mythos* (Reinbek: Rowohlt Verlag, 1993).

8. It goes without saying that I am exaggerating the broad traits of a style of thought in order to draw out its internal logic. A direct contradiction to my portrait was furnished by one of the slogans of May 1968 in France: "tu fais la révolution pour toi" ("you make the revolution for yourself"). Many, however, were repelled by this "hedonism" and preferred to take their stand with the working class of Billancourt or Flins, standing on the side of a curiously unhistorical interpretation of history that assumes the existence of an essentially unchangeable working class and its proletarian politics.

9. See "Droits de l'homme et politique," in Claude Lefort, *L'invention démocratique. Les limites de la domination totalitaire* (Paris: Fayard, 1981). See also the discussion of this point in chapters 5 and 7 above.

10. See the debate between Ulrike Poppe, Wolfgang Ullman, Michael Brie, Uwe Ewald, and Rainer Land, "'Schuld' im Räderwerk der Institutionen" in *Berliner Debatte. Initial*, 2 (1993), 11–22. The position just described is similar to that of Michael Brie, who is sharply challenged by Ulricke Poppe.

11. Dieter Henrich, *Nach dem Ende der Teilung. Über Identitiäten und Intellektuelität in Deutschland* (Frankfurt am Main: Suhrkamp Verlag, 1993). The book is a collection of essays, so the argument is repeated at various points. See, for example, pages 62ff, 111, 115, 119, and 173.

12. See *Nach dem Ende*, "Die Krise der Universität im vereinigten Deutschland" (125–56) as well as "Warnzeichen für die Wissenschaftspolitik," which was published originally in the *Frankfurter Allgemeine Zeitschrift* and concludes by proposing an "Um-wicklung" rather than an "Abwicklung." On the other hand, Henrich blames the problems of the Western universities, at least in part, on the reaction to the radical student movement, which led to the rapid expansion of the university system and created life-time jobs for many mediocre assistant professors who happened to be around. He fears that the *Abwicklung* in the East will produce similar results.

13. *Nach dem Ende* (160), in an essay titled "Das Ende einer Befangenheit? Intellektuelle in der Bundesrepublik nach der deutschen Teilung." A more critical account of the actual role played by the German intellectuals is offered by Thomas Schmid, "Pinscherseligkeit. Über die deutschen Intellektuellen und ihre Unfähigkeit, mit der jüngsten Geschichte zurechtzukommen," *Die Zeit*, No. 15, 3 April 1992.

14. See the long interview on this subject that Weizsäcker gave to Gunter Hofmann and Werner A. Perger, *Die Zeit*, No. 26, 19 June 1992. The book from which this is taken was published as *Richard von Weizsäcker im Gespräch mit Gunther Hofmann und Werner A. Perger* (Frankfurt am Main: Eichborn-Verlag, 1992).

15. Wolfgang Engler, "Die Etabliertendemokratie," in Unseld, *Politik ohne Projekt*, 207.

16. There have been some exceptions recently, most notably Dubiel, Frankenberg, and Roedel, *Die demokratische Frage* (Frankfurt am Main: Suhrkamp Verlag, 1989), which picks up some of the French analyses and applies them to preunification West Germany. Ulrich Beck's recent *Die Erfindung des Politischen* (Frankfurt am Main: Suhrkamp Verlag, 1993) notes the way in which the lack of an analysis of totalitarianism by the West German Left has had harmful effects on its ability to enter into dialogue with the East (222n), but does not itself propose such an analysis—with the result that an otherwise interesting analytic proposal for a "self-reflexion of modernity" ends with a plaidoyer for "an art of doubting" and a renewal of sociology as a complement to the "sub-politics" that the author seems to make interchangeable with "the political." The interdependence of democracy and totalitarianism should forbid the sociologist from pretending somehow to know better what is really happening in society. Beck, on the other hand, claims constantly to see the emperor's new clothes; a typical sentence reads: "Precisely when one holds before one's eyes the drama of the contradiction between citizen and soldier, one asks with a certain perplexity how this could have been accepted for so long almost without anyone noticing it" (130). The reason Beck is so self-

confident, ultimately, is that within the German sociological tradition, as he himself recognizes, all currents agree that "modernization" has been the dominant force; and, as Beck presents it, democracy has nothing to do with such modernization—which was indeed, if unfortunately, the case for Germany.

17. The rocky, paradoxical, and contradictory adventure of citizenship in the wake of the French Revolution has been traced subtly in Pierre Rosanvallon, *Le sacré du citoyen* (Paris: Gallimard, 1992). In a more contemporary vein, the same author has published "La nouvelle crise de l'Etat-Providence" (in *Notes de la Fondation Saint-Simon*, September 1993) in which he argues that the solidarity that founded the "Bismarckian" welfare state was that of a group insurance policy against accidents; today's sociological methods and social realities make it far more difficult to argue that "we are all in the same boat." Those with secure jobs, good health, or private pension plans are increasingly less willing to contribute to maintain those who are excluded. The abstract necessity that insured *de facto* social solidarity no longer produces even the appearance of a normative justification of (increasingly expensive) welfare measures.

18. Frank's speech is reprinted as "Nachdenken über Deutschland. Aus Anlaß der Kommemoration der Reichspogromnacht vom 9. November 1938," in Unseld, *Politik ohne Projekt*, 250–82. Jürgen Habermas immediately came to Frank's defense in *Die Zeit*, with an article, "Die zweite Lebenslüge der Bundesrepublik: Wir sind wieder 'normal' geworden," which is reprinted in the same volume, 283–97.

Index

Abensour, Miguel, 27n11
Ackerman, Bruce, 206n31, 207n35
Adieux au prolétariat, 244
Adorno, Theodor, 17, 69, 88, 160,
   165–67, 168n4, 170n17, 203n5, 235,
   286, 293n23, 297
Aiguillon, duke of, 106
Almond, Gabriel A., 265
Althusser, Louis, 252n5
American Left. *See* Left
American Revolution, xiii, xiv, 3, 6, 7,
   11–12, 15, 19–20, 23, 24, 28n18, 31,
   72, 80–81, 88, 90, 93, 95–96, 126n30,
   239–40, 242, 248, 287, 309; democracy and, 4, 79, 91; and the political,
   79, 82, 95
Amerika, 138
ancien régime. *See* Old Regime
*Ancien Régime et la Révolution. See
   Old Regime and the Revolution,
   The*
Anderson, John, 273n1
Anti-Intellectualism in American Life,
   35
antipolitics, xii, 4–5, 13–14, 16, 25,
   26n3, 31, 42–43, 48n23, 119, 154,
   237–38, 258, 264, 265, 269, 300, 303,
   308, 315; democracy and, 18, 39;
   totalitarianism and, 9, 10–12, 17, 19,
   28n21, 39–40

Apel, Karl-Otto, 168n6, 209n51
Arato, Andrew, 28n16, 292n16
Arendt, Hannah, 31, 43, 71–73, 88, 92,
   98n23–24, 208n44, 228, 230, 231n2,
   301, 310–13
Aristotle, xiii, 93, 139, 296, 305–6,
   315, 316n6
art, 133–38, 145, 151, 213; modern,
   138, 213–14, 226. *See also* modernism
Assembly of Notables, 106, 125n23
Aufhebung, 35, 185
Austin, J. L., 120n1
autonomy, 24, 30n29, 41, 69, 81, 90,
   104–5, 154, 177, 179, 186–87, 189,
   190–92, 197, 200–201, 207n36,
   208n43, 209n51, 242, 246–48, 251,
   260–61, 264, 274n10, 281, 287, 309,
   314–15; of the political. *See* political, the
avant-garde, 133–35, 136–37, 138,
   140–43, 145, 147, 151, 153–54

Babbit, Bruce, 278n32
Babeuf, François, 12, 85, 149, 295
Bahro, Rudolf, 32, 211, 246
Bailly, Jean-Sylvain, 110
Baker, Keith M., 124n21, 125n27
Barnave, Joseph, 121n4
Bastille, 12, 60, 110, 112, 149

About the Author

Dick Howard teaches political philosophy at SUNY, Stony Brook. He is also a Correspondant of the Collège International de Philosophie in Paris, France, and an associate of the Center for European Studies at New York University. He has also been a fellow at the Ecole des Hautes Etudes en Sciences Sociales and of the Centre de Recherche en Epistémologie Appliquée (CREA) in Paris, and a Humboldt Fellow at the Max Planck Institut and the Universities of Tübingen and Frankfurt in Germany.

Howard has published and lectured on philosophical, sociological, and political themes in North America and Europe since the 1960s. His 1987 study, *La naissance de la pensée politique américaine* (*The Birth of American Political Thought*, 1990), was awarded the Prix France-Etats-Unis. A former editorial board member of the journal *Telos*, he participates editorially in a number of journals, including *Constellations, Esprit, Berliner Debatte. Initial, Philosophy and Social Criticism*, and *Thesis Eleven*. His commentaries on contemporary political developments are broadcasted on radio and television in France, Canada, and the United States.

Howard is the author of *From Marx to Kant*, 2d edition, revised (1993, French translation in 1995), *Defining the Political* (1989), *The Marxian Legacy*, 2d revised edition with new afterword (1988), and *The Politics of Critique* (1988). The present volume was originally published in Germany under the title *Die Politisierung der Politik* (Suhrkamp, 1996), and a French version is now in preparation.